CHILDREN
OF
DIVORCE

CHILDREN
OF
DIVORCE

Empirical Perspectives on Adjustment

Edited by **Sharlene A. Wolchik,** Ph.D.
and **Paul Karoly,** Ph.D.

Arizona State University

Gardner Press, Inc. • New York & London

This volume is dedicated to our parents—Olga and Leon Wolchik
and
Dora and Harry Karoly.

GARDNER PRESS, INC.
19 UNION SQUARE WEST
NEW YORK, NEW YORK 10003

ALL FOREIGN ORDERS EXCEPT CANADA AND SOUTH AMERICA
TO:

AFTERHURST LIMITED
CHANCERY HOUSE
319 CITY ROAD
LONDON, N1, ENGLAND

Library of Congress Cataloging-in-Publication Data
Main entry under title:

Children of divorce.

Bibliography: p.
Includes index.
1. Children of divorced parents—United States—
Addresses, essays, lectures. 2. Divorce—United States—
Addresses, essays, lectures. 3. Custody of children—
United States—Addresses, essays, lectures.
4. Remarriage—United States—Addresses, essays,
lectures. I. Wolchik, Sharlene. II. Karoly, Paul.
HQ777.5.C44 1988   306.8′9   85-20565
ISBN 0-89876-120-4

Designed by Sidney Solomon
PRINTED IN THE UNITED STATES OF AMERICA

CONTENTS

I.
CONCEPTUAL FOUNDATIONS

II.
SOCIAL/CONTEXTUAL FACTORS

III.
PERSONAL/DEVELOPMENTAL FACTORS

IV.
INTERVENTIVE APPROACHES

CONTRIBUTORS

Jeffrey D. Arnett
Department of Psychology
University of Virginia

Sanford L. Braver
Department of Psychology
Arizona State University

W. Glenn Clingempeel
Department of Psychology
Pennsylvania State University

Robert D. Felner
Department of Psychology
University of Illinois

Paul G. Glick
Department of Sociology
Arizona State University

John Guidubaldi
Department of Early Childhood Education
Kent State University

Elizabeth Heiss
Department of Psychology
Temple University

E. Mavis Hetherington
Department of Psychology
University of Virginia

E. Ann Hollier
Department of Psychology
University of Virginia

Melanie A. Katzman
The Regent Hospital
New York City

Paul Karoly
Department of Psychology
Arizona State University

Lawrence A. Kurdek
Department of Psychology
Wright State University

Jessica Pearson
Center for Policy Research, Denver

Richard T. Rowlison
Department of Psychology
University of Illinois

Irwin N. Sandler
Department of Psychology
Arizona State University

Mitch A. Shuwall
Department of Psychology
Long Island University

Arnold L. Stolberg
Department of Psychology
Virginia Commonwealth University

Lisa Terre
Department of Psychiatry and Human Behavior
University of Mississippi Medical Center

Nancy Thoennes
Center for Policy Research, Denver

Patricia Walsh
Department of Psychology
Virginia Commonwealth University

Sharlene A. Wolchik
Department of Psychology
Arizona State University

Preface and Acknowledgments

Living in a household with both biological parents is a part of growing up that no longer can be taken for granted. Many of today's children will experience the breakup of their families before they reach the end of adolescence, and a significant portion of these children will face other changes in family structure when one or both of their parents remarry. As the boundaries of the concept of the American family are being enlarged to include single-parent, binuclear, and blended-family structures, there is a pressing need for psychologists, social workers, and educators, as well as professionals from many other disciplines, to understand how these altered family structures affect the unwilling participants—the children. Assessing the form and force of the upheaval engendered by divorce and identifying those environmental dimensions and personal competencies most likely to facilitate subsequent adjustment are difficult endeavors. Yet these are the tasks that must be addressed if social scientists are to be responsive to the needs of these children. The contributors to this volume recognize the challenges inherent in studying children of divorce. Some have sought to capture the impact on children of a multistage, multifaceted life transition involving an extensive reorganization of roles and relationships. Others have focused on the children's active processing and structuring of events that both shape their adjustment and change the nature of their social worlds. In working toward their unique and shared goals, these investigators have employed a diversity of methodologies and theoretical orientations.

This volume provides a comprehensive state-of-the-art review of the challenges of divorce for children and their parents, and for the researchers and clinicians who study and intervene in the all-too-common unraveling of the fabric of the American family. The contributors, many of whom are leading scholars in the field, address four key topics: frameworks for conceptualizing the processes of divorce and remarriage, social and contextual factors influencing divorce adjustment, personal and developmental factors that shape children's coping with transitional events, and the efficacy of preventive and treatment programs.

In the initial chapter, Paul Glick, a distinguished demographer, examines the shifting composition of the American family. He details the rise in divorce rates over the past two decades, and thoughtfully links fluctuations in those rates to changes in the social and economic milieu. Glick then identifies the number of children who will face the breakup of their family of origin and highlights the fact that many of these children will encounter multiple changes in family structure as it shifts from a two-parent to a one-parent and then back to a two-parent household. In his concluding section, he looks ahead to the next decade and speculates about the future of the American family.

In Chapter 2, Robert Felner, Lisa Terre, and Richard Rowlison present their transitional-event model, which captures the richness and complexity inherent in the *process* of divorce adjustment. The adaptive challenges set in motion by divorce, the active interplay between children and their environments, and the environmental and social contextual factors that shape the adjustment process are central features of this model. Felner and his co-workers compare their model with more traditional perspectives, and articulate the fit between their framework and the available database on children's adjustment to divorce. These authors also provide an indepth discussion of five contextual factors that have significant implications for children's efforts to cope with divorce.

In Chapter 3, Mavis Hetherington, Jeffrey Arnett and Ann Hollier shift our focus from divorce to the next challenge facing most children of divorce—adjusting to life in a stepfamily. Hetherington and her colleagues cogently review critical conceptual and methodological concerns in the study of stepfamilies and highlight the need for rigorous, multimethod investigations. In addition to outlining a life transition model of the effects of remarriage, these authors paint a rich picture of the changes that remarriage engenders among individual family members and among dyads within the stepfamily. They then summarize current knowledge about developmental outcomes of stepchildren. Finally, Hetherington and her coauthors examine how the quality of children's relationships with members of their stepfamilies influences adjustment to the changes that occur within this evolving family structure.

In Chapter 4, Irwin Sandler, Sharlene Wolchik and Sanford Braver provide a methodology for quantifying the significant events in children's postdivorce environments. These authors first outline several conceptual and methodological considerations relevant to constructing their divorce events schedule. They then illustrate the value of this inventory by presenting findings of several studies on children's divorce environments. Whether parents and children agree in their perceptions of the stressfulness of divorce events, whether divorce events differ across custody arrangements, and whether the occurrence of divorce events is related to children's adjustment are some of the issues explored. The chapter concludes with a section on fruitful directions for furthering our understanding of divorce adjustment.

In their chapter, Glenn Clingempeel, Mitch Shuwall, and Elizabeth Heiss address a topic with significant policy implications—the consequences of custody arrangements for children's well-being. These authors propose that the impact of custody arrangements is mediated by variables operating at an individual, family, or social system level and, using this framework, they review empirical research on the effect of such arrangements. Clingempeel and his co-workers then consider how remarriage affects custody arrangements, as well as the other side of the coin—how various patterns of contact with the nonresidential parent influence the quality of relationships within the stepfamily.

Using the extensive database from the nationwide National Association of School Psychologists study, John Guidubaldi examines age and gender differences in adjustment to divorce. The many methodological strengths of this project—large sample size, multiple informants, assessment of functioning across different settings, and longitudinal assessments—increase one's confidence in Guidubaldi's conclusion that divorce is hurting America's children, and in particular, its sons. Guidubaldi speculates about why these gender differences occur and why they are more marked for early elementary versus middle elementary school-aged children. He also discusses some provocative policy implications of the findings of this project.

Lawrence Kurdek focuses on cognitive factors that may influence divorce adjustment. He first sets the stage by discussing the basic premises of cognitive-developmental theories and by reviewing data linking children's cognitions and stress. Kurdek then presents results of his programmatic research projects that document the utility of a cognitive-developmental model of children's reactions to divorce. His discussion of the relevance of these data for improving assessment strategies and interventions should be useful to both researchers and clinicians.

A frequent complaint about policies that affect children of divorce is that they are made without consideration of empirical findings. In part this policy–research schism is the fault of social scientists who have been reluctant to accept the complexities inherent in studying such issues as mediation. In their chapter, Jessica Pearson and Nancy Thoennes describe their pioneering efforts to assess the benefits of mediation as an increasingly frequent alternative to the adversarial process. In comparing children's adjustment across four dispute categories, these researchers found limited differences between children whose parents participated in mediation versus the use of more traditional adjudication processes. The authors consider several explanations for these results, and conclude that the benefits of mediation appear to fall short of our expectations. This chapter highlights the need for dialogue between researchers and policy makers.

How effective are current interventions for children of divorce? In Chapter 9, Arnold Stolberg and Patricia Walsh address this important question. Organizing interventions in terms of their fit with a four-stage model of the divorce process, these authors discuss a variety of approaches ranging from the education of "primary decision influencers" (such as attorneys, physicians, and clergy) to the involvement of children in divorce intervention programs. In evaluating these approaches, Stolberg and Walsh consider not only whether there is empirical evidence of the programs' effectiveness, but also the availability of a vehicle for program dissemination. This latter criterion is particularly significant given the large number of children who will face divorce.

The book concludes with a chapter devoted to strengthening marital relationships, written by Melanie Katzman and Paul Karoly. After critically reviewing the efficacy of competency-based preventive interventions for distressed couples, nondistressed couples, and couples who are considering marriage, the authors identify methodological problems that are common in this literature. Katzman and Karoly then outline several intriguing and significant questions for future study.

Taken together, the chapters in this volume provide an empirical foundation for an emergent understanding of divorce and its aftermath. The slow process of replacing conjecture with solid data is definitely under way—wedded to a multidimensional framework capable of eventually capturing inherent, systemwide complexities rather than smoothing them out for simplicity's sake (as has been done in the past). The volume also reveals some of what we don't know—and why. Hence we have a "good beginning" to what will surely be a continuing self-correcting process of discovery, confirmation, and redirection, all in the service of improving the quality of life for America's families. What the field can least afford today are easy answers and the failed social policies they engender.

Partial support for editing this volume was provided by NIMH grant #MH39246-02 to establish the Program for Prevention Research at Arizona State University. We wish to thank each of the authors for his or her contributions to this volume. Also, we appreciate the careful work of the staff at Gardner Press, particularly Suzi Tucker. The clerical assistance of Lavaun Habegger and Claudia Bean deserves acknowledgment. Our spouses, Philip Poirier and Linda Ruehlman, merit special recognition for their encouragement, support, and understanding throughout all phases of this project. Finally, we thank our children, Lauren Ann and Michael, for helping us to rediscover the wonders of life and for motivating our attempts to enhance the quality of children's experiences.

PART I
CONCEPTUAL
FOUNDATIONS

The Role of Divorce in the Changing Family Structure:
Trends and Variations

PAUL C. GLICK

A generation ago, the impact of divorce on American family life was slight as compared with the situation today. The baby boom was near its crest and the familistic era of the 1950s had kept the divorce rate at a relatively low level. The number of young children who were living with a divorced parent was no higher in 1960 than the number living with a widowed parent. Mothers commnly bore three or four children, and so most mothers were kept busy with family responsibilities. By contrast, mothers of the 1980s more typically have only one or two children to care for, and more than half of these mothers work at jobs outside the home. And, not incidentally, there are now four times as many young children in the homes of divorced parents as in the homes of widowed parents.

A declining birth rate and a closely related increase in the employment of women are by no means the only reasons for the changing role of divorce in U.S. society, but they have probably played leading parts in the transformation (Cherlin, 1981; Ross & Sawhill, 1975). Many other factors will be mentioned here as contributors to the increased divorce rate. Clearly, however, some factors, including the increasing age at first marriage, have operated to curb the upward trend of divorce.

This chapter features published and unpublished results of research on divorce obtained from national vital statistics, decennial censuses, and large sample surveys made available by the federal government. The treatment is mainly descriptive, with some effort to show how different types of research findings are interrelated, and also with some speculation about future changes.

The first major section deals with divorce trends and differentials. It covers changes in divorce and remarriage a well as fluctuations over time in the number of children involved in divorce. This section includes some projections of the proportion of young adults who may eventually end both first and second marriages in divorce. Also, information is presented on the age distribution of adults at divorce and remarriage and on how much time elapses between these martial events.

The second major section compared the socioeconomic level of divorced persons and other adults. It shows that the status of divorced persons, on the average, is clearly higher than that of other unmarried adults. The third major section features changes since 1960 in the composition of the families of divorced persons and other adults. It also shows changes in the living arrangements of young children in terms of the marital status of their parents. Special subsections examine the extent to which divorced persons are cohabiting outside marriage and describe how child custody arrangements by divorced parents differ according to the sex of the child. Finally, some information is presented about young adult divorced sons and daughters who have returned to their parental homes.

TRENDS AND VARIATIONS IN DIVORCE

The Longtime Upward Trend of Divorce

Divorce rates for the United States are available for each year since 1867. In that year there was only one divorce for every 3000 people (U.S. National Center for Health Statistics, 1973). It was a time when most of the population had grown up on farms or in small nonfarm areas where being married was considered necessary to ensure the successful operation of the family business, and when the marital problems that would be likely to lead to divorce today were rarely considered justification for voluntarily dissolving a marriage. With the gradual growth of urbanization and associated modern developments, the divorce rate slowly rose to the level of 1.0 per 1000 population in 1911 and to around 1.5 during the 1920s. (See Table 1.1). Then, in 1933, in the worst part of the economic depression, it dropped to 1.3. During the subsequent economic recovery, the divorce rate regained its upward momentum and reached 2.0 per 1000 population in 1940.

The unsettled social conditions during World War II were associated with a continual and substantial rise in the divorce rate. With the discharge of millions of members of the armed forces after the war, the divorce rate zoomed—to an unprecedented 4.3 per 1000 population in 1946. Thereafter it declined sharply, and remained low for about a decade while the baby boom was gaining momentum and the age at marriage was low. By 1958 the divorce rate stood a 2.1 per 1000 population. This rate was nearly as low as it had been in 1940, and lower than it has been in any year since 1958. But a turning point was just ahead.

The demographic and social changes that occurred after 1960 had the net effect of starting the divorce rate on an upward climb that continued for two decades. Some of these changes were the increase in education and employment of women during the war in Vietnam, the resurgence of the women's movement, the decline in the birth rate, and the ebbing of conformity to traditional religious social norms relating to marriage. The divorce rate moved steadily upward, from 2.2 per 1000 population in 1960 to a peak of 5.3 in 1979.

The most rapid increase in the divorce rate occurred during the first half of the 1970s. During this period the marriage rate also reached a peak (in 1972), and divorces are most likely to occur two to four years after marriage, as will be shown. One contributing factor was demobilization after the end of the war in Vietnam in 1973, but its impact on the divorce rate was much less than that after World War II, when far more military personnel were released.

The rise in the divorce rate eased during the second half of the 1970s,

Table 1.1
Divorce Rate per 1000 Population: United States, 1920–1984

Year	Divorce Rate	Year	Divorce Rate	Year	Divorce Rate
1920	1.6	1955	2.3	1977	5.0
1925	1.5	1958	2.1	1978	5.1
1930	1.6	1960	2.2	1979	5.3
1933	1.3	1965	2.5	1980	5.2
1935	1.7	1970	3.5	1981	5.3
1940	2.0	1972	4.0	1982	5.1
1946	4.3	1975	4.8	1983	5.0
1950	2.6	1976	5.0	1984	4.9

Source: U.S. National Center for Health Statistics, 1982, 1984a, 1984b, 1985.

and virtually ceased for awhile before fluctuating slightly downward during the early 1980s. It is still too early to predict with confidence that a major decline in divorce has set in. The divorce rate in 1983 was about one-fifth above the 60-year trend between 1920 and 1980 (Glick, 1984a). Even if the rate were to decrease to four per 1000 population by 1990 (which this writer does not expect), it would remain in line with the trend since 1920.

The divorce rate for blacks is typically higher than that for whites, and because divorced blacks tend to be slower to remarry, the proportion of adults who are currently divorced is significantly higher for blacks than for whites (Espenshade, 1984).

Trends of First Marriage, Divorce, and Remarriage

As compared with the divorce rate shown in Table 1.1, more refined rates of divorce for the period since 1921 are shown in the Table 1.2, along with correspondingly refined rates of first marriage and remarriage. These rates have bases tailored to relate to the population in the most relevant age and marital status group. Rates of first marriage, divorce, and remarriage hit low levels during the depression, high levels soon after the end of World War II, and lower levels during the relatively stable period of the 1950s. Thus a pattern was established that suggested a tendency for changes in social and economic coditions to cause all three types of rates to move in the same direction. But, after the 1950s, the three rates began to

Table 1.2
Rates of First Marriage, Divorce, and Remarriage: United States, 1921–1981

Period	First Marriage*	Divorce†	Remarriage‡
1921–1923	99	10	98
1927–1929	94	12	84
1930–1932	81	10	61
1939–1941	106	14	103
1945–1947	143	24	163
1951–1953	122	16	136
1957–1959	112	15	129
1966–1968	107	20	166
1975–1977	85	37	134
1978–1980	83	40	134
1981	86	40	128

*First marriages per 1000 never-married women 14–44 years old.
†Divorces per 1000 married women 14–44 years old.
‡Remarriages per 1000 widowed and divorced women 14–54 years old.
Source: Norton & Glick, 1979; rates for 1978–1981 estimated by the author.

diverge. First marriages continued to deline for another two decades, while divorce rates climbed steadily upward. And, as the divorce rates increased, remarriage rates also climbed, and then peaked during the lat 1960s; thereafter they declined in spite of the continuing rise in divorce. One reason why young adults postponed their entrance into first marriage was the existence of a large pool of divorced persons who competed for potential marriage partners.

These developments evidently imply that an early and permanent first marriage became less attractive after 1960, and that more remarriages were being deferred longer, or entirely forgone. If more of these persons had married sooner, the pool of married persons eligible for divorce would have been still larger. That condition might have led to a greater increase in the divorce rate. In the meantime, vastly increasing numbers of young couples were living together without being married, thereby helping to keep the marriage rate relatively low and adding nothing to the divorce rate when these POSSLQs (partners of opposite sex sharing living quarters) decided to separate. This subject is discussed more fully in the following.

Children Involved in Divorce

Even more germane here than the divorce rate is the extent to which children are involved in divorce. Two measures that reveal the trend of this involvement between 1950 and 1981 are presented in Table 1.3. The first shows the average number of children in the custody of their parents when the divorce occurred. These children averaged about eight years of age. The trend of their involvement in divorce, therefore, tended to vary according to the level of the birth rate roughly eight years earlier. Thus this

Table 1.3
Children Under 18 Years Old Involved in Divorce: United States, 1950–1981

Year	Children Under 18 per Divorce	Percent of Children Under 18	Year	Children Under 18 per Divorce	Percent of Children Under 18
1950	0.78	0.63	1975	1.08	1.67
1958	1.08	0.65	1977	1.00	1.67
1960	1.18	0.72	1978	1.01	1.77
1967	1.34	0.89	1979	1.00	1.84
1970	1.22	1.25	1980	0.98	1.73
1972	1.20	1.47	1981	0.97	1.87

Source: U.S. National Center for Health Statistics, 1984[a].

trend peaked at 1.34 children per divorce in 1967, about eight years after the crest of the baby boom. By contrast, it was much lower in 1950, at least partly because the children 10–17 years of age who were involved in divorce at that time had been born during the depression of the 1930s when birth rates were very low. Similarly, this measure was also low in 1981, thus reflecting the decline in birth rates during the preceding two decades.

A relatively small proportion of children are involved in divorce during a given year, but this proportion is cumulative throughout childhood. As Table 1.3 shows, less than 1 percent (0.6 percent) of all children in the United States under 18 years of age in 1950 were involved in divorce during that year, but more than three times that amount, 1.9 percent, were involved during 1981. The largest five-year increase occurred between 1970 and 1975, when the divorce rate went up faster than during any other five-year period since 1950.

By the early 1980s, approximately 2 percent of all children under 18 were involved in divorce in a given year. At this rate 36 percent of the children would be involved in divorce before they reached the age of 18 years. This figure is consistent with an estimate made in 1983 by Arthur J. Norton of the U.S. Bureau of the Census, namely, that 59 percent of all children born in 1983 were likely to live for an extended period with only one parent before they reached the age of 18 years. It has been estimated that close to two-thirds of these children are likely to have lived with a divorced parent (Bumpass, 1984: Glick, 1984b). Thus, in round numbers about 60 percent of all young children today are likely to spend part of their childhood with one parent, including close to 40 percent with a divorced parent.

Projections of Divorce and Redivorce

Although persons between 25 and 39 years of age are in the period of life during which most divorces occur, the actual divorce rate characteristic of that period is one-third to one-half of the rate for the entire life span. Therefore, methods have been developed to project the total number of divorces this group of persons will have experienced by the time they have reached old age (U.S. Bureau of the Census, 1977; Cherlin, 1981; Weed, 1982; Glick, 1984a).

The projections—the result of applying the method developed by Glick—are presented in Table 1.4. They show the projected proportion of both first marriage and remarriages that may eventually end in divorce. Along with the projections, the table shows the proportions of marriages that had already ended in divorce by the survey date in 1980. The assumption underlying the projection method is that the same increments in divorce that occurred between 1975 and 1979 for each five-year age group will be experienced by younger adults during succeeding five-year periods until they reach 70–74 years of age. For example, it is assumed that persons 25–29 years of age in 1980 will add as much divorce experience between 1980 and 1984 as persons 30–34 in 1980 had between 1975 and 1979. In other words, because the projections are based on divorce experience during the late 1970s, the method implies that the future amount of change will be smaller than that during the early 1970s when the increase in divorce was at its height.

The projections may be too high or too low—or about right—depending on the actual future levels of divorce. They have the merit of being based on data for a recent period, and of being extensions of divorce levels that were current when the younger persons involved were forming their attitudes about divorce as a solution to unhappy marriages.

Table 1.4 shows that the proportion of persons divorced after first marriage was somewhat higher than for men under 45 years of age, reflecting the usually earlier age at marriage of women and consequently their longer exposure to the risk of divorce by a given age. By age 35–44

Table 1.4

Percent of First and Second Marriages That Ended in Divorce by 1980 and That May Eventually End in Divorce, by Age and Sex: United States

Age in 1980 and Sex	Percent of First Marriages Ending in Divorce by 1980	Percent of First Marriages That May End in Divorce	Age in 1980 and Sex	Percent of Second Marriages Ending in Divorce by 1980	Percent of Second Marriages That May End in Divorce
Men:			Men:		
25–34	20	49	30–39	19	61
35–44	25	39	40–49	22	46
45–54	22	28	50–59	26	36
55–64	19	20	60–69	21	23
65–74	15	15	70–74	19	19
Women			Women		
25–34	24	49	30–39	22	54
35–44	27	37	40–49	27	42
45–54	22	27	50–59	26	31
55–64	19	20	60–69	25	27
65–74	15	15	70–74	18	18

Source: U.S. Bureau of the Census, derived from unpublished Current Population Survey data for June 1980.

the proportion divorced was higher than that for older persons, as a result of the upswing in divorce during the past two decades.

About one-half (49 percent) of all *first* marriages for persons 25–34 years old in 1980 may end in divorce by the time they reach their early 70s, according to the projections. That is close to twice the proportion for persons 20 years older and more than three times that for persons 40 years older. These differences across age groups reflect a tremendous lowering of the threshold for divorce among members of the younger generation as compared with that of their parents (or grandparents), who ended only 15 percent of their first marriages in divorce. Whereas the older generations evidently included many couples who felt constrained to endure disagreeable marriages, the younger generation evidently includes a far larger share of couples who are mutually liberating themselves from such marriages, as well those in which one partner is an unwilling participant in the separation.

As another indication of the rising divorce rate, the proportion of persons 30–39 years old in 1980 who had ended their *second* marriage in divorce was about the same as that for persons five years younger, 25–34, who had ended their *first* marriage in divorce. Moreover, women under 50 years of age had higher proportions redivorced by 1980 than men under 50 in comparable age groups, again reflecting the younger age at second marriages for women. And persons in their 50s had already experienced more redivorce than those in their 70s because of the general increase in the amount of divorce among adults of all age groups.

About 61 percent of the men and 54 percent of the women in their 30s in 1980 may expect to end their *second* marriage in divorce, according to the projections. These levels are somewhat higher than those for first marriages. Perhaps there are selective background and personality characteristics typical of adults with one divorce that tend to make them particularly subject to redivorce. These individuals apparently know from previous experience how to obtain a divorce and the probable consequences of becoming divorced again.

One may speculate as to why 61 percent of men, but only 54 percent of women, are likely to end their second marriage in redivorce. Part of the difference may be related to the higher remarriage rates for men than for women. Thus divorced men are more likely to marry never-married women than divorced women are to marry never-married men, and this pattern may carry over to marriages of a higher order. In addition, men continue to marry and divorce later than women do, and at succeeding marriages, the gap between the ages of the bride and groom tends to increase.

In brief, the projections imply that about one-half of the first marriages of young adults today are likely to end in divorce, and that 55–60 percent of their second marriages are also likely to end in divorce. These projections apply to persons who are young enough to have been strongly affected by the recent upsurge in divorce.

Projections of Divorce by Educational Level

There are clear tendencies for the divorce projections to vary according to educational level (see Table 1.5). The highest proportion of young adults in 1980 who may end their first marriage in divorce are those who did not complete a high school education, or who attended college but did not complete a full four-year course. The lowest proportions for women are for those who graduated from college but did not go on to graduate school.

Among young women, those with five or more years of college had significantly higher projected levels of divorce than those who terminated their education after four years of college. Probably a substantial proportion of the women with graduate school training had delayed marriage after college graduation and had started to concentrate on a professional career before they finally married. Conflicts between career and marriage, as well as the establishment of many fixed habits before marriage, may

Table 1.5
Projected Percent of Ever-Married Persons Who May Eventually End Their First Marriage in Divorce, by Age, Education, and Sex: United States

Age in 1980 and Sex	Total	Years of School Completed by 1980				
		0–11	12	13–15	16	17+
Men						
25–34	49	51	51	58	40	41
35–44	39	41	41	45	33	32
45–54	28	30	27	33	20	25
55–64	20	23	19	23	14	15
65–74	15	16	14	15	10	9
Women						
25–34	49	53	48	55	39	52
35–44	37	43	34	43	33	42
45–54	27	30	24	31	22	30
55–64	20	22	18	20	18	22
65–74	15	17	13	12	11	*

*Very small number of women.
Source: U.S. Bureau of the Census, derived from unpublished Current Population Survey data for June 1980.

have contributed to the ending of the first marriage in divorce for these highly educated woman.

These findings are interpreted as evidence that the social backgrounds, individual characteristics, and perhaps good fortune that inspire people to persist until they attain the traditional goals of high school or college graduation also help them to maintain intact marriages. This has been referred to as the Glick effect (Bernard, 1966). By the same kind of reasoning, if there should become a new norm of continuing one's education until an associate-of-arts degree or its equivalent is attained after two years of college, a logical expectation would be that the level of divorce for those with 14 years of education would gradually decline.

As more women voluntarily choose to acquire graduate school training, one may expect that an increasing share of them will simultaneously achieve a successful career and a continuing marriage. Evidence that a beginning has been made in this direction is demonstrated by the 84 percent increase between 1970 and 1977 in the number of married couples in which both the husband and the wife reported having completed five or more years of college. The only combination of educational levels with a larger increase (114 percent) was that for married couples in which the husband reported having completed five or more years of college, and the wife only four years of college (U.S. Bureau of the Census, 1972, 1978).

Remarriage by Age at Divorce and Number of Children

The vast majority of divorced persons eventually remarry and thereby signify that marriage continues to be their preferred life-style during the fully mature phase of their lives. Within this context it is useful to note the great extent to which the likelihood of remarriage after divorce is correlated with the age at which the divorce occurs. The "Current Population Survey" data for 1975 on women under 75 years of age whose first marriage ended in divorce yielded the following information about remarriage. For women who became divorced before they were 30 years old, 76 percent had remarried by the survey date, as compared with 56 percent for those divorced during their 30s, 32 percent for those divorced during their 40s, and only 11 percent for those divorced after 50 years of age. Obviously the chances for remarriage were clearly the highest for the two-thirds of all the divorced women who had terminated their first marriage before the age of 30 years (U.S. Bureau of the Census, 1977).

Chances for remarriage are negatively correlated with the number of children, but much of the correlation can be accounted for by one's age at divorce. Even so, 80 percent of women below the age of 30 at divorce were remarried before the survey date if they had borne no children, as compared with 73 percent of the women in this age group who had three or more children. For women who were above 30 years old at divorce, those with no children or with one child had a slightly better chance of becoming remarried than those with two or more children. Being both young and childless at divorce, as expected, greatly improves the odds that a remarriage will occur. But women with these characteristics can usually be more deliberate about entering a remarriage than can divorced mothers with children to support; otherwise the correlation between remarriage and number of children probably would be higher.

Age at Marital Events

Just as women tend to be two or three years younger than men at first marriage, they also tend to be a few years younger than men at divorce, remarriage, and redivorce (see Table 1.6). Speculation about this traditional pattern of age at marriage would include the earlier physical maturation of women and a likely preference on the part of women for men who are older and generally more secure economically than men of their own age. Once this difference has been established at the time of first marriage, it presumbaly carries over to later marital events.

Between 1975 and 1980, when the divorce rate was still rising rapidly, the median age at first marriage went up by more than a year for men (from 23.5 to 25.2 years) and also for women (from 21.1 years to 22.5 years), as measured by the U.S. Bureau of the Census (1984b). During this period a growing number of young adults were delaying marriage, and many of them were living in marriagelike situations outside marriage. A corresponding increase in the median age at divorce occurred for men, and also in the median age at remarriage for both men and women. But a much larger change took place in the opposite direction, toward a younger median age at redivorce. These changes and other evidence (Norton, 1980) provide a somewhat mixed indication of a general tendency in recent years for successive marital events to take place within shorter intervals than formerly. Further evidence of this development is presented in the next section.

Divorces after first marriage are most heavily concentrated among persons in their 20s, after which the percentages by age at divorce gradually taper off until very few occur after the early 50s. Remarriages are less narrowly distributed, but the great majority take place among persons in their 20s and 30s, again with few occurring after the early 50s. Redivorces most often happen during a span of 20 years but somewhat later, from the

Table 1.6

Age at Marital Events for Men and Women 15–74 Years Old: United States, 1980 and 1975

Age at Marital Event	Age at Divorce After First Marriage		Age at Remarriage After First Marriage Ended in Divorce		Age at Redivorce After Second Marriage	
	Men	Women	Men	Women	Men	Women
1980						
Total (%)	100	100	100	100	100	100
Under 20	4	10	1	5	0	1
20–24	23	28	14	22	6	10
25–29	25	25	25	28	18	20
30–34	18	15	22	19	20	22
35–39	12	9	15	12	18	18
40–44	8	6	10	7	13	12
45–49	5	4	7	4	10	9
50–74	5	3	6	3	15	8
Median years	30	27	32	29	36	34
1975						
Median years	29	27	33	29	41	38

Source: U.S. Bureau of the Census, 1976b, and unpublished Current Population Survey data for June 1980.

mid-20s through the early 40. For each type of marital event, men are more heavily concentrated toward the older end of the age distribution and the women toward the younger end, as would be expected.

Thus if first marriages last until the marital partners have reached the age of 40 years, there appears to be only about 15 percent chance, on the average, that these marriages will end in divorce later on. Only about 10 percent of remarriages after divorce occur after the age of 45 years, and only about 10 percent of redivorces take place after the age of 50 years. Increases in the divorce rate have been found at all ages during the past decade or two, but the increase has been the fastest among persons between the ages of 20 and 39 years, where the heaviest concentration of divorces is found.

Interval Between Marital Events

For those who end their first marriage in divorce, the median interval between marriage and divorce is seven years. In spite of all the social changes during the past several decades, this interval has hovered close to the same level. Yet this is not evidence of a seven-year itch because there is no concentration of divorces during the seventh (or eighth) year of marriage. But as the divorce rate has risen, the median interval between divorce and second marriage became shorter by about one year during the last half of the 1970s. This development suggests, among other things, that there may have been an increase in the proportion of persons who knew who their prospective partner in remarriage was going to be before they obtained a divorce.

As shown in Table 1.7, in both 1975 and 1980, the median interval between divorce and remarriage was relatively brief (two or three years), but this was a period of relatively low remarriage rates, as compared with those of the late 1960s. Persons who obtained a second divorce took two years less time to do so, on the average, than did those who obtained a first divorce. Moreover, the median interval from second marriage to redivorce became shorter during the late 1970s. In brief, persons who divorced between 1975 and 1980 displayed a marked tendency to shorten each of the succeeding intervals by a year or so. Concurrently, as can be seen in Table 1.6, the median age at second divorce was about four to five years earlier in 1980 than in 1975.

More men who obtain divorces after a first marriage do so during the second, third, or fourth year of marriage than during any other three-year period, according to the figures in Table 1.7. The slightly longer intervals for women than for men suggest that some women may have misreported

the date of their marriage so as to mask the fact that they had borne a
child, or at least had become pregnant, before marriage. Very few first
divorces are reported during the first year of marriage—about the same
number as for those after 25 years of marriage.

Close to four of every five persons in 1980 who remarried after a first
marriage ended in divorce did so rather quickly, within the first five years
after the divorce. Over one-fourth did so during the first year after divorce,
and almost none did so after an interval of 15 years.

A little over one-half of the remarried persons in 1980 who became
divorced again reported that they had done so during the first five years
after their remarriage. One-tenth had redivorced before the end of the first
year. Perhaps a substantial number of those who remarried quickly after
their first marriage are represented among those whose second marriage
did not last very long. Likewise, that 20 percent of remarried persons who
obtained a second divorce after having been remarried for ten or more
years may be overrepresented by persons who had changed their earlier
marital statuses after fairly lengthy deliberation.

Table 1.7
**Intervals Between Marital Events for Men and Women 15–74 Years Old:
United States, 1980 and 1975**

Interval	Between First Marriage and Divorce		Between Divorce and Second Marriage		Between Second Marriage and Redivorce	
	Men	Women	Men	Women	Men	Women
1980						
Total (%)	100	100	100	100	100	100
Under one year	6	5	28	27	13	10
One year	9	7	21	20	13	14
Two years	9	9	14	14	11	12
Three years	8	8	10	9	9	10
Four years	7	8	7	7	9	8
Five to nine years	26	28	14	14	25	25
10–14 years	15	15	4	6	11	11
15–19 years	9	9	1	2	6	5
20 years and over	11	11	1	1	3	5
Median years	6.7	6.9	2.1	2.2	4.5	4.5
1975						
Median years	6.7	7.3	3.1	3.2	6.0	5.5

Source: U.S. Bureau of the Census, 1976b, and unpublished Current Population Survey data for June
1980.

RELATION BETWEEN MARITAL STATUS AND SOCIOECONOMIC STATUS

The adults in each marital status category range from one extreme of the socioeconomic scale to the other; but there is a distinct tendency for those in a given phase of their marital history to be concentrated at a certain position along that scale. For example, married adults tend to have relatively high socioeconomic status, whereas the various categories of unmarried adults tend to have lower status. This finding no doubt reflects many different circumstances, such as the degree to which people of a given socioeconomic level value the need to follow the norm of being married during their middle adult years.

In this section, three measures of socioeconomic status are presented—education, labor force participation, and income. The purpose is to orient the reader as to how currently divorced women compare with other women, on the average, with respect to their standing in society, as reflected by the measures that are used. The focus is on women because most of the children who live with a divorced parent live with the mother.

Relation Between Marital Status and Educational Level

As shown in Table 1.8, the average educational level of divorced women is strikingly similar to that of women in intact marriages, and well above that of separated and remarried women. The presentation is made by race because of the grossly heavier concentration of black women at the lowest educational level. Data are provided for women in their late 30s to early 50s, because after this period of life relatively few marital events occur. The relatively small number of never-married mothers in this age range is not shown. The data are for 1975, the most recent date for which data have been published by the Census Bureau. The women who had married were at high risk of divorce during the decade before the survey date, when divorce rates went up fastest.

Divorced women and married women were most likely to have completed high school or college. Separated women had the largest rate of high school dropouts, probably associated with premarital pregnancy before high school graduation followed by early marriage and later unstable marital experience. Poorly educated divorced mothers seem most likely to try to remarry soon in order to have a husband to help support the children, but they are probably much less likely to be asked to be marital partners than better educated divorced women.

Women with graduate school training tend to be least likely to marry, most likely to become divorced, and least likely to remarry (U.S. Bureau of the Census, 1972). They are usually in a better financial position to maintain a household for themselves and their children, if any. They can also afford to wait longer to find an appropriate partner in remarriage. This waiting period is ordinarily rather long for divorced mothers with careers that require a high level of education.

Relation Between Marital Status and Labor Force Status

Divorced mothers of young children are the most likely to be in the labor force, and never-married mothers are the least likely. As shown in Table 1.9, worker rates for separated and married mothers fall between these two extremes. The labor force participation rates vary with the children's age. For example, in 1981, 83 percent of divorced mothers of school-age children were in the labor force, as compared with only 41 percent of never-married mothers of children under three years of age.

Table 1.8
Marital Status of Women 35–54 Years Old, by Education and Race: United States, 1975

Years of School and Race	Intact First Marriage	Separated	Divorced	Remarried*
White, 35–54				
Total				
(thousands)	14,346	539	1,543	2,735
Percent	100	100	100	100
0–11 years	26	45	28	38
12 years	50	40	46	46
13–15 years	13	9	15	10
16 or more	11	6	11	6
16 years	7	2	6	3
17 or more	4	4	5	3
Black, 35–54				
Total				
(thousands)	1,135	393	274	319
Percent	100	100	100	100
0–11 years	45	63	48	56
12 years	39	31	36	33
13–15 years	8	4	10	6
16 or more	8	2	6	5

*Predominantly remarried after divorce.
Source: U.S. Bureau of the Census, 1977.

Of special interest are some of the factors behind the high labor force rates for divorced mothers. These women are a very special group in that they consistently have the highest rates of labor force participation for women in each group according to age and race. Their relatively high educational level implies that they usually possess a high degree of employability. Also, many divorced mothers do not receive much financial support from their former husbands, and that stimulates them to earn a living for themselves and their children. Divorced women have the smallest average number of young children per mother, and as the Table 1.10 shows, they have much higher incomes than other unmarried women.

For women in the other marital status groups, the circumstances relating to employability are generally quite different. For example, separated women not only tend to have the lowest education, but also usually have the most children. Married women also have a relatively large number of children to care for, on the average, but they have a husband to help share living costs; therefore, many of them do not feel the urgency to find work outside the home. Besides, the ranks of employed married women are constantly being depleted through divorce, and at the same time being expanded by the less employable divorced women who "hasten back into marriage." The very low worker rate for never-married mothers reflects, in large part, their concentration in the teens and early 20s and their generally low educational level, and hence low employability. Many of these young mothers live with their parents, as shown later.

An especially rapid rate of increase in labor force participation is found among mothers of preschool children. To illustrate, the proportion of married mothers of preschool-age children in the labor force was over twice as high in 1982 (49 percent) as in 1960 (19 percent), according to the U.S. Bureau of the Census (1983). For divorced mothers the corresponding 1982 worker rate (67 percent) was well above average.

Table 1.9
Percent of Mothers in the Labor Force, by Marital Status and Race of Mother and Age of Children: United States, 1981

Age of Children and Race	Divorced	Separated	Married	Never Married
Total, with children under 18	78	62	56	52
With some 6–17, none younger	83	70	63	65
With some under six	65	51	48	46
With some three to five, none younger	70	54	55	55
With some under three	58	49	44	41
White with children under 18	79	62	55	49
Black, with children under 18	72	62	66	54

Source: U.S. Bureau of Labor Statistics, 1983.

Relation Between Marital Status and Income Level

The superior income level of divorced women as compared with other unmarried women is demonstrated in Table 1.10. Here the best available recent information is for adults 25–64 years old who reported their income for 1982. Obviously married women with husbands in this age range have by far the greatest income advantage, as a rule. Their median family income considerably exceeds twice the corresponding level for women who maintain a home with no husband present. A large proportion of the women who are living apart from a husband are divorced and have custody of children. They generally have only one earner in the family, whereas about one-half of the married couples have two earners. Moreover, the median personal income for husbands in 1982, $20,600, was nearly twice as high as that for divorced women, $11,450 (U.S. Bureau of the Census, 1984c).

Also, by way of contrast, the median personal income of divorced women in 1982 was nearly twice as high as that for separated women—and for married women. Thus divorced women not only have more education and higher worker rates than separated women, but also receive far more income for the work they do from other sources. One reason is that they are more likely to work full time during the entire year. Married women are most likely to have no income at all. In this context it is relevant to point out that the higher a man's income, the more likely he is to be

Table 1.10

Family Income of Married Couples and Lone Women, and Personal Income of Women by Marital Status: United States, 1982

Income	Family Income, Householder 25–64		Personal Income, Woman 25–64		
	Married Couple	Woman, No Husband	Divorced Woman	Separated Woman	Married Woman
Total (thousands)	39,542	7,330	5,925	2,568	40,313
Percent	100	100	100	100	100
Under $5000	3	20	22	41	52
$5000–$9999	5	22	22	26	18
$10,000–$14,999	9	18	22	14	14
$15,000–$19,999	11	14	16	9	8
$20,000–$24,999	12	10	9	5	4
$25,000–$29,999	13	6	5	2	2
$30,000–$34,999	11	4	2	1	1
$35,000 and over	36	6	2	1	1
Median (dollars)	28,800	12,200	11,450	6,850	6,100

Source: U.S. Bureau of the Census, 1984c.

married, whereas the higher a woman's income, the more likely she is to be divorced (U.S. Bureau of the Census, 1972).

Women with high incomes usually have a relatively high educational level, but the marital history pattern for high-income women differs significantly from that for high-education women. Both groups have a relatively high percent of never married and a high percent of divorced, but high-income women have a high percent of remarried, whereas high-education women have a low percent of remarried (U.S. Bureau of the Census, 1972). During recent years there has been a steady upward trend in the proportion of wives who received more income, the same amount of income, or almost as much income as their husbands. Currently about 20 percent of wives fit this description. This trend suggests that more men are willing to remain married to a wife with about equal or higher income than their own without the situation becoming one of the major grounds for seeking a divorce.

Divorced men are usually in a much better financial situation than divorced women. The median personal income of divorced men 25–64 years old in 1982 was $16,400, as compared with $11,450 for divorced women (U.S. Bureau of the Census, 1984c). These figures are inclusive of adults with and without the custody of children, but the children usually live with the mother, and the typical divorced man does not provide full financial support for the children in his ex-wife's custody. It is safe to say, in light of this incomplete information, that divorced fathers with child custody are much more financially able to provide care for their children outside the home while they work than can divorced women.

TRENDS AND VARIATIONS IN FAMILY STRUCTURE

In view of the rapid increase in divorce during recent decades, one would expect to find that changes in divorce have played a large part in the dynamics of family structure during that period. Evidence to that effect is presented in here. Attention is focused on families with children under 18 years of age at successive dates from 1960 to 1983, with projections to 1990 in some of the tables. Children under 18 in 1960 were born between the years 1942 and 1960, whereas those under 18 in 1990 will have been born between 1972 and 1990.

The social and economic milieu during the intervening period ranged from the low-birth-rate years of the early 1940s through World War II; the baby boom of the late 1940s through the early 1960s; the war in Vietnam;

the social upheaval of the late 1960s, including the revitalization of the woman's movement; and the upswings in divorce and unmarried cohabitation, especially during the 1970s; to a period of relative stability of vital rates during shifting economic conditions thus far in the 1980s. The impact of such developments on the trends and variations in family structure will be referred to from time to time in the following.

The definition of a family as used here is the one that has been used by the Census Bureau for 35 years. Thus a family is defined as a group of two or more persons related by birth, marriage, or adoption, and who live together in the same household. All persons so related are regarded as one family. For example, a married couple or a parent–child group living in the home of relatives as a subfamily is treated as a part of the relatives' family.

Changes in Family Composition

In 1960, when the end of the baby boom was approaching, there were considerably more American families with young children than without any (see Table 1.11). Thereafter the proportion of families with young children declined, and by 1983 there were equal numbers of families with

Table 1.11
Composition of Families by Presence of Children, with Marital Status of Parents: United States, 1960–1990

Composition	1960	1970	1975	1983	1990
All families (thousands)	45,149	51,143	55,712	61,393	65,654
Percent	100	100	100	100	100
With no children under 18	43	45	46	50	52
With children under 18	57	55	54	50	48
Two parents present	52	48	45	40	36
One parent present	5	7	9	10	11
Mother present	4	6	8	9	10
Father present	1	1	1	1	1
Families of married couples	88	86	84	81	79
With no children under 18	36	38	39	41	43
With children under 18	52	48	45	40	36
Families of divorced persons	2	3	5	7	8
With no children under 18	1	1	1	2	2
With children under 18	1	2	4	5	6
Mother present	1	2	3	4	5
Father present	0	0	1	1	1
Families of other persons	10	11	11	12	13

Source: U.S. Bureau of the Census, 1963, 1973a, 1976a, and 1984a projections for 1990 made by the author.

and without young children in the home. The primary contributing factors were the decline in fertility and the aging of the population. The latter caused a substantial increase in "empty nest" families with no more grown children in their parental home.

If the projections shown in Table 1.11 for 1990 prove reliable, the tide will have turned so that there will be, for the first time, fewer families with young children than without any. The basic assumption underlying this projection is that the various components of family composition will continue to move in the same direction between 1983 and 1990 as between 1975 and 1983, but that the rate of change will be a little slower. This assumption is consistent with the expectation that the amount of social change influencing family structure during the rest of this decade will remain stable or diminish. Thus it is anticipated that birth rates will remain low rather than declining as they did after the baby boom, that the rapid increase in education has about run its course, and that the employment rate for women will continue to increase but at a slower pace.

Between 1960 and 1983, the proportion of families maintained by a married couple fell sharply, by almost one-fourth. In the meantime the proportion maintained by only one parent doubled, as the number of homes kept up by mothers grew at a record rate. The quite small number of father–child families actually increased a little faster than the number of mother–child families, but there were still so few of them by 1983 that their proportion of all families rounded off to only 1 percent.

The families of *divorced persons* increased at a faster rate than the families of persons in any other major category shown in Table 1.11. These families are expected to be four times as large a proportion of all families by 1990 as in 1960. And the families of divorced parents are expected to be six times as large a proportion of all families in 1990 as in 1960. Even so, these families seem likely to constitute only 6 percent of all families by the end of the present decade.

A far more impressive impact of divorce on family structure results from changing the perspective to the proportion of adults who will *ever* have maintained a family as a divorced person sometime during their life. Besides the young adults who are currently divorced, many others have already been divorced but are currently remarried, and still others who are currently in an intact first marriage will become divorced later on. Therefore, the chances are that close to one-fifth of the young adults today will eventually maintain a home as a divorced person.

Three of every four families of divorced persons have *young children* (below the age of 18 years) in their homes, and perhaps most of the remainder already have, or will eventually have, *young adult* sons and daughters (some of them divorced) living with them. These and the other points made in the foregoing reinforce the impression that divorce has become a pervasive factor in some families in the United States. And this picture does not include the intact families that feel the impact of divorce indirectly through the experiences of their close relatives.

Nearly one-half of all one-parent families are maintained by a divorced person. The other half consist of approximately equal numbers of families of separated and never-married parents. Families of separated parents have been increasing less rapidly than those of divorced parents, whereas families of never-married parents (mostly mothers) have increased even faster. These facts reflect, among other things, the more rapid processing of divorce cases as well as the tremendous increase in the number of births to unmarried mothers, which amounted to only 5 percent of all births in 1960, and was 19 percent in 1981.

Unmarried Couples with Children

The households of men and women who are living together without being married increased far more rapidly than did any other type of household during the 1970s. From a little over a half million in 1970, the number had climbed to 1.9 million by 1983. The most rapid rate of increase occurred during the last half of the 1970s, when the number of such couples went up by 15–20 percent per year. But the increase in cohabitation outside marriage only partially offset the postponement of marriage. Between 1980 and 1983, the growth in the number of these cohabiting couples diminished sharply, so that the future direction and amount of change in this group is hard to predict (U.S. Bureau of the Census, 1984b).

Cohabiting couples with children, however, increased more slowly during the 1970s than did those with no children in their home. By 1983 about 28 percent, or 525,000, of these homes included children under 15 years old. The unmarried couples with children most often consisted of two divorced adults, typically between 25 and 34 years of age. Twenty-five percent of all the cohabiting adults with children involved a divorced man living with a divorced woman (see Table 1.12). To consider the cohabiting men and women separately, half of all the cohabiting fathers (or surrogate fathers) were divorced; the corresponding proportion for the mothers (or surrogate mothers) was about four-tenths. The next most frequent marital status of the cohabiting parents was "never married." Moreover, one-half of all cohabiting parents consisted of either two divorced persons or two never-married persons. Still another perspective is that three of every four of the cohabiting parents included combinations of divorced and never-married adults. Quite obviously only relatively small numbers of cohabiting parents were classified in each of the other marital status categories.

Nearly three-fourths of the children in the homes of unmarried couples in 1983 were the women's sons or daughters, even though only about a third of the unmarried couples were living in homes maintained by women. Of the remaining children, twice as many were the men's children as were children born to the cohabiting couple, according to unpublished data for 1983. Census reports show these children as members of one-parent families, and, as a matter of fact, most of them are the natural children of one but not both of the cohabiting "parents." The children in these homes constitute about 5 percent of all children classified as members of one-parent families.

The nearly two million unmarried couples in 1983 constituted about 4 percent of all couples (married and unmarried) in the United States. Those with children represented only about 1 percent of all households in that year. These figures give just a snapshot picture of the situation at a given time. Some adults had been cohabiting outside marriage previously but were not doing so at the survey date, and others who had not yet cohabited will do so in the future. Therefore, even if cohabitation rates do not change from now on, a reasonable estimate of *lifetime* cohabitation for young adults today is that it may be three times as high as the *current* level. The corresponding lifetime level for cohabiting couples with children is probably somewhat lower, perhaps less than twice the current level. On this basis, less than 2 percent of children born this year may be expected to live with cohabiting parents sometime before they reach adulthood.

The information in this section is based on the household relationships, sex, and marital status of adults as reported to the Bureau of the Census. No questions were asked about whether the adults involved were engaging

Table 1.12

Unmarried Couples with Children under 15 Years of Age in the Home, by Marital Status of the Man and Woman: United States, 1983

Marital Status of Man	Total		Marital Status of Woman			
	(thou-sands)	%	Never Married	Divorced	Separated	Widowed
Total (thousands)	525	—	187	262	53	23
Percent	—	100	36	50	10	4
Never married	233	44	22	16	3	3
Divorced	214	41	9	27	4	1
Separated	71	14	5	6	3	0
Widowed	7	1	0	1	0	0

Source: U.S. Bureau of the Census, 1984b.

in marriagelike behavior. However, because the majority of them are under 40 years of age, most of them probably were doing so. This implication is supported by the Census Bureau's restriction of the term "unmarried couples" to members of households that included only two adults, one man and one woman unrelated to each other.

Living Arrangements of Children

Although children of divorced parents are the primary focus of this book, the present section deals extensively with a comparison of the living arrangements of children of divorced parents with those of children of other parents. A large minority of today's infants who will make their childhood home with parents who have been divorced will also have lived at one time or another with a never-married, separated, or stepparent, besides having lived with their two natural parents.

In this section the unit of analysis is the child, whereas the family was featured as the unit in preceding sections. As recently as 1960, the vast majority of young children lived with two parents. But the proportion

Table 1.13

Children Under 18 Years of Age, by Marital Status and Sex of Parents: United States, 1960–1990

Living Arrangements	1960	1970	1975	1983	1990
Total under 18 (thousands)	64,310	69,523	66,350	64,058	64,776
Percent	100	100	100	100	100
Living with two parents	88	83	79	73	71
Two natural parents:					
Both married once	73	69	64	58	55
One or both remarried	6	5	5	4	4
One stepparent	9	9	10	11	12
Living with one parent	9	14	17	22	26
Mother only	8	12	15	20	24
Divorced	2	4	5	8	11
Separated	4	5	6	5	5
Widowed	2	2	2	2	2
Never married	0	1	2	5	6
Father only	1	2	2	2	2
Divorced	0	0	1	1	1
Living with no parent	3	3	3	3	3

Source: U.S. Bureau of the Census, 1964, 1973b, 1975, 1984b; projections for 1990 prepared by the author.

shrank from 88 percent at that time to 73 percent in 1983, and may be expected to keep on shrinking until it reaches a projected estimate of 71 percent by 1990 (see Table 1-13). This projection is based on the same assumption mentioned in the discussion of Table 1.11, namely, that the recent trend will continue, but the rate of change for each category will slow down.

Most of the young children who are living with two parents live with a father and a mother both of whom are in an intact first marriage; currently this applies to an estimated 58 percent of all children under 18. But the decline in the proportion of children in the homes of two never-divorced parents has gone down even more sharply than that for the entire group of children living with two parents. Moreover, the proportion of children living with their two natural parents one or both of whom had remarried has also decreased somewhat. Unpublished data from the 1975 "Current Population Survey" show that about one-third of the children of women now past their reproductive years had been born after their divorced mothers had entered their current second marriage. But because remarried mothers or fathers are usually older than their counterparts in first marriages, and because the birth rate has declined most among women approaching the end of the reproductive period, the downward trend of children with remarried parents should not be too surprising.

Children living with a stepparent and a natural parent (usually the mother) are of special interest. These children have constituted a gradually increasing segment of all young children, whereas some students of the family might have expected the huge increase in divorce since 1960 to have caused the proportion living with a stepparent to have gone up much faster. But divorced persons who remarry are likely to have had few children or none, and, as was shown in Table 1.3, the average number of children involved in divorce (and hence in remarriage) is down sharply since the mid-1960s. Even so, the projections for 1990 point to an expected 12 percent of all children under 18 at that time living with a natural parent and a stepparent. In view of an expected 71 percent of young children to be living with two parents at that time, this 12 percent in a stepfamily will amount to one child in every six living with a father and a mother.

The prospects of a young child ever living in a stepfamily, rather than currently living in one, are obviously still greater. With half of marriages ending in divorce, and most of the divorced parents remarrying, the chances of a child being a member of a stepfamily before the age of 18 years these days must be of the order of one in three or four. Considered in this manner, the stepparenting situation looms much larger than the snapshot picture showing that about one-ninth of all children under 18 live in a stepfamily today. And surely the problems of adjustment in remarriage must be considerably greater for a divorced parent than for a childless divorced person who remarries.

Currently a little over one-fifth of the children under 18 are in one-parent families; most of them are in transition to another two-parent family (Ross & Sawhill, 1975). Many of these children will have lived through several phases of single parenting and double parenting. Some start out living with a never-married parent who later marries, becomes separated, divorced, remarried, and then redivorced. Considerable resilience must be required for children to make an average or better social adjustment while passing through all of these changes in living arrangements.

Most of the children living with a separated parent relatively soon will be living with a divorced parent, particularly children of white mothers (McCarthy, 1978). Little is known about how many estranged spouses become reconciled and establish a stable marital relationship once again, but the proportion may be larger than it had been believed to be (Kitson, 1985). As pointed out, the evidence seems clear that at least some of the parents reported as separated have never been married, in view of the fact that the number of separated women substantially exceeds the number of separated men in census reports.

Very few young children live with a widowed mother. This is attributable to the quite low death rates for young adults and to the fact that young widowed parents have about the same remarriage rates as divorced parents of similar age (U.S. Bureau of the Census, 1977).

Fastest growing since 1970 has been the number of children living with a parent who has never married. The reason, of course, is the notable increase, mentioned earlier, in the proportion of births to unmarried mothers. Because this growth has been by far the heaviest among black women, they were the parents of two-thirds of all children under 18 living with a never-married mother in 1983. Currently the number of children under 18 residing in the homes of their never-married mothers is more than half as large as the number living with divorced mothers.

Fathers continue to have custody of only 2 percent of the children under 18 years of age. About half of these fathers are divorced. One, probably minor, reason why divorced men have custody of so few children as compared with divorced women is that divorced fathers apparently enter more quickly into remarriage, and so appear in the statistical tables as married parents.

Some 3 percent of young children live with neither parent; most of these live with grandparents or other close relatives while their parents, mostly divorced or never married, live elsewhere. The proportion of young black children living apart from their parents with other relatives or nonrelatives was 8 percent in 1982, four times the corresponding figure, 2 percent, for white children. Many of their mothers probably leave the children with relatives while they move to another location where they can find better employment opportunities, and then send support money to those who are taking care of their children.

Relation Between Sex of Children and Living Arrangements

The ratio of young boys to girls in the home varies widely among families of different types. At birth there are about 105 boys to every 100 girls in the United States. In 1983 the ratio for those under 18 in two-parent families was also 105. But in the same year, there were 103 boys for every 100 girls in the families of divorced parents (U.S. Bureau of the Census, 1984b). The difference is far more striking on the basis of some other sources. For example, the June 1975 "Current Population Survey" showed that mothers of two young children were 18 percent more likely to be in an intact first marriage if both of the children were boys (Spanier & Glick, 1981).

Boys were much more likely to be living with their father than with their mother, if the mother was still divorced, according to a special tabulation of data from the June 1980 "Current Population Survey." Nine percent of the children under 18 of currently divorced women were living with their father. As shown in Table 1.14, among these children living with their

Table 1.14

Mothers of Children under 18 Years of Age, by Mother's Education, Living Arrangements of the Children, and Ratio of Sons to Daughters: United States, 1980

Years of School Completed by Mother	Mother with Children in Her Home		Mother with Children in the Father's Home	
	Mother Married*	Mother Divorced	Mother Remarried†	Mother Divorced
Total (thousands)	42,661	4,061	447	396
Sons per 100 daughters in the home, total	114	105	109	187
Mother completed				
0–11 years of school	109	109	107	245
12 years	112	106	84	158
13–15 years	122	106	343	252
16 years or more	119	89	115	163

*Predominantly mothers in their first marriage.
†Predominantly mothers remarried after divorce.
Source: U.S. Bureau of the Census, unpublished Current Population Survey data for June 1980.

father, there were 187 boys to every 100 girls. By contrast, among the children living with their currently divorced mother, there were only 105 boys for every 100 girls. This preponderance of sons living with their father was particularly notable if their divorced mother had dropped out of high school or college before graduation. Under these circumstances there were about 250 boys for every 100 girls living with their fathers.

Mothers were found to be more likely to have sons under 18 in their homes if they were married than if they were currently divorced. As Table 1.14 shows, the ratio of boys to girls was 114 to 100 for those in the home of a married mother and 105 to 100 for those in the home of a divorced mother. Here, again, is evidence that married couples tend to be more likely to stay married if they have sons in the home. These facts also suggest that divorced mothers tend to feel less urgency to remarry if they have daughters rather than sons in their custody. An alternative interpretation is that divorced mothers may feel less reluctant to take sons than daughters into remarriage because the relationship between stepfathers and stepsons might involve fewer personal problems than that between stepfathers and stepdaughters. Although the study on which this research was based did not provide information about whether the fathers had remarried, in all likelihood most of them had done so.

In brief, sons are significantly more likely than daughters to be living with a father, regardless of whether the father is married or divorced. In this context divorced mothers with child custody are evidently more likely to bring sons than daughters with them into a remarriage or to remarry rather promptly.

Sons are more likely to be found in homes where there is a father for a number of reasons, perhaps the most important of which is the greater difficulty in rearing boys than girls (Hetherington et al., 1979). Parents in their first marriage may be more likely to remain married if they have sons, as the mother might have to take care of the sons alone after divorce. And if a divorced mother has custody of sons, she may feel a special need to remarry to have a husband not only to help pay the bills, but also to help with the child rearing. Alternatively the preference for sons may have survived from generations ago, before social security and other pensions were available, when most families lived on farms, or perhaps had shops in small towns or cities, and felt that sons would be more useful in the family enterprise than daughters. This preference appears to be found most often among parents of low socioeconomic status, and it seems likely it will diminish in the future (Spanier & Glick, 1981).

Young Adult Children Living with Their Parents

Along with the rising divorce rate, one might expect a corresponding rise in the number of young adults who return to live with their parents after they are divorced (Shehan et al., 1983). According to the U.S. Bureau of the Census (1973c, 1984b), the proportion of young adults in their 20s who were living in the homes of their parents rose by nearly one-half, from 21 percent to 29 percent, between 1970 and 1983. Primarily, more young adults were postponing marriage and staying at home with their parents. A majority were employed, but about one-fourth of the never-married persons were unemployed or attending school (Glick & Lin, 1986).

Most of the young adults who became divorced had a home of their own. Divorced men were more likely to maintain an apartment or house alone (or with an unrelated woman), whereas divorced women were more likely to maintain an apartment or house with one or more of their children (or with an unrelated man). In 1983, however, an estimated 22 percent of divorced persons in their 20s were living with their relatives (mainly parents). And in 1970, when a far smaller proportion of divorced persons was cohabiting outside marriage, an even larger proportion—29 percent—of divorced persons in their 20s was living with parents (U.S. Bureau of the Census, 1973b). In 1980 about three-fourths of live-in divorced sons and daughters were employed, with 15 percent unemployed. Very few were attending school. These divorced adults presumably were unable financially to keep up a home apart from their parents, although a substantial majority of the divorced mothers worked outside the home while the grandmother apparently took care of the children. One of the reasons why more parents make room in their homes for their young adult children these days is the fact that such divorced children bring with them fewer preschool- and school-age children now that the birth rate is low.

OUTLOOK

Divorce has surely played a major role in the changing American family structure since 1960. But what about the future? Will divorce increase, decrease, or stay about the same? Of course, no one can predict the answer with great confidence. Divorce rates have fluctuated in the past, and may be expected to do so in the future. But as for the next decade or so, there are several reasons to expect that the divorce rate may gradually resume its historic upward trend, and other reasons why it may decline.

One reason the divorce rate may increase is that the number of persons in the period of life when most divorces occur, ages 25–39 years, will not reach a peak until about 1990. Other potential developments that would tend to increase divorce include a continuing upward trend in the employment of women, in the equality of the sexes, in the secularization of life, and in the acceptance of divorce as a reasonable way to resolve serious marital difficulties.

A different set of potential developments might cause pressure toward a decline in divorce (Kempler, 1983). They include a substantial rebounding of the birth rate associated with a decrease in the employment of young women, an easing of the entry of young men into the labor force because of the current maturing of persons born during the period of declining birth rates in the 1960s, an associated decline in cohabitation outside marriage as more young couples marry early with more commitment to each other, and an increasingly "conservative trend" that could reflect a growing disfavor for divorce as a cure-all for serious marital problems.

What really happens to the divorce levels during the coming years will depend on the net effect of counteracting forces that affect the stability of marriage. It is only realistic to expect the divorce rate to remain high in this modern era, especially if the economy continually provides jobs for most of the women who seek them. At the same time, it should not be surprising if an increasing proportion of young adults decide to opt for a lifetime of singlehood or for spending the remaining years of their life in the single state after having experienced several years of marriage. In the words of Westoff (1978), "The future seems less and less compatible with long-term traditional marriage." And yet this does not seem inconsistent with a realistic expectation that the vast majority of men and women will continue to prefer the benefits of a stable married life, either after their first venture into marriage, or during their second time around.

Probably most people would agree that children are most likely to enjoy healthy development if they spend their entire childhood in the home of their two natural parents, provided their parents are compatible. But under present conditions, the quality of the child care seems more important than who renders it. Finally, despite the many changes in family structure during recent decades, it is of interest to note that three-fourths of the people in the United States are still living in the homes of married couples (Glick, 1979, 1984a).

REFERENCES

Bernard, J. (1966). Marital stability and patterns of status variables. *Journal of Marriage and the Family, 28*(4), 421–439.

Bumpass, L. L. (1984). Children and marital disruption: A replication and update. *Demography, 21*(1), 71–82.

Cherlin, A. J. (1981). *Marriage, Divorce, Remarriage*. Cambridge, Mass.: Harvard University Press.

Espenshade, T. J. (1984.). Black-white differences in marriage, separation. and remarriage, Unpublished report to National Institute of Child Health and Human Development. Urban Institute, Washington, D.C.

Glick, P. C. (1979). Children of divorced parents in demographic perspective. *Journal of Social Issues, 35*(4), 170–182.

Glick, P. C. (1984a). Marriage, divorce, and living arrangements: Prospective changes. *Journal of Family Issues, 5*(1), 7–26.

Glick, P. C., & Lin, S. L. (1986). More young adults are living with their parents: Who are they? *Journal of Marriage and the Family, 48* 107–112.

Hetherington, E. M., Cox, M., & Cox, R. (1979). Family interaction and the social, emotional and cognitive development of children following divorce. In V. C Vaughn & T. B. Brazelton (Eds.), *The family: Setting priorities. (pp. 71–87). New York: Science & Medicine Publications.*

Kemper, T. D. (1983). Predicting the divorce rate: Down? *Journal of Family 4*(3), 507–524.

Kitson, G. C. (1985). Marital discord and marital separation: A county survey. *Journal of Marriage and the Family, 47*(3), 693–700.

McCarthy, J. (1978). A comparison of the probability of the dissolution of first and second marriages. *Demography, 15*(3), 345–359.

Norton, A. J. (1980). The influence of divorce on the traditional life cycle measures. *Journal of Marriage and the Family, 42*(1), 63–69.

Norton, A. J., & Glick, P. C. (1979). Marital instability in America: Past, present, and future. In G. Levinger & D. C. Moles (Eds.),*Divorce and Separation: Context, Causes, and Consequences* (pp. 6–19). New York: Basic Books.

Ross, H. L., & Sawhill, I. V. (1975). *Time of transition: The Growth of Families Headed by Women.* Washington, D.C.: Urban Institute.

Shehan, C., Berardo, D., & Berardo, F. (1983, October). The empty-nest is filling again: A look at extended families in America in hard times. Paper presented at the annual meeting of the National Council on Family Relations, St. Paul, Minn.

Spanier, G. B., & Glick, P. C. (1981) Marital instability in the United States: Some correlates and recent changes. *Family Relations, 31*(3), 329–338.

U.S. Bureau of the Census (1963). 1960 Census of Population, *II* (4A), Families. Washington, D.C.: U.S. Government Printing Office.

U.S. Bureau of the Census (1964). 1960 Census of Population, *II*(4B), Persons by family characteristics. Washington, D.C.: U.S. Government Printing Office.

U.S. Bureau of the Census (1972). 1970 Census of Population, *II*(4C), Marital status. Washington, D.C.: U.S. Government Printing Office.

U.S. Bureau of the Census (1973a). 1970 Census of Population, *II*(4A), Family composition. Washington, D.C.: U.S. Government Printing Office. U.S. Bureau of the Census (1973b). 1970 Census of Population, *II* (4B), Persons by family characteristics. Washington, D.C.: U.S. Government Printing Office.

U.S. Bureau of the Census (1973c). 1970 Census of Population, *I*(D1), Detailed characteristics. Washington, D.C.: U.S. Government Printing Office.

U.S. Bureau of the Census (1975). Current population reports, *20*(287), Marital status and living arrangements: March 1975. Washington, D.C.: U.S. Government Printing Office.

U.S. Bureau of the Census (1976a). Current population reports, *20*(291), Household and family characteristics: March 1975. Washington, D.C. U.S. Government Printing Office.

U.S. Bureau of the Census. (1976b). Current population reports, *20*(297), Number, timing, and duration of marriages and divorces in the United States: June 1975. Washington, D.C.: U.S. Government Printing Office.

U.S. Bureau of the Census (1977). Current population reports, *20*(312), Marriage, divorce, widowhood, and remarriage by family characteristics: June 1975. Washington, D.C.: U.S. Government Printing Office.

U.S. Bureau of the Census (1978). Current population reports, *23*(77), Perspectives on American husbands and wives. Washington, D.C.: U.S. Government Printing Office.

U.S. Bureau of the Census (1983). Statistical abstract of the United States. Washington, D.C.: U.S. Government Printing Office.

U.S. Bureau of the Census (1984a). Current population reports, *20*(388), Household and family characteristics: March 1983. Washington, D.C.: U.S. Government Printing Office.

U.S. Bureau of the Census (1984b). Current population reports, *20*(389), Marital status and living arrangements: March 1983. Washington, D.C.: U.S. Government Printing Office.

U.S. Bureau of the Census (1984c). Current population reports, *60*(142), Money income of households, families, and persons in the United States: 1982. Washington, D.C.: U.S. Government Printing Office.

U.S. Bureau of the Census (1983). Statistical abstract of the United States: 1984. Washington, D.C.: U.S. Government Printing Office.

U.S. Bureau of Labor Statistics (1983). Marital and family patterns of workers: An update (Bulletin 2163). Washington, D.C.: U.S. Government Printing Office.

U.S. National Center for Health Statistics (1973). Vital and health statistics, *21*(24), 100 years of marriage and divorce statistics: United States, 1867–1967. Washington, D.C.: U.S. Government Printing Office.

U.S. National Center for Health Statistics (1980). Vital statistics of the United States: 1976, *III*, Marriage and divorce. Washington, D.C.: U.S. Government Printing Office.

U.S. National Center for Health Statistics (1982). Monthy vital statistics report, *30*(13), Annual summary of births, deaths, marriages, and divorces: United States, 1981. Washington, D.C.: U.S. Government Printing Office.

U.S. National Center for Health Statistics (1984a). Monthly vital statistics report, *32*(9, supplement), Advance report on final divorce statistics, 1981. Washington, D.C.: U.S. Government Printing Office.

U.S. National Center for Health Statistics (1984b). Monthly vital statistics report, *31*(13), Annual summary of births, deaths, marriages, and divorces: United States: 1982. Washington, D.C.: U.S. Government Printing Office.

U.S. National Center for Health Statiistics (1985). Monthly vital statistics report, *33*(12), Births, marriages, divorces, and deaths for 1984. Washington D.C.: U.S. Government Printing Office.

Westoff, C. F. (1978). Some speculations on the future of marriage and fertility. *Family Planning Perspectives, 10*(2), 79–83.

Weed, J. A. (1982). Divorce: American style. *American Demographics, 4*(3), 12–17.

2

A Life Transition Framework for Understanding Marital Dissolution and Family Reorganization

ROBERT D. FELNER, LISA TERRE,
and RICHARD T. ROWLISON

As do so many chapters dealing with the subject of children's adaptation following divorce, we were going to begin this chapter with a discussion of incidence rates to document the extent of the problem. Following that, and again in keeping with the typical chapter on this issue, we were going to provide a brief overview of findings and arguments relating to the types and increased incidence of adaptive problems specific to children who have experienced divorce as compared with children from intact families. This would be done, of course, with the idea that we were demonstrating that divorce is "an event which places children at greater risk for emotional disorder" (Felner et al., 1980b). We would then launch into a discussion of models for understanding the effects of divorce and their implications for intervention and prevention. However, after careful deliberation, we decided that "standard" opening would not have really fit well with where we hope to end up. Instead we begin with the assertion that, *"Divorce has little or no adaptive impact on children whatsoever!"* Now let us attempt to explain what has led us to make a statement that, at best, could be termed highly controversial.

Let us examine what we mean by a divorce. It must be recognized that the legal divorce is often not a part of the experience of the children. The parents may meet several times in the company of attorneys to work out issues, sign some papers, file them with the court, and, at some later point, with only the judge and clerk present, the papers are finalized and the "divorce" occurs. To be sure, there are exceptions that involve emotionally taxing courtroom scenarios for the child. But this is generally not the case, since less than 15 percent of all divorces actually go to court on the initial custody agreement, and even fewer require the child to be present (Felner & Terre, 1987; Foster & Freed, 1980; Johnston et al., 1985). The reader may say that our exaggerated focus on the legal "stamping" of the divorce fails to capture the tremendous upheaval, stress, and adaptive challenges that are often features of the process surrounding the divorce. This, however, is exactly the point we are trying to make. That is, what is essential for understanding the effects of divorce is a focus not on the divorce, but rather on those characteristics of the developmental context (e.g., the child's relationships to care givers, the stability of the environment) that characterize and shape the divorce experience for the child (as well as for adults). As noted elsewhere, "The data make it clear that a perspective which views divorce as a unitary stressful event is, at best, misleading. It appears far more helpful to focus not only on the brief period surrounding that 'event', but also on its aftermath and the repercussions it precipitates in the lives of family members which may continue to engender new stressors and changes and demand new adaptations for some time to come" (Felner et al., 1980b, pp. 102). Instead of seeking to understand divorce as a unique and circumscribed developmental phenomenon, we suggest that it may well be best understood as a "special case" instance of normative development, at least in our attempts to identify and elaborate salient adaptive processes. The implications of this view of divorce for the frameworks that we employ to explore the consequences of divorce, as well as for the nature of the questions asked or answered, and for the interventions that may derive from them, are quite broad. And, since systematic frameworks are necessary if we are to develop a better understanding of how contextual factors interact with child-related ones to shape adaptation (Sameroff, 1982), it is to a consideration of current and emergent models that we now turn.

In this chapter we first briefly consider two perspectives, which, in the past, have been the most widely employed for viewing the process by which individuals adapt to significant life events or changes. Following that we discuss in greater detail an evolving model for viewing significant life transitions. As was hinted earlier, this latter model and its applicability to understanding the divorce process, developed by the senior author and his colleagues (Felner et al., 1975; Felner et al., 1980b, 1983; Felner, 1984; Felner et al., 1986; Felner & Terre, 1987), is one that emphasizes the prolonged period of adapatation to such transitions and the adaptive tasks that characterize them. Further, we feel that our model is particularly well-suited for understanding of the effects of occurrences such as divorce on children because, of those life events models that exist, it is the one that may be most compatible with general developmental perspectives on risk, resilience and vulnerability (Sameroff et al., 1982), while at the same time it provides the best fit for the data pertaining to divorce. Finally, it is a model that has as its explicit goal the facilitation of programs aimed at both the primary prevention of disorder and the enhancement of development.

Before discussing this conceptual framework, let us turn to a consideration of two of the more frequently used models for understanding the effects of life events, and what these offer for our understanding of the effects of divorce. These models, and their more general implications for considering the adaptive consequences of life events and changes, have been discussed by us in greater detail elsewhere (c.f. Felner, 1984; Felner et al., 1980b, 1983, 1986). Thus in this chapter, we briefly summarize these discussions rather than consider them in detail.

CRISIS THEORY AND LIFE CRISES

No discussion of models for understanding the adaptive significance of life events would be complete without a bow to crisis theory. This model is heavily based on ego-analytic conceptualizations of personality development (Erikson, 1959), early efforts by mental health professionals to develop brief interventions for individuals who had experienced traumatic events, particularly bereavement, and attempts to understand the processes by which such events influenced development (Lindemann, 1944, 1979). Crisis theory has been perhaps most systematically developed and articulated by Caplan (1964). He viewed crises as occurring when individuals encountered significant life problems that they could neither avoid nor deny, and that exceeded their ability to cope with effectively, given their coping resources. The actual crisis itself is a state of homeostatic imbalance or disequilibrium that develops in the organism when coping efforts fail. This in turn results in heightened levels of tension, anxiety, and "acute psychological upset" (Caplan, 1964, p. 35), which disrupt the more typical steady-state equilibrium of the individual and leave the system open to rapid change. While in a state of crisis, individuals are seen as being particularly susceptible to outside influence, and thus are good candidates for intervention. Caplan (1964) argues further that: (1) crisis resolution generally occurs within four to six weeks; (2) the outcome may be positive or negative, with the crisis providing the opportunity for growth as well as for the development of disorder; and (3) whatever the outcome, crises have important implications for long-term adaptation.

Even from this limited discussion of crisis theory, it should be evident that the focus is neither on the event per se nor on the particular relationship between the individual and the environmental context, except insofar as the environment may be a precipitant of the problem or a possible source of coping resources. Rather the focus is almost exclusively on the internal, affective state of the organism. The primary tasks confronting the individual include the reestablishment of a state of internal homeostatic balance, the "realignment of forces both inside [the] personality and in relationship with meaningful people in [the] milieu" (Caplan, 1964, p. 43), and the development of new patterns of problem solving. If we remember that this model is heavily rooted in dynamic formulations of development and disorder, such an emphasis is not surprising. Freudian roots are particularly evident, for example, when, in discussing factors that relate to crisis onset and outcomes, Caplan (1964) notes the importance of determining whether or not the present situation is "symbolically link(ed)" to similar problems in the past. He remarks that, "It is a characteristic finding during crises that memories of old problems which are in some way linked to the present one are stimulated and either emerge spontaneously into consciousness or can be uncovered by simple psychiatric interviewing" (p. 41).

This view of life events as crises may be particularly useful for understanding the individual's efforts to cope with the feelings that may be aroused immediately preceding or following the divorce. But it has little utility for understanding the more prolonged adaptive efforts that may be required both prior to and after the divorce. Indeed an exclusive reliance on this framework may lead to a tendency to view divorce as a relatively brief and unitary "crisis-predisposing event" (Felner et al., 1975, 1980b), thereby diverting our focus from the prolonged and complex process of adaptation that is called for during this transition. Additionally, with the exception of the role of external agents as sources of influence, a crisis model tells us little about the nature of the person–environment transactions that are necessary for successful adaptation. Finally, this model is not applicable to all individuals who are experiencing any particular life event, because stressful life events may not precipitate a state of crisis among all who experience them. Recall that a crisis only occurs when a person's coping abilities are taxed beyond his or limits. Such a person-centered approach is not helpful for understanding the full range of adaptive efforts demanded by significant life events or changes. Rather an idiographic focus is only appropriate for understanding a circumscribed subset of coping efforts and adaptive outcomes in à particular subset of the population experiencing the life problem. That is not to say that crises are not important, or that incorporation of the crisis concept into a more general model for understanding adaptation to transitional events or life events may not be helpful. We merely point out that an exclusive reliance on crisis theory may be far too limiting to allow for the full consideration of the adaptive implications of divorce and similar major life changes. A final, generally unrecognized but critical contribution of crisis theory is that it may be seen as an attempt to understand the adaptive processes called for by significant life changes or events as "special case" instances of more general developmental processes and patterns.

STRESSFUL LIFE EVENTS

A second widely employed perspective for understanding the adaptive significance of life events is rooted in epidemiology and public health (Dohrenwend, 1979; Dohrenwend & Dohrenwend, 1984) and emphasizes the relationship between the experience of single or multiple life-change events and current population levels of physical or mental disorder. This "stressful-life-events" position identifies psychosocial stress as the mediator that links the experience of the life event and dysfunction. Consistent with its conceptual heritage, the primary focus of much of the work in this area has been on predicting dysfunction and identifying agents of etiological significance therein (e.g., the stressful properties of life events and changes). Oddly, what needs to be clearly understood here is that the stressful-life-events model primarily is interested neither in life events per se nor in their general significance for the full range of human functioning and development, but rather provides a means by which to explore the nature and consequences of stress broadly conceived (Felner et al., 1983, 1986). Perhaps this viewpoint can best be illustrated by noting that among the most salient guiding questions in this area are those that pertain to what a stressful life event is and what makes it stressful (Felner et al., 1986) with the primary goals being the development of instruments or markers to predict disorder as well as the articulation of models of life stress that allow for the exploration of hypotheses about specific stress–disorder links. Further, as has been discussed in detail by the present authors (Felner et al., 1986), the search for answers to these questions have generally fallen into three broad categories. These are: (1) attempts to identify personal dispositions or psychological characteristics influencing the degree to which the event is appraised as stressful by the individual experiencing it; (2) efforts to elaborate aspects of the events that relate to the degree to which they are appraised as stressful; and (3) environmental or situational factors that may mediate people's appraisal of an event, the demands it places on them, and coping resources they have available to deal with the resultant stress.

Although much more may be said about the voluminous literature on stressful life events, it is not our intent to review material that has been so thoroughly discussed elsewhere (cf., Dohrenwend & Dohrenwend, 1978, 1984; Felner et al, 1983, 1986; Monroe, 1982; Perkins, 1982; Sarason et al., 1978)—nor is it our intent to evaluate fully the adequacy of this model for understanding the impact of divorce on children (cf. Felner et al., 1980, for a detailed discussion of this topic). Rather, given its general significance and widespread use, it is important to note this model briefly and discuss its limitations for viewing the adaptive significance of divorce for children. It is also important to note that stressful-life-events models have not been without value for advancing our understanding of the processes by which individuals cope with life events. Such models have made important contributions in: (1) clarifying factors that may mediate adaptation to stress resulting from a life event; (2) highlighting the level of risk associated with such events; and (3) explicitly recognizing individual differences in response to the same event. Nonetheless this model is seriously deficient for guiding efforts to understand fully the adaptive significance of occurrences, such as parental divorce, and it is to these limitations that we now turn.

A TRANSITIONAL-EVENTS PERSPECTIVE

One of the primary limitations of a stressful-life-events framework is that it leads to a misleading view of divorce as a circumscribed, unitary stressful event (Felner et al., 1980b). As noted at the outset of this chapter, it is believed necessary to focus on the entire transitional period that may extend temporally for some time around the actual "event", if we are to understand fully the resultant adaptive process. That is, it may not be possible to talk about "a divorce" with any precision, because the divorce experience may be dramatically different for each person, with the level and degree of additional stressors and changes, and the resultant adaptive tasks that accompany the divorce, varying markedly across individuals.

Illustratively, Sandler, and colleagues (1986) argue, "Stress impact differs across divorce-related events and . . . divorces in which many highly stressful events occur will more adversely affect children than will divorces in which fewer or less stressful events occur."

A second limitation of the stressful-life-events approach that may be less obvious, but just as critical, is the truncation of range of the phenomenon of concern that, at least implicity, accompanies the use of this model. Because of its epidemiological roots in the search for factors related to risk for disorder,the focus is on those characteristics of events and individuals that are linked to the level of stress experienced and to the concomitant risk for disorder that ensues. Exemplifying this stance are arguments by Dohrenwend and Dohrenwend (1984), who take the position that the life events with which researchers in this area are primarily concerned are those that occur in *close temporal proximity* to the onset of disorder, and by Bloom (1979), who argues that a means of identifying significant life events is to "identify a stressful life event that appears to have undesirable consequences in a significant proportion of the population" (p. 183). While such a pathology-focused stance may be useful in highlighting the need to target preventive interventions toward individuals who are experiencing divorce, it draws attention away from the fact that positive life changes may also have important adaptive implications and pose serious adaptive challenges (Felner et al., 1983).

A third limitation of a stressful-events approach is the generally static and passive model of the coping process that it has represented. Factors in the environment are seen to "mediate" the stressfulness of an event and to interact with personal factors ultimately influencing the individual's appraisal of the event's stressfulness (Felner et al., 1983). Little attention is paid to how environmental circumstances may shift or be actively influenced by the individual's coping efforts. For example, social support may be seen as a relatively static element of the environment that is salient only insofar as it may "buffer" the effects of stress or contribute to the individual's appraisal of the event as stressful. In contrast, from a transitional perspective, social support is seen as an aspect of the environment that the individual must actively modify and that is similarly influenced by the characteristics and coping efforts of the individual (Felner et al., 1983).

THE LIFE TRANSITION FRAMEWORK

The "transitional-events" model of Felner and colleagues (cf., Felner, 1985; Felner et al., 1983, 1986), while building upon the preceding models, differs from them in a number of important ways. First, the period of time that is of concern is significantly greater. In contrast to the four- to six-week focus of crisis theory or the circumscribed-event view of stress models, the emphasis of the transitional-events model is on the extended adaptive processes that may be called for both prior to and following the labeled "event." This transitional period, during which the organism may face multiple adaptive tasks, challenges, and further life changes, may require several years for a new stable equilibrium to be attained. Indeed, in some instances, the changed life circumstances may pose challenges that are never actually resolved, but either must be reworked on a continuing basis or may reemerge due to normative developmental changes or other transitional events.

A second point of departure of the transitional framework from prior ones is that, in keeping with the crisis model, but quite different than the stressful-life-event perspective, the transitional-event approach seeks to shift the focus of stress and its pathogenic effects to a concern with the ways in which such events relate to the full range of developmental processes and outcomes. That is, transitional events are seen as special instances of more general developmental patterns that have been disrupted, or intensified, or are in need of reorganization in specific ways. However, by contrast with the crisis model, which had as its central concern the reestablishment of homeostatic balance in the organism, the emphasis is now on the changes and modifications in the organism's environment that characterize such transitional events, the adaptive tasks that they pose, given the existing or emerging characteristics of the person, and the nature of the transactions between the person and the developmental context that relate to positive or negative outcomes (Bronfenbrenner, 1979; Sameroff et al., 1982). Significant changes that occur include those in the relationship between persons and the elements of the social environment in which they live. These changes may involve not only the restructuring of the individual's cognitive representations of reality, but also an active restructuring of their interactions with the environmental systems with in which they function. Such challenges are seen to underlie and define the adaptive tasks the person confronts (Felner et al., 1986).

Characteristics of the transitional-events model are captured by Felner and colleagues (1986) in the discussion of the choice of this term. They state:

> This juxtaposition [of the terms event and transition] was chosen with the intent of capturing the unique nature of the phenomenon we seek to explain. On the one hand, the inclusion of the term transition is meant to underscore our concern with a process that involves change and the ways individuals adapt to it . . . . That is, we are not only concerned with the event proper but

also the adapative efforts which lead up to and follow it. The term 'event' is nonetheless included as it needs to be recognized that we are dealing with a particular type of transition. . . .

The focus of this framework is on those transitions that are characterized by fundamental and clearly identifiable shifts in the organism's environment rather than those that are attributed to normative, less observable, and sharp maturational changes in the organism,—that is, "those transitions marked by identifiable events in the life history where the event signals that the individual is in the midst of, or at one of the end points of, a profound and extensive reorganization of their place in the social environment" (Felner et al., 1986). Further, it is a model that views the organism as actively engaged in transactions in order to shape the environment and master the adaptive tasks that confront it.

It must be understood that a transitional-events framework does not preclude the use of elements of crisis or stressful-life-events perspectives. Rather, while allowing for a consideration of some of the issues of concern to these two earlier models, the transitional-events framework is more inclusive in its focus upon the adaptive processes and outcomes of interest. Several excellent examples already exist of ways in which these models may be combined in the study of parental divorce, and they are discussed later in this chapter (e.g., the work of Sandler and Wolchik and their colleagues). However, a brief discussion of the more general issues involved in how this may be done is included so as to clarify a key element of the transitional-events perspective—its emphasis on more proximal rather than distal environmental circumstances.

What do we mean by proximal versus distal conditions, changes, and events? Here the work of De Longis and colleagues (1982), which focuses on the distinction between day-to-day stress processes and major stressful life events, may be instructive. These authors argue that a distinction should be made between major life events and the actual stressors they precipitate or exacerbate in the individual's daily life. This distinction is based on the conceptual proximity of the events. Put otherwise, major events are considered distal because they do not directly describe the life circumstances in which they result or the adaptive processes they require. In contrast, proximal stressors are those more immediate, daily transactions that describe a person's actual experiences and adaptive efforts. From a transitional-events perspective, the incorporation of a similar component is vital, although somewhat broadened. We are still concerned with proximal stressors or "hassles," as are DeLongis and colleagues (1982), but so too are we concerned with the full range of daily experiences, tasks, and more immediate changes in the child's environment that accompany divorce.

An emphasis on the person-in-environment is another essential element of the transitional-events model. Compared with the hoary tradition that stressed the importance of child-related variables on children's adaptation to life events, interest in the role of environmental influences is relatively new, and the development of true transactional models is even more recent. The nascent state of development of transactional-contextual views applicable to development in general, and life events in particular, is underscored by Bronfenbrenner (1979). In writing about the difference in our understanding of person versus environment factors Bronfenbrenner states, "What we find . . . is a marked asymmetry, a hypertrophy of theory and research focusing on the properties of the person and only the most rudimentary conception and characterization of the environment in which the person is found" (p. 16). Sameroff and Seifer (1983) make a similar observation, noting that the study of high-risk children may have been, at least in part, responsible for the shift in the attention of developmental psychologists from a primary focus on the "processes of development (e.g., learning and perception) to a greater interest in the context of development. . . ." (p. 1254). For those concerned with the developmental significance of life events or transitions, the need for models that are more sophisticated than those previously employed may be particularly critical. Again, Bronfenbrenner, writing on our understanding of contextual factors on development, states, "On the environmental side, however, the prospect is bland by comparison, both in theory and data. The existing concepts are limited to a few crude and undifferentiated categories that do little more than locate people in terms of their social address—the setting from which they come" (1974, p. 17). Among those crude categories to which he then refers are single- versus two-parent households and such personal characteristics as ethnic background or social class. For us, these issues are the heart of a shift to the transitional-events model we espouse. That is, if we are to further our understanding of the developmental significance of such occurrences, we need to develop frameworks that allows us to attend to the full complexity of the environmental circumstances in which the individual resides and, more specifically, to understand better the process underlying the experience of, and adaptation to, various life transitions.

An example of what we mean here may help. It is very difficult even to begin to consider what specific actions are required for effective coping with such a broad and ambiguous problem as a divorce if we keep our attention focused on the relatively immediate affective response to the separation decision, with its consequent demands for expression of feelings, support, and reintegration. However, if we know that there are certain adaptive tasks that characterize transitions, (such as the reorganization of one's assumptive world, daily routines, and social networks, and the redefinition of roles (Felner et al., 1983, 1986), then we can begin to identify and focus upon more specific aspects of each of these areas that may have been affected by the divorce. As Felner et al. (1983) posit:

> We would like to suggest that a key aspect of a transitional perspective on life change must be an emphasis on identifying the specific types of changes which confront the individual during the transition as tasks which must be actively mastered by the individual . . . we are no longer concerned with the individual's affective response to the change (that is, the experienced level of stress). Rather, from this perspective we are concerned with what the individual must do, cognitively and/or behaviorally, to achieve satisfactory levels of adaptation to the new circumstances in their life from events and the transitional tasks they precipitate. (p. 209)

Given the preceding comments, we must now stop to make a critical point. That is, because transitional events often involve a shift from one or more social systems to others, or modifications in the individual's existing social system, the characteristics of these systems may be significant factors in shaping the degree of difficulty of the adaptive tasks the person confronts. Thus considering the extent to which the family system defines the child's developmental context and the shifts in family structure and organization inherent in the divorce process, if we are truly to move to a transactional model of life change, then the child's coping efforts cannot be considered apart from the nature of the family system and the tasks, changes, and coping efforts with which it is involved.

THE TRANSITIONAL EVENT OF DIVORCE

There is considerable empirical support for the view that parental divorce is best understood as a marker of more extended multifaceted processes that involve complex transactions between family members and environmental variables, both of which shift and evolve over time (e.g., Felner et al., 1980b; 1983; Lazarus & Folkman, 1984). On the one hand, for example, children's cognitive abilities, problem-solving skills, and coping styles may act to shape both perceptions and appraisals of the changes occurring around them as well as efforts to shape these circumstances (Kurdek et al., 1981; Lazarus & Folkman, 1984). On the other hand, the environmental context that children experience defines the specific array of changes, tasks, and stressors with which they must attempt to cope, and, it must be understood, this context continues to evolve and change further over time. A detailed consideration of all the environmental challenges, adaptive tasks, and moderators of the developmental outcomes that may be associated with divorce is well beyond the scope of this chapter; and we will not attempt to review them here. [The reader is referred to Felner et al. (1980b), Felner and Terre (1987), and a number of the other chapters in this volume for a more thorough discussion of this literature.] Rather, by drawing on representative work and focusing on key issues in the divorce literature relating to children, an attempt will be made to demonstrate the utility of a transitional-events perspective for understanding the child's adaptive efforts and to identify personal and situational factors that may be central to shaping the transactions between the child and his or her environment during this critical transition.

CHILD CHARACTERISTICS AND THE IMPACT OF DIVORCE

The search for systematic adjustment problems or "effects of divorce" has been marked by inconsistent findings and has provided little support for any particular adaptive outcome being specific to children of divorce (Felner & Terre, 1987). Indeed, it was precisely this inconsistency that led to both a search for moderator variables and the recognition of the long-term adaptive process involved (Felner et al., 1980b). Illustratively, when the child's age and gender are considered as they relate to divorce outcomes, a markedly inconsistent pattern of results is found (Felner et al., 1980b; Felner & Terre, 1987). The evidence pertaining to differences in children's responses to parental divorce associated with these variables indicates that they are far more consistently correlated with the pattern of adjustment than with the severity of trauma or the magnitude of the problems displayed. In attempting to account for these findings, Felner and Terre (1987) argue that the child's age or sex may be most important by acting to influence the coping efforts children are able to bring to bear upon the situation, thereby both shaping their appraisal of the situation and limiting their ability to act on it. In other words, it is not the child's age gender per se that is central to shaping the outcome, but, as in other developmental challenges, it is the child's age- and gender-related competencies or socialization experiences that are important determinants of the differential patterns of adjustment. In support of such a position, Longfellow (1979) argues that differential child reactions to divorce at varying ages may be due to the social-cognitive abilities that children bring to the situation and their attempts to understand or deal with it. Similarly, other authors (e.g., Kurdek & Siesky, 1979, 1980a, 1980b; Kurdek et al., 1981) note that children's age-related social or cognitive abilities may affect their ability to draw on available coping resources in their environment as well as their perception of the divorce. In this vein Kurdek and Siesky (1980b) note that locus of control and interpersonal reasoning are important mediators of children's adjustment to divorce (see Larry Kurdek's chapter in this volume for a detailed discussion of this topic).

In addition to the evidence that children react differently to divorce depending on their developmental status or socialization experiences, it is also becoming increasingly clear that children's reactions and coping patterns may vary during different phases of the divorce process (Hancock, 1980; Hetherington et al., 1978a; Messinger & Walker, 1981; Wallerstein, 1983). Based on a longitudinal study, Wallerstein (1983), drawing heavily upon ego psychology, has argued that children of divorce face a *series of coping tasks* that change throughout the process. Further, although the focus of Wallerstein's structural perspective is on ego processes and psychic integrity rather than specific environmentally linked challenges and problem-solving strategies required (and hence differs substantially from our own), it does address, to some extent, the transitional task of reorganization of the individual's assumptive world, which elsewhere (Felner et al., 1983) we have identified as being common across transitional events.

A significant exception to this pattern of inconsistent effects relates to the increased level of acting-out, antisocial, or aggressive behaviors that have been repeatedly found to be associated with divorce (e.g., Felner et al., 1975; Felner et al., 1981; Hetherington et al., 1978b; Hodges & Bloom, 1984; Hodges et al., 1984; McDermott, 1968, 1970; Wallerstein & Kelly, 1975). Given the central thesis of this chapter, these findings are particularly instructive. First, as we see in our discussion of environmental conditions and changes associated with divorce, such a pattern of results would be predicted for most children, whether from intact or divorced households, who had similar developmental circumstances. Second, related to this finding are a number of studies that have sought to disentangle the effects of divorce from the more general case of father absence, and, in so doing, have highlighted how the processes surrounding divorce may be critical to shaping adaptive outcomes. A number of authors (Felner et al., 1975, 1981; Glueck & Glueck, 1950; Hetherington, 1972) have shown that antisocial or acting-out problems are far more prevalent in children from households where a divorce had occurred than from those in which a parent had died. Similarly, Felner et al. (1981) reported lower levels of frustration tolerance and more difficulties in following rules among children experiencing divorce versus those dealing with parental death or coming from intact households. These findings further highlight the fact that it is not the family disruption or parental absence per se that acts to shape outcomes, as much as it is the circumstances and the changes in them that accompany this change in family organization. It is to these circumstances that we now turn.

THE DIVORCE CONTEXT AND CHILDREN'S ADAPTATION

Felner and Terre (1987) have elucidated a set of contextual factors that may be critical to the child's development, and which may be changed, disrupted, or otherwise in need of attention or alteration during the transitional process accompanying divorce. Among these are (1) interaction patterns between the parents, (2) parent–child interaction patterns and relationships, (3) the degree of stability of routine and organization in the daily life of the child, (4) the emotional well-being of the parents, and (5) changes in the material circumstances of the family and household in which the child lives. For the sake of clarity, we first consider each of these issues separately. However, at the end of our discussion, we consider ways in which these factors may be related, and discuss several recent efforts that have demonstrated how cumulative change and stress across areas may interact to influence children's adjustment.

For children and adolescents, both the level of family organization and interaction prior to the divorce and continuations or shifts in the circumstances that follow it may be among the most salient aspects of the developmental context that shape adaptation. In particular, parental conflict, both pre- and postseparation, appears to have a pronounced effect on the coping efforts of children, and has been repeatedly identified as a precursor of dysfunction, particularly conduct disorders, among both children and adolescents in intact as well as divorcing families (Ellison, 1983; Emery & O'Leary, 1982; Farber et al., 1985; Felner et al., 1975; Luepnitz, 1979; Nelson, 1981; Porter & O'Leary, 1980; Rosen, 1979). Further, marital conflict has also been shown to influence other factors, such as inconsistent disciplinary practices (Emery, 1982; Emery & O'Leary, 1984) and lower levels of parental well-being (Felner & Terre, 1987), which in themselves may be associated with increased adaptive difficulties.

A crucial point is that these factors affect children similarly across intact and divorced families. Because divorce may frequently follow a prolonged period of heightened conflict between the parents, it may be argued that at least some of the negative effects of divorce that have been found are not attributable to any aspect of the divorce or its associated environmental changes, but to the conditions that existed while the family was intact. Recent reviews of literature in this area (e.g. Emery, 1982; Felner, 1984; Felner et al., 1980b; Felner & Terre, 1987; Peterson et al., 1984; Rutter, 1981) lend support to this position, generally concluding that predivorce parental discord may be a more potent influence on children's subsequent adjustment than is the separation or divorce itself. Drawing on these data and a transitional-events perspective, we argue that one of the critical tasks that confront a family is the development of a new organization and style of interacting that minimizes the level of postdivorce conflict between the parents. That such an outcome may be beneficial to the child's well-being and potentially lead to the reversal of some of the negative consequences of exposure to predivorce conflict is suggested by several studies that have compared children from high- and low-conflict intact or divorced families. Hetherington and colleagues (1979) report that two years after divorce, children from high-conflict divorced families display the greatest adjustment problems, and children from high-conflict intact families fare only slightly better, manifesting significantly more difficulties than those from divorced families characterized by lower levels of postdivorce conflict. A similar reduction in adjustment problems was found by Rutter (1981) to be associated with a reduction in parental conflict following the separation. More generally, both of these studies are consistent with the findings of other studies comparing high- and low-conflict family groups (McCord et al., 1962; Nye, 1975; Rutter, 1979).

It should be noted at this juncture that parental conflict in and of itself is not sufficient to account for the adjustment difficulties that are frequently associated with divorce. Indeed we need to be careful not merely to replace the overly simplistic question of "What are the effects of divorce on children?" with the equally overly simplistic answer that parental conflict accounts for any and all adverse effects found. Parental conflict may act directly to influence the child's adjustment. However, as we shall see, so too, may it be associated with a number of other conditions (e.g., chronic disorganization, inconsistent parenting) in the child's environment that are developmentally hazardous and contribute to the difficulties.

Another set of factors related to family organization that may have significant implications for children's efforts to cope with divorce and its related tasks or stressors involves the nature and quality of parent–child relationships before, during, and after the separation. Here the data make clear that the stresses and increases in adaptive demands associated with the divorce, whether they result from living in the high-conflict environment that may characterize the predivorce household or from the changed living conditions postseparation, may result in significant alterations in parent–child relationship patterns. Thus another of the tasks faced by families during this transition is the establishment of new, stable, and developmentally enhancing patterns of parent–child interactions. Several studies underscore the fact that this is a task that must be actively attended to, as well as the salience of this issue for children's adaptive efforts and the degree to which these critical relationships may be influenced by other transactions among family members or between the family system and the environment. Hetherington and colleagues (1978a) and Wallerstein and Kelly (1980b) have noted that a deterioration in custodial parent–child relationships may frequently occur in the first year or two following divorce, and that the pattern of this deterioration may closely parallel the types and degrees of behavioral problems shown by young children. Consistent with these findings, a number of other studies (e.g., Felner, Farber, et al. 1981; Hess & Camara, 1979, Hodges et al., 1984; Pett, 1982) have found that when divorced parents or children of divorce rated their relationships with each other positively, the children's adjustment was also found to be more positive. The deterioration in parent–child relationships that has been found is not a function of divorce per se but depends heavily on the conditions that surround it. This point is illustrated by a quote from Wallerstein and Kelly (1980a), who, in commenting on the strong correlation between the custodial mother–child relationship and the psychological status of the child at follow-up, conclude, "Our data underscore the fragilility of the relationship between the single parent and the preschool child and the extraordinary susceptibility of this relationship to conflictual stresses from within, and pressures and deprivations from without" (p. 614).

Underscoring the fact that these processes may merely be special instances of more typical developmental transactions and outcomes is a study by Hodges and co-workers (1984), who report on a study of children in intact versus divorced households, and who find that while family type did not predict child adjustment, the levels of maternal warmth and permissiveness did predict better child outcomes across family constellations.

In addition to the need to protect, maintain, or restructure the relationship with the custodial parent, the relationship with the noncustodial parent also must be actively attended to by the child and family system. Generally the amount and quality of contact between noncustodial parents and their children have been shown to be associated with more positive adjustment of children following divorce (Hess & Camara, 1979; Hetherington et al., 1978a; Rosen, 1979; Wallerstein & Kelly, 1980a). However, in keeping with the contextual arguments of this chapter, it must be noted that these findings have typically been related to broader positive family interaction patterns. That is, other studies and reviews (e.g. Ahrons, 1981, 1983; Dominic & Schlesinger, 1980; Felner & Terre, 1987) have shown that patterns of contact with the noncustodial parent beneficial to the child development most typically occur when there are relatively low levels of conflict between the parents. Further, the ease with which noncustodial parents are able to visit (Dominic & Schlesinger, 1980; Tepp, 1983), the ambiguity of their role (Tepp, 1983; Wallerstein & Kelly, 1980a, 1980b), their own psychological conflicts over the divorce, remarriage of either of the spouses, and the degree to which the noncustodial parents perceive themselves as rejected by their children have also all been shown to relate to frequency and quality of contact (Dominic & Schlesinger, 1980; Hetherington et al., 1978a, 1978b; Tepp, 1983; Tropf, 1984; Wallerstein & Kelly, 1980a, 1980b). Indeed, where conflict between the ex-spouses is high, or where the noncustodial parent displays signs of psychopathology, not only has a positive association not been found between visitation frequency and adjustment (Felner, 1984; Hess & Camara, 1979; Hetherington et al., 1978a; 1978b), but frequent visitation may actually *hamper* the child's coping efforts by exacerbating interparental conflict (e.g., Clingempeel & Reppucci, 1982; Ellison, 1983; Kurdek et al., 1981; Westman et al., 1970), thus having a negative impact on the well-being of the custodial parent and making the development of a stable postdivorce level of organization in the child's life more difficult (Felner & Terre, 1987). Felner and Terre (1987) summarize these issues by noting, "When high levels of involvement by the non-custodial parent with the child exist following the divorce it most often does so in the context of a broader set of stable, satisfying, and low conflict interactions among the members of the family system that has been dissolved by divorce. Further, when such conditions do not exist but where the contact between the child and the non-custodial parent remains high, the child's adaptive efforts do not seem to be enhanced." Here we might add that such efforts may actually be impeded in the latter circumstances.

The increased vulnerability of divorced adults to mental health problems and decreased well-being has been a frequently reported finding (e.g., Bloom, 1978; Bloom et al., 1978; Goetting, 1981). Although early research in this area sought to document the risk of dysfunction associated with marital disruption, more recent studies have centered on understanding the specific factors that may moderate both negative and positive outcomes. For example, Kazak and Linney (1983) found that among divorced mothers, different competencies predicted life satisfaction at various points in the postdivorce adjustment process. Specifically, for women separated less than three years, social participation was the best predictor of life satisfaction, while for those separated more than three years, competence as self-supporters was the best indicator.

The extent to which parents are able successfully to master the adaptive tasks, changes, and challenges set in motion by their divorce has also been directly linked to the efficacy of the child's coping efforts. Zill (1978) found that children whose mothers were psychologically troubled were more likely to feel rejected and unhappy than those whose mothers were psychologically healthy. Vaughn and colleagues (1979) noted an association among less stable caretaking environments, maternal anxiety, and attachment problems in children. Further, Colletta (1983) found that the presence of such specific stress factors as low income, number of children, or sex of the child, when associated with divorce, predicted reduced parental role functioning and parenting practices that related to poorer adaptive outcomes for children of divorce (Felner et al., 1981).

In a study of factors bearing on parental role functioning and children's adjustment, Stolberg and Anker (1983) found a consistent relationship between which parent initiated the divorce and the adjustment of mother-custody children. That is, children whose fathers initiated the divorce displayed higher prosocial, interpersonal skills than did children whose mothers initiated the divorce or whose parents made a mutual decision to end the marriage. In accounting for these results, Stolberg and Anker argue that the process of initiating divorce is associated with an anticipatory problem focus at the expense of child-focused behaviors. Inasmuch as mother-initiated divorces may thus reduce children's psychological access to their primary caretakers during this period (for mother-custody children), this situation is seen to be second only to mutually-initiated divorces (which psychologically remove both parents) in affecting children's behavior.

The results of the Stolberg and Anker study must be tempered somewhat in light of findings pertaining to the relationship between the mother's coping efficacy and her appraisal of the desirability of the divorce. That is, when the mother is the custodial parent, and she views the divorce as a desirable occurrence (and thus, we would assume, a condition that might be most often associated with her seeking the divorce), reduced problems or risk levels for the children are found (Biller, 1974; Santrock & Warshak, 1979). Additionally, when she perceives the divorce as an unwanted event, the risk of child difficulties may be greater (Kopf, 1970). In attempting to integrate these findings, it may be helpful again to consider the prolonged transitional process involved. Initially the decision to divorce and the preparation for seeking it may reduce the psychological accessibility of the mother, or, when mutually sought, both parents, thus resulting in greater difficulties for children during this phase of the process.

The parents' psychological acceptance of and accommodation to the divorce, subsequent to the separation, however, may be far better when they both sought or wanted the divorce, and hence may ultimately result not only in better psychological functioning on their part, but in conditions that facilitate the child's coping efforts.

It should also be noted, given the transactional model espoused here, that child behavior has likewise been found to influence the affective and coping responses of mothers following divorce. Hetherington and others (1978b), for example, found mothers' feelings of confidence, self-esteem, state anxiety, and level of depression to be synchronously correlated with children's (especially sons') frequency of noxious and aggressive behavior. In a related set of findings, Patterson (1976) indicated that children and their parents often become involved in a cyclical process of coercion, with the mother's and child's responses inextricably intertwined.

In addition to these studies, other works have yielded contradictory findings, at times indicating only weak relationships between parent and child postdivorce outcomes (Hingst, 1981), or, as in one case (Kurdek ct al., 1981), reporting a negative relationship between the custodial parents' general personal competence (not, it should be noted, parenting behaviors per se) and the children's divorce adjustment. To say that parent and child well-being are complexly related is to state the obvious. Nevertheless, given our rudimentary understanding of the nature of these transactions, it seems clear that efforts to understand divorce outcomes that are focused exclusively on either the parents or the children are certain to be short-sighted.

Yet another set of changes and associated tasks that may accompany divorce relates to shifts in material circumstances. The correlation between divorce and a drop in standards of living for female-headed (but not male-headed) families has been documented in several studies (Bahr, 1983; Bradbury et al., 1979; Espenshade, 1979; Felner et al., 1980a; Hetherington, 1978; LeMasters, 1971; Wolff, 1969). That the association between divorce and financial difficulties in mother-headed households may negatively impact children's adjustment is clear from the frequency with which these sudden downward shifts in socioeconomic status have been noted to be correlates of child adjustment difficulties (Bahr, 1983; Desimone-Luis et al., 1978; Fulton, 1979; Hodges et al., 1979; Hetherington et al., 1978a, 1978b; Nelson, 1981; Pett, 1982). Of particular note, given our emphasis on the contextual factors associated with divorce as being of prime concern in determining its adaptive significance, are those studies that show that when family income is statistically equated, differences in behavior problems between children from divorced and from intact families drop out (Adams & Horovitz, 1980; Colletta, 1979,

1983; MacKinnon, et al., 1982; Svanum et al., 1982). On the basis of these data, MacKinnon and colleague argue that children within divorced households often spend several years in milieus that contain the stresses found in low-income environments'' (p. 1397).

Demands for adaptation to the precipitous changes in economic status following divorce, and the ways in which such shifts may exacerbate other stressors and make the mastery of the other divorce related adaptive tasks more difficult, may be equally or more important to understanding the links between children's postdivorce adjustment and economic conditions than is low economic status per se. For example, Desimone-Luis and co-workers (1979) found that children who showed the most pronounced behavioral difficulties following divorce were from homes that had experienced the most severe decreases in economic status immediately following the divorce. Consistent with this finding, Felner and Terre (1987) summarize the findings relating postdivorce economic circumstances and children's well-being by stating: "Economic deprivation accompanying divorce may influence the child's adjustment not only directly, by decreasing the level of material resources available to the child, but also less directly by leading to additional alterations such as [in] mother–child interaction patterns, daily routines, or the quality and/or location of the child's domicile or through contributing to the stress experienced by the custodial parent." They also note that the findings in this area "reinforce the importance of the change associated with divorce as being among the most significant factors influencing adjustment."

In addition to studies that have focused on somewhat discrete changes in the child's postdivorce environment, other studies have attempted to examine the cumulative effects of such stressors and changes. The latter emphasize the range of shifts or disruptions in the child's environment with which the child must cope and which define a general context for development that is in some disarray. The degree of flux and disorganization in such a context may have a significant effect on the child's postdivorce adjustment. Thus reestablishment of a well-organized, predictable milieu that reflects at least as good a level of functioning as the predivorce circumstances is a critical task confronted by the family system.

That divorce engenders multiple environmental changes that disrupt family organization and daily routines or functioning has been frequently noted, as has the adaptive significance of such disruption (Felner, 1984; Felner et al., 1980b, 1983, 1986; Felner & Terre, 1987; Wolchik et al., 1984). Conflicts experienced by the custodial parent between employment or divorce-related demands and child care demands are often reflected in difficulties in coping with routine household tasks as well as in regulating and scheduling events of family life (e.g., bedtime, meals, arrival at school) (Johnson, 1983; Weinraub & Wolf, 1983). Other work has shown that the maintenance or reestablishment of stable, predictable patterns of family functioning and household routine may significantly enhance a child's adaptation to parental divorce (Farber et al., 1984; Hetherington et al., 1978a, 1978b).

Further highlighting the notion that rather than dealing with an "event," children of divorce are actually attempting to cope with a more extensive and prolonged reorganization of their environments, are the results of a recent series of studies. For example, Felner et al. (1980a) report that children in divorced households experienced lower levels of educational stimulation and parental attention, and greater economic stress and higher levels of general family problems, than those from intact homes or homes that were disrupted by parent death. Further, certain of these problems (e.g., lack of educational stimulation) have been shown to be related to increased levels of acting-out problems in both intact and divorced households (Boike et al., 1978). Stolberg and Anker (1983) also examined changes in the time spent with each parent, the level of demands on the custodial parent, and changes in economic circumstances and residential shifts following divorce. Children of divorce tended to perceive their environments as more disorganized than children from intact families, and frequency of total changes was associated with children's perceptions of being less able to control their environments. Similarly, Kurdek and Blisk (1983) found that high degrees of change in a number of areas (e.g., the number of people living in the home, family income, hours of parent–child interactions, quality of living quarters) were associated with child difficulties in social and psychological functioning.

Recent work by Sandler and Wolchik and their colleagues (Sandler et al., 1986; Wolchik et al., 1985a, b) has attempted further to address questions as to the types, extent, and effects of the environmental changes experienced by children whose parents divorce. In these efforts they have provided an excellent example of how a life transitions framework may incorporate a life stress model while at the same time informing and enriching what is done. These authors have developed and evaluated a life-events questionaire that focuses on the changes that a child may experience during the process of divorce. Further, in keeping with the transitional-events model, they have elected to focus not only on negative changes but on positive ones as well. More generally the target is those more specific, minor events that occur during the divorce process. This is a strategy that is consistent with the transitional-events model's shift from attempting simply to evaluate the impact of distal, large events, to a position that includes a concern with more proximal "hassles," "uplifts"

(DeLongis et al., 1983; Lazarus & Folkman, 1984), or daily experiences (Stone & Neale, 1984) that more directly impact on/or describe the immediate developmental transactions and context in which the individual is involved. Using a key informant's strategy (i.e., children or parents who had experienced divorce, lawyers, clinicians) to identify events that may have been experienced in association with the divorce and that had a significant impact on the child, 62 items were selected (Wolchik et al., 1985b). The authors assert that they were careful to exclude any events that were not objectively verifiable, could be viewed as a symptom of disorder, or were within the child's control. They do point out, however, that some critical events on the list may reflect the responses of the social environment to the child's adaptive or maladaptive behaviors (e.g., Mom gets mad at you or tells you that you are bad). Findings indicate that children tended to report that the items included were associated with less stress than parents or clinicians perceived them to be (Wolchik et al., 1985b) and that the number of positive events children reported experiencing related to differential custody arrangements (Wolchik et al., 1985a).

Of all the psychlogical and situational factors that may serve to shape the developmental context of children and the nature of their transactions with it, none are more important than the custody and visitation arrangements and the degree to which the parents and children can master the tasks associated with such arrangements. If we consider that the child's entire milieu is, to a great extent, structured by the particular child care arrangements the parents enter into, and that these arrangements will also, in large part, determine the nature and frequency of contact between the parents, it is clear that not only may these arrangements act directly upon the child's well-being, but, through their interaction with other changes, stressors, and conditions associated with the divorce, they may become even more critical in determining adaptive outcomes (Felner & Terre, 1987). Yet despite the broad scope and complexity of the issues involved, and the impact of child-custody arrangements, we show signs of repeating the errors we made in considering the effects of divorce in our exploration and discussion of child custody. That is, we have generally not phrased our questions in this area in ways that are consistent with transitional-events frameworks or transactional perspectives on development. Instead social scientists and legal professionals have once again become caught up in an overly simplistic question similar to that which has guided studies of divorce effects, namely, "Which type of custody arrangement is best?" (Felner & Terre, 1987). Even worse, some mental health professionals have allowed themselves to move from studies asking and purporting to answer this question to advocating that a "presumption" of a particular type of custody be incorporated into state statutes to mandate what is best in the *general case*. The degree to which this is misguided and unwise should be evident from the discussion of the complex factors that are involved in shaping adaptive outcomes following divorce.

Lending further support to this position is a recent review of the child-custody literature by Felner and Terre (1987). They conclude that there is little evidence to support advocating one type of custody arrangement over others as "best." Instead, they argue, it is critical to consider the full set of family circumstances involved in determining what custody/visitation arrangements are viable and best for the well-being of the child. They state, "Perhaps the clearest statement that can be made is that there is no one custody arrangement which is best. Arguments in favor of a presumption of one form over another are ill-suited to the realities of family life and child development." They also note that the level of interparental conflict and discord appears to be particularly critical both in itself and as it may interact with other variables to determine the adaptive consequences of different custody conditions for children. Across different types of custody conditions, such discord was found to be more strongly associated with negative child adjustment than was the particular type of custody arrangement. Further, when discord is high, increased contact between parents due to more frequent visitation or greater parity in custodial responsibilities (i.e., joint versus sole custody) is consistently found to relate to such additional child stressors as reduced parental well-being, greater disorganization in day-to-day routines, and increased re-litigation and continued conflict. By contrast, when conflict is low, parental cooperation is high, and extensive involvement in parenting by both parents is mutually sought or desired, then greater contact and more equal responsibilities are related to better outcomes for children. Even here, however, the additional demands often associated with joint custody and, where shared physical custody is in force, the continuing instability of the environment, are often found to be hard on the children even when the parents express satisfaction with the arrangements.

These comments point to some of the most severe limitations of the literature that has been used in support of the joint-custody bandwagon (Reppucci, 1984). That is, most of the individuals who have been included in the samples to date have either actively sought joint custody or have agreed to it with little external threat of it being imposed. As is clear from this, a transactional approach to the question of the effects of divorce on children raises serious concerns about what will happen when couples who are less motivated or are still heavily involved in conflict, as is the more modal case for divorcing couples (Johnston et al., 1985), enter into joint-custody arrangements either because of coercion or having it imposed on them by the court. Such arrangements have not been shown to be associated with clearly better outcomes than sole-custody arrangements, even when the couples are highly motivated (Felner & Terre, 1987). A full discussion of the issues of differential custody arrangements and outcomes is beyond the scope of this chapter (for a more complete discussion, c.f. Clingempeel & Reppucci, 1982; Felner & Terre, 1987; Reppucci, 1984; Weithorn, 1987). The essential point for this work, however, is that such arrangements must be considered as critical factors that both shape and interact with other important elements of the child's postdivorce environment and which may have profound implications for the degree of success families have in their coping efforts. To consider this or related issues outside the framework of a transitional-events model may lead to conclusions that are seriously misleading and that result in policies that neither serve the child's interests nor result in optimal functioning.

CONCLUDING COMMENTS

Divorce involves a prolonged process of adaptation to extensive reorganization and change in the child's environment. It is clear that a transitional perspective, which emphasizes that the child and other family members are involved in active transactions with their environment while attempting to adapt to divorce-related changes, stressors, and adaptive tasks, nicely captures the complexity of this process and fits well with the data that have been compiled thus far. Further, the transitional perspective appears to be a useful heuristic for guiding future work. One of the most important attributes of our transitional-events model is that it puts the study of children's divorce adaptation back into the broader context of developmental research and theory, thereby helping further to clarify and identify potentially salient shapers of adaptive outcomes and eliminating the need to "reinvent the wheel" at each turn. Indeed we may now advocate the position that instead of asking what the effects of such events on children are, we would be far better served to attempt to understand the ways in which such events relate to systematic disruptions, changes, and alterations in important developmental processes and conditions.

The importance of this shift in perspective, not only for guiding more basic research, but also for intervention, may be made clearer by considering an evolving model for preventive interventions developed by Lorion and his colleagues (Lorion, 1983a, 1983b; Lorion, 1985; Lorion & Lounsbury, 1981; Felner & Lorion, 1985), which defines preventive interventions within a developmental paradigm. Here preventive interventions are seen to involve the systematic manipulation of processes related to the development of adaptive or maladaptive outcomes (i.e., to increase the occurrence of the former while reducing the incidence of the latter). That is, interventions are not targeted to outcomes per se, but are targeted at the developmental processes and mechanisms that result in those outcomes. In this chapter we have identified a number of possible elements of the transitional process that may be salient to the adaptive efforts of children who are attempting to cope with parental divorce and the circumstances that accompany it. In addition we have articulated a model for viewing the more general processes involved, which we feel allows for a more precise definition of what it is the child is actually trying to cope with than does either a stressful-life-events model or a crisis model. If this is indeed the case, such a transitional-events framework should facilitate our efforts to develop effective programs and policies that reduce the level of risk associated with divorce and result in enhanced developmental outcomes for children. At the very least, it should shift our focus from the divorce to the processes and the context in which it is experienced.

REFERENCES

Adams, D., & Horovitz, J. (1980). Psychopathology and fatherlessness in poor boys. *Child Psychiatry and Human Development, 10,* 135–143.

Ahrons, C. (1981). The continuing co-parental relationship between divorced spouses. *American Journal of Orthopsychiatry, 51,* 415–428.

Ahrons, C. (1983). Predictors of paternal involvement post-divorce: Mothers' and fathers' perceptions. *Journal of Divorce, 6,* 55–69.

Bahr, S. (1983). Marital dissolution laws: Impact of recent changes for women. *Journal of Family Issues, 4*(3), 455–466.

Biller, H. B. (1974). *Paternal Deprivation: Family, School, Sexuality and Society.* Lexington, Mass: Heath.

Bloom, B. (1978). Marital disruption as a stressor. In D. G. Forgays (Ed.), *Primary Prevention of Psychopathology: Vol. 2, Environmental Influences* (pp. 81–101). Hanover, N.H.: University Press of New England.

Bloom, B. (1979). Prevention of mental disorders: Recent advances in theory and practice. *Community Mental Health Journal, 15,* 179–191.

Bloom, B. C., Asher, S. J., & White, S. W. (1978). Marital disruption as a stressor: A review and analysis. *Psychological Bulletin, 85,* 867–894.

Boike, M., Ginter, E., Cowen, E., Felner, R., & Francis, R. (1978). The relationship between family background problems and the competencies of young normal children. *Psychology in the Schools, 15,* 283–290.

Bradbury, K., Danziger, S., Smolensky, E., & Smolensky, P. (1979). Public assistance, female headship, and economic well-being. *Journal of Marriage and the Family, 41,* 519–535.

Bronfenbrenner, U. (1979). *The Ecology of Human Development: Experiments by Nature and Design.* Cambridge, Mass.: Harvard University Press.

Callahan, E. J., & McCluskey, K. A. (1983). *Life-Span Developmental Psychology: Nonnormative Life Events*. New York: Academic Press.

Caplan, G. (1964). *Principles of Preventive Psychiatry*. New York: Basic Books.

Clingempeel, W., & Reppuci, N. (1982). Joint custody after divorce: Major issues and goals for research. *Psychological Bulletin, 91,* 102–127.

Colletta, N. D. (1979). The impact of divorce: Father absence or poverty? *Journal of Divorce, 3*(1), 27–35.

Colletta, N. D. (1983). Stressful lives: The situation of divorced mothers and their children. *Journal of Divorce, 6,* 19–31.

DeLongis, A., Coyne, J. C., Dakof, G., Folkman, S., & Lazarus, R. S. (1982). Relationships of hassels, uplifts, and major life events to health status. *Health Psychology, 1,* 119–136.

Desimone-Luis, J., O'Mahoney, K., & Hunt, D. (1979). Children of separation and divorce: Factors influencing adjustment. *Journal of Divorce, 3,* 37–42.

Dohrenwend, B. P. (1979). Stressful life events and psychopathology: Some issues of theory and method. In J. E. Barrett (Ed.), *Stress and Mental Disorder*. New York: Raven Press.

Dohrenwend, B. S., & Dohrenwend, B. P. (1978). Some issues in research on stressful life events. *Journal of Nervous and Mental Disease, 166,* 7–15.

Dohrenwend, B. S., & Dohrenwend, B. P. (1984). Life stress and illness: Formulations of the issues. In B. S. Dohrenwend & B. P. Dohrenwend (Eds.), *Stressful Life Events and Their Contexts* (pp. 1–27). New Brunswick, N.J.: Rutgers University Press.

Dominic, K., & Schlesinger, B. (1980). Weekend fathers: Family shadows. *Journal of Divorce, 3,* 241–247.

Ellison, E. (1983). Issues concerning parental harmony and children's psychosocial adjustment. *American Journal of Orthopsychiatry, 53,* 73–80.

Emery, R. (1982). Interparental conflict and the children of discord and divorce. *Psychological Bulletin, 92,* 310–330.

Emery, R., & O'Leary, K. D. (1982). Children's perceptions of marital discord and behavior problems of boys and girls. *Journal of Abnormal Child Psychology, 10, 11–24.*

Emery, R., & O'Leary, K. D. (1984). Marital discord and child behavior problems in a nonclinic sample. *Journal of Abnormal Child Psychology, 12,* 411–420.

Espenshade, T. (1979). The economic consequences of divorce. *Journal of Marriage and the Family, 41,* 615–625.

Erikson, E. (1959). Identity and the life cycle. *Psychological Issues Monographs, 1*. New York: International Universities Press.

Farber, S., Felner, R., & Primavera, J. (1985). Parental separation/divorce and adolescents: An examination of factors mediating adaptation. *American Journal of Community Psychology, 13,* 171–185.

Felner, R. D. (1984). Vulnerability in childhood: A preventive framework for understanding children's efforts to cope with life stress and transitions. In M. C. Roberts & L. H. Peterson (Eds.), *Prevention of Problems in Childhood: Psychological Research and Applications.* (pp. 133–169). New York: Wiley-Interscience.

Felner, R., Farber, S., Ginter, M., Boike, M., & Cowen, E. (1980a). Family stress and organization following parental divorce or death. *Journal of Divorce, 4,* 67–76.

Felner, R., Farber, S., & Primavera, J. (1980b). Transitions and stressful life events: A model for primary prevention. In R. H. Price, R. F. Ketterer, B. C. Bader, & J. Monahan (Eds.), *Prevention in Mental Health: Research, Policy, and Practice* (pp. 81–108). Beverly Hills, Calif.: Sage Publications.

Felner, R., Farber, S., & Primavera, J. (1983). Transitions and stressful life events: A model for primary prevention. In R. D. Felner, L. A. Jason, J. N. Moritsugu, & S. S. Farber (Eds.). *Preventive Psychology: Theory, Research, and Practice* (pp. 199–215). New York: Pergamon Press.

Felner, R., Ginter, M., Boike, M., & Cowen, E. (1981). Parental death or divorce and the school adjustment of young children. *American Journal of Community Psychology, 9,* 181–191.

Felner, R. D., & Lorion, R. P. (1985). Clinical child psychology and prevention: Toward a workable and satisfying marriage. *Proceedings from the Conference on Training Clinical Child Psychologists,* Hilton Head Island, S.C.

Felner, R., Rowlison, R., & Terre, L. (1986). Unraveling the Gordian knot in life change events: A critical examination of crisis, stress, and transitional frameworks for prevention. In S. M. Auerbach & A. L. Stolberg (Eds.), *Children's Life Crisis Events: Preventive Intervention Strategies.* (pp. 39–63). New York: Hemisphere/McGraw-Hill.

Felner, R., Stolberg, A., & Cowen, E. (1975). Crisis events and school mental health referral patterns of young children. *Journal of Consulting and Critical Psychology, 43,* 305–310.

Felner, R., & Terre, L. (1987). Child custody and children's adaptation following divorce. In L. A. Weithorn (Ed.), *Psychology and Child Custody Determinations: Knowledge, Roles and Expertise.* Lincoln, Neb.: University of Nebraska Press, (Divisions 37 and 41 sponsored monograph).

Foster, H., & Freed, D. (1980). Joint custody: Legislative reform. *Trial,* June, 22–27.

Fulton, J. (1979). Parental reports of children's post-divorce adjustment. *Journal of Social Issues, 35,* 126–139.

Glueck, S., & Glueck, E. (1950). *Unraveling Juvenile Delinquency.* Cambridge, Mass.: Harvard University Press.

Goetting, A. (1981). Divorce outcome research. *Journal of Family Issues, 2,* 350–378.

Hancock, E. (1980). The dimensions of meaning and belonging in the process of divorce. *American Journal of Orthopsychiatry, 50*(1), 18–27.

Hess, R., & Camara, K. (1979). Post-divorce relationships as mediating factors in the consequences of divorce for children. *Journal of Social Issues, 35,* 79–96.

Hetherington, M. (1972). Effects of father absence on personality development in adolescent daughters. *Developmental Psychology, 7,* 313–326.

Hetherington, M., Cox, M., & Cox, R. (1978a). The aftermath of divorce. In J. H. Stevens, Jr., & M. Matthews (Eds.), *Mother-Child, Father-Child Relations.* (pp. 149–176). Washington, D.C.: National Association for the Education of Young Children.

Hetherington, M., Cox, M., & Cox, R. (1978b). The development of children in mother-headed families. In H. Hoffman & O. Reiss (Eds.), *The American Family: Dying Or developing.* New York: Plenum Press.

Hetherington, M., Cox, M., & Cox, R. (1979). Play and social interaction in children following divorce. *Journal of Social Issues, 35,* 26–49.

Hingst, A. (1981). Children and divorce: The child's view. *Journal of Clinical Child Psychology,* Fall, 161–164.

Hodges, W., & Bloom, B. (1984). Parent's report of children's adjustment to marital separation: A longitudinal study. *Journal of Divorce, 8,* 33–50.

Hodges, W., Buchsbaum, H., & Tierney, C. (1984). Parent-child relationships and adjustment in preschool children in divorced and intact families. *Journal of Divorce, 7,* 43–58.

Hodges, W., Wechsler, R., & Ballantine, C. (1979). Divorce and the preschool child: Cumulative stress. *Journal of Divorce, 3,* 55–67.

Johnson, P. (1983). Divorced mothers' management of responsibilities. *Journal of Family Issues, 4,* 83–103.

Johnston, J., Campbell, L., & Tall, M. (1985). Impasses to the resolution of custody and visitation disputes. *American Journal of Orthopsychiatry, 55,* 112–129.

Kazak, A., & Linney, J. A. (1983). Stress, coping, and life change in the single-parent family. *American Journal of Community Psychology, 11,* 207–219.

Kopf, K. (1970). Family variables and school adjustment of eight grade father-absent boys. *The Family Coordinator, 17,* 145–150.

Kurdek, L., & Blisk, D. (1983). Dimensions and correlates of mothers' divorce experiences. *Journal of Divorce, 6,* 1–24.

Kurdek, L., Blisk, D., & Siesky, A. (1981). Correlates of children's long-term adjustment to their parents' divorce. *Developmental Psychology, 17,* 565–579.

Kurdek, L., & Siesky, A. (1979). An interview study of parents' perceptions of their children's reactions and adjustment to divorce. *Journal of Divorce, 3,* 5–17.

Kurdek, L., & Siesky, A. (1981a). Sex role self-concepts of single divorced parents and their children. *Journal of Divorce, 3,* 249–261.

Kurdek, L., & Siesky, A. (1980b). Children's perceptions of their parents' divorce. *Journal of Divorce, 3,* 339–378.

Kurdek, L., & Siesky, A. (1981). Effects of divorce on children: The relationship between parent and child perspectives. *Journal of Divorce, 4,* 85–99.

Lazarus, R., & Folkman, S. (1984). *Stress, Appraisal, and Coping.* New York: Springer.

LeMasters, E. E. (1971). Parents without partners. In A. S. Skolnick & J. H. Skolnick (Eds.), *Family in Transition.* Boston, Little, Brown.

Lindemann, E. (1944). Symptomatology and management of acute grief. *American Journal of Psychiatry, 101,* 141–148.

Lindemann, E. (1956). The meaning of crisis in individual and family living. *Teachers College Record, 57,* 310–315.

Lindemann, E. (1979). *Beyond Grief: Studies in Crisis Intervention.* New York: Jason Aronson.

Longfellow, C. (1979). Divorce in context: Its impact on children. In G. Levinger & O. C. Moles (Eds.), *Divorce and Separation: Context, Causes and Consequences* (pp. 287–306). New York: Basic Books.

Lorion, R. P. (1983a). Evaluating preventive interventions: Guidelines for the serious social changes agent. In R. D. Felner, L. Jason, J. Moritsugu, & S. S. Farber (Eds.), *Preventive Psychology: Theory, Research, and Practice in Community Interventions.* (pp. 257–268). New York: Pergamon Press.

Lorion, R. P. (1983b). Research issues in the design and evaluation of preventive interventions. In J. Bowker (Ed.) *Education for Primary Prevention in Social Work.* New York: Council on Social Work Education.

Lorion, R. P. (1985). Environmental approaches to prevention: The dangers of imprecision. *Prevention in Human Services, 4,* 193–205.

Lorion, R. P. & Lounsbury, J. W. (1981). Conceptual and methodological considerations in evaluating preventive interventions. In W. R. Tash & G. Stahler (Eds.) *Innovative Approaches to Mental Health Evaluation.* New York: Academic Press.

Luepnitz, D. (1979). Which aspects of divorce affect children? *The Family Coordinator,* January, 79–85.

MacKinnon, C., Brody, G., & Stoneman, Z. (1982). The effects of divorce and maternal employment on the home environments of preschool children. *Child Development, 53,* 1392–1399.

McCord, J., McCord, W., & Thurber, E. (1962). Some effects of paternal absence on small children. *Journal of Abnormal and Social Psychology, 64,* 361–369.

McDermott, J. F. (1968). Parental divorce in early childhood. *American Journal of Psychiatry, 124,* 118–126.

McDermott, J. F. (1970). Divorce and its psychiatric sequelae in children. *Archives of General Psychiatry, 23,* 421–427.

Messinger, L., & Walker, K. (1981). From marriage breakdown to remarriage: Parental tasks and therapeutic guidelines. *American Journal of Orthopsychiatry, 1,* 429–438.

Monroe, S. M. (1982). Life events assessment: Current practices, emerging trends. *Clinical Psychology Review, 2,* 435–454.

Nelson, G. (1981). Moderators of women's and children's adjustment following parental divorce. *Journal of Divorce, 4,* 71–83.

Nye, F. I. (1957). Child adjustment in broken and in unhappy, unbroken homes. *Marriage and Family Living, 19,* 356–361.

Patterson, G. (April, 1976). Mothers: The unacknowledged victims. Presented at the Society in Child Development Meeting, Oakland, Calif.

Perkins, D. (1982) The assessment of stress using life events scales. In L. Goldberger & S. Breznitz (Eds.), *Handbook of Stress* (pp. 320–331). New York: Free Press.

Peterson, G., Leigh, G., & Day, R. (1984). Family stress theory and the impact of divorce on children. *Journal of Divorce, 7,* 1–20.

Pett, M. (1982). Correlates of children's social adjustment following divorce. *Journal of Divorce, 5,* 25–39.

Porter, B., & O'Leary, D. (1980). Marital discord and childhood behavior problems. *Journal of Abnormal Child Psychology, 8,* 287–295.

Rapoport, L. (1965a). The state of crisis: Some theoretical considerations. In H. J. Parad (Ed.) *Crisis Intervention: Selected Readings* (pp. 23–31). New York: Family Service Association of America.

Rapoport, L. (1965b). Working with families in crisis: An exploration in prevention intervention. In H. J. Parad (Ed), *Crisis Intervention: Selected Readings* (pp. 129–139). New York: Family Service Association of America.

Reppucci, N. D. (1984). The wisdom of Solomon: Issues in child custody determination. In N. D. Reppucci, L. A. Weithorn, E. P. Mulvey, & J. Monahan (Ed.), *Children, Mental Health and the Law* (pp. 59–78). Beverly Hills, Calif.: Sage Publications.

Rosen, R. (1979). Some critical issues concerning children of divorce. *Journal of Divorce, 3,* 19–25.

Rutter, M. (1981). Stress, coping and development: Some issues and some questions. *Journal of Child Psychology and Psychiatry, 22,* 323–356.

Rutter, M. (1979). Protective factors in children's responses to stress and disadvantage. In M. W. Kent & J. E. Rolf (Eds.), *Primary Prevention of Psychopathology: Social Competence in Children* (Vol. 3) (pp. 49–75). Hanover, N.H.: University Press of New England.

Sameroff, A. J., Seifer, R., & Zax, M. (1982). Early development of children at risk for emotional disorder. *Monographs of the Society for Research in Child Development, 47,* 1–82.

Sameroff, A. (1982). Development and the dialectic: The need for a systems approach. In W. A. Collins (Ed.), *Minnesota Symposium of Child Psychology (Vol. 15).* Hillsdale, N.J: Erlbaum.

Sameroff, A. J., & Seifer, R. (1983). Familial risk and child competence. *Child Development, 54,* 1254–1268.

Sandler, I., Wolchik, S., Braver, S., & Fogas, B. (1986). Significant events of children of divorce: Toward the assessment of risky situations. In S. M. Auerbach & A. Stolberg (Eds.), *Crisis Intervention with Children and Families.* (pp. 65–83). New York: Hemisphere.

Santrock, J., & Warshak, R. (1979). Father custody and social development in boys and girls. *Journal of Social Issues, 35,* 112–125.

Sarason, I., Johnson, J., & Seigel, J. (1978). Assessing the impact of life changes: Development of the life experiences survey. *Journal of Consulting and Clinical Psychology, 46,* 932–946.

Stolberg, A., & Anker, J. (1983). Cognitive and behavioral changes in children resulting from parental divorce and consequent environmental changes. *Journal of Divorce, 7,* 23–41.

Stone, A., & Neals, J. (1984). New measure of daily coping: Development and preliminary results. *Journal of Personality and Social Psychology, 4,* 892–906.

Svanum, S., Bringle, R., & McLaughlin, J. (1982). Father absence and cognitive performance in a large sample of 6–11 year old children. *Child Development, 53,* 136–143.

Tepp, A. (1983). Divorced fathers: Predictors of continued paternal involvement. *American Journal of Psychiatry, 140,* 1465–1469.

Tropf, W. (1984). An exploratory examination of the effect of remarriage on child support and personal contacts. *Journal of Divorce, 7,* 57–73.

Vaughn, B., Egeland, B., Sroufe, L. A., & Waters, E. (1979). Individual differences in infant-mother attachment at 12 and 18 months: Stability and change in families under stress. *Child Development, 50,* 971–975.

Wallerstein, J. (1983). Children of divorce: The psychological tasks of the child. *American Journal of Orthopsychiatry, 53,* 230–243.

Wallerstein, J., & Kelly, J. (1975). The effects of parental divorce: Experiences of the preschool child. Journal of the American Academy of Child Psychiatry, 14, 600–616.

Wallerstein, J., & Kelly, J. (1980a). Effects of divorce on the visiting father-child relationship. *American Journal of Psychiatry, 137,* 1534–1539.

Wallerstein, J., & Kelly, J. (1980b). *Surviving the Breakup: How Children and Parents Cope with Divorce.* New York: Basic Books.

Weinraub, M., & Wolf, B. (1983). Effects of stress and social supports on mother-child interactions in single- and two-parent families. *Child Development, 54,* 1297–1311.

Weithorn, L. A. (1987). *Psychology and Child Custody Determinations: Knowledge, Roles and Expertise*. Lincoln, Neb.: University of Nebraska Press. (Divisions 37 and 41 sponsored monograph).

Westman, J., Cline, D., Swift, W., & Kramer, D. (1970). Role of child psychiatry in divorce. *Archives of General Psychiatry, 23,* 416–421.

Wolchik, S., Braver, S., & Sandler, I. (1985a). Maternal versus joint custody: Children's post-separation experiences and adjustment. *Journal of Clinical Child Psychology, 14,* 5–10.

Wolchik, S., Fogas, B., Sandler, I. (1984). Environmental change and children of divorce. In J. H. Humphrey (Ed.), *Stress in Childhood.* (pp. 79–96). New York: AMS Press.

Wolchik, S. A., Sandler, I. N. Braver, S. L. & Fogas, B. A. (1985b). Events of parental divorce: Stressfulness ratings by children, parents and clinicians. *American Journal of Community Psychology, 14,* 59–74.

Wolff, S. (1969). *Children Under Stress.* New York: Basic Books.

Zill, N. (1978). Divorce, marital happiness and the mental health of children: Findings from the Foundation for Child Development National Survey of Children. Prepared for the National Institute of Mental Health Workshop on Divorce and Children, Bethesda, Md.

3

Adjustment of Parents and Children to Remarriage

E. MAVIS HETHERINGTON, JEFFREY D. ARNETT,
and E. ANN HOLLIER

When his first wife, Queen Catherine of Aragon, failed to produce a male heir to the royal throne, King Henry VIII sought to divorce her and marry his mistress, Anne Boleyn. His appeal to the pope for an annulment denied, Henry resorted to drastic measures to clear the way for his second marriage. In 1534 the English Reformation began when the pope was declared to have no authority in England. The Act of Supremacy established the Church of England as an institution separate from the Roman Catholic church, with the king as its supreme head and divine representative. The king's first marriage was declared invalid shortly thereafter, and Anne Boleyn was swiftly installed as England's new queen. Henry's eldest daughter, the future Queen Mary I of Scotland, was an unusual stepdaughter, as she never saw her mother again after Henry renounced her, and her father's remarriage was soon terminated with the beheading of Anne Boleyn.

Although contemporary divorce and remarriage have less dramatic ramifications for political and religious change than Henry's radical marital shifts, they are markedly affecting the experiences of a substantial segment of American families. Divorces are considerably easier to obtain today than they were in Henry's day, and American adults are shedding their spouses in record numbers, without the expedient of shedding their heads. However, many of these newly single adults will show no greater satisfaction with single life than did King Henry. As noted by Paul Glick in his chapter, the vast majority of divorced persons eventually remarry, half within three years of the divorce. The picture painted by these statistics is complicated by the fact that most couples separate months, or even years, before the divorce decree, and by the increase in cohabitation among divorced adults prior to remarriage. Yet it seems clear that singlehood is "a waystation rather than a destination" (Furstenberg, 1980, p. 446) in the family life cycle of most divorcing adults.

Even with the precipitous rise in the divorce rate that this century has seen, many unhappily wedded parents formerly felt obliged to stay together "for the sake of the children." Now, however, the voluntary sundering of families with chidlren has become commonplace. As noted earlier in Paul Glick's chapter, 40 percent of children born in the 1980s will experience parental divorce before they reach the age of 18, and approximately 25 percent will be a member of a stepfamily before they reach adulthood. For many children even more family disruptions lie ahead, just as they did for the unfortunate Princess Mary who had a succession of five stepmothers. Over 55 percent of remarriages can now be expected to end within ten years (Furstenberg & Spanier, 1984). In addition, as noted earlier by Paul Glick, when divorces occur in remarried families, they tend to occur more rapidly than in first marriages. Adults who have once gone through a divorce seem less reticent to leave an unsatisfying subsequent marriage.

With such a large proportion of today's youth growing up in stepfamilies, the question arises: Do divorce and remarriage make a difference in terms of developmental outcomes for children? The high rates of divorce and remarriage come on the heels of the heyday of the traditional American nuclear family as it was romanticized during the 1950s, making today's shifting marital alliances stand out in sharp relief. Many professionals uncritically have assumed therefore that any variation from the nuclear family structure is detrimental to children, yet we still have relatively little sound evidence regarding the impact of this alternative family form on child development. Now that stepfamilies have become so common, there is a pressing need for educators, legislators, judges, welfare workers, pediatricians, clinicians, and other professionals to discern what the needs, difficulties, and strengths of these children and their families may be. In formulating the answers, they turn to behavioral scientists, who, thus far, have been slow in providing reliable information, largely because in studying stepfamilies a number of complex and often interlocking issues must be simultaneously addressed.

STRUCTURAL COMPLEXITY IN STEPFAMILIES

Stepfamilies comprise a wide array of structurally distinct family forms. If we consider all possible combinations of remarriages of a divorced couple, including multiple divorces and remarriages, and the offspring and kin involved in the sequence of marital relationships, the classification of stepfamilies becomes a formidable task. Most studies of stepfamilies have classified families in terms of the structure of the custodial household and have not considered links with consanguinal kin and relatives by marriage outside of the household. The three stepfamily forms that have received the most attention are *stepfather households, stepmother households,* and *blended households.* Stepfather households, in which a woman with custody of children from a previous marriage takes a new husband, comprise 70 percent of stepfamily households. In addition, nearly 20 percent of children living in stepfamilies have a residential stepmother, and some stepfamily households are actually blended, that is, both partners bring children to the household from a previous marriage. Moreover, many stepfamilies modify the household structure by giving birth to children from the remarriage. Because of the readier availability of the families, most research has been done on stepfather households. However, it is likely that the experiences and outcomes for these families will differ from those in other stepfamily households.

Not only are stepfamily households structurally complex compared with nondivorced households, but stepfamilies are much more profoundly influenced by kinship ties outside of the immediate household. The boundaries of the stepfamily are more permeable than are nondivorced family boundaries (Walker & Messinger, 1979). Whereas "household" and "family" usually are synonymous concepts for the child in the nondivorced family, this is not the case in stepfamilies (Visher & Visher, 1978). While the nuclear family usually functions as a relatively well-defined and self-contained unit, in the stepfamily the child has one natural parent who does not live in the same household, and the child often serves as an ongoing link between the households of the two former spouses (Sager et al., 1980). It has been proposed that a *linked stepfamily system* occurs if there is a remarriage of either the custodial or noncustodial visiting parent (Jacobson, 1984b).

The kinship network of the stepfamily is larger and more complex than it is in nuclear families, not only because of the possible variations in residential household structure, but also because of the possible variety of nonresidential siblings, stepsiblings, and half-siblings; quasi-kin (the ex-spouse, ex-spouse's blood kin, and new mate); and step-kin. Appropriate behavior in such a complex kinship system may be uncertain and it has been suggested that ambiguity of role relationships may be a major problem in remarriage (Cherlin, 1978). One study investigating the attitudes of remarried spouses concerning appropriate interaction between their current and ex-spouses (Goetting, 1978) found that the only thing more than half of the subjects could agree upon was that their current and former mates should say hello. Other investigators, however, have commented that over time most members of divorced and remarried families do remarkably well in coping with their changing life situation and alterations in family relations (Furstenberg & Spanier, 1984). Moderate levels of contact with quasi-kin are associated with higher marital satisfaction than either very high or very low levels of contact (Clingempeel, 1981). This suggests that the kinship network can provide the stepfamily with important resources and support, but that with very high contact, kinship ties can become intrusive and interfere with the remarried family's ability to function effectively. (See the chapter by Glenn Clingempeel in this volume for a more detailed presentation of this topic.)

The greater potential for competing obligations and responsibilities to kin also makes itself felt in other ways in stepfamilies. Structurally complex stepfamilies, in which a custodial mother marries a stepfather who has either nonresidential or residential children of his own, report lower marital satisfaction and less positive interactions among family members and more conflict about child rearing than families in which only one spouse has children from a previous marriage (Clingempeel, 1981; Clingempeel & Brand, 1985; Clingempeel et al., 1984). This is most marked in blended families where two sets of children live in the same home (Hetherington et al., 1981b). In contrast, the birth of a baby to remarried couples is associated with increased marital satisfaction.

Recent interest has focused on the impact of divorce and remarriage on childrens' relationships with their grandparents. After divorce the custodial mother generally disengages from the kin of the ex-spouse and increases contact with her own kin as she seeks financial assistance and help with child care (Anspach, 1976; Furstenberg & Spanier, 1984; Hetherington et al., 1981b; Marsden, 1969; Spicer & Hampe, 1975). Continued contact with the maternal grandmother is related to positive outcomes for children (Hetherington et al., 1981b; Kellam et al., 1977). Moreover, involvement of grandfathers is associated with improved skills and social development in sons of divorced custodial mothers (Hetherington et al., 1981b). However, many middle-class divorced women feel ambivalent about their need to rely on their mothers and conflicts about child rearing, discipline and authority may arise that are accompanied by increased feelings of regressive dependency and powerlessness in the custodial mother. If adequate financial and child care facilities are available, most middle-class white women prefer not to live with their mothers, although they value having them in close geographic proximity (Hetherington et al., 1981b). Little is known about the effects of remarriage on the ties of grandparents to the family, or about how the stepgrandparents are received into the family system. In a recent study, sustained contact with parents of the noncustodial parent was found to be mediated by the relationship between the child and noncustodial parent (Furstenberg & Spanier, 1984). Frequent visits by the noncustodial parent were associated with frequent contact with the noncustodial grandparents. In addition, remarriage did not appear to subtract, but rather to add, grandparents for children. Contact with stepgrandparents did not lessen the child's interaction with the family of the noncustodial parent.

HISTORICAL AND DEMOGRAPHIC VARIATION

The experience of living in a stepfamily is almost certainly different today from what it was a generation ago. Two historical factors contribute to these differences. The first is the difference in the cause of dissolution of the initial marriage; the second is the increased frequency of divorce and remarriage. Remarriage is far more likely now to follow divorce than the death of a spouse. There is evidence that the reason for loss of the absent parent has a differential impact on later behavioral and social adjustment, at least for girls (Hetherington, 1972). It seems likely that such differences persist into a remarriage and have consequences for the child's successful adjustment to living with a stepparent (Bowerman & Irish, 1962; Duberman, 1975).

The increase in both divorce and remarriage changes the way we view stepfamilies, and may affect the stepfamily experience for all family members. Four out of every ten marriages now involve at least one partner who has been formerly married (Cherlin & McCarthy, 1983), and as noted earlier by Paul Glick, one-ninth of the children in the nation live in remarried-couple households. Cherlin (1981) has argued that changes in attitudes often follow rather than precede social change, as they have in attitudes toward maternal employment and divorce. Stepfamilies have met with acceptance and support from both their kinship group and the community as remarriage becomes more frequent. In addition, with remarriages constituting a much larger proportion of families now than they did just a decade or two ago, it seems probable that the characteristics of remarried families are more similar to those of nondivorced families in this cohort than in any preceding cohort. Such cohort effects are rarely discussed, and must be taken into account in evaluating the relevance of older research findings for understanding contemporary stepfamilies.

Other demographic variations that must be considered in evaluating the effects on children of growing up in stepfamilies include such factors as the race, sex, income, and education of family members; the child's age at time of divorce and time of remarriage; and the length of time spent in a single-parent home. In addition, factors relating to the complexity of family structure, such as age and number of siblings in the home, the presence or absence of new half-siblings from the current marriage, and other kin and quasi-kin within and outside of the home, are important. Furthermore, such variables must be considered not only in terms of their independent effects, but also of their possible interactions (Price-Bonham & Balswick, 1980). [For a more detailed discussion of demographic factors and problems in research methodology in the study of remarriage, see Furstenberg & Spanier (1984); and Ganong and Coleman (1984).] Differences in the characteristics of the family, the social milieu in which it is embedded, and the history from which it springs all intertwine to create a matrix of experiences and expectations that each family member brings to the new marriage, with the potential to influence profoundly reactions to it and adjustment within it.

REMARRIAGE AS A LIFE TRANSITION

Perhaps the most important consideration in developing a comprehensive model of the effects of remarriage on children is that, similar to divorce, remarriage does not represent a unitary event, but a process. It calls upon all family members to make a *series* of adjustments over time. It has multiple levels of impact and short-term, as well as long-term, consequences. The factors that mediate successful or deleterious short-term outcomes may differ from those that mediate delayed outcomes. Moreover, remarriage implies that some of the family members have undergone the dissolution of a previous marriage through death or divorce and also have spent a period of time in a one-parent household. If the earlier marriage was ended by divorce, the parent and child may have experienced a period of family conflict and multiple life changes frequently associated with separation and divorce.

Longitudinal studies indicate that in the period surounding separation and divorce there is a crisis period of family disequilibrium as the individuals involved attempt to adapt to the many changes occurring in their altering life situation. However, most families have adjusted and re-stabilized within three years following divorce (Hetherington et al., 1981b; Weiss, 1975). For this reason an understanding of the effects of remarriage on family members and family functioning depends on recognizing that the family members' experiences alter and are modified throughout the process of family reorganization that has preceded and that follows remarriage. The importance of controlling for the timing of events associated with marital transitions is evident in the Hetherington et al. (1981b) divorce study. In this investigation it was found that there were substantial changes in family functioning in the six years following divorce. For the members of divorced families, there are considerable difficulties at two months, which become more acute at one year, and then abate substantially by two years as the adjustment process in many of the families stabilizes. At six years following divorce, patterns of adaptation vary among families in which divorced mothers had remarried, and in which they had remained single, and in never-divorced families.

Although scant longitudinal data on remarriage are available, it seems likely that a similar pattern of adaptation may occur. The remarriage may initially bring with it family disorganization, and perhaps crisis, as families seek to clarify roles and relationships. In successful remarriages these events will be followed by recovery and the eventual reorganization of the family system. In unsuccessful remarriages this restabilizing may never occur, or there may be an initial "honeymoon" period, where the family members strive to make the marriage succeed, followed by discouragement, conflict, and the eventual dissolution of the marriage. The success of the family's adaptation to the stresses of the remarriage depends on the resilience and coping strategies family members can bring to bear in meeting the challenges they face. It also depends on whether there are stressors in addition to the change in family structure, such as financial difficulties, custody battles, or child behavior problems; and it will be affected by the family's perceptions and interpretations of the situation, and by the availability of personal and extrafamilial resources and support systems.

In any case it is important to keep in mind that the stresses, perceptions, and resources accompanying remarriage change over time and may result in different impressions of family functioning, depending on whether we are looking at children who are still adjusting to a new stepparent or those who have spent most of their lives in stepfamilies (Ganong & Coleman, 1984). Furthermore, the stress that accompanies life transitions such as this one may not necessarily be undesirable. There is some suggestion that children who successfully cope with changes and stressful life events may emerge as more resilient and competent adults than those who are exposed to very few challenges or stresses in their formative years (Glick & Kessler, 1980; Garmezy & Rutter, 1983; Hetherington, 1984).

METHODOLOGY IN STEPFAMILY RESEARCH

There is a growing awareness that the study of stepfamily functioning must become much more multidimensional if we are to assess adequately the characteristics and effectiveness of stepfamilies as child-rearing environments. The studies available to date, however, are notably lacking in their recognition of and accounting for the complexity of important variables. Much of the literature is based on clinical impressions and case studies. Those articles reporting research findings often have methodological shortcomings. Many studies are based on small samples of convenience, or are drawn from clinical or other nonrepresentative populations. Most studies have used nonprobability sampling techniques because of the expense and difficulty of obtaining an adequate sample size even without the use of large-scale random sampling techniques. Others fail to investigate or control for variables identified in the literature as potentially important *covariates,* and the heterogeneity of the groups studied masks any group differences that might be present. And most studies only sample the responses of a single family member or lack appropriate comparison groups. Almost no longitudinal data exist, and conclusions about causal linkages and directions of effects are, therefore, speculative at best. The vast majority of the studies have employed only self-report measures despite their well-known problems of bias and retrospective distortion. Moreover, few of those measures were standardized, with most having been developed by the authors.

It may be because of these deficiencies in the methods employed that research reports of significant differences between children reared in stepfamilies and those from nondivorced homes have been inconsistent. Perhaps the differences really are more meager than the clinical literature on troubled stepfamilies would suggest, but it is becoming increasingly clear that in order to find out we must develop more sophisticated conceptual models and more rigorous, multimethod approaches.

A *developmental-ecological process-oriented* perspective is beginning to emerge in the study of marital transitions and family reorganization. It is recognized that it is not the restructuring of the family per se, but the changes in family functioning and altered life experiences associated with divorce and remarriage that mediate the impact of these events on family members. There is increased concern with how the changes in family process interact with the developmental stage of the child as well as of the family life cycle, and with how the characteristics of the family members and their environments influence outcomes of remarriage (Ganong & Coleman, 1984; Price-Bonham & Balswick, 1980). Finally, we are also beginning to see a movement away from the "deficit-comparison model" and toward a greater interest in identifying what skills and resources stepfamilies have at their disposal, and how successful remarriages bring these to bear on dealing with their new life situation (Fast & Cain, 1966; Knaub et al., 1984; Sager et al., 1980). Marital transitions and periods of family reorganizations are being recognized as increased opportunities for change. These changes may be associated with short- or long-term developmental delays, and with disruptions and declines in psychological well-being, or with personal growth and enhanced social, cognitive, and emotional development.

THE STEPFAMILY SYSTEM

It has been argued that the stepfamily system lacks clear, socially defined roles (Cherlin, 1978; Messinger, 1976; Walker & Messinger, 1979). At one time remarriage most often followed widowhood, and the new parent assumed the roles of the deceased natural parent. With the rise in the divorce rate during the 20th century, this is no longer the case. Usually a remarriage involves a surviving natural parent living outside the household. In many stepfamilies the child has little contact with the outside parent, and, as with the death of the natural parent, the biological parent is replaced by the stepparent (Furstenberg & Seltzer, 1983). Frequently, however, the nonresidential parent continues to participate in economic, decision-making, and emotional roles, particularly where the child is concerned (Cherlin, 1978; Furstenberg & Spanier, 1984). This complicates the process of integrating the stepparent into the household, as our culture provides no clear guidelines regarding which roles are to be retained by the natural parents, which assumed by the stepparent, and which shared among them. The stepparent's personal style in adopting parental roles, and the other family members' reactions to the stepparent and to issues raised by the remarriage, have consequences that affect the whole family system (Fast & Cain, 1966).

The Marital Relationship

The marital relationship in a remarriage must be considered in relation to the previous marital experiences of the couple. A study by Furstenberg and Spanier (1984) found that, although immediately after divorce two-thirds of divorced adults express reluctance about remarriage, this does not predict the occurrence or rapidity of subsequent remarriage. In courtship and the decision to remarry, remarried couples feel that in second marriages, in contrast to first, they are less romantic, less pressured by expectations of friends and families, and less prone to jump into marriage because of pregnancy or the wish to escape a dreary family situation. Couples in second marriages were described as more pragmatic, honest, and willing to discuss the shortcomings of the relationship and the possibility of divorce. Moreover, remarried spouses are less likely to be swayed by status-enhancing attributes such as appearance, occupational status, and ambition, and are more likely to choose spouses whom they feel are stable and considerate, and have similar interests.

Problem solving, communication, and assumption of responsibilities appear to be more open and egalitarian in second marriages (Hetherington et al., 1981b; Furstenberg & Spanier, 1984). However, a remarried spouse may be particularly sensitized to conflict, and fear it as a threat to the stability of the new family (Goldstein, 1974). In well-functioning remarried families, this may lead to more open expression of differences of opinion and sensitivity to the viewpoint of the spouse (Furtstenberg & Spanier, 1984). In some remarriages, however, the remarried partner may bring to the second marriage unresolved issues from the first, and may respond to conflict that does erupt in maladaptive ways (Cherlin, 1978; Messinger & Walker, 1981). In dysfunctional remarriages this may result in what Goldstein (1974) has termed "pseudomutuality," the repression and denial of marital hostility—a denial that may extend even to the children's intolerance of any open expression of anger between the spouses. The result is an inability to cope effectively with, or even recognize the presence of, tensions before they become explosive. Not surprisingly, there is a modestly higher incidence of divorce in second and subsequent marriages (e.g., Bumpass & Sweet, 1972; Cherlin, 1977). But when we examine the statistics more closely, we find that the higher divorce rate is largely attributable to couples who remarry and quickly divorce again. Remarriages that do not quickly end in divorce are about as enduring as first marriages, and while marital satisfaction is slightly lower for remarried women that for once-married women, there is no significant difference for first-married and remarried men (Glenn & Weaver, 1977). In fact, remarried men actually score significantly higher on measures of global happiness (White, 1979). Furthermore, even among the least satisfied group, remarried women, a majority report being very happy with their marriages (Furtstenberg & Spanier, 1984; Glenn & Weaver, 1977).

In the early stages of remarriage, the former spouse may loom as a standard of comparison, as a target of mutual contempt or hostility used to increase solidarity in the new marriage, or sometimes as a continued object of mixed feelings or attachment (Hetherington et al., 1981b; Furstenberg & Spanier, 1984; Wallerstein & Kelly, 1980b; Weiss, 1975). If no children were involved in the first marriage, there is little interaction with former spouses. If children were involved, contact between former spouses is usually restricted to child-rearing issues and is more often controlled, tense, or hostile than actively cordial.

The situation in remarriages involving children differs greatly from that of childless remarriages. Whereas in nondivorced families, or in remarried families with no children from a previous union, the marital relationship usually predates the parental one, spouses in stepfamilies with children lack the time alone early in the relationship for stabilizing that relationship and for establishing its privacy (Fast & Cain, 1966; Ransom et al., 1979). Instead their time alone together must be stolen from time with the children, who may be particularly needy emotionally immediately following the remarriage. Marital relationship needs may be ignored, thus creating resentment and prolonging the conflict that is an inevitable part of the reorganization of the family system (Bitterman, 1968; Keshet, 1980; Visher & Visher, 1978).

Some of this conflict is generated by the negotiation of the stepparent's role-to-be in the family. The stepparent is in a particularly precarious situation, for, in the stepfamily, the biological parent and his or her children share a history of experiences and customs to which the stepparent is not privy. This serves as a divisive influence and sets the stage for several related conflicts. The stepparent often feels called upon to assume a parental role immediately without the benefit of having participated in the establishment of the family rules and customs regarding the children (Visher & Visher, 1978), lacking the clear, socially defined roles inherent in the status of natural parent (Cherlin, 1978; Walker & Messinger, 1979), and the time to learn marital and parental roles gradually (Fast & Cain, 1966). The stepparent must carve spheres of influence out of areas that were previously the prerogatives of the residential and nonresidential biological parents. The residential parent may welcome and encourage this on some levels, but ambivalence about relinquishing sole authority in the family is likely also to be present and to go unrecognized (Fast & Cain, 1966; Messinger & Walker, 1981; Visher & Visher, 1978). To the extent that the stepparent's ideas about appropriate discipline and affection differ from the practices of the previous marriage, they are likely to be met with resistance by both their stepchildren and their spouse (Visher & Visher, 1978). Not surprisingly, parents in stepfamilies identify disagreements over children as the major source of conflict in their marital relationship (Messinger, 1976).

In spite of these problems, mothers who have remarried report that the remarriage does make it less difficult to manage the various tasks of raising children (Furstenberg & Spanier, 1984). This seems to be mediated by the emotional support found in a satisfactory marital relationship, which is associated with lower maternal depression and a higher sense of well-being and competence, which in turn is reflected in greater maternal responsiveness and affection (Arnett, 1984; Hetherington et al., 1984). Although no systematic longitudinal data on the issue are available, it seems likely that the relation between marital satisfaction and stress, competence, and satisfaction in child rearing may become more closely related over the course of the remarriage, as patterns of family relationships become integrated and stabilized.

The Nonresidential Parent–Child Relationship

The child's relationship with the noncustodial parent has typically evolved in an inhospitable and unsupportive environment. Most children are distressed by their parents' separation and divorce, even when it is preceded by long periods of recurrent conflict or violence between the parents, to which the children are often exposed (Wallerstein & Kelly, 1980a). After the divorce the visiting parent often receives little legal, social, or emotional support for continued participation in the parenting role (Keshet, 1980), and may find his or her efforts to sustain contact with the child actively thwarted by the custodial parent (Furstenberg, 1981). It is little wonder, then, that the child's relationship with the nonresidential divorced parent is quite variable. Although most children maintain some relationship with the nonresidential parent (Messinger, 1976), the frequency of contact declines rapidly over the first two years following divorce, and a majority have seen their nonresidential parent rarely, or not at all, in the past year (Furstenberg & Seltzer, 1983). On the other hand, infrequent visits may be compensated for a certain extent by longer contact when visitation does occur (Tropf, 1984). Frequency of visitation is associated not only with the length of time since divorce, but also with such variables as the extent of financial support provided by the outside parent; the race, social class, and sex of the visiting parent; the age and sex of the child; the marital status of the two ex-spouses; and the distance between their homes (Furstenberg, 1981, 1982, 1983; Furstenberg & Seltzer, 1983; Hetherington, 1981; Hetherington et al., 1981a, 1981b; Tropf, 1984; Weiss, 1975).

There appears to be a strong association between frequency of contact and quality of the parent–child relationship as reported by the child. Children who see their outside parent frequently are much more likely to report feeling close to their nonresidential parent and being satisfied with their relationship (Furstenberg, 1983). In contrast, the nonresidential parent is likely to report being very close to the child, even with less frequent contact, while residential parents give consistently low ratings to the quality of the child's relationship with the outside parent (Furstenberg, 1981).

There appears to be little, if any, connection between the quality of the child's relationship with the nonresidential father before the final separation and that found 18 months later (Hetherington, 1981; Wallerstein & Kelly ,1980a). In a classic clinical study of divorce by Wallerstein and Kelly (1975, 1976, 1980a, 1980b; Kelly & Wallerstein, 1976), a sample of 58 families and their children were followed for ten years after the final separation. These investigators report that, over the first 18 months following separation, about half of the nonresidential parent–child relationships remained essentially unchanged, and of the other 50 percent, about half had deteriorated dramatically whereas the rest had remarkably improved. They suggest that the child's relationship with the nonresidential parent is strongly influenced by the nonresidential parent's ability to cope with the divorce. Their findings indicate that if the father is depressed or feels guilty about ending the marriage, he is likely to find visitation uncomfortable and will avoid it. If he is psychologically well-adjusted, and sees the children as a source of companionship or as a boost to his self-esteem, visitation will be increased. More frequent contact is also associated with higher income and education, and with an amicable relationship with the former spouse. However, some nonresidential parents maintain a high level of contact for less savory reasons, such as reluctance to leave the children with a depressed or emotionally disturbed mother, or competition with the former spouse for their children's affection, or as a way of continuing hostilities. Perhaps this is part of the reason why residential parents are *less* satisfied with the child's relationship with the nonresidential parent when the amount of contact is very high (Furstenberg, 1983).

Whatever the reasons for maintaining contact, the nonresidential father's relationship with his child does continue to influence the child. His continued positive involvement is associated with more positive outcomes for his child, particularly for boys (Hetherington et al., 1981a, 1981b). Nonresidential fathers are more likely to maintain a stable and frequent pattern of contact with sons of preschool and elementary school age than with daughters (Hess & Camara, 1979; Hetherington, 1981). This sex difference in frequency of contact is not found, however, with older children, who generally have been separated from their parents for longer periods of time. Finally, frequency of contact is lowest of all for adolescent children of both sexes who were very young when their parents divorced (Furstenberg, 1983).

In cases in which the father obtains custody of the child and the nonresidential parent is the mother, a different pattern of visitation results. Nonresidential mothers are much less likely than nonresidential fathers to terminate contact with their children (Furstenberg, 1983), and are much more likely to maintain a regular, frequent pattern of visitation. This finding contradicts to some extent the assumption that mothers who give up or lose custody of their children following divorce are less capable of or less committed to parenting than are other divorced mothers.

It is not only the frequency, but the quality, of contact that differs for residential and nonresidential parents. The contact with the noncustodial parent involves social exchanges such as going to movies, taking trips, or dining out; seldom does it include instrumental exchanges such as helping with school work or monitoring the performance of household tasks (Furstenberg & Spanier, 1984; Hetherington et al., 1981b). This pattern frequently leads to complaints by custodial parents and custodial stepparents about the nonresidential parent's lack of involvement in child care.

Remarriage affects the frequency of visitation. In a recent survey of stepfamilies (Furstenberg & Spanier, 1984), it was found that two-thirds of nonresidential parents see their children at least several times a month if neither they nor their former spouses have remarried. According to the survey, if both are remarried, only one-third continue to see their children as often, a finding that has since been replicated (Tropf, 1984). (See the chapter by Glenn Clingempeel in this volume for a more detailed presentation of this topic.)

Remarriage also affects the extent of the nonresidential parent's influence in decisions regarding children. Influence decreases dramatically if the nonresidential parent remarries first, perhaps indicating a disengagement on that parent's part when faced with new family ties and responsibilities. However, what may appear to be a contradictory finding may also occur, if we look at the relations between shifts in marital status and shifts in custody rather than solely at the influence of the nonresidential parent on child-rearing decisions. If both of the divorced spouses remain single or both remarry, shifts in custody are unlikely to occur, and about four out of five couples maintain the same custody arrangement. Custodial change is most likely to occur when one spouse, either the husband or wife, remarries and the other does not. In such a case, if the husband is the one who remarries, the ex-wife may fail to retain custody of the children—because, perhaps, of the difficulty of rearing disturbed or difficult-to-manage sons, or a feeling of being overburdened if a working mother, or arguments by the married fathers, that he can offer the children a more stable home environment (Furstenberg & Spanier, 1984; Hetherington et al., 1981b).

In the long run, however, it appears that divorce and remarriage often result in a permanent rupture in the nonresidential parent's and particularly the father's, ability to function as a parent (Furstenberg & Seltzer, 1983). The child, on the other hand, often continues to have an emotional attachment to the absent parent, and feelings of grief and anger concerning the loss of the parent are reactivated by the remarriage of the residential parent. In addition, fantasies of reunion of the divorced parents often come to an abrupt end at this time (Ransom et al., 1979). The child's ability to resolve these feelings, and the ability of the adults involved to understand and assist in this process, appear to have a great deal to do with how successfully the child will adapt to the residential parent's remarriage.

The Residential Parent–Child Relationship

The quality of the child's relationship with the custodial parent may play a pivotal role in the ability to adjust to living with a stepparent. This may be particularly true for children who have spent longer periods prior to the remarriage in a single-parent household. The residential parent plays an increasingly central role in the child's development, and the nonresidential parent is less able to buffer the deleterious effects of living with an inadequate parent (Hetherington, 1981). The custodial parent–child relationship is affected by the course of the family history extending from the original marriage of the biological parents through separation, divorce, life in a single-parent household, and into the remarriage. The relationship of the residential parent and the child, like that of the nonresidential parent and child, suffers from the divorce, particularly in the early postdivorce period.

Hetherington (1981) found that, in single-parent mother-headed households, the mother's relationship with her child often becomes ineffectively authoritarian. It is characterized by an increase in orders and negative behaviors directed toward the child by the mother, coupled with a decrease in her warmth and responsiveness to the child's needs. Mothers in single-parent households are less playful, less affectionate, and less approving with their children as compared with mothers in intact families. This behavior on the part of the mother is matched by higher rates of noxious behavior and noncompliance on the part of her child. Negativity between mother and child is especially pronounced in interactions with male children, and the pair is likely to become caught in an escalating cycle of antagonism and coercion. While the mother–child dyad appears to be stabilizing and functioning more effectively two years after the divorce, it is still not completely comparable in its pattern of interaction to a mother–child dyad from an intact family, particularly when comparing mothers and sons.

As noted above, the remarriage may precipitate an emotional crisis for the child, who must now confront the finality of the divorce (Visher & Visher, 1978). This reactivated sense of loss is often further aggravated by the greater unavailability of the nonresidential parent following the residential parent's remarriage (Furstenberg & Seltzer, 1983), and the loss of the residential parent's undivided attention and affection, which must now be shared with the stepparent.

Many professionals describe the single-parent household entering remarriage as a closed system (Messinger & Walker, 1981). The parent–child relationship often differs in important respects from those of parents and children in nondivorced families. Power is more symmetrically distributed, with children playing a greater role in important decision making and assuming greater responsibility for organizing and carrying out household maintenance tasks, including supervising and caring for younger siblings (Weiss, 1979). While this pattern may result in more responsible, mature, and independent children, the parent–child relationship often becomes inappropriately intense as parents turn to their children for companionship, emotional support, and nurturance after the dissolution of their marriage (Keshet, 1980; Messinger & Walker, 1981; Ransom et al., 1979; Wallerstein & Kelly, 1980; Weiss, 1979). This parental dependency can lead to insecurity and distress for children who must give up at an early age their illusions of parental invulnerability or omnipotence. Yet, many children also feel great pride in their competence as compared with their age mates, and value the special closeness of their relationship with their parent. The child often views the parent's new spouse as a rival and resents the encroachment upon what had previously been a privileged relationship, or fears desertion by the remaining parent (Fast & Cain, 1966; Ransom et al., 1979; Wallerstein & Kelly, 1980). These feelings may manifest themselves in the parent–child relationship as angry resistive behavior, insecure attention-seeking demands, or depression and with-drawal (Fast & Cain, 1966; Hetherington & Clingempeel, 1984; Messinger & Walker, 1981; Podolsky, 1955; Peterson & Zill, 1983).

On the other hand, there is some evidence that remarriage can benefit the parent–child relationship. While remarried mothers report lower well-being than mothers in nondivorced families, they nevertheless are happier than divorced mothers (Arnett, 1984; Weingarten, 1980; White, 1979); and this enhanced well-being may make them more able and tolerant as parents. Mothers whose new husbands are warm and supportive may become more effective, authoritative parents, displaying greater warmth, communication, and control (Hetherington et al., 1981a). This is par-ticularly true for parents of boys. In fact, in one study boys in stepfather families demonstrated more warmth and less hostility in their rela-tionships with their remarried mothers than is seen in the mother–son relationship in nondivorced families (Santrock et al., 1982). It may be that after the stress and conflict custodial mothers and sons experience in a single-parent household, they have little to lose and much to gain by welcoming a stepparent into their family. Boys are generally found to be more adversely affected by divorce than are girls (Hetherington, 1981; Wallerstein & Kelly, 1980), at least in part because of the fact that they suffer the rupture of their relationship with their same-sex parent when the father leaves the home. For a similar reason, girls may be more adversely affected by remarriage than are boys (Hetherington & Clingempeel, 1984; Peterson & Zill, 1983). They usually develop relatively harmonious rela-tionships with their divorced mothers after an initial period of adjustment, and they may experience stronger feelings of loss when the special close-ness they developed with their mothers in the aftermath of divorce is disrupted by the remarriage. It should be noted that this discussion is based on studies of stepfather households. There is not a sufficient body of literature as a basis for comment on what may occur in stepmother households.

The Stepparent–Stepchild Relationship

The stepparent is faced with striking a delicate balance between par-ental and nonparental roles (Fast & Cain, 1966). To become successfully integrated into the family and develop an appropriate relationship with the stepchild, the stepparent must negotiate two tasks that involve somewhat incompatible behaviors. First, the stepparent must develop a warm and appropriately affectionate relationship with the child. Second, the stepparent must also establiish a role as a legitimate parental authority and disciplinarian (Ransom et al., 1979).

These tasks are made still more difficult by several factors. The non-custodial parent, for example, may exercise considerable influence through his or her continuing relationship with the child, or through the child's continuing attachment (Fast & Cain, 1966), as well as through continuing economic and decison-making roles (Walker & Messinger, 1979). In addition, the stepparent is often subjected to a continual comparison with the absent parent, particularly by the child (Fast & Cain, 1966). Third, many of the stepparent's roles will have previously been the exclusive domain of the spouse, and the child as well as the spouse may be somewhat ambivalent about acknowledging these new parental prerogatives as valid and appropriate for the stepparent (Fast & Cain, 1966). Finally, the vagueness of the stepparent role is often accentuated by considerable ambivalence in the feelings of stepparent and stepchild for each other (Fast & Cain, 1966; Messinger, 1976). This ambivalence has a number of sources and can express itself in a variety of ways familiar to clinicians.

Most children express a preference for living in a two-parent household (Wallerstein & Kelly, 1980). Some children, particularly the younger ones, may transfer their former attachment to their nonresidential parent to the stepparent, and may come eventually to accept him or her fully as a parent figure (Podolsky, 1955). However, the child's reactivated feelings of loss over the divorce, and the lessened accessibility of both the residential and nonresidential parents at this time, may cause the child to feel abandoned by both biological parents. The child may view the stepparent as an intruder trying to take the "real" parent's place, and may then attempt to drive a wedge between the newly married couple (Fast & Cain, 1966). The clinical literature also often refers to the child's attempt to resolve the anger and hurt over the loss of the nonresidential parent by idealizing that relationship and transferring compartmentalized negative feelings to the stepparent relationship (Schulman, 1972; Visher & Visher, 1978). This pattern is not supported by one of the few studies to compare explicitly children's assessments of their stepfathers and nonresidential fathers, however (Halperin & Smith, 1983). Using adjective checklists, children rated their residential stepfathers and nonresidential biological fathers similarly, and both were perceived more negatively than were the fathers of children from nondivorced homes. It may be that this idealization of the absent parent, if it is truly characteristic of a nonclinical sample of stepchildren, is more often found in children younger than those in this sample (Kelly & Wallerstein, 1976). It is also plausible to hypothesize that, if present, it is activated selectively in response to stressful events—such as conflict with the stepparent.

The child may also resist developing an emotional bond with the stepparent out of feelings that to do so would be a demonstration of disloyalty to the natural parent (Fast & Cain, 1966; Goldstein, 1974; Ransom et al., 1979). This resistance to accepting the stepparent as a parent figure or to forming a close relationship is particularly common in families with pre-adolescent and young adolescent children (Bowerman & Irish, 1962; Hetherington et al., 1981a; Ransom et al., 1979). Children in this age range are less likely than younger and older children to accept even a warm and authoritative stepparent.

These ambivalent feelings on the part of the child may be compounded by the stepparent's own ambivalence and, often, unrealistic expectations (Messinger, 1976; Schulman, 1972; Visher & Visher, 1978). The stepparent has little guidance in formulating what his or her proper parental rights and responsibilities should be (Cherlin, 1978), the means to attain them, or a realistic idea of how long it should take to develop a satisfactory parental relationship with the child (Stern, 1978; Visher & Visher, 1978). Meanwhile the stepparent often feels called upon to love the child instantly as one of his or her own (Visher & Visher, 1978), even while struggling with many antagonistic feelings toward the child—as a reminder of the spouse's previous marriage, as a source of competition for the spouse's affection and attention, or as an additional financial or emotional responsibility (Fast & Cain, 1966; Visher & Visher, 1978). The stepparent may feel guilty about any less than noble feelings toward the child (Messinger, 1976; Schulman, 1972) and may overcompensate for them. Stepparents often insist that they feel and act toward their stepchildren as a parent, or they may press too prematurely for a close relationship. Because they are often hypersensitive to any evidence that they are not accepted or viewed as parents, if their overtures are rebuffed, an excalating cycle of resentment and hurt feelings can result (Fast & Cain, 1966; Visher & Visher, 1978).

The stepfamily has been identifed as a high-risk family setting for adolescents in terms of both destructive parent–child relations and the development of problem behavior in children (Burgess & Garbarino, 1983; Daly & Wilson, 1981; Garbarino et al., 1984; Hetherington, et al., 1981a, 1981b). Stepfamilies with adolescent children have more divergent perceptions about family functioning and areas of conflict (Pasley & Thinger-Tallman, 1984). Parent–child relations in adolescence are disrupted in many families, not just in stepfamilies, due to the growing independence and developing sexuality and the adolescent. The handling of privacy issues and physical affection can show marked changes in this period. It has been speculated that, in stepfamilies, affectional relationships can be complicated in cross-sex relationships with older children by the lack of an explicit incest taboo. It is proposed that this can lead to considerable tension in stepfamilies with adolescent children (Whiteside & Auerbach, 1978), particularly stepfather families with adolescent girls (Kalter, 1977). A recent study by Hetherington and Clingempeel (1984) of nine- to 12-year-old stepchildren found that, in the first six months following remarriage, stepfathers were more restrained than fathers in nondivorced families in expressing physical affection toward their stepchildren. However, it should be noted that this was true in relations with both stepsons and stepdaughters, which suggests that it may not be based on inhibitions associated with incest fears but on a general problem in expression of physical intimacy.

In forming a new relationship with a stepchild, stepfathers may find it easier to be verbally affectionate or to grant children special privileges than to use more intimate, physical forms of affection. Clinicians also have suggested that family members with adolescents may resist any acknowledgement of intergenerational sexual feelings, thus creating a potentially explosive situation in stepfamilies that lack some of the implicit controls governing such intergenerational sexual expression. It is common for family members to use conflict to maintain an acceptable distance among themselves when they cannot trust other mechanisms to do so, and this may occur in stepfamilies in dealing with issues of physical and emotional intimacy that cannot be dealt with successfully in a more open manner (Goldstein, 1974).

The disciplinary role of the stepparent in remarried families presents some unique problems. The stepparent frequently has child-rearing policies that differ from those to which family members are accustomed, and both the child and the residential parent are likely to resist abrupt and extreme change in, child-rearing styles and strategies. The stepparent risks being considered the "bad guy" by the other family members, who are drawn together by their common family history against the "intruder" (Visher & Visher, 1978; Walker & Messinger, 1979). This may be particularly true of the stepparent who comes into the family with the intention of "straightening that kid out" (Hetherington, 1981), and tries immediately to assert an authoritarian style of parenting. On the other hand, the stepparent may abdicate all responsibility for monitoring the child's behavior, which is an equally maladaptive strategy (Hetherington et al., 1981a, 1981b; Visher & Visher, 1978). In a recent survey of remarriage, it was found that many stepfathers, when asked who was in their family, did not even report stepchildren, but named only their biological children (Pasley & Thinger-Tallman, 1984).

There is some suggestion that the most successful stepparent–stepchild relationships are those in which the stepparent focuses first on developing a warm, friendly relationship with the child (Stern, 1978). Once the stepparent has established a solid base of mutual respect and affection on which to build, attempts to assert authority are more likely to be accepted as legitimate by the child, and the parent is more likely to be successful in discipline. This whole process of fully integrating the stepparent into the family system takes longer than many parents anticipate (Schulman, 1972), as the stepparent's role may continue to evolve for as long as two years (Stern, 1978).

No systematic longitudinal data are available on how the disciplinary role and areas of conflict change over time in stepfamilies. However, in the previously cited study by Hetherington and Clingempeel (1984), it was found that in the first six months following remarriage, conflicts between stepfathers and stepchildren were likely to occur when fathers were backing up mothers' attempts at rule enforcement, particularly those rules regarding household routines and tasks. Mothers in stepfamilies report conflict with their children, especially daughters, over household routines and with their sons over grooming. It should be noted that it would not be accurate to report that more overall conflict was occurring between the stepfather and stepchildren. Fathers in nondivorced families may be more involved with their sons than are stepfathers in the early state of remarriage. They grant their sons more special privileges and are more physically affectionate; however, they also get into more disputes with their sons about monitoring their sons' activities, companions, whereabouts, and grooming. Information on shifts in patterns of discipline and areas of conflict as the stepfamily adjusts to its new organization will await the collection of further data in this longitudinal study.

In summarizing the available studies, it must be concluded that, although clinicians speculate that stepfamilies encounter many problems, the research literature is not consistent in showing how well or how poorly they cope with them. Most self-report, questionnaire, or single-interview studies find few consistent differences in family relations between stepfamilies and nondivorced families (Bohannon & Yahres, 1979; Raschke & Raschke, 1979; Fox & Inazu, 1982). The higher divorce rate in remarried families and the high incidence of behavior problems in children from stepfamilies reported in two recent relatively well-designed studies (Peterson & Zill, 1983; Hetherington et al, 1985) suggest that such families may have more unresolved problems. Studies involving multiple informants or measures assessing highly specific behaviors more frequently reveal differences between stepfamilies and nondivorced families (Garbarino et al., 1984; Hetherington & Clingempeel, 1984). The inconsistency in findings may be attributable not only to measurement differences, but also to the differences in ages of the children in the families sampled, and to the failure of most studies to control for time since remarriage.

Stepmothering

If the available research on stepparent–stepchild relationships in step-father families is scarce, it seems abundant compared with research on stepmother families. Of the studies done on stepfamilies, many do not include stepmother families at all, and many of those that do make no mention of separate analyses or comparisons of stepmother and stepfather families.

Stepmothers have been portrayed in an unflattering light in fairy tales "Cinderella," and "Hansel and Gretel." Whether this mythology of the "wicked stepmother" has some basis in fact, or the mythology itself makes filling the role of stepmother more difficult, there are some indications that stepmothers have a more difficult time becoming integrated into the stepfamily than do stepfathers, and that their relationships with their stepchildren are poorer (Bowerman & Irish, 1962; Duberman, 1972, 1975; Schulman, 1972). This may be partly due to their being more committed than stepfathers to "earning" their status as a parent in the stepfamily, and to the greater amount of time that mothers spend with children than do fathers. Clinicians report that whereas stepfathers will often withdraw from the parenting role if they face initial rejection and hostility from their stepchildren, stepmothers are more likely to persist in trying to fill the role (Visher & Visher, 1978), often fueled by a fantasy of themselves as saviors "fulfilling all the longing for love and nurturance which [their] new children no doubt have" (Goldstein, 1974, p. 436). Unfortunately these good intentions may be interpreted as intrusive by the children, and the step-mother's persistence may result in continuing hostility by her stepchildren.

Stepmothers report "lower quality" relationships with their step-children than do stepfathers (Duberman, 1973), and many fewer step-mothers than stepfathers report having parental feelings for their stepchildren, acting in the role of socializing agent, or feeling mutual love in their relationships with their stepchildren (Duberman, 1975). This senti-ment is shared by their stepchildren, half of whom report feeling little affection toward their stepmothers, and who are far more likely than children of stepfather families to wish they lived in a different family (Bowerman & Irish, 1962).

There are some indications that there may be age and sex differences in children's relationships with and reactions to stepfathers and stepmothers. Wallerstein and Kelly (1980b) report age differences, with younger chil-dren more likely than older children to develop a close relationship with their stepmother, just as Hetherington et al. (1981a, 1981b) found to be true in stepfather families. Both stepmothers and stepfathers report more positive relationships with sons than with daughters (Reaves, 1982), and adolescent daughters are particularly likely to resent stepmothers. Adolescent children may blame the stepmother for the breakup of their parents' marriage, and a young stepmother may be unprepared for and uncomfortable with adolescent stepchildren.

Though little evidence is in at this point, it should be particularly interesting to see if there are sex differences in children's adjustment to living in a stepmother family. There is some suggestion that children fare better following divorce when in the custody of their same-sex parent (Santrock & Warshak, 1979). For girls there are indications that this advantage following divorce may be undone by their poorer adjustment to living in a stepfather family. For example, girls in stepfather families have more difficulty on several aspects of school behavior compared with girls of other family types, including stepmother families, while this is not true of boys (Burchinal, 1964); and adolescent girls in stepfamilies have an unusually high rate of referral for psychological counseling, particularly regarding substance abuse and sexual behavior problems (Kalter, 1977). Whether boys who go from father custody to living in a stepmother family face similar risks remains an open question.

Stepparenting in Perspective

"It is likely that there is no single stepparenting style that would work in all stepfamilies, just as there is not parenting style that works in all nondivorced families. What will succeed in a given family depends on several factors. The child's age heavily influences what the child needs and will accept from the stepparent. Young children are likely to accept an authoritative stepparent, while preadolescent and early adolescent children may have more difficulty accepting a stepparent no matter how competent a parent he or she may be (Hetherington et al., 1981a, 1981b). For children below age eight, consistent discipline, accompanied by warmth and responsiveness, is likely to be most appropriate and effective. Adolescents, on the other hand, are generally less likely than other children to accept stepparents, even those who are relatively competent, stable, and responsive. The temperaments, personalities, attitudes, and relationsips to other family members of the individuals involved will also influence the appropriateness and success of various stepparenting styles. In addition, cultural and subcultural variations may shape the adjustment and relations in stepfamilies.

Sibling Relationships

Of all aspects of stepfamily research, sibling and stepsibling relationships remain the *terra incognita* in our understanding of stepfamily functioning. In single-parent families, older children are frequently expected to assume responsibility for the care and supervision of their younger siblings (Weiss, 1979), and it has been shown that a father surrogate, such as an older brother, can have a significant positive impact on the social adjustment of boys in father-absent families (Hetherington et al., 1981a, 1981b; Santrock et al., 1982; Wohlford et al., 1971; Zill, 1982). What, then, becomes of this sibling bond when the parent remarries? Do siblings provide an alernate source of guidance and emotional gratification for one another while the parent is distracted by the demands of the new marital relationship? Or are sibling conflicts, perhaps over rivalry for the parental attention that is available, one arena in which the stresses of adjusting to a stepfamily can be "safely" expressed, thus channeling attention away from unresolved issues between the spouses? Virtually nothing appears in the literature, although the few shreds of available evidence suggest that sibling relationships in stepfamilies may be somewhat disengaged, or even abrasive. Wagner (1984) reports that stepchildren are less involved with and showed less empathy and concern for their siblings than is true of children in nondivorced families. Bowerman and Irish (1962) report that children more often feel discriminated against in favor of siblings in stepparent families, suggesting that sibling rivalry may be particularly keen. Clearly, however, more research in this area is needed.

Evidence of stepsibling relationships is scarcely more abundant, and much of what is available is drawn from the clinical literature. When stepsibling conflict is the focus of family pathology, clinicians suggest that it may be a result of a more dominant, older, or more numerous sibling cluster attempting to shut the other out or use it as a scapegoat. It has been proposed that in the case of families with adolescent stepsiblings, conflict may be a way of maintaining distance in the absence of an explicit incest taboo (Ransom et al., 1979; Whiteside & Auerbach, 1978), although Duberman (1973) found cross-sex stepsibling relationships to be more satisfactory than same-sex relationships. Often stepsiblings do not live in the same household. Typically the mother's children live with her whereas the father's children visit during weekends, summer vacations, or holidays. Duberman (1973) found less positive relationships among stepchildren under these circumstances than when they lived in the same household.

A third piece in the stepfamily sibling relationships' puzzle is the question of the child's feelings toward half-siblings produced in the new marriage. The birth of a younger sibling can be a stressful event in any family (Dunn, 1983; Dunn et al., 1981). Yet there is a dearth of information on how children in stepfamilies receive this event. Related evidence would suggest, though, that rapport, at least in the long run, may be quite good. While remarried households including children from a previous marriage are more likely to fail, the birth of a child in the new marriage is associated with greater marital stability (Becker et al., 1977). The presence of half-siblings is also associated with greater harmony between the stepparent and child (Duberman, 1975), as well as between stepsiblings (Duberman, 1973). Perhaps the new child serves as a tangible symbol of the blending together of the disparate family subsystems.

CHILD OUTCOMES

A central concern of clinicians and developmental psychologists has been whether there are differences in developmental outcomes and adjustment for children in nondivorced families versus stepfamilies. Because remarriages have been preceded by the divorce or death of a parent, without a one-parent nonremarried comparison group it is impossible to discern whether differences between children in stepfamilies and those in nondivorced families are attributable to the remarriage or to the experiences that preceded it. Studies involving such one-parent nonremarried comparison groups are rarely found. Moreover, reports of differences in outcome are again found to vary with the methods used, the source of the report, the age and sex of the child, and time since remarriage. The following review of the literature attempts to focus on the more methodologically sound studies and on studies that may illuminate how these various factors may mediate developmental outcomes. In general it will be seen that differences between stepchildren and those in other family types are more often found on measures of conduct disorders involving antisocial, impulsive externalizing behavior, and not on those related to internalizing behaviors or self-concept.

Self-Concept

Self-concept is obviously an area where the child usually is the best source of information. Because of differences in the ability and cognitive capacity of children of different ages, the instruments used across ages vary and may not be comparable. The majority of studies have reported no difference in self-esteem between stepchildren and children in nondivorced or single-parent families (Parish & Taylor, 1979; Parish, 1981; Raschke & Raschke, 1979; Wilson et al., 1975). However, length of time since remarriage was uncontrolled in these studies. Studies with findings of no differences in self-esteem between children from stepfamilies and those from nondivorced families have tended to involve younger grade-school children, while those reporting poorer self-images have been based on the reports of preadolescents (Hetherington & Clingempeel, 1984), adolescents (Rosenberg, 1965), or adults (Kaplan & Pokorny, 1971). Kaplan and Pokorny (1971) found that children whose mothers had remarried before the children were eight years old had self-concepts similar to those of children in nondivorced families, whereas children whose mothers had married when the child was older than eight had lower self-concepts than children of nondivorced families.

There is also little consistency in the reports of sex differences in self-esteem among these families. Two studies reporting sex differences found significant differences for boys only—but in markedly different directions, and a third study reports significant differences only for girls. Nunn and Parish (1983) report that, among fifth- to tenth-graders, boys in step-families have lower self-concepts than boys in divorced or nondivorced families, with no differences among girls. In contrast, Santrock et al. (1982) compared children in stepfamilies and nondivorced families and found the self-concepts of boys in stepfamilies to be *higher* than for boys in nondivorced families, with no differences among the girls. However, the two studies used radically different methodologies. Parish used the child's self-report on the Personal Attribute Inventory for Children, while Santrock and colleagues based their conclusions on observers' global ratings of parent–child interactions. It is also possible that the stepfathers in Santrock's sample were exceptional. In contrast to the findings in other studies (Hetherington et al., 1981a, 1981b; Hetherington & Clingempeel, 1984), compared with fathers in nondivorced families, these stepfathers were more attentive to the needs of the children and were more authoritative parents.

Results of two recent longitudinal studies suggest that time since remarriage and sex of the child may be important factors mediating the effects of remarriage on self-esteem. In the Hetherington and Clingempeel (1984) study, at six months after remarriage, no differences in self-esteem were found in the reports of preadolescent boys from remarried, nondivorced, and single-parent mother-custody homes. However, girls in stepfather families rated themselves lower than girls in nondivorced families on issues of social responsibility, ego strength, and cognitive agency. In a second study, Hetherington and colleagues (1985) examined self-esteem in ten-year-old children whose parents had been divorced six years earlier. If custodial mothers had been remarried for more than two years, their sons and daughters did not differ in their reports of self-esteem from children in divorced, nonremarried mother-custody families, or nondivorced families. However, if there had been a stepfather in the home for less than two years, the self-esteem of girls, but not of boys, was lower than for the other family types. This suggests that initially remarriage is more stressful for girls than for boys, but that girls eventually adjust to their new family situation.

In summary, the kindest statement that can be made about this confused literature on self-esteem is that the results are inconclusive and that the topic warrants further study with more systematic attention paid to such variables as the child's sex, age at divorce and remarriage, past experience of divorce and life in a one-parent family, quality of the parent–child and stepparent relationships, and the method of measuring self-concept.

Externalizing Disorders

Evidence indicates that stepchildren generally exhibit more externalizing, acting-out, impulsive antisocial behavior than do children in nondivorced families. Once again, however, the evidence is mixed, and is complicated by age and sex differences. Self-reports of children in remarried families indicate no more delinquent behavior than for children of nondivorced families (Perry & Pfuhl, 1963; Wilson et al., 1975). However, their teachers report that children in remarried families exhibit more conduct problems than do children in nondivorced families (Furstenberg & Seltzer, 1982; Touliatos & Lindholm, 1980). Both boys and girls in remarried families are more likely to bring home critical notes from teachers, and stepdaughters also are more likely to have been expelled than are girls in nondivorced or divorced mother-headed households (Peterson & Zill, 1983). It has been suggested that teachers may be biased in their perceptions of children living in nontraditional types of families. Parents, however, also report more conduct problems for children in remarried families, at least in the early stages of remarriage (Hetherington & Clingempeel, 1984; Hetherington et al., 1985; Zill & Peterson, 1983; Garbarino et al., 1984). Perhaps children's reports are likely to be biased in their own favor but until more studies are published that compare reports from more than one source, this remains an open question.

Several studies have looked intensively at differences in conduct between children in stepfamilies and children of other family types. Generally it appears that living in a stepfamily is most difficult for girls, and for adolescents. Kalter (1977) found both age and sex differences in aggression toward parents as well as other conduct problems among children from divorced, remarried, and nondivorced families. For children under age seven, there were no differences by family type or the sex of the child. For children seven to 11, boys in divorced families exhibited more problems than boys of the other two family types, while there were no differences among the girls. For children over 12, however, those in stepfamilies exhibited more problems than those of the other two family types, and the differences were strongest for girls.

Jacobson (1984a) conducted a study of four family types: (1) child lives with single mother, visits remarried father; (2) child lives with remarried father, visits single mother; (3) child lives with remarried mother, visits remarried father; and (4) child lives with remarried mother, visits single father. In comparing conduct-related, affect-related, and overall behavior problems, the results indicated that children in stepmother families had more overall behavior problems than children living with a single mother, and that they had both more conduct problems and more overall behavior problems than children in stepfather families where the biological father had remarried. It was also found that, for all stepfamily types combined, boys under 12 and older children of both sexes had more overall behavior problems, more conduct-related problems, and more affect-related problems than the nonclinical sample of children on whom the Achenbach Child Behavior Checklist, which they used (Achenbach, 1978), was standardized.

Zill and Petersen (1983) used parents' reports on items selected from the Achenbach Child Behavior Checklist to measure antisocial behavior; immature, impulsive-hyperactive behavior; and depressed withdrawn behavior in a large-scale survey of nondivorced, divorced, and remarried families. Girls in stepfamilies were more prone to antisocial behavior than those in divorced or nondivorced families. In contrast, boys in remarried families were reported to be as low in antisocial behavior as those in low-conflict nondivorced families. Boys in single-parent families or high-conflict nondivorced families were more prone to externalizing disorders than the former two groups. At the same time, stepfamily boys were found to exhibit the most impulsive-hyperactive immature behavior, whereas girls in single-parent families were the most extreme of the three groups on impulsive-hyperactive behavior. This study also replicated a finding by Santrock and his colleagues (1979) that, in one-parent households, children show less antisocial behavior if they are in the custody of a parent of the same sex.

In an ongoing lontigudinal study (Hetherington & Clingempeel, 1984) of adaptation during the first two years following remarriage, mothers and stepfathers reported that, in the first six months, both boys and girls in stepfather families showed more externalizing behavior than those in nondivorced families as measured on the Achenbach Child Behavior Checklist. Finally, Hetherington et al. (1981a, 1981b), in a follow-up to their longitudinal study of divorce, found that the behavior of boys improves notably at home and at school following their mother's remarriage to a warm, authoritative stepfather. However, if the parents had been remarried for less than two years, boys showed more externalizing behavior than those in nondivorced families but less than those in single-parent mother-custody households. In contrast, when the remarriage had occurred longer than two years before, no differences were found between boys in nondivorced and in remarried families. On the other hand, girls whose mothers had been remarried less than two years showed the most antisocial behaviors, and no differences were found among the three groups more than two years after remarriage (Hetherington et al., 1985). The findings of these five studies suggest that the effects of divorce and life in a mother-custody single-parent family are more adverse for boys while the presence of a stepfather is more stressful for girls. Zill and Peterson (1983) and Hetherington et al. (1985) also report that, with time, both boys and girls adapt to their stepfamilies, with boys actually benefiting from the presence of a stepfather.

Internalizing Behavior

The pattern of findings for the effects of remarriage on internalizing behaviors such as anxiety, withdrawal, and depression are less consistent than those for externalizing behaviors. Internalizing behaviors tend to be more subtle and less readily observed by others and less reliably assessed than are conduct disorders. There are some studies that show children of stepfamilies to be functioning less well than children in nondivorced families, and others that find no differences. Where there are sex differences, it is usually, though not exclusively, girls in stepfamilies who are having the most difficulty.

The bulk of the evidence indicates that stepchildren are as happy as children from nondivorced families (Bohannon & Yahres, 1979), are no more likely to have psychosomatic complaints (Burchinal, 1964; Perry & Pfuhl, 1963), and are as psychologically healthy as those from nondivorced families (Burchinal, 1964; Manosevitz, 1976; Touliatos & Lindholm, 1980), while those from single-parent homes tended to have more problems (Manosevitz, 1976). Two studies did find significant differences between stepchildren and children from nondivorced homes, with stepchildren being lower in well-being (Kellam et al., 1977) and higher in internalizing pathology (Garbarino et al., 1984). Both of these samples, however, are drawn from high-risk populations, where the stress and disruption of divorce and remarriage are more likely to be compounded by a number of other environmental stressors. In one instance the sample was drawn from lower-class, inner-city black families, while the subjects for the other study were adolescents at risk for physical abuse by their parents. But sampling bias can also work in the other direction. For example, Manosevitz (1976) may have failed to find differences in the functioning of college students from nondivorced and remarried families in part because those children who are most emotionally and cognitively disabled by their inability to cope with stressful life events are also less likely to enter college.

It is important as well to take into account the perspective of the informant. In data drawn from reports during the first six months of remarriage (Hetherington & Clingempeel, 1984), findings of sex differences varied dramatically, depending on the source of the report. Self-reports revealed no significant differences in depression by sex or by family type, regardless of whether the data were drawn from a specific inventory of behaviors of the last 24 hours, the depression subscale of the Achenbach Child Behavior Checklist assessing behavior over the previous three months, or global mood ratings. In contrast, mothers in stepfamilies rated their sons as significantly more depressed than did mothers of sons in nondivorced families on both the Achenbach depression subscale and the 24-hour behavior inventory, while stepfathers rated both stepdaughters and stepsons as more depressed compared with the reports of nondivorced fathers on the Achenbach depression subscale but not on the 24-hour inventory. Finally, teachers' reports on the Achenbach subscale indicate that girls from remarried families are moodier and more withdrawn at school compared with girls from nondivorced families. It is quite possible that children exhibit somewhat different behavior in their relationships with different adults or across different settings, particularly early in the remarriage. However, the possibility that adults' perceptions are biased by subjective feelings or expectations clearly merits further investigation. It is noteworthy that the most consistent findings came from the reports of the children themselves, and that they do not perceive themselves as being particularly unhappy, at least in the first few months following remarriage.

With regard to sex differences, some studies using observer ratings and parent reports suggest that girls in stepfamilies experience greater anxiety and depression than do girls in divorced or nondivorced families, while boys in stepfamilies experience these affective problems no more than boys in nondivorced families, and less than boys in divorced families (Hetherington et al., 1985; Santrock et al., 1982; Zill & Petersen, 1983).

However, these studies are relatively restricted in terms of the time since remarriage, and it seems probable that remarriage could have different short- and long-term effects on children's affective functioning.

In summary, most studies of internalizing behavior comparing children of stepfamilies with children of nondivorced families find little difference in functioning, with children of both groups generally functioning better than children in divorced families. There is some indication that girls in stepfamilies are impaired in this area, based on observers' and parents' reports. But, contradictory findings based on reports of the children themselves call this into question, and there is a need to separate the study of children's short-term adjustment from the examination of more enduring outcomes.

Social Adjustment

There is some indication that children of stepfamilies do not function as well socially as children of nondivorced families. They report poorer peer relations (Nunn & Parish, 1983), their social adaptation is observed to be poorer by their parents and teachers (Kellam et al., 1977), and they are reported to be more agressive toward their peers (Kalter, 1977).

Although children in stepfamilies might not function as well in their social relationships as children in nondivorced families, there is evidence that a good relationship with a stepfather, older brother, or grandfather is associated with improved social and personal functioning for boys in divorced families (Hetherington et al., 1981a, 1981b; Santrock et al., 1982; Wohlford et al., 1971; Zill, 1982). The presence of a stepmother may not have the same ameliorative effect for boys. In one study, boys in step-mother families reported fewer friends than boys in nondivorced, step-father, or divorced families, while there were no differences among girls (Burchinal, 1964).

As for outcomes in studies of internalizing behavior, there seem to be some method-related differences occurring in reports of problems in social behavior and adjustment. There is a trend for studies in which self-reports are used to find few differences between children in stepfamilies and other children, however, parents and teachers are more likely to report adverse behaviors in stepchildren. In addition, adverse effects are more likely to be reported when children are studied shortly after remarriage (Dahl et al., 1977; Hetherington et al., 1985; Kellam et al., 1977; Peterson & Zill, 1983), than when families have had the opportunity to adapt to their remarried family situation.

Cognitive Development

Few studies are available that examine the impact of remarriage on cognitive development and achievement, and the results are inconsistent. Although some studies report that stepchildren perform as well academically as children of nondivorced families (Bohannon & Yahres, 1979; Burchinal, 1964; Perry & Pfuhl, 1963), a large-scale survey finds stepchildren to perform less well academically (Furstenberg & Seltzer, 1982).

Chapman (1977) examined field independence and SAT scores among college students of father-absent, nondivorced, and stepfather families, and found among males that those of nondivorced families were most field independent, followed by males from stepfather families, with males from father-absent families the least field independent. Females of stepfather families actually scored higher on field independence than females of the other two family types, and had higher SAT verbal scores than females of intact families. Again, it should be noted that individuals who have been able to enter college may represent a select group.

Santrock (1972) found the presence of a stepfather to have somewhat positive effects on the cognitive development of boys, in a study of children's third- and sixth-grade IQ and achievement. However, the effect was significant only for the third-grade achievement of boys whose biological fathers had left the home before the boys were five years old, compared with father-absent boys whose fathers had left after that time, and there was no correspondingly positive effect on girls. Finally, Hetherington and co-workers (1981), in a review article, conclude that the presence of a father surrogate (i.e., older brother, grandfather, or stepfather) has not been shown to have a postive effect on achievement and intellectual functioning, and may, in fact, be detrimental.

Racial Differences in Children's Adjustment

Little noted thus far in remarriage research is the possibility that the remarriage experience may be quite different for children of white and of black families. Research has indicated the importance of kin as influences in the lives of black children (McAdoo, 1978; Nobles, 1978; Stack, 1974). With regard to remarriage, this is illustrated in a study by Kellam et al., (1977). Conducted on an inner-city, economically deprived, black population, the results of this study differed somewhat from studies on white populations that have indicated a beneficial effect of a stepfather on the social functioning of boys (Hetherington et al., 1981a, 1981b; Santrock et al., 1982). In contrast, Kellam et al. found the social adaptation of children in stepfather families to be no better than for children living with a single mother, with both of these groups having poorer social adaptation than both intact (nondivorced) and mother–grandmother households.

It is also possible that the prevalence of mother-headed families among blacks has implications for the social significance and role expectations of stepfathers. Since mother-headed families are more common in black communities, the addition of a stepfather to the family may have less value among black children in terms of making their own family more like a "modal" two-parent family. Futher, in a community where so many mothers are raising their children without the aid of a male figure, stepfathers may feel less compelled to take on parental responsibilities. These differences in extended family networks, socialization, and normative family types may affect black children's adjustments to living in a stepfamily in ways quite different from those of white children. The understanding of these relationships awaits further research.

SUMMARY

Although research in the area of stepfamilies is meager, there are indications that stepchildren, as compared with children in nondivorced families, are more likely to have higher rates of acting-out impulsive behaviors, conduct disorders, and problems in social relationships. In contrast, on measures of self-concept and internalizing disorders such as depression, withdrawal, and anxiety, and in cognitive development, stepchildren usually are found to be similar to children in nondivorced families.

In considering factors that may mediate these outcomes, sex and age of the child and length of time since remarriage are proving to be particularly salient variables. In addition, the quality of the relationship with kin and quasi-kin both inside and outside of the home, particularly with the custodial and noncustodial parents and the residential stepparent, moderate the effects of remarriage. Although less is known about the role of siblings and grandparents, it seems likely that they, too, will be important in helping the child adjust to his or her restructured family.

Young children seem to adapt more readily to their parents' remarriages than do late-preadolescent or adolescent children. Remarriage seems to exacerbate the conflict, need for independence, and resistance to authority often found in adolescents. As adolescents become older and are oriented toward leaving the home, or have left the home, as in the case of college students, they are better able to accept their parents' remarriage.

Boys in divorced mother-custody families tend to show no adverse effects or may benefit from the addition of a stepfather, while girls in such families are more likely to exhibit at least short-term disruptions in behavior. It seems likely that this is attributable, in part, to the relationship of the children with the custodial mother in a one-parent household in the period following divorce. Divorced mothers and daughters usually are able to establish close supportive relationships whereas divorced mothers and their sons are more likely to become involved in mutually coercive conflictual relationships. The introduction of a stepfather may be perceived as an intrusion into the mother–daughter relationship, whereas stepsons may have little to lose and much to gain from the addition of a supportive stepfather. Little is known about the effects of the introduction of a stepmother into a father-custody household. However, there may be differences in the impact of residential stepmothers and residential stepfathers on boys and girls. Certainly there is some evidence in the divorce literature that children do better in the custody of a same-sex parent.

Changes in the relationship between the custodial parent and child may be particularly important. If the parent's response to remarriage is to invest heavily in the new marriage to the neglect of the child, the child's ability to cope with this stressful transition may be overtaxed. If, on the other hand, the parent draws on the emotional support in the new marital relationship, the increased support in finances and household duties, and his or her own increased well-being to support the child emotionally and to spend more time more positively with the child, long-term adjustment may be enhanced. Certainly, the child's contribution to any change in the relationship following remarriage, either from resentment over the remarriage or from feeling more secure and taking pleasure in the parent's happiness, should be considered as well. Children play an active role not only in parent–child adjustment, but also in supporting or undermining the new marital relationship. Whatever the relative contribution of parent and child, the quality of that relationship is likely to have broad repercussions on the child's functioning (Hetherington et al., 1981a, 1981b; Zill & Petersen, 1983).

The quality of the child's relationship with the stepparent and noncustodial parent must also be considered. Following remarriage the relationship with the stepparent could be a more important factor in determining the effects of remarriage on the child than the child's relationship with the noncustodial biological parent, although the relationship with the noncustodial parent continues to be important (Furstenberg & Seltzer, 1983). Many stepfathers tend to be disengaged in the early stages of remarriage, although a significant minority may be extremely intrusive and restrictive (Hetherington et al., 1981a). In cases where the stepfather is able to find an authoritative middle ground and behave in a warm, responsive, and appropriately controlling manner, the child is likely to benefit. It seems that the most beneficial family system for stepchildren is one in which the custodial parent, stepparent, and noncustodial parent have a supportive relationship with the child and little overt conflict among themselves. Again, it should be kept in mind that in considering the restructuring of the family following remarriage, family changes both inside the household of residence and external to it may interact to affect the child's adjustment.

Finally, families change over time and adjust to the new situations, experiences, and challenges they encounter in marital trasitions. In the case of divorce, the first two years following the divorce may be particularly disruptive and stressful for the family, but after that initial transition period, restabilizing of the family and successful adjustment occur in most cases. Following remarriage it also will take time for the family system to stablize and for relationships to develop among family members, particularly between the stepparent and children, so that any beneficial effect of living in a successful stepfamily may not be apparent for some time. There is some evidence that this is the case since investigators who study children in the early stages of remarriage are more likely to find adjustment problems than those who examine later stages of remarriage. It has been show that, after remarriage, large numbers of children in stepfamilies are seen by their parents as needing psychological help, while among children who have lived in a stepfamily for at least four years, the perceived need for psychological help has greatly decreased (Zill & Peterson, 1984). However, one should be alert to the fact that such perceived needs for psychological help may reflect the parents' anxieties, the past experiences of the children going through divorce and life in a one-parent family, or the actual adjustment of the child. Moreover, because the divorce rate is higher in remarried than first-married families, many stepchildren will confront subsequent marital disruptions and family reorganizations. These children have been reported to show even higher rates of needing or getting psychological help than those in stable remarriages (Zill & Peterson, 1984). This underlines the need to examine remarriage as part of a series of family formations and reorganizations that begin with first marriage.

In some ways it is premature to review the literature on remarriage. Within five years the data from several reasonably well-designed investigations currently under way will provide a much richer empirical basis for such a review. It is hoped, however, that the present review will alert investigators to significant issues, problems, and promising directions to pursue in the study of remarriage and stepparenting.

REFERENCES

Achenbach, T. M. (1978). The child behavior profiles. I: Boys aged 6–11. *Journal of Consulting and Clinical Psychology, 46,* 478–88.

Achenbach, T. M., & Edelbrock, C. S. (1979). The child behavior profiles. II: Boys aged 12–16 and girls aged 6–11 and 12–16. *Journal of Consulting and Clinical Psychology, 47,* 223–233.

Anspach, D. (1976). Kinship and divorce. *Journal of Marriage and the Family, 38,* 343–350.

Arnett, J. (1984). Mother's and children's adjustment to stepfamilies at one to six months following remarriage. Unpublished master's thesis, University of Virginia.

Bachrach, C. (1983). Children in families: Characteristics of biological, step- and adopted children. *Journal of Marriage and the Family, 45,* 171–179.

Becker, G., Landes, E., & Michael, R. (1977). An economic analysis of marital instability. *Journal of Political Economy, 85,* 1141–1187.

Bernard, J. (1956). *Remarriage: A Study of Marriage.* New York: Dryden.

Bitterman, C. (1968). The multi-marriage family. *Social Casework, 49,* 218–221.

Bohannon, P., (Ed.) (1970). *Divorce and After.* New York: Doubleday.

Bohannon, P. (1981). Stepfamilies: A partially annotated bibliography. Prepared for *Stepfamily Association of America, Inc.,* Palo Alto, Calif.

Bohannon, P., & Yahres, H. (1979). Stepfathers as parents. In E. Corfman (Ed.), *Families Today: A Research Sampler on Families and Children* (pp. 347–362). NIMH Science Monograph. Washington, D.C.: U.S. Government Printing Office.

Bowerman, C., & Irish, D. (1962). Some relationships of stepchildren to their parents. *Marriage and Family Living, 24,* 113–121.

Bumpass, L. (January, 1983). Children and martial disruption: A replication and update. Working Paper 82-67, Center for Demography and Ecology, University of Wisconsin, Madison.

Bumpass, L., & Rindfuss, R. (1979). Children's experience of marital disruption. *American Journal of Sociology, 85,* 49–65.

Bumpass, L., & Sweet, A. (1972). Differentials in marital instability: 1970. *American Sociological Review, 37,* 754–766.

Burchinal, L. G. (1964). Characteristics of adolescents from unbroken, broken, and reconstituted families. *Journal of Marriage and the Family, 26,* 44–50.

Burgess, B., & Garbarino, J. (1983). Doing what comes naturally? An evolutionary perspective on child abuse. In D. Finkelhorn, R. Gelles, G. Hataling, & M. Straus (Eds.), *The Dark Side of Families.* (pp. 88–101). Beverly Hills, Calif.: Sage.

Chapman, M. (1977). Father absence, stepfathers, and the cognitive performance of college students. *Child Development, 48,* 1155–1158.

Cherlin, A. (1977). The effects of children on marital dissolution. *Demography, 14,* 265–272.

Cherlin, A. (1978). Remarriage as an incomplete institution. *American Journal of Sociology, 84,* 634–650.

Cherlin, A. (1981). *Marriage, Divorce, Remarriage.* Cambridge, Mass.: Harvard University Press.

Cherlin, A., & McCarthy, J. (April, 1983). Remarried couple households. Paper presented at the annual meeting of the Population Association of America. Pittsburgh, Pa.

Clingempeel, W. G. (1981). Quasi-kin relationships and marital quality in stepfather families. *Journal of Personality and Social Psychology, 41,* 890–901.

Clingempeel, W. G., & Brand, E. (1985). Quasi-kin relationships, structural complexity, and marital quality in stepfamilies: A replication and extension. *Family Relations, 34,* 401–409.

Clingempeel, W. G., Ievoli, R., & Brand, E. (1984). Structural complexity and the quality of stepfather-stepchild relations. *Family Process, 23,* 547–560.

Dahl, B. B., McCubbin, H. I., & Lester, G. R. (1976). War-induced father absence; Comparing the adjustment of children in reunited, non-reunited and reconstituted families. *International Journal of Sociology and the Family, 6,* 99–108.

Daly, M., & Wilson, M. (1981). Child maltreatment from a sociological perspective. *New Directions for Child Development,* no. 11, 31–52.

Duberman, L. (1973). Stepkin relationships. *Journal of Marriage and the Family, 35,* 283–292.

Duberman, L. (1975). *The Reconstituted Family: A Study of Remarried Couples and Their Children.* Chicago: Nelson-Hall.

Dunn, J. (1983). Sibling relationships in early childhood. *Child Development, 54,* 787–811.

Dunn, J., Kindrick, C., & MacNamee, R. (1981). The reaction of first-born children to the birth of a sibling: Mothers' reports. *Journal of Child Psychology and Psychiatry, 22,* 1–18.

Fast, I., & Cain, A. (1966). The stepparent role: Potential for disturbances in family functioning. *American Journal of Orthopsychiatry, 36,* 485–491.

Fox, G. L., & Inazu, J. K. (1982). The influence of mothers' marital history on the mother-daughter relationship in black and white households. *Journal of Marriage and the Family, 44,* 143–153.

Furstenberg, F. (1980). Reflections on remarriage. *Journal of Family Issues,* 1, 443–453.

Furstenberg, F. (April, 1981). Renegotiating parenthood after divorce and remarriage. Paper presented at the biennial meeting of the Society for Research in Child Development, Symposium on Changing Family Patterns, Boston.

Furstenberg, F. (November, 1982). Child care after divorce and remarriage. Paper presented at the MacArthur Foundation's Conference on Child Care: Growth Fostering Environments, Chicago.

Furstenberg, F. (1983). Martial disruption and childcare. Unpublished manuscript, Pennsylvania State University, University Park.

Furstenberg, F., Nord, C., Peterson, J., & Zill, N. (April, 1982). The life course of children of divorce: Marital disruption and parental contact. Paper presented at the Population Association of America Meeting, San Diego.

Furstenberg, F., & Seltzer, J. (April, 1983). Divorce and child development. Paper presented to the American Orthopsychiatric Association Panel on Current Research in Divorce and Remarriage, Boston.

Furstenberg, F. F., & Spanier, G. B. (1984). *Recycling the Family: Remarriage After Divorce.* Beverly Hills, Calif.: Sage.

Ganong, L., & Coleman, M. (1984). The effects of remarriage on children: A review of the empirical literature. *Family Relations, 33,* 389–406.

Garbarino, J., Sebes, J., & Schellenbach, C. (1984). Families at risk for destructive parent-child relations in adolescence. *Child Development, 55,* 174–183.

Garmezy, N., & Rutter, M. (Eds.) (1983). *Stress, Coping and Development in Children.* New York: McGraw-Hill.

Glenn, N., & Weaver, C. (1977). The marital happiness of remarried divorced parents. *Journal of Marriage and the Family, 39,* 331–337.

Glick, I., & Kessler, D. (1980). *Marital and Family Therapy.* New York: Grune & Stratton.

Goetting, A. (September 1978). The normative integration of the former spouse relationship. Paper presented at the meeting of the American Sociological Association, San Francisco.

Goldstein, H. (1974). Reconstituted families: The second marriage and its children. *Psychiatric Quarterly, 48,* 433–440.

Halperin, S. & Smith, T. (1983). Differences in stepchildren's perceptions of their stepfathers and natural fathers: Implications for family therapy. *Journal of Divorce, 7,* 19–30.

Hess, R. D., & Camara, K. A. (1979). Post-divorce family relationships as mediating factors in the consequences of divorce for children. *Journal of Social Issues, 35,* 79–96.

Hetherington, E. M. (1972). Effects of father absence on personality development in adolescent daughters. *Developmental Psychology, 7,* 313–326.

Hetherington, E. M. (1981). Children and divorce. In R. Henderson (Ed.), *Parent-Child Interaction: Theory, Research and Prospects* (pp. 33–58). New York: Academic Press.

Hetherington, E. M. (1984). Stress and coping in children and families. In A. Doyle, D. Gold, & D. S. Maskowitz (Eds.), *Children in Families Under Stress.* (pp. 7–33). New Directions for Child Development, no. 24. San Francisco: Jossey-Bass.

Hetherington, E. M., Camara, K. A., & Featherman, D. L. (1981). Achievement and intellectual functioning of children in one-parent households. In J. Spence (Ed.), *Assessing Achievement.* (pp. 206–284). San Francisco: W. H. Freeman.

Hetherington, E. M., & Clingempeel, G. (1984). A longitudinal study of remarriage and stepparenting. Study in progress. Preliminary results.

Hetherington, E. M., Cox, M., & Cox, R. (April, 1981a). Divorce and remarriage. Paper presented to the Society for Research in Child Development, Boston

Hetherington, E. M., Cox, M., & Cox, R. (1981b). Effects of divorce on parents and children. In M. Lamb (Ed.), *Nontraditional Families* (pp. 233–288). Hillsdale, N.J.: Lawrence Erlbaum.

Hetherington, E. M., Cox, M., & Cox, R. (1985). Long-term effects of divorce and remarriage on the adjustment of children. *American Journal of Orthopsychiatry, 24,* 518–530.

Jacobson, D. S. (May, 1984a). Factors associated with healthy family functioning in stepfamilies. Paper presented to Society for Research in Child Development, Workshop on Remarriage and Stepfamilies, Lexington, Ky.

Jacobson, D. (1984b). Family type, visiting and children's behavior problems in the stepfamily: A linked-family system. Unpublished manuscript.

Jones, S. (1978). Divorce and remarriage: A new beginning, a new set of problems. *Journal of Divorce, 2,* 217–227.

Kalter, N. (1977). Children of divorce in an outpatient psychiatric population. *American Journal of Orthopsychiatry, 47,* 40–51.

Kaplan, H. B., & Pokorny, A. D. (1971). Self-derogation and childhood broken home. *Journal of Marriage and the Family, 33,* 328–337.

Kellam, S. G., Ensminger, M. E., & Turner, J. (1977). Family structure and the mental health of children: Concurrent and longitudinal community-wide studies. *Archives of General Psychiatry, 34,* 1012–1022.

Kelly, J., & Wallerstein, J. (1976). The effects of parental divorce: Experiences of the child in early latency. *American Journal of Orthopsychiatry, 46,* 20–32.

Keshet, J. (1980). From separation to stepfamily. *Journal of Family Issues, 1,* 517–532.

Knaub, P., Hanna, S., & Stinnett, M. (1984). Strengths of remarried families. *Journal of Divorce, 7,* 41–55.

Marsden, D. (1969). *Mothers Alone: Poverty and the Fatherless Family.* London: Allen Lane, Penguin Press.

McAdoo, H. P. (1978). Factors related to stability in upwardly mobile black families. *Journal of Marriage and the Family, 40,* 761–778.

Messinger, L. (1976). Remarriage between divorced people with children from previous marriages. A proposal for preparation for remarriage. *Journal of Marriage and Family Counseling, 2,* 193–300.

Messinger, L., & Walker, K. (1981). From marriage breakdown to remarriage: Parental tasks and therapeutic guidelines. *American Journal of Orthopsychiatry, 54,* 429–437.

Nobles, W. W. (1974). Africanity: Its role in black families. *The Black Scholar,* 10–17.

Nunn, G., & Parish, T. (1983). Perceptions of personal and familial adjustment by children from intact, single-parent and reconstituted families. *Psychology in the Schools, 20,* 166–174.

Nye, F. I. (1957). Child adjustment in broken and in unhappy unbroken homes. *Marriage and Family Living, 19,* 356–361.

Oshman, H. P., & Manosevitz, M. (1976). Father absence: Effects of stepfathers upon psychoscial development in males. *Developmental Psychology, 12,* 479–480.

Parish, T. S. (1981). Young adult's evaluations of themselves and their parents as a function of family structure and disposition. *Journal of Youth and Adolescence, 10,* 173–178.

Parish, T., & Dostal, J. (1980). Evaluations of self and parent figures by children from intact, divorced, and reconstituted families. *Journal of Youth and Adolescence, 9,* 347–351.

Parish, T. S., & Nunn, G. (1981). Children's self-concepts and evaluations of parents as a function of family structure and process. *Journal of Psychology, 107*(1), 105–108.

Parish, T. S., & Taylor, J. C. (1978). The Personal Attribute Inventory of Children: A Report on its validity and reliability as a self-concept scale. *Educational Psychology Measures, 38,* 565–569.

Parish, T. S., & Taylor, J. C. (1979). The impact of divorce and subsequent father absence on children's and adolescents' self-concepts. *Journal of Youth and Adolescence, 8,* 427–432.

Pasley, K., & Thinger-Tallman, M. (1982). Remarried family life: Supports and constraints. In G. Rowe (Ed.), *Building Family Strengths 4.* (pp. 367–383). Lincoln, Neb.: University of Nebraska Press.

Perry, J. B., & Pfuhl, E. H. (1963). Adjustment of children in "solo" and "remarriage" homes. *Marriage and Family Living, 25,* 221–223.

Peterson, J. L., & Zill, N. (April, 1983). Marital disruption, parent/child rela-
    tionships, and behavioral problems in children. Paper presented at the
    Society for Research in Child Development Meetings, Detroit.
Podolsky, E. (1955). The emotional problems of the stepchild. *Mental Hygiene, 39,*
    49–53.
Price-Bonham, S., & Balswick, J. (1980). The noninstitutions: Divorce, desertion
    and remarriage. *Journal of Marriage and the Family, 42,* 959–972.
Ransom, J., Schlesinger, S., & Derdeyn, A. (1979). A stepfamily in formation.
    American Journal of Orthopsychiatry, 49, 36-43.
Raschke, H. J. & Raschke, V. J. (1979). Family conflict and children's self-
    concepts: A comparison of intact and single-parent families. *Journal of*
    Marriage and the Family, 41, 367–374.
Reaves, J. (1982). Stepfamily and noncustodial parent interaction. *Dissertation*
    Abstracts International, 4(6-B), 2000.
Robinson, M. (1980). Step-families: A reconstituted family system. *Journal of*
    Family Therapy, 2, 45–69.
Rosenberg, M. (1965). *Society and the Adolescent Self-Image.* Princeton, N.J.:
    Princeton University Press.
Sager, C., Steer, H., Crohn, H., Rodstein, E., & Walker, E. (1980). Remarriage
    revisited. *Family and Child Mental Health Journal, 6,* 19–33.
Santrock, J. W. (1972). Relation of type and onset of father absence to cognitive
    development. *Child Development, 43,* 455–459.
Santrock, J., & Warshak, R. (1979). Father custody and social development in
    boys and girls. *Journal of Social Issues, 35*(4,), 112–125.
Santrock, J., Warshak, R., Lindbergh, C., & Meadows, L. (1982). Children's and
    parent's observed social behavior in stepfather families. *Child Development,*
    53, 472–480.
Schulman, G. (1972). Myths that intrude on the adaptation of the stepfamily. *Social*
    Casework, 53, 131–139.
Spicer, J., & Hampe, G. (1975). Kinship interaction after divorce. *Journal of*
    Marriage and the Family, 38, 113–119.
Stack, C. B. (1974). *All Our Kin: Strategies for Survival in a Black Community.*
    New York: Harper & Row.
Stern, P. N. (1978). Stepfather families: Integration around child discipline. *Issues*
    in Mental Health Nursing, 1, 49–56.
Thies, J. (1977). Beyond divorce: The impact of remarriage on children. *Journal of*
    Clinical Child Psychology, 6(2), 59–61.
Touliatos, J., & Lindholm, B. W. (1980). Teachers' perceptions of behavior prob-
    lems in children from intact, single-parent, and stepparent families. *Psy-*
    chology in the Schools, 17, 264–269.
Tropf, W. (1984). An exploratory examination of the effect of remarriage on child
    support and personal contacts. *Journal of Divorce, 7,* 57–73.
U.S. Center for Health Statistics (1977). Vital Statistics Report, Advance Report,
    Final Marriage Statistics, 1974. Washington, D.C., U.S. Government Print-
    ing Office.
Visher, E., & Visher, J. (1978). Major areas of difficulty for stepparent couples.
    International Journal of Family Counseling, 6(2), 70–80.
Wagner, A. (1984). Family conflict in original and stepfather families: An examina-
    tion of sibling, parent-child and parental discord. Unpublished master's
    thesis, University of Virginia.

Walker, L., Brown, H., Crohn, H., Rodstein, E., Zeisel, H., & Sager, C. (1979). An annotated bibliography of the remarried, the living together and their children. *Family Process, 18,* 193–212.

Walker, K., & Messinger, L. (1979). Remarriage after divorce: Dissolution and reconstruction of family boundaries. Family Process, 18, 185–192.

Wallerstein, J., & Kelly, J. (1975). The effects of parental divorce: Experiences of the preschool child. *Journal of American Academic Child Psychiatry, 14,* 600–616.

Wallerstein, J., & Kelly, J. (1976). The effects of parental divorce: Experiences of the child in later latency. *American Journal of Orthopsychiatry, 46,* 256-269.

Wallerstein, J., & Kelly, J. (1980a). Effects of divorce on the visiting father-child relationship. *American Journal of Psychiatry, 137,* 1534–1539.

Wallerstein, J., & Kelly, J. (1980b). *Surviving the Breakup: How Children and Parents Cope with Divorce.* New York: Basic Books.

Weingarten, H. (1980). Remarriage and well-being. National survey evidence of social and psychological effects. *Journal of Family Issues,* 1(4), 533–559.

Weiss, R. (1975). *Marital Separation.* New York: Basic Books.

Weiss, R. (1979). Growing up a little faster: The experience of growing up in a single-parent household. *Journal of Social Issues, 35,* 97–111.

White, L. (1979). Sex differential in the effect of remarriage on global happiness. *Journal of Marriage and the Family, 41,* 869–876.

Whiteside, M., & Auerbach, L. (1978). Can the daughter of my father's new wife be my sister? *Journal of Divorce, 1,* 271–283.

Wilson, K. L., Zurcher, L. A., MacAdams, D. C., & Curtis, R. L. (1975). Stepfathers and stepchildren: An exploratory analysis from two national surveys. *Journal of Marriage and the Family, 37,* 526–536.

Wohlford, P., Santrock, J. W., Berger, W. E., & Liberman, D. (1971). Older brothers' influence on sex-typed aggressive and dependent behavior in father absent children. *Developmental Psychology, 4,* 124–134.

Young, E., & Parish, T. (1977). Impact of father absence during childhood on the psychosocial adjustment of college females. *Sex Roles, 3,* 217–227.

Zill, N. (1982). *Happy, Healthy and Insecure.* New York: Doubleday.

Zill, N., & Peterson, J. L. (April, 1983). Marital disruption, parent-child relationships, and behavior problems in children. Paper presented at the Society for Research in Child Development, Detroit.

PART II
SOCIAL/CONTEXTUAL FACTORS

4

The Stressors of Children's Postdivorce Environments

IRWIN N. SANDLER, SHARLENE A. WOLCHIK
and SANFORD L. BRAVER

There is increasing consensus in the literature that divorce should be studied as a process rather than a single discrete experience. That is, divorce represents a process of transition in family structure that lasts until a new structure is established and stablized. For example, Felner and colleagues (1983) have proposed that divorce be viewed as a marker "of the unfolding of major changes in an individual's life which may engender new stresses and changes and demand adaptive effort . . ." (p. 209). It follows from this that a critical task for researchers is the identification of life changes that create the adaptive tasks for children during this time of transition.

Several authors have begun to identify these critical divorce related life changes. For example, Stolberg and Anker (1983) developed a 19-item scale to assess the objective environmental changes that occur for children after a divorce (e.g., changes in residence, family income, health of parents or other family members). They reported that environmental change was positively associated with parents' ratings of more behavior pathology in children. Also, high levels of environmental change were correlated with children's perceiving their environment as being less under

Partial support for writing this chapter was provided by NIMH grant #MH38474-01 to the three authors and by NIMH grant #MH39246-02 to establish the Program for Prevention Research at Arizona State University.

their own or their parents' control and being more disorganized. Other researchers have further described the nature of the major post divorce changes that have an impact on children. These changes include decreased income, decreased time with both the custodial and the noncustodial parent, increased parental psychological disorder, disruption in family household routine, increased conflict between the parents, and less effective, consistent, and positive parenting (Hetherington, 1979; Kurdek, 1981; Wolchik et al., 1984).

We agree with this line of thinking that research on the effects of divorce needs to include an assessment of the critical experiences that take place during this time. When we began our work we felt that there was a need for a valid and reliable measure to assess these experiences in a standardized, systematic way. Toward that end we have developed a Divorce Events Schedule for Children (DESC), and have used this instrument as a central measure in our research on children of divorce. In this chapter we describe the development of the DESC, some of our research findings to date, and future directions for research using this measure.

The DESC utilizes life-events methodology to assess the significant post-divorce experiences of children. It is similar in that sense to other life events scales, such as those developed by Holmes and Rahe (1967) for adults and by Coddington (1972) for children and adolescents. These scales have been used extensively in epidemiological research to study the contribution of stressful life conditions to mental and physical health problems. The strengths and limitations of such life-event measures have recently been the subject of several critical reviews (Monroe 1982; Sandler & Guenther, 1985; Zimmerman, 1983). In our adaptation of the life-events methodology, we were conscious of the recent criticisms but believed that the methodology had many advantages as an approach to assessing the postdivorce environment. In our development of the DESC, we specifically addressed the following criticisms of previous life-event scales: ambiguous definition of what an event is, unrepresentative sampling of events, confounding of events with symptomatology of psychological disorder, and questionable reliability of scores derived from life-event scales.

We defined events as "objectively verifiable occurrences in an individual's environment of which the individual is aware and which have a significant impact on the individual" (Sandler et al., 1986). Positive and negative occurrences were included because both have been found to contribute in different ways to indices of psychological well-being and distress (Zautra & Reich, 1980). It should be noted that this definition does *not* include the concept of change. Although several authors have proposed that change is the common element assessed by life-events scales, a review of prior such scales indicated that many contain items that are not necessarily changes—for example, 28 percent on Johnson and Mc-Cutchen's Life Events Checklist; 16 percent on the Dohrenwend et al. and PERI scales (Sandler & Guenther, 1985). There is also considerable controversy in the literature about whether change is the central stress dimension of life events (Gersten et al., 1974). Instead of including change in the *definition* of events, we assessed whether each event did or did not involve a change. In our response format, subjects were first asked whether an event occurred or did not occur in a specified time period (the previous three months), and then whether this represented a change in their environment. That is, if a child reported that an event occurred, we asked whether this was "more than usual, less than usual or the same amount as usual." If a child reported that an event did not occur, it was possible that this was a decrease in the rate of occurrence of that event. To assess this we asked, "Is this a change from (less than) the way it usually was?" By assessing events both as occurrences and as changes we were able empirically to address the issue of how change contributes to the stressfulness of events.

Prior life-events scales have also been criticized for not including a representative sample of events for the population under study (Dohrenwend et al., 1978; Sandler, 1979). To develop a representative sample of events, we asked knowledgeable informants to nominate events that might have a significant impact on children of divorce. Our informants included approximately 40 parents and children who had experienced divorce and 20 professionals (e.g., psychologists, lawyers) who worked with divorcing families. The informants' list of 210 events was reduced to 62 events using the following criteria. First, redundant items were combined into a single item. Second, items that were clearly contaminated with psychological symptomatology were eliminated (Dohrenwend & Dohrenwend, 1978)—such items primarily referred either to an internal state of the child (e.g., "You feel sad"), or to observable behavior that might be a direct indicator of children's maladaptive behavior (e.g., "Your school grades decline," "You have more arguments with your parents"). We attempted to eliminate items that were *primarily* within the child's control. It should be noted however, that because many of the critical postdivorce events involve transactions between the child and his or her environment, we could not completely eliminate items that might reflect the response of the social environment to children's adaptive or maladaptive behavior (e.g. "You do fun things with Dad," "Mom gets mad at you or tells you that you're bad"). These items were retained despite the fact that they may be affected by the child's behavior because they may also reflect critical effects of the divorce process on the child's environment. For example, a child's mother may get angry with him or her either because the parent is under great stress or because of the child's "bad" behavior (Longfellow et al., 1982; Weissman & Paykel, 1974).

The issue of whether events are likely to be caused by the child or by some factor external to the child is particularly important in interpreting relations between scores derived from this scale and measures of child disorder. Because we were interested in maximizing our ability to make inferences about the effects of the postdivorce environment on child disorder, this issue of event contamination was important for our research. Thus we were interested in classifying events in terms of their likelihood of being caused by the child. Twelve researchers familiar with life-events methodology and children's divorce experiences (psychology faculty, graduate students, and child clinicians) rated each event using the following instructions.

> Attached are a list of events that sometimes happen to children when their parents divorce. We are interested in learning how likely it is that each of these events might be caused by the child as opposed to being the result of some other factor. Children can cause events in several ways. For example, they may directly cause events to happen, or events may be a response of the social environment to the child's adaptive or maladaptive behaviors. On the other hand, events may be caused by a variety of other factors that the child did not cause. For example, events may be due to the way parents feel about each other, stresses on the parent such as loneliness or economic stresses, or changes in living arrangements.
>
> Rate each event on the attached scale to indicate how likely or unlikely it is that the event might be caused by the child. Use your best judgment in making these ratings without regard to whether or not you are using the entire range of the scale over the set of events.
>
> How likely is it that each event would be caused by the child?

1	2	3	4	5	6	7
Extremely likely	Very likely	Likely	Equally likely and unlikely	Unlikely	Very unlikely	Extremely unlikely

Events were classified as either likely to be caused by the child or unlikely to be caused by the child if 75 percent of the raters agreed in scoring the event on that side of the neutral point. Using this criterion, three events were classified as likely to be caused by the child and 29 as unlikely to be caused by the child, and the remaining 30 events were classified as being ambiguous as to their causality.

Events were also classified as being consensually desirable or undesirable. This was done using the judgments of 131 children of divorce (ages eight to 15). All children who reported that an event had occurred to them were asked whether it was positive, neutral, or negative, and how positive or negative it was (using a seven-point scale). Events were classified as consensually desirable or undesirable if 80 percent of the children rated them in that direction. Sixteen events were classified as consensually undesirable and 18 as consensually desirable. The 62 events on the scale and their consensual desirability and locus of causality categorization are presented in Table 4.1.

The reliability of subjects' reports of life events has been a continuing concern of life-event researchers (Neugebauer, 1981). We assessed test–retest reliability of both individual reports of whether or not each event occurred and summary scores derived from these reports using a sample of 36 children of divorce (age eight through 15) (Sandler et al., 1986). Median item reliability, calculated as the phi coefficient, was 0.61, with a range of 1.00 to −0.07. Individual item reliabilies are presented in Table 4.1. The subjects' reports of the occurrence of the consensually undesirable and desirable events can be summed to yield undesirable and desirable event scores, the two most commonly used scores from life-event scales. Test–retest reliability of these total scores was 0.85 for undesirable events and 0.65 for desirable events. Because the time for reporting events was three months and the interval between scale administration was two weeks, we regard these reliability estimates as encouraging.

We have used the DESC to study several aspects of the postdivorce environment, including children's and parents' perceptions of the stressfulness of divorce experiences, the frequency of occurrence of these events, correlates of occurrence of different divorce experiences, and the relation between divorce experiences and children's postdivorce adjustment.

The sample used to study the correlates of event occurence and the frequency of event occurence consisted of 158 children who had experienced divorce. The sample was derived by inviting the participation of people listed in court records as having been divorced within the prior 30 months (mean time since separation of the parents was 16.5 months), and by volunteers who responded to media articles about the study. The sample included 56 percent girls and 44 percent boys, ages eight through 15 (mean age = 11.5). Child-custody arrangements of the sample included 65 percent maternal custody, 7.2 percent paternal custody, 27.8 percent joint custody. A subsample of 58 of these children and their mothers completed additional forms to report their perceptions of how stressful each event would be for the typical child to whom it occurred. Although this sample of 158 children formed the basis for most of the analyses presented in this chapter, the sample for the study to be discussed on the divorce events experienced by children in joint versus maternal custody

Table 4.1
**Desirability, Locus of Causality, and Test–Retest Reliability
of Divorce Events[a]**

	Desirability[b]	Causality[c]	Reliability
1. Mom and Dad differ in how they want the child to be (activities they want the child to do or the child's ideas about things).	A	E	0.26
2. People in the child's neighborhood say bad things to the child about his/her parents.	U	E	0.83
3. The child has chores to do around the house (like making meals or cleaning his/her room).	A	A	0.63
4. The child's dad is unhappy.	U	A	0.63
5. The child's friends tease him/her or are mean to him/her.	U	A	0.85
6. The child's dad does extra nice things for him/her that he/she likes.	D	A	0.61
7. Mom tells the child that she doesn't like the child spending time with Dad.	U	A	0.71
8. The child's mom is strict.	A	A	0.23
9. The child does fun things with his/her dad.	D	A	0.91
10. The child has to watch out for, or take care of, his/her brothers and sisters.	A	A	0.78
11. The child's dad takes care of the things that need to get done for the child (like giving him/her a ride or making his/her meals).	D	A	0.61
12. The child's mom asks him/her about the child's dad's private life.	A	A	0.67
13. The child's dad says bad things about the child's mom.	U	E	0.75
14. The child's dad is strict.	A	A	0.50
15. The child's mom says bad things about the child's dad.	U	E	0.43
16. The child has free time to do things he/she likes (playing, relaxing).	D	A	−0.02
17. The child's mom gets mad at him/her or tells him/her that he/she is bad.	A	C	0.64
18. The child's mom and dad argue in front of him/her.	U	E	0.61
19. The child's relatives say bad things to him/her about his/her parents.	U	E	0.64
20. The child's dad asks him/her about the child's mom's private life.	U	E	0.77

Table 4.1 (continued)

21. The child spends time with his/her dad's family.	D	A	0.64
22. The child's *(noncustodial parent)* misses scheduled visits.	U	E	0.40
23. The child's mom does extra nice things for him/her, that he/she likes.	D	A	0.49
24. Household routines get done smoothly (like dinner on time, regular bedtime, the child's clothes get washed, the child gets ready for school on time).	D	A	0.30
25. The child does fun things with his/her mom.	D	A	−0.07
26. The child gets toys, clothes, and other things he/she likes.	D	A	—d
27. The child's dad tells him/her not to tell some things to his/her mom.	A	E	0.51
28. The child's dad tells him/her that he doesn't like the child spending time with his/her mom.	U	E	0.36
29. The child's dad gets mad at him/her or tells the child that he/she is bad.	A	C	−0.47
30. The child's mom takes care of the things that need to get done for the child (like giving him/her a ride or making his/her meals).	D	A	−0.07
31. The child's mom tells him/her not to tell some things to his/her dad.	A	E	0.44
32. The child spends time with Mom.	D	A	—d
33. The child spends time with his/her mom's family.	D	A	0.82
34. The child gets to see his/her old friends.	D	A	0.61
35. The child's dad tells him/her about things in his life, like problems, or his feelings about things.	A	A	0.44
36. The child's mom is unhappy.	U	A	0.56
37. The child is making new friends.	D	C	0.46
38. The child spends time with his/her dad.	D	A	0.68
39. The child spends time alone, by him/her-self.	D	A	0.36
40. The child has to give up pets or other things that he/she likes.	U	E	0.25
41. The child's mom tells him/her about things in her life, such as problems, or her feelings about things.	A	A	0.37

Table 4.1 (continued)

42. The child's mom or dad talks to him/her about why they were divorced.	A	A	0.34
43. The child's mom or dad talks to him/her about which parent he/she wants to live with.	A	A	0.58
44. The child's mom and dad make him/her follow different rules while the child is at their house.	A	E	0.72
45. The child's *(custodial parent)* works. (For joint custody, "Mom and Dad.")	A	E	0.53
46. The child's mother's boyfriend or husband tells the child to do things.	A	E	0.43
47. The child's parents hit each other or physically hurt each other.	U	E	0.69
48. The child's father's girlfriend or wife tells the child to do things.	A	E	0.61
49. The child's dad starts to go on dates.	A	E	0.64
50. The child's dad remarries or has a girlfriend live with him.	A	E	0.76
51. The child's dad or mom told him/her the divorce took place because of the child.	U	A	−0.02
52. The child changes schools.	A	E	0.87
53. The child's mom remarries or has a boyfriend live with her.	A	E	0.61
54. The child's dad gets a steady girlfriend.	A	E	0.76
55. The child's mom gets a steady boyfriend.	D	E	0.63
56. The child's mom starts to go on dates.	D	E	0.56
57. The child's *(noncustodial parent)* moves out of town.	U	E	0.85
58. The child's brothers and sisters live in a different house than the child.	A	E	0.89
59. The child moves to a new house.	A	E	0.83
60. The child changes which parent he/she lives with.	A	A	—d
61. The child talks to a lawyer or judge.	A	E	—d
62. New kids move into the child's house.	A	E	1.00

a Items were rewritten for this table in which the word "child" was substituted for the pronoun "you."

b A = ambiguous
U = undesirable
D = desirable

c E = externally caused
C = child caused
A = ambiguous

d Test–retest reliability could not be calculated for these items because there was no variance in one of the measures.

arrangements included only cases in which the parents had been physically separated for 30 months or less.

PERCEPTIONS OF THE STRESSFULNESS OF DIVORCE EVENTS

The relative stressfulness of events is a topic that has received considerable attention in the life-events literature. One way to approach this issue is to have knowledgeable informants rate the stressfulness of the events. We did this in a study (Wolchik et al., 1985b) in which 58 children of divorce, 58 divorced mothers, and 50 child-mental-health professionals rated how stressful each of the DESC events would be for the "typical child."* Subjects rated how upsetting each event would usually be for the *typical* child using a seven point scale (1 = not all upsetting, 7 = very upsetting). In addition 123 children whose parents had divorced within the past 30 months indicated whether or not each event had occurred to them, and, if it had occurred to them, how positive or negative it was for them (using a seven-point scale in either the positive or negative direction). It should be noted that for this study all paternal custody cases in the larger data set were excluded. Thus we utilized three groups of raters and two rating approaches to assess the perceived stress value of the events.

There was a high level of consistency across both methods and raters as to the relative stress value of the events. The Spearman rank order correlation was 0.81 between children's mean ratings of the stressfulness of events for the typical child and their mean ratings of how "bad" these events were when they had actually experienced them. The rank order correlation between the mean stressfulness ratings of events for the typical child was 0.87 for children versus parents, 0.69 for children versus clinicians, and 0.73 for parents versus clinicians. Nine of the events rated as most stressful by children who actually experienced them were also rated among the ten most stressful in children's ratings for the typical child. These events are shown in Table 4.2.

Similarly, of the ten events rated as least stressful by children who experienced them, eight were also rated among the ten least stressful in children's ratings for the typical child. These events are shown in Table 4.3. In comparing parent and child ratings, there was agreement on seven of the events that were considered to be among the ten most stressful and

---

*Because this study focused on stress experiences, the positive events on the DESC were rewritten to reflect negative changes in the environment. For example, the item "the child does fun things with Mom" was rewritten as "the child does *less* fun things with Mom."

seven of the events that were considered to be among the ten least stressful.

While it is difficult to abstract general themes from the events that parents and children identify as most or least stressful, the most stressful events appear to involve blaming the child for the divorce, derogation of the parents, and interparental conflict. The least stressful appear to involve parental dating, parents confiding in the children, and household routines. It is interesting to note that in the ratings of the event stressfulness for the typical child, the Spearman correlations between the ratings of clinicians and those of parents (0.73) and children (0.69) were somewhat lower than those between parents and children (0.87). This may be so because clinicians are basing their ratings on the experiences of a somewhat atypical group of children: those they see in psychotherapy.

In a second set of analyses on this same data, we were interested in

Table 4.2
Rank Order of Events Rated as Among the Ten Most Stressful

	Ranking by Children Who Experienced Event	Ranking for the "Typical Child" Rater		
		Child	Parent	Clinician
Dad or Mom tells child the divorce took place because of the child.*	1	1	1	1
Child's parents hit each other or physically hurt each other.	2	2	2	2
Child's relatives say bad things to his/her parents.	3	4	4	14.5
Dad tells child that he doesn't like child spending time with Mom.*	4	5	13.5	8.5
Mom and Dad argue in front of child.	5	3	7	10.5
Dad says bad things about child's Mom.	6	7	6	4
Child has to give up pets or other things that he/she likes.	7	8	16	16
Mom acts unhappy.	8	9	19	23.5
Dad asks child questions about Mom's private life.	9	30	31	25
People in the neighborhood say bad things to the child about his/her parents.	10	6	10	26.5
Dad gets mad at child or tells child that she/he is bad.	20	10	5	11.5

*These events occurred to less than ten children and, therefore, the obtained ratings may not represent stable ratings.

whether there were differences among the three groups of raters in the magnitude of event stressfulness ratings for the typical child. A highly significant multivariate effect for rater was obtained $F(124, 162) = 3.10$, p <0.001. Univariate analysis of variance for each event and cell comparisons using Tukey tests revealed that children reported events as being less stressful than did clinicians (on 19 items) or parents (on ten items). Mothers and clinicians differed significantly on nine items, with mothers rating seven of these items as less stressful and two as more stressful.

Taken together, our findings suggest that there is considerable consensus across raters about the *relative* stress value of divorce-related events for children. At the same time, children rated many of these events as less stressful than did parents or clinicians. The differences may be

Table 4.3
Rank Order of Events Rated as Among the Ten Least Stressful

	Ranking by Children Who Experienced Event	Ranking for the "Typical Child"		
		Rater		
		Child	Parent	Clinician
Dad tells child about things in his life, such as problems, or his feelings about things.	40.5	62	58.5	50.5
Mom or Dad talk to child about why they got divorced.	29	61	51	59
Mom starts to go on dates.	44.5	60	62	36
Child has more chores to do around the house (like making meals or cleaning his/her room).	40.5	59	60	60
Child has to watch out for, or take care of, brothers and sisters more often.	43	58	55	47.5
Dad starts to go on dates.	42	57	52	37
Household routines get done less smoothly (like dinner on time, regular bedtime, getting ready for school on time).	—*	56	50	57.5
Mom tells child about things in her life, such as problems, or her feelings about things.	38	55	57	47.5
Child spends more time alone, by him/herself.	46	54	49	40
Mom gets a steady boyfriend.	39	53	54	32.5

*The wording of this item differed in the rating for the "typical child" and on the DESC. The stress ratings on the DESC item thus were not seen as comparable and are not presented.

attributable in part to the different postdivorce coping patterns of children and their parents. For example, children may minimize the stressfulness of their experiences to maintain a belief in their ability to cope. On the other hand, parents' ratings may be affected by their own psychological issues, such as their feelings of guilt. The idea that parents' views of their children's reactions are affected by their own needs is supported by our finding that the best single predictor of parental reports of child psychological symptomatology was the parent's own symptomatology (Fogas et al., 1985; Sandler et al., 1985).

Another approach to the issue of differential perceptions of divorce experiences is to ask whether stressfulness ratings differ as a function of the type of event being rated. We felt that this analysis could be particularly interesting for comparing stress perceptions of events that involved the mother and the father (Braver et al., 1984). On the 62-item DESC, there are 34 items that are identical for mother and father (e.g., "Dad is unhappy"; "Mom is unhappy"). These 34 items may be subdivided into three categories of events: parent–child (e.g., "You spend less time with Dad"; nine items for each parent); parent–parent (e.g., "Mom says bad things to you about Dad"; four items for each parent); and parent–new partner (e.g., "Mom gets married"; four items for each parent). The data used in this analysis are parent, child, and clinician ratings of event stressfulness for the typical child as described in the study presented above.

The main analysis used here was three (type of rater: child, parent, or clinician) times two (mother versus father event) analysis of variance with the mother-versus-father factor treated as a repeated measures factor. The multivariate approach to repeated measures was used. Separate analyses were performed for each type of event: parent–child, parent–parent, or parent–new partner. This, too, was treated multivariately (SPSS-X, 1986).

Table 4.4
Mean Ratings for Mother and Father Events by Children of Divorce, Their Mothers, and Clinicians

Type of Event	Rater		
	Children	Mothers	Clinicians
Father			
Parent to child	4.49	4.64	4.62
Parent to other parent	5.02	5.54	5.71
Parent to new other	4.23	4.38	5.10
Mother			
Parent to child	4.92	4.83	4.63
Parent to other parent	4.48	5.44	5.61
Parent to new other	4.63	4.69	5.44

The mean stressfulness rating made by each rater for each type of event is presented in Table 4.4.

The results showed significant multivariate effects for both the main effects and the interaction. In exploring the effects for each univariate analysis, we found (as noted before) that clinicians and parents rated events as more stressful than did children, and that "mother events" were rated generally more stressful than "father events." The interaction revealed that clinicians rated mother events about equally stressful as father events, while children rated mother events as substantially more stressful than father events. Parent ratings tend to fall in the middle, with mother events being rated as slightly more stressful than father events. The differences are particularly pronounced for events that involve one parent being derogated by the other or negative parent–child interactions. Children are more prone than either parents or clinicians to give higher stress ratings when the mother rather than the father is being derogated, or when the negative interaction is with the mother rather than the father. These results may be due to the greater primacy that children who live with their mothers give to their relationship with them. It is surprising, however, that both mothers and clinicians are less likely to perceive this differential reaction than children.

CORRELATES AND FREQUENCY OF EVENT OCCURRENCE

Although we know a fair amount about what experiences occur and have an impact on children after divorce, we have relatively little normative information about these experiences. For example, while several researchers (e.g., Hetherington et al., 1981; Jacobson, 1978) have reported that interparental hostility is associated with negative child adaptation, we have very little information about how frequently children actually perceive interparental conflict, and what factors are associated with more or less of these experiences. Such information is important for several reasons. The attention devoted to any type of experience in the planning of educational or intervention programs should be a joint function of the impact of that type of experience and the frequency with which it occurs. Furthermore, analysis of how the frequency of events covaries with other factors may be useful for designing and evaluating programs to change the rate of occurrence of events. For example, it would be interesting to know whether factors such as different custody arrangements, or a policy of mandatory mediation of divorce disputes rather than litigation, affect the postdivorce experiences of children.

The utility of normative information on the occurrence of divorce-related events can be illustrated by examining our data on events in the realm of interparental conflict and derogation of parents. The 13 items on our scale that involve this domain of experience and the percentage of our sample who reported the occurrence of these events during the past three months are presented in Table 4.5. The rank orders of their stressfulness ratings are also provided.

As can be seen in Table 4.5, some overt conflict experiences are fairly common, and are also among the most stressful divorce-related experiences (e.g., items 13, 15 and 18). It is interesting to note that the 30 percent occurrence rate for these three events is similar to Wallerstein's (1983) estimate that one-third of her sample continued to experience open interparental hostility up to five years after the divorce. While reports of hostility have been frequently noted in the literature, other parent conflict events that are rarely noted in the literature also seem to occur frequently. These other events involve the child's indirect exposure to conflict between the parents. Experiences where one parent asks the child about the other parent's private life would fall into this category (items 20 and 12). For example, 22 percent of our sample reported that Dad asked questions about Mom's private life while 33 percent of the children were asked by Mom about Dad's private life. While these items are perceived as being among the most stressful events by children to whom they occur, they are rated as much less stressful in both parents' and children's ratings for the typical child. Apparently one really needs to "be in the child's shoes" to appreciate the stress engendered by such experiences. A second noteworthy finding in these data is that derogation of parents by the child's relatives or neighbors is not uncommon, and is rated as very stressful across all rating methods (items 19 and 2). A considerable amount has been written about the support and assistance children can receive from their extended network (Cochran & Brassard 1979; Guidubaldi et al., 1983). The data in Table 4.5 indicate that when families divide, the extended network members take sides, and their expression of negative feelings to the children is an important source of stress.

While normative data on event occurrence are helpful in telling us what happens after the divorce, they tell us little about why these events occur. Toward the aim of clarifying causal mechanisms, it is useful to identify individual and environmental factors that relate to the frequency of event occurrence. Individual factors include stable characteristics of the child, such as age, birth order, gender, and ethnicity, as well as characteristics of the child that are potentially subject to change, such as his or her social skills or interpersonal reasoning abilities. Likewise one can conceptualize environmental factors that are not subject to manipulation (e.g., length of separation) and others that are potentially changeable (e.g., custody arrangements, parental mental health, payment of child support). Knowledge of changeable factors which affect event occurrence has obvious implications for the development of preventive interventions. On the other

Table 4.5
Interparental Hostility and Conflict Events

Item Number	Occurrence (percent reporting)	Rank Order of Stressfulness Ratings		
		Child Rater, Ratings for Events Experienced	Child Rater, Ratings for Typical Child	Parent Rater, Ratings for Typical Child
1. Mom and Dad differ in how they want the child to be.	37	31	50	29.5
19. The child's relatives say bad things to him or her about his/her parents.	15	3	4	4
2. People in the child's neighborhood say bad things to the child about his/her parents.	18	10	6	10
13. The child's dad says bad things about the child's mom.	26	6	7	6
15. The child's mom says bad things about the child's dad.	32	16	11	11
7. Mom tells the child that she doesn't like the child spending time with Dad.	11	19	18	8
28. The child's dad tells the child that he doesn't like the child spending time with Mom.	4	4	5	13.5
27. The child's dad tells him/her not to tell some things to his or her mom.	39	21	52	32.5
31. The child's mom tells him/her not to tell some things to his or her dad.	43	27	48	43
18. The child's mom and dad argue in front of him/her.	34	5	3	7
47. The child's parents hit each other or physically hurt each other.	4	2	2	2
20. The child's dad asks him/her about the child's mom's private life.	22	9	30	31
12. The child's mom asks him/her about the child's dad's private life.	33	15	44	43

hand, the identification of unchangeable factors can be useful in helping to anticipate the occurrence of events (e.g., across time) or in helping to understand the postdivorce experiences across different groups of children (e.g., boys versus girls).

Individual Child Characteristics

Prior research has indicated that age and gender are related to children's postdivorce adjustment. Hetherington and colleagues (1978) and Wallerstein and Kelly (1980) reported that boys manifest more psychological symptomatology in the years following divorce than do girls. Santrock and Warshak (1979), on the other hand, found that the match between the gender of the child and that of the custodial parent, rather than the gender of the child per se, is critical in affecting postdivorce adjustment. They found that both boys and girls had more symptomatology when they lived with the opposite-sex parent. Wallerstein and Kelly (1980) have reported relationships between age of the child and both the extent and types of postdivorce adjustment problems. Preschool children are more likely to blame themselves and to experience nightmares, enuresis, and eating disturbances. Early-school-age children have academic problems, withdrawal, and depression. Older school-age children are more likely to blame one parent for the divorce and to feel intense anger at one or both parents. Adolesents experience the intense anger of the older school-age child, and also exhibit problems with developmental issues of independence and interpersonal relationships. Other research (Kurdek et al., 1981) has found that older children show less psychological symptomatology following divorce than do younger children. It is reasonable to hypothesize that age and gender differences in postdivorce adjustment are mediated both by the different experiences that occur and by differential responses to these experiences.

We investigated age and gender differentces for both the total number of positive and negative events that occurred and the occurrence of each individual event. Age of child was dichotomized as older (12–15) versus younger (eight to 11) and analysis of variance was used to test age and gender differences in the occurrence of total positive and negative events. The sole significant effect for the summary event scores indicated that girls ($\bar{X}=8.88$) reported *more* negative events than did boys ($\bar{X}=6.90$), $F(1,129)=5.13$, $p<0.05$. This is indeed a surprising finding, given the expectation that negative events are positively correlated with psychological disorder and that previous findings show girls experiencing *less* postdivorce symptomatology than boys. It is instructive to note that the individual events girls experience more frequently than boys often involve being caught in conflicts between Mom and Dad (e.g., "Dad asks questions about Mom's private life"; "Mom says bad things about Dad").

Environmental Factors

We investigated the effects of four environmental factors: household income, length of time since parental separation, custody arrangement, and parental psychological disorder. It is reasonable to expect that each of these might affect the events that take place in the postdivorce environment. Higher household income has been related to lower postdivorce symptomatology in children (Fulton, 1979) and it was expected that low income would result in more negative postdivorce experiences.

Investigators are also increasingly recognizing the importance of time as a dimension in children's postdivorce adjustment. For example, Wallerstein (1983) describes six "tasks" of divorce adjustment for children, which are encountered at different times after the divorce. Hetherington et al. (1981) identify one year after divorce as a time when family distress is at a peak. From our perspective, that divorce is not a unitary experience but a process of transition to a new family structure, a fundamental question is: "What happens over time?" Or: "What are the stressors with which children cope at different times after parental separation?"

Currently considerable change is being seen in how the courts are now handling custody issues. After a prolonged period in which mothers were viewed as the preferred custodial parent (Clingempeel & Repucci, 1982), there is now an increased emphasis on joint custody, in which both parents share responsibility for decisions about the children's health, education, and welfare. While joint custody may or may not involve a greater equality of contact between the parents and children, it is possible that it may affect the kinds of postdivorce experience children encounter. There is considerable evidence that parental psychiatric disturbance is often manifested in the parents' relationships with their children (Weissman & Paykel, 1974; Longfellow et al., 1982). This is particularly significant for children of divorce, because their parents are likely to be experiencing high levels of life stress and high psychiatric symptomatology (Bloom et al., 1978, Hetherington et al., 1981).

The Findings

The effects of length of parental separation and income on the total positive and negative events scores were analyzed as the significance of the linear trend (Sandler et al., 1986). Negative events did not differ as a function of either length of separation or income. A significant linear trend was found for positive events, indicating more positive events with increasing income [F linear, $(1,121) = 6.20$ p <0.05]. Analysis of the effects of length of separation and income on each item using Kendall's tau indicated 11 significant item differences for each of these factors. These item differences clearly indicate greater contact with the noncustodial parent for higher income children, possibly reflecting a general trend for fathers of higher social class to be more involved in their children's lives. Alternatively, the higher income families may derive that income from child support payments received from the father. It is possible that payment of child support and paternal involvement are positively related. While a consistent pattern is not evident for the events that differ as a function of length of separation, three items involving parental dating are found more frequently with increasing time since separation.

Our sample included 44 children in joint-custody arrangements and 89 in sole maternal custody (Wolchik et al., 1985a). It is important to note that joint custody refers to the legal status of the parents and not the residency arrangements of the children. In the joint-custody sample, 29 children resided primarily with their mother, four lived primarily with their father, and 11 alternated residences. The effects of custody arrangements were analyzed using two-way (custody × gender of child) multivariate analyses of covariance in which age of child, time since parental separation, and household income were used as covariates. The results indicated that children in joint custody reported more positive events than did children in maternal custody. Although the custody multivariate main effect for negative events was not significant, a marginally significant custody × gender multivariate interaction was found, $F(2,112) = 2.58$, $p<0.08$. Examination of the univariate effects disclosed that this finding was due to a significant sex × custody interaction for negative events.* Joint-custody boys (but not girls) reported fewer negative events than did maternal-custody boys. These results are important because they contradict prior speculation that joint custody provides a less healthy postdivorce environment for children (Benedek & Benedek, 1979; Goldstein et al., 1973). It should be noted, however, that our analyses did not find differences in child psychopathology as a function of custody arrangements. Furthermore, because parents self-select custody arrangements, we cannot say whether custody arrangement per se, or the characteristics

---

*It should be noted that this effect was significant only for the negative event score that was based on the children's own ratings of the quality of the events. No significant effect was found for the negative event score derived from normative rating of the quality of the events. Thus, the finding must be considered as suggestive only.

of the families who select different custody arrangements, is the critical variable affecting the occurrence of postdivorce events.

The psychological disorder of the custodial parent was assessed using the Global Severity Index (Derogatis et al., 1974) from the Hopkins Symptom Checklist. We were also interested in assessing the effects of the parents' recent life experiences on the events that relate to the children. Divorce is clearly a time of transition for the parents, and is marked by a wide range of changes, both positive and negative. The recent life experiences of the parents were assessed using the Life Experiences Scale (Sarason et al., 1978), which yields a score for recent positive and negative events. Pearson product moment correlations were calculated between parental stress and disorder scores and measures of children's events. Parental negative events were correlated with higher child negative-events scores ($r(129) = -0.17$, $p<0.05$) and lower parent positive-event scores ($r(129) = -0.22, p<0.01$). Parental psychological disorder was correlated with lower child positive-event scores ($r(129) = -0.16, p<0.05$), but was not significantly related to children's negative events. Although the magnitude of these relations is small, the results tend to confirm the negative impact of parental stress and distress on the children's experiences.

Relation Between Events and Psychological Symptomatology

There is much empirical support for the prediction that more divorce events will be related to higher levels of psychological disorder in children. Studies using general life-events scales with children and adolescents have consistently reported that more events (particularly negative events) relate to higher levels of psychological disorder, physical illness, and school-adjustment problems (Johnson, 1982; Sandler & Block, 1979). Three studies have specifically examined the effects of life events on children of divorce. As already noted, Stolberg and Anker (1983) found that the total amount of experienced change related to higher levels of psychological symptomatology. Stolberg and co-workers (in press), using a general measure of child life events, reported that life-change events were the single best predictor of postdivorce adjustment. Because the scale they used contained primarily negative events, they further concluded that it was aversive events that primarily led to psychological disorder. Farber and colleagues (1985) used a divorce "hassle" scale for children, and reported that more divorce hassles are related to higher levels of psychological symptomatology.

Unlike the above event measures, the Divorce Events Scale for Children (DESC) is comprised of a representative sample of divorce events. What is the advantage of assessing a representative list of events? Prior work with life-events scales constructed to contain a representative list of events for specific populations—for example, college students (Sandler & Lakey, 1982)—have *not* found that scores derived from such scales are more strongly related to psychological disorder than are those derived from more omnibus life-events scales. Despite this, it is our contention that use of the DESC has several advantages over omnibus life-events scales because it will better enable us to understand the impact of experiences on child psychological disorder. We will first present data analyses, which are analogous to traditional life-events research, that examine the relation between events and disorder. These analyses are primarily simple correlations between negative events scores and measures of child disorder. We will then discuss some relatively new research directions that will enable us to use the DESC to advance our understanding of how postdivorce events affect psychological disorder. As will be seen, these analyses require a life-events scale that includes a representative list of events that occur to children of divorce.

RELATION BETWEEN DIVORCE EVENTS AND DISORDER

As previously discussed, events on the DESC were categorized as positive, negative, or ambiguous based on a consensus of the ratings of children to whom the events had occurred (Sandler et al., 1986). Sixteen of the events were categorized as undesirable, and 18 as desirable. Separate undesirable and desirable events scores were generated by summing the reported occurrence (in the past three months) of the events in each category. Measures of children's psychological disorder were obtained from parent ratings [total pathology on the Achenbach Child Behavior Checklist (Achenbach, 1978)] and from children's reports of anxiety (Reynolds & Richmond, 1978), depression (Kovacs, 1981), and hostility (Braver, 1983)]. Correlations between the life-events scores and measures of psychological disorder for the total sample are presented in Table 4.6. Analyses for subsamples divided by gender and age are presented in Table 4.7.

The results indicate that across age and gender, more negative divorce events (but not positive events) are significantly correlated with a higher level of psychological symptomatology. The finding that negative but not positive events relate significantly to psychological disorder is consistent with the general findings in the life-events literature (e.g., Sandler & Guenther, 1985) and confirms the Stolberg et al. (1985) speculation about the importance of negative events.

One criticism of studies that report significant correlations between life-events scores and psychological disorder concerns the confounding of life events with disorder, or the tendency of symptomatic people to cause the negative events to occur [Zimmerman, 1983]. For example, McCrae and Costa (1984) found that the confounded events on their life-events list completely accounted for the relation between the event scores and measures of physical illness. Because of this concern, we were interested in whether the relations between negative divorce events and psychological disorder found in our sample were due to this type of confounding. As previously described, events for the scale were selected so that they would be primarily beyond the control of the child, and not confounded with symptomatology. Based on the consensus of our judges, 29 of these events

Table 4.6
Relations Between Life-Events Scores and Measures of Psychological Disorder

	Positive Events	Negative Events
Achenbach total pathology	−0.13	0.09
Anxiety	0.01	0.36[a]
Depression	−0.08	0.28[a]
Hostility	0.03	0.26[b]

Note: N is 152. Ns for specific correlations vary slightly due to missing data on different variables.
[a] $p<0.001$
[b] $p<0.01$

Table 4.7
Relations Between Life Event Score and Psychological Disorder by Age and Gender

	Boys (N=67)		Girls (N=85)		Old (N=75)		Young (N=77)	
	Positive Events	Negative Events	Positive Events	Negative Events	Positive Events	Negative Events	Positive Events	Negative Events
Achenbach total pathology	−0.01	0.12	−0.29[b]	0.16	−0.11	0.14	−0.17	0.07
Anxiety	0.02	0.38[a]	0.00	0.32[a]	0.03	0.40[a]	−0.02	0.29[a]
Depression	−0.09	0.35[a]	−0.07	0.24[b]	−0.14	0.28[b]	−0.04	0.27[b]
Hostility	0.20	−0.28[b]	−0.14	0.28[a]	0.09	0.39[a]	−0.02	0.16

[a] $p<0.01$
[b] $p<0.08$

were rated as unlikely to be caused by the child; 11 were also consensually designated (as described previously) as being undesirable. We reasoned that a relation between psychological symptoms and a negative events score composed of these 11 events could not be attributed to the tendency for disturbed children to cause negative events. As can be seen in Table 4.8, the significant relations between negative events and disorder are indeed maintained using this restricted sample of events.*

FUTURE DIRECTIONS IN THE ASSESSMENT OF DIVORCE EVENTS

The results with the DESC to date have provided useful information about (1) what positive and negative events occur in children's postdivorce environments, (2) factors related to the occurrence of these events, and (3) how these events relate to children's mental health. We feel that several additional steps are needed to further our understanding of the ways in which divorce affects children's postdivorce adjustment. These steps include (1) assessment of the more specific characteristics of the postdivorce environment that have an impact on children's adjustment, (2) assessment of the relation between events and children's divorce-adjustment tasks, and (3) testing of causal inferences about the effects of

Table 4.8
Relations Between Nonchild-Caused Negative Events and Psychological Disorder

	Total Sample (N = 152)	Boys (N = 67)	Girls (N = 85)	Young (N = 77)	Old (N = 75)
Achenbach total Pathology	0.02	0.07	0.07	0.03	0.03
Anxiety	0.34[a]	0.36[b]	0.29[b]	0.25[c]	0.42[a]
Depression	0.24[b]	0.30[c]	0.21[d]	0.20[d]	0.27[c]
Hostility	0.22[b]	0.28[c]	0.24[b]	0.12	0.37[a]

[a]$p<0.001$
[b]$p<0.01$
[c]$p<0.05$
[d]$p<0.07$

*The same analysis could not be done in a meaningful way for a similarly restricted positive event score because only three positive events were consensually rated as not being caused by the child.

divorce-related processes on children's disorder. These directions will be described briefly in turn.

Characteristics of Events that Correlate with Adjustment Problems

An important question still to be answered concerns the identification of specific events or characteristics of events that account for the relation between events and disorder. Specifically, can we use the DESC to identify the most damaging aspects of divorce for children? Two steps in studying this question would be (1) to develop a way of identifying different characteristics of events and (2) to develop event scores that reflect these different event characteristics. The analysis showing that undesirable but not desirable events correlate significantly with children's adjustment problems (discussed earlier in this chapter) is one example of this type of research.

A question that has been posed frequently in the life-events literature concerns whether the undesirability or the change quality of events is the central stressful component leading to psychological disorder (Vinokur & Selzer, 1975; Gersten et al., 1974). Although the results generally have favored the undesirability model, the positive relation found in most life-events scales between aversiveness of events and their change value has hindered a definitive empirical test of the predictions made by the two models (Dohrenwend & Dohrenwend, 1981). Because event valence and change are independently assessed on the DESC, the problem of correlation of event aversiveness and change is reduced. Scores can be derived that represent negative changes, and positive changes, as well as positive and negative events that are not changes. Preliminary analyses in which these scores were correlated with measures of psychological symptomatology indicated that positive *and* negative changes are *both* related to *higher* levels of psychological symptomatology while stable positive events relate to lower symptomatology. (Sandler et al., 1984). Although this evidence is preliminary, it is consistent with the view that *change* and quality are a critical stressful characteristics of postdivorce environments.

The different stressful characteristics of events might also be identified using statistically derived dimensions (based on factor analysis or cluster analysis) or a rationally derived categorization system. Illustratively, Sandler and Ramsay (1980) used a technique developed by Mangusson (1971) to ascertain the dimensions that clinicians used to structure their conceptualization of children's life events. They identified seven interpretable dimensions: loss, entrance, family troubles, sibling problems, primary environment change, physical harm, and positive events. Using a sample of inner-city elementary school children, Sandler and Ramsay (1980) demonstrated that two of these dimensions (entrance and family troubles) were primarily responsible for the relation between events scores and parent- and teacher-rated child psychological disorder.

An intriguing question to raise, once an event categorization system has been developed, is whether there is some specificity between different kinds of postdivorce experiences and different psychological disorders. Children of divorce are at risk for a wide range of disorders, including aggression, anxiety, depression, school-adjustment problems, and peer-adjustment problems (Felner et al., 1981; Guidubaldi et al., 1983; Hetherington, 1979; Wallerstein & Kelly, 1980). One might speculate that this wide range of adjustment problems occurs because divorce involves a wide range of stressful experiences. However, if different types of experiences can be assessed separately, it may be possible to specify which kinds of experiences lead to specific outcomes. On the basis of prior research, for example, it may be hypothesized that loss events lead to depression (Brown & Harris, 1978; Paykel, 1979), while family conflict events lead to aggression problems (Emery, 1982).

Divorce Events and Children's Adaptive Tasks

The concept of "adaptive tasks" has recently been proposed as a framework for organizing our thinking about children's divorce adjustment (Felner et al., 1983; Wallerstein, 1983). As discussed in detail in their chapter in this volume, Felner and his colleagues propose that divorce is best viewed as a period of family transition in which the child must accomplish important cognitive and behavioral tasks in order to adapt to the changes in the family environment. These tasks include reconstructing social networks, redefining family relationships, and reestablishing household routines. Wallerstein's (1983) view of children's divorce-adjustment tasks is more intrapsychically based than Felner and his colleagues' model. She defines six adaptive tasks: acknowledging the reality of the divorce; resuming customary, developmentally appropriate activities; dealing with feelings of loss and rejection; resolving feelings of anger and forgiving the parents; accepting the permanence of the divorce; and achieving realistic hope for future loving relationships. According to both Wallerstein and Felner, the adaptive or maladaptive outcomes of divorce are the result of the kinds of mastery children achieve over these tasks. Thus, children can either maintain or resolve feelings of anger or rejection and these outcomes determine the children's long-term view of themselves and their world.

The contrast between these models and a stress model (e.g., McGrath, 1970; Selye, 1956) is important to note. In the stress model as usually articulated, the stressor is viewed as a change from a state of equilibrium (Dohrenwend & Dohrenwend, 1981; Holmes & Masuda, 1974; Selye, 1956). Adapting to the change requires effort, but too much effort exhausts the individual's adaptive capacity, leaving the individual vulnerable to physical and psychological disorder (Selye, 1956). A cognitive variant of the stress model views the interpretation of the events as the key determinant of their stressfulness, particularly the interpretation of threat or physical harm rather than challenge (Lazarus & Launier, 1978). From the cognitive point of view, adjustment might primarily involve management of the state of negative arousal caused by the stressful experiences. In contrast, the adaptive task models of both Felner et al. and Wallerstein envision some extended core issues to be addressed in the divorce-adjustment process. Resolution of these tasks over time determines how the child thinks, feels, and behaves in the new family environment.

Although life-events schedules have been used traditionally within a stress model, it is interesting to consider how they might relate to an adaptive task model. Within Felner et al.'s (1983) model, the divorce events represent the daily experiences that provide the setting for the unfolding of adaptive tasks. Thus we could categorize life events according to the adaptive tasks they involve (e.g., dealing with interparental conflict or establishing new household routines).

In Wallerstein's model, where the tasks are more intrapsychic, events may be seen as promoting either adaptive or maladaptive resolution of the tasks. Illustratively, consider the task of dealing with feelings of loss and rejection. The child needs to deal with the partial loss of a parent, maintain a sense of self-worth, and redefine her or his relationship with the departed parent. Clearly, how the feelings of loss and rejection are resolved will be greatly affected by the *specific events* that occur. Some events may entail a profound sense of loss, such as the noncustodial parent missing visits, the child spending less time with the noncustodial parent, and the noncustodial parent moving away. Other events may mitigate the sense of loss, such as the child spending more time with parents, the child making regular visits to the noncustodial parent, the parent confiding in the child, and the child developing new relationships. While events can be organized by their relevance to adaptive tasks, we should not overlook the possibility that events may also act as generalized stressors, bringing about a state of negative arousal, which makes accomplishment of any adaptive task more difficult. Our preliminary findings that the change involved in events (regardless of the valence of the change) leads to higher levels of anxiety is consistent with this generalized stress effect.

Development of Inferences About the Causal Relationships Between Divorce-Related Processes.

What is the state of our current ability to make confident inferences about the causal relationships between postdivorce experiences and adjustment? How can we pursue research with the DESC (and similar measures of the postdivorce environment) to strengthen the causal inferences we draw? In this section we propose that, despite considerable research, we currently cannot place much confidence in assertions about those factors that are causally related to differential adaptation. We will, however, suggest three research directions that should be pursued to strengthen our understanding of causal relationships.

Before proceeding with our argument, it is useful to agree on a criterion for considering a relationship as causal. We propose the following: a manipulation of the putative causal factor will result in a predicted change in the putative effect. While this is only one of many concepts of causality (Cook & Campbell, 1979), it is particularly appropriate if we intend that our research lead to the development of interventions that will set the stage for improved postdivorce adaptation. To make confident causal assertions, it is necessary to satisfy three conditions: time precedence, relationship, and nonspuriousness (Kenny, 1979). Although research with children of divorce has identified many factors that relate to postdivorce adaptation, rarely have researchers examined these relationships in a way that satisfies the conditions of time precedence and spuriousness. Rarely, also, are the putative causal factors and effects assessed over time so as to test the hypothesis that the causal factor at time one was related to the effect at time two. Furthermore, although numerous alternative causal models are proposed to account for observed relationships, rarely are such models tested.

Illustratively, let us consider the statement that the level of interparental conflict is causally related to the quality of child postdivorce adjustment. This statement is generally accepted as being in accord with common sense, as well as empirical evidence (Hetherington, 1979; Kurdek, 1981; Wolchik et al., 1983). Studies that have investigated the relation between interparental conflict and child maladjustment have relied on simple correlations between measures of these constructs (Fulton, 1979; Kurdek & Blisk, 1983; Jacobson, 1978), which, with some exceptions (Hetherington, et al., 1981), were obtained concurrently. These studies do establish an association between postdivorce family conflict and child disorder that is consistent with the literature on intact families (Emery, 1982). However, there remain plausible rival hypotheses about the causal role of family conflict for children of divorce. It is conceivable, for example, that postdivorce family conflict is highly related to predivorce family conflict. If so, it may be that children in families with high postdivorce conflict had higher levels of psychological disorder before the divorce and simply continue to evidence disorder after the divorce. Likewise, other variables, such as parental psychopathology or family income, may account for the relation between interparental conflict and child disorder. It is time that we move beyond a simple assessment of the relation between postdivorce variables to a probing of causal pathways.

One approach to exploring causal models of postdivorce variables involves the use of structural equations (Kenny, 1979). Causal modeling requires that we think through our theoretical understanding of the causal relationships, and specify one or more competing models based on our best theory (Cooley, 1979). Structural equation analysis then provides a means for statistically testing whether the observed pattern of relationships is consistent or inconsistent with the specified model. If it is inconsistent with the specified model, we reject the model in its proposed form and respecify it. If the model is not inconsistent with the observed relationships, the model is not rejected (although it is recognized that other models may also be consistent with the data).

Illustratively, our research is based on the assumption that the postdivorce environment is causally related to adjustment problems. Within this model the undesirable change score of the DESC can be used to assess environmental stress. Although it is beyond the scope of this chapter to specify fully a causal model of how the postdivorce environment affects mental health, the important constructs and some causal paths between them can be specified. There is empirical evidence that variables such as parental mental health, parental stress, parental support, family income, negative divorce-related events, and children's cognitive competencies are associated with postdivorce adjustment. From a stress and coping theoretical framework, we can specify how some of these effects may be causally interrelated. For example, one can hypothesize that the effect of parent psychological disorder on children's postdivorce adjustment is mediated by its impact on children's negative events and the support the parent provides.

A second important step in exploring causal models is the use of longitudinal designs that allow the criterion of time precedence to be satisfied in order to strengthen causal inferences. Hetherington et al., (1981), for example, have considered the relation between parent psychological disorder and child psychological symptomatology. They argued that child psychological symptomatology causes parental pathology, and tested and confirmed this hypothesis in a longitudinal design by finding a significant relation between child symptomatology at time one and parent pathology at time two. Thus, with longitudinal designs, it is possible to address the issue of the child's influence on the environment as well as of the environment's influence on the child. As a second illustration, consider the effect of interparental conflict on child psychological disorder. We can utilize a subset of events from the DESC to represent interparental conflict that occurred in the past three months. As discussed previously in this chapter, the often observed relation between these two variables may be due to the stability of these constructs over time and may not reflect the causal impact of recent interparental conflict on child disorder. This model can be tested, along with the alternative model in which there is a causal path between interparental conflict at time one and child disorder at time two.

Finally, we can probe the causal relationship between variables by taking advantage of "natural experiments" that may change the postdivorce environments of children. Major changes are taking place in the legal processes involved in divorce (e.g., mediation of custody disputes) and in the postdivorce structure of the family (e.g., joint custody) (Repucci, 1984). Different legal arrangements may result in specific kinds of postdivorce experiences that affect children's adjustment. For example, it may be that joint-custody (or particularly joint-residency) arrangements result in more parental social support. Because joint custody is more likely to be granted in some jurisdictions than in others, it may be possible to test joint custody as a naturally occurring quasi-experiment. Similarly, an experimental approach may be taken in which interventions designed to improve some aspects of the postdivorce environment are implemented and the effects of these changes on children's adaptation are assessed.

SUMMARY

The reasonable assumption upon which most current divorce research is based is that the experiences that mark the divorce process play an important role in explaining the effects of divorce on children. The current research task is to elucidate what these experiences are and to predict and explain their impact more specifically. The Divorce Event Schedule for Children (DESC) was developed as an instrument to be used in this line of inquiry, as a measure of children's perceptions of significant postdivorce events.

The DESC has acceptable test–retest reliability, face validity, and construct validity. We have illustrated the utility of the scale to study the key participants' perceptions of the stressfulness of the postdivorce environment, and to study factors (e.g., custody arrangements) that influence the divorce-related experiences of children. As our research progresses, we have come to appreciate more fully the complexity of the processes involved and to sharpen the questions we pose. The most critical issues that remain are to identify the postdivorce processes that have the strongest impact on children, and to improve children's divorce outcomes by intervening in these processes.

REFERENCES

Achenbach, T. M. (1978). The child behavior profile: I. Boys aged 6–11. *Journal of Consulting and Clinical Psychology, 46,* 478–489.

Benedek, E. P., & Benedek, R. S. (1979). Joint custody: Solution or illusion? *American Journal of Psychiatry, 136,* 1540–1544.

Bloom, B. L., Asher, S. J., & White, S. W. (1978). Marital disruption as a stressor: A review and analysis. *Psychological Bulletin, 85,* 867–894.

Braver, S. L. (1983). Development of a hostility scale: The Braver Aggression Device (BAD). Unpublished manuscript, Arizona State University, Tempe.

Braver, S. L., Fogas, S. B., Wolchik, S. A., & Sandler, I. N. (August, 1984). Ratings of stressfulness of mother versus father divorce events. Paper presented at the American Psychological Association Convention, Toronto, Ont., Canada.

Brown, G. W., & Harris, T. (1978). *Social Origins of Depression.* New York: Free Press.

Clingempeel, W. G., & Repucci, N. D. (1982). Joint custody after divorce: Major issues and goals for research. *Psychological Bulletin, 91,* 102–127.

Cochran, M. M., & Brassard, J. A. (1979). Child development and personal social networks. *Child Development, 50,* 601–616.

Coddington, R. D. (1972). The significance of life events as etiologic factors in the diseases of children: I. A survey of professional workers. *Journal of Psychosomatic Research, 16,* 7–18.

Cook, T. D., & Campbell, D. T. (1979). *Quasi-experimentation: Design and Analysis Issues for Field Settings.* Chicago: Rand-McNally.

Cooley, W. W. (1978). Structural equations and explanatory observational studies. *Educational Researcher, 7,* 9–15.

Derogatis, L. R., Lipman, R. S., Rickels, K., Uhlenhuth, E. H., & Covi, L. (1974). The Hopkins Symptom Checklist (HSCL): A self-report symptom inventory. *Behavioral Science, 19,* 1–15.

Dohrenwend, B. S., & Dohrenwend, B. P. (1978). Some issues in research on stressful life events. *Journal of Nervous and Mental Disease, 166,* 7–15.

Dohrenwend, B. S., & Dohrenwend, B. P. (1981). What is a stressful life event? In H. Selye (Ed.), *Selye's Guide to Stress Research* (pp. 1–21). Vol. 1. New York: Van Nostrand Rinehold.

Dohrenwend, B. S., Krasnoff, L., Askenasy, A. R., & Dohrenwend, B. P. (1978). Exemplification of a method for scaling life events: The PERI life events scale. *Journal of Health and Social Behavior, 19,* 205–229.

Emery, R. E. (1982). Interpersonal conflict and the children of discord and divorce. *Psychological Bulletin, 92,* 310–330.

Felner, R. D., Farber, S. S., & Primavera, J. (1983). Transitions and stressful life events: A model for primary prevention. In R. D. Felner, L. A. Jason, J. N. Moritsugu, & S. S. Farber (Eds.), *Preventive Psychology: Theory, Research and Practice* (pp. 199–215). New York: Pergamon Press.

Felner, R. D., Stolberg, A., & Cowen, E. L. (1975). Crisis events and school mental health referral patterns of young children. *Journal of Consulting and Clinical Psychology, 43,* 305–310.

Farber, S. S., Felner, R. D., & Primavera, J. (1985). Parental separation/divorce and adolescents: An examination of factors mediating adaptation. *American Journal of Community Psychology, 13,* 171–185.

Fogas, B. S., Sandler, I. N., Dannenbaum, S. E., Wolchik, S. A., & Braver, S. L. (March, 1985). Assessment of child psychopathology in children of divorce. Paper presented at the Western Psychological Association Convention, San Jose, Calif.

Fulton, J. A. (1979). Parental reports of children's post-divorce adjustment. *Journal of Social Issues, 35,* 126–139.

Gersten, J. C., Langner, T. S., Eisenberg, J. G., & Orzeck, L. (1974). Child behavior and life events: Undesirable change or change per se? In B. S. Dohrenwend & B. P. Dohrenwend (Eds.), *Stressful Life Events: Their Nature and Effects* (pp. 159–171). New York: Wiley.

Goldstein, J., Freud, A., & Solnit, A. (1973). *Beyond the Best Interests of the Child.* New York: Free Press.

Guidubaldi, J., Cleminshaw, H. K., Perry, J. D., & Kehle, T. J. (August, 1983). Factors affecting the adjustment of children from divorced families. Paper presented at the American Psychological Association Convention, Anaheim, Calif.

Guidubaldi, J., Perry, J. D., & Cleminshaw, H. K. (1983). The legacy of parental divorce: A nationwide study of family status and selected mediating variables on children's academic and social competencies. *School Psychology Review, 12,* 300–323.

Hetherington, E. M. (1979). Divorce: A child's perspective. *American Psychologist, 34,* 851–858.

Hetherington, E. M., Cox, M., & Cox, R. (1981). Effects of divorce on parents and children. In M. Lamb (Ed.), *Nontraditional families* (pp. 233–288). Hillsdale, N.J.: Erlbaum.

Hetherington, E. M., Cox, M., & Cox, R. (1978). The aftermath of divorce. In J. H. Steven, Jr., & M. Matthews (Ed.), *Mother-Child Father-Child Relations* (pp. 149–176). Washington, D.C.: NAEYLC.

Holmes, T. H., & Masuda, M. (1974). Life change and illness susceptibility. In B.

S. Dohrenwend & B. P. Dohrenwend (Eds.), *Stressful Life Events: Their Nature and Effects* (pp. 45–73). New York: Wiley.

Holmes, T. H., & Rahe, R. H. (1967). The social readjustment rating scale. *Journal of Psychosomatic Research, 11,* 213–218.

Jacobson, D. S. (1978). The impact of marital separation-divorce on children. II. Interparental hostility and child adjustment. *Journal of Divorce, 2,* 3–19.

Johnson, J. H. (1982). Life events as stressors in childhood and adolescence. In B. B. Lakey & A. E. Kazdin (Eds.), *Advances in Clinical Child Psychology,* Vol. 5 (pp. 219–253). New York: Plenum Press.

Kenny, D. A. (1979). *Correlation and Causality.* New York: Wiley.

Kovacs, M. (1981). Rating scales to assess depression in school-aged children. *Acta Paedopsychiatrica, 46,* 305–315.

Kurdek, L. A. (1981). An integrative perspective on children's divorce adjustment. *American Psychologist, 36,* 856–866.

Kurdek, L. A., & Blisk, D. (1983). Dimensions and correlates of mothers' divorce experiences. *Journal of Divorce, 6,* 1–24.

Kurdek, L. A., Blisk, D., & Siesky, A. E. (1981). Correlates of children's long term adjustment to their parents' divorce. *Developmental Psychology, 17,* 565–579.

Lazarus, R. S., & Launier, R. (1978). Stress related transactions between person and environment. In L. A. Pervin & M. Lewis (Eds.), *Perspectives in Interactional Psychology* (pp. 287–327). New York: Plenum Press.

Longfellow, C., Zelkowitz, P. & Saunders, E. (1982). The quality of mother-child relationships. In D. Belle (Ed.), *Lives in Stress: Women and Depression* (pp. 163–176). Beverly Hills, Calif.: Sage.

Magnusson, D. (1971). An analysis of situational dimensions. *Perceptual and Motor Skills, 32,* 851–867.

McGrath, J. E. (1970). A conceptual formulation for research on stress. In J. E. McGrath (Ed.), *Social and Psychological Factors in Stress* (pp. 10–21). New York: Holt, Rinehart & Winston.

Monroe, S. M. (1982). Life events assessment: Current practices, emerging trends. *Clinical Psychology Review, 2,* 435–453.

Neugebauer, R. (1981). The reliability of life event reports. In B. S. Dohrenwend & B. P. Dohrenwend (Eds.), *Life Events and Their Contexts* (pp. 85–107). New York: Prodist.

Paykel, E. S. (1979). Causal relationships between clinical depression and life events. In J. E. Barrett (Ed.), *Stress and Mental Disorder* (pp. 71–86). New York: Raven Press.

Reynolds, C. R., & Richmond, B. O. (1978). What I think and feel: A revised measure of children's manifest anxiety. *Journal of Abnormal Psychology, 6,* 271–280.

SPSS, Inc. (1986). *SPSSX User's Guide* (2nd ed.). New York: McGraw-Hill.

Sandler, I. N. (1979). Life stress events and community psychology. In I. G. Sarason & C. D. Spielberger (Eds.), *Stress and Anxiety,* Vol. 6. (pp. 213–232). New York: Hemisphere.

Sandler, I. N., & Block, M. (1979). Life stress and maladaptation of children. *American Journal of Community Psychology, 7,* 425–440.

Sandler, I. N., & Guenther, R. R. (1985). Assessment of life stress events. In P.

Karoly (Ed.), *Measurement Strategies in Health Psychology* (pp. 555–600). New York: Wiley.

Sandler, I. N., & Lakey, B. (1982). Locus of control as a stress moderator: The role of control perceptions and social support. *American Journal of Community Psychology, 10,* 65–81.

Sandler, I. N., & Ramsay, T. B. (1980). Dimensional analysis of children's stressful life events. *American Journal of Community Psychology, 8,* 285–302.

Sandler, I. N., Wolchik, S. A., & Braver, S. L. (August, 1984). Development of a divorce event schedule for children. Paper presented at the American Psychological Association Convention, Toronto, Ont., Canada.

Sandler, I.N., Wolchik, S. A., & Braver, S. L. (August, 1985). Relationship between parental distress and children's post divorce adjustment. Paper presented at the American Psychological Association Convention, Los Angeles, Calif.

Sandler, I. N., Wolchik, S. A., Braver, S. L., & Fogas, B. (1986). Significant events of children of divorce: Toward the assessment of a risky situation. In S. M. Auerbach & A. Stolberg (Eds.), *Crisis Intervention with Children and Families.* (pp. 65–83). New York: Hemisphere.

Santrock, J. W., & Warshak, R. (1979). Father custody and social development in boys and girls. *Journal of Social Issues, 2,* 233–240.

Sarason, I. G., Johnson, J. G., & Siegel, J. M. (1978). Assessing the impact of life changes: Development of the life experiences survey. *Journal of Consulting and Clinical Psychology, 46,* 932–946.

Schroeder, D. H., & Costa, P. T., Jr. (1984). Influence of life events stress on physical illness: Substantive effects or methodological flaws? *Journal of Personality and Social Psychology, 46,* 853–863.

Selye, H. (1956). *The Stress of Life.* New York: McGraw-Hill.

Stolberg, A. L., & Anker, T. M. (1983). Cognitive and behavioral changes in children resulting from parental divorce and consequent environmental changes. *Journal of Divorce, 7,* 23–41.

Stolberg, A. L., Camplain, C., Currier, K., & Wells, M. J. (in press). Individual, familial and environmental determinants of children's post-divorce adjustment and maladjustment. *Journal of Divorce.*

Vinokur, A., & Selzer, M. L. (1975). Desirable versus undesirable events: Their relationship to stress and mental distress. *Journal of Personality and Social Psychology, 32,* 329–377.

Wallerstein, J. S., & Kelly, J. B. (1980). *Surviving the Breakup: How Children and Parents Cope with Divorce.* New York: Basic Books.

Wallerstein, J. S. (1983). Children of divorce: Stress and developmental tasks. In N. Garmezy & M. Rutter (Eds.), *Stress, Coping and Development in Children* (pp. 265–303). New York: McGraw-Hill.

Weissman, M. M., & Paykel, E. S. (1974). *The Depressed Woman.* Chicago: University of Chicago Press.

Wolchik, S. A., Braver, S. L., & Sandler, I. N. (1985a). Maternal versus joint custody: Children's post-separation experiences and adjustment. *Journal of Clinical Child Psychology, 14,* 5–10.

Wolchik, S. A., Fogas, B. S., & Sandler, I. N. (1984). Environmental change and children of divorce. In J. H. Humphrey (Ed.), *Stress in Childhood* (pp. 79–97). New York: AMS Press.

Wolchik, S. A., Sandler, I. N., Braver, S. L., & Fogas, B. S. (1985b). Events of parental divorce: Stressfulness ratings by children, parents and clinicians. *American Journal of Community Psychology, 14,* 59–74.

Zautra, A., & Reich, J. W. (1980). Positive events and reports of well-being: Some useful distinctions. *American Journal of Community Psychology, 8,* 657–670.

Zimmerman, M. (1983). Methodological issues in the assessment of life events: A review of issues and research. *Clinical Psychology Review, 3,* 339–370.

5

Divorce and Remarriage: Perspectives on the Effects of Custody Arrangements on Children

W. GLENN CLINGEMPEEL, MITCH A. SHUWALL,
and ELIZABETH HEISS

The high rates of family disruption and reconstitution have increased and complicated the decisions that must be made as to where children will live and who will be responsible for their welfare. Divorcing parents usually make custody decisions without court intervention, but there is evidence that the incidence of contested cases that must be decided by the courts is increasing (Bodenheimer, 1977).

A Pandora's box of complications engendered by shifting social and economic conditions, and a dramatically changing American family, are now confronting family courts. For example, the traditional practice of giving custody to one parent (usually the mother) and visitation rights to the other (usually the father) has recently come under attack by joint custody advocates, who argue that both parents have equal right to their children (e.g., Abarbanel, 1979; Canackos, 1981; Roman & Haddad, 1979). Moreover, the high rate of remarriage and redivorce has also presented the courts with a variety of difficult questions: In what situations should remarriage of either biological parent result in a shift of custody arrangements? When should the stepparent be allowed to adopt the stepchild without the consent of the noncustodial biological parent? What are the child-rearing rights and obligations of stepparents after their divorce from the child's biological parent?

Social science research has been largely irrelevant to custody policy and to onerous custody decisions faced by the courts and by divorcing and remarrying parents. There are at least two reasons for this policy–research schism. Not only have researchers failed to examine the complexity of factors at multiple levels of analysis that might mediate the effects of custody arrangements on children, but they have ignored the effects of custody arrangments over time—particularly the results when or both biological parents remarry.

Clingempeel and Reppucci (1982) proposed a multilevel/multivariable/ life-cycle perspective to guide research on the effects of custody arrangements on children. Their literature review and conceptual guidelines for research focused on debates regarding the relative merits and demerits of joint versus single-parent custody. They elucidated an array of variables operating at two interdependent levels of analysis—the divorced-family level and the social system level—that may mediate the effects of custody arrangements. They also emphasized the importance of a family life-cycle perspective, that is, examining how the effects of custody arrangments may vary over time and as a function of predictable ecological transitions (e.g., shifts in the developmental status of children, remarriage of parents).

In this chapter we largely follow the Clingempeel and Reppucci (1982) conceptual guidelines. We update their review, however, with more recent empirical research, and we depart from their framework in at least two important ways. First, we focus less on the effects of legally designated types, such as joint versus single-parent custody, and instead place more emphasis on variations in de facto arrangements (e.g., frequency of contacts and duration of stays with each parent) and their consequences for children. De jure types are gross classifications and do not differentiate the multiple variations within and between each type. Moreover de facto arrangements are related to but not determined by legally designated types. (Some children in joint custody may have a less even distribution of stays with each parent than children in sole-custody arrangements.) Second, we focus more extensively on remarriage of the biological parents as a predictable change in the family life cycle that may alter the effects of custody arrangements on children. The high rate of remarriage after divorce and the shrinking intermarriage interval strongly suggest that any discussion of postdivorce custody arrangements is incomplete without a discussion of postremarriage custody exigencies.

This chapter has two major goals: (1) to review recent empirical research on the effects of postdivorce and postremarriage custody arrangements on children, and (2) to raise empirical questions and stimulate future research that may fill lacunae in the extant literature. First, however, we review briefly the history of child custody adjudication in the United

States, and we examine some contemporary issues and trends in family law.

DIVORCE, REMARRIAGE, AND CHILD CUSTODY: HISTORY AND CURRENT ISSUES IN FAMILY LAW

Historical Overview

The ancient Roman tradition of granting absolute authority over children to the father persisted, with few exceptions, until the 1800s. The Judeo-Christian tradition of paternal supremacy, coupled with the presumption that the father, as property owner, was better equipped financially to care for children, contributed to the preference for the father as custodial parent. It was not until the latter 1800s that children came to be regarded as independent parties with special interests, rather than their father's chattel (Haralambie, 1983).

By the turn of the century, the preference for the father as custodial parent had begun to erode. The shift from an agrarian to an industrialized economy, with the concomitant demand for a mobile labor force, resulted in the separation of work and home, and contributed to the assumption that child rearing was an exclusively female undertaking (Hutterli, 1982). By the 1920s the "tender years doctrine," which prescribes the routine awarding of custody of young children to the mother, became the guiding consideration in custody decisions. The mother–child relationship was sanctioned and maternal instinct revered. In 1938 one judge proclaimed, "There's but a twilight zone between a mother's love and the atmosphere of heaven . . ." (*Tuber v. Tuber*, 1938).

Today the majority of states have expunged the tender years doctrine from their statutes. Even in states that retain the principle of maternal preference, it is usually not considered the primary determinant of custody (*Jenkins v. Jenkins*, 1979), but rather an important consideration among other factors (*Albright v. Albright*, 1983), or a tiebreaker in difficult cases *(Grubbs v. Grubbs, 1981)*. In practice, however, the tender years doctrine still influences custody decision making, with 90 percent of all contested cases resolved in favor of the mother (Gouge, 1980). In 1925 Judge Cardozo, ruling in *Finlay v. Finlay,* introduced the "best interests of child standard," which directs the courts to assume the role of *parens patriae* and to guarantee the well-being of minors. Today the best interests standard has replaced the tender years doctrine in most states (Meyer &

Schlissel, 1983). More recently, joint custody after divorce has received the attention of the legal and mental health professions. Although a plethora of variations is possible, joint custody has assumed two general forms: (1) *joint physical custody,* in which the children alternate living with each parent for a specified period of time; and (2) *joint legal custody,* in which parents share the decision-making responsiblity, yet not the physical custody of their children. Several social and economic factors may have contributed to the emergence of joint custody: the recognition of parenting rights for fathers, the women's movement, the questionable constitutionality of the tender years doctrine, disillusionment with the adversarialness of sole-custody proceedings, and social science research suggesting that children benefit from a continuing relationship with both parents (Gouge, 1980; Mills & Belzer, 1982; Robinson, 1982; Schulmann & Pitt, 1982).

Joint Custody and Family Law

Recent proponents of joint custody have offered several supporting arguments, including: (1) *both* parents have a fundamental constitutional right to their children after divorce (Canackos, 1981); (2) joint custody (in conjunction with mediation and counseling services) would reduce the incidence of the "seize–run–sue" syndrome, in which approximately 100,000 children are abducted yearly by their noncustodial parents (Hutterli, 1982); and (3) joint custody would eliminate the winner-take-all mentality of sole-custody proceedings and would attenuate both pre- and postdivorce interparental conflict (Gouge, 1980). Critics of joint custody have countered with their own arguments: (1) joint custody would disrupt continuity of care and given children less sense of control over their environments (e.g., Goldstein et al., 1973); and (2) joint custody would exacerbate interparental conflict, particularly in cases where it is permitted on the petition of only one parent (Steinman, 1983).

The justification and rationale underlying awards of joint custody have varied across jurisdictions. In most cases, the courts have awarded joint custody only when it is desired by both parents, but there are case law exceptions where awards have occurred despite the objections of one parent (e.g., *Beck v. Beck,* 1981). Usually, however, joint custody is denied when parents are overtly hostile toward each other (e.g., *Mastropole v. Mastropole,* 1981).

The proximity of maternal and paternal homes has been debated as a criterion in joint-custody decisions. In cases where maternal and paternal homes are far apart, some courts have denied joint physical custody and offered joint legal custody as an alternative (e.g., *Rusin v. Rusin,* 1980). Other courts have argued that joint physical custody may be the solution when the distance between homes is great and prohibits regular visitation (e.g., *Lumbra v. Lumbra,* 1978). In these cases, the pattern of alternations between parental homes is usually fashioned around the child's school year.

The age of the child has been a factor in joint custody decisions. A number of courts have ruled that joint physical custody is not appropriate for children of "tender years" (e.g., *Utley v. Utley,* 1976). The reluctance of the courts, however, sometimes dissipates when the homes of parents are geographically close to each other and similar (e.g. *Kilgore v. Kilgore,* 1976). A compromise approach adopted by some courts is joint legal custody, in which one parent has physical custody and the other has liberal visitation rights (e.g., *Daniel v. Daniel,* 1977).

Remarriage, Postdivorce Relationships, and Family Law

Most parents establish new romantic relationships and eventually remarry after divorce; some turn to alternative life styles (cohabitation, homosexual relationships). One by-product of these new and varied postdivorce relationships is the reenactment of custody disputes and attempts to modify initial postseparation custody arrangments. As a result, judges who must make custody decisions are confronted with novel and enigmatic questions.

In custody decisions triggered by new relationships, the courts have attempted to protect the parent's freedom to develop new relationships as long as parent behavior is not deemed detrimental to children. In many cases, however, it may be exceedingly difficult, if not impossible, to determine unambiguously how children are affected by new parental relationships. Explicit guidelines and social science research are lacking. Four situations that may prove difficult for judges are cohabitation, homosexual relationships, interracial relationships, and remarriage and redivorce.

Cohabitation

Cohabitation of an unmarried parent has occasionally resulted in modification of custody decisions. Courts consider the child's awareness of the parent's sexual conduct. (*DiStefano v. DiStefano,* 1978), the transience of the parent–third-party relationship (*Rupp v. Rupp,* 1979), and the desirability of the proposed home (*In re Boyer,* 1980). In the landmark case of *Jarrett v. Jarrett* (1979), the Supreme court of Illinois deemed custody modification necessary to protect the children from the potential moral harm of witnessing their mother's cohabitating relationship. In reaching its decision, the court cited the custodial parent's violation of state fornication and moral conduct laws. *Jarrett,* however, does not represent the current trend in custody decision making (Gottsfield, 1984). Usually the courts have required evidence that the parent's cohabiting relationship has already harmed the child and that modification would serve the child's best interests (*Lapp v. Lapp,* 1983). In most cases cohabitation is not assumed harmful a priori, but is investigated in conjunction with the totality of the child's circumstances (*In re Marriage of Thompson,* 1983).

Homosexual Relationships

Courts have been divided in their treatment of homosexual relationships of the custodial parent. In *Bezio v. Patenaude* (1980), the court failed to find a connection between the mother's lesbian relationship and her fitness as a parent. In *Kallas v. Kallas* (1980), however, the custodial parent's homosexuality per se did not warrant custody change—but the overt display of the homosexual relationship was considered relevant to custody proceedings. In *Complainant v. Defendant* (1983) the court adopted a moderate position and allowed a homosexual father to retain custody of his daughter, yet stipulated that he not share the bedroom with his male lover when the child was present in the home. Propriety in conducting the homosexual relationship and the strength of the parent–child relationship have been used as defenses against the shifting of custody to the heterosexual parent (*M.P. V. S.P.,* 1979).

There are numerous cases where the homosexual parent has been denied custody. In *M.J.P.V.J.G.P.* (1982), for example, the court held that the mother's homosexual relationship represented "sufficient change of conditions" to warrant custody modification. The court reasoned that the child would be subjected to societal prejudice due to the mother's unconventional life-style. In *Hall v. Hall* (1980) the demonstration that, in the event of conflict, the custodial parent would opt for a continued homosexual relationship, rather than custody of her children, was sufficient to deny custody to a lesbian mother. Moreover vociferous advocacy of the homosexual life-style may also damage a parent's chances of obtaining custody (Gottsfield, 1984).

Interracial Relationships.

In most custody cases where parents develop postdivorce relationships with interracial partners, race has been considered irrelevant as a custody decision-making criterion (e.g., *Edel v. Edel,* 1980; *Palmore v. Sidoti,* 1984). In *Edel v. Edel* (1980) the court failed to find evidence that a white custodial mother's impending marriage to a black man would harm the child. Similarly, in *Palmore v. Sidoti* (1984) the U.S. Supreme Court ruled unanimously that the risk of the child being subjected to racial discrimination was insufficient grounds to take custody away from a white woman whose remarriage was to a black man.

The race of the parents has been a decision-making criterion more often in cases where children are born from interracial marriages that later dissolve (e.g., *Farmer v. Farmer,* 1981). Often the "minority race" parent has been preferred in custody awards because the courts have assumed that this parent is better prepared to help the child cope with racial prejudice and societal alienation (Meyer & Schlissel, 1983).

Remarriage and Redivorce

The changed circumstances associated with remarriage of the custodial or noncustodial biological parent (e.g., shift from a one- to a two-parent family, increase in economic resources) may precipitate custody modification disputes (*Abel v. Hadder,* 1981). When the noncustodial parent remarries and the custodial parent remains single, several factors are considered by the courts: the relative stability of the remarried and nonremarried parents' homes; the character of the stepparent; the quality of the relationship between stepparent and child; and the degree of harmony in the parent–stepparent marital relationship ("Remarriage of Parent," 1980).

Some courts, on the other hand, emphasize continuity of care, focusing less on the remarriage of the noncustodial parent than on the adequacy of the child's situation with the custodial parent (*Wiggins v. Wiggins,* 1982). When the petition to shift custody to the remarried noncustodial parent is denied, the court may adopt the compromise solution of granting increased visitation privileges to the nonresidential parent (*K.B. V. S.B.,* 1981).

Likewise, the remarriage of the custodial parent may necessitate reconsideration of the custody arrangement. A problematic stepparent–stepchild relationship is one of the more common situations that may result in a change of custody to the noncustodial parent (*In re Custody of Yuhas,* 1980).

Remarriage of the custodial parent may also precipitate a petition for adoption by the custodial stepparent. If this petition is granted, the stepparent is given the status of a biological parent and all legal ties with the noncustodial, biological parent are severed. When the noncustodial parent agrees to the adoption, the process usually continues unhindered. When the parent denies consent, the petition to adopt is often denied. Yet under certain conditions—as when abandonment of the child has been demonstrated—the need to obtain consent from the noncustodial biological parent may be obviated (*In re Robert J.,* 1974). Moreover, in recent years the courts have increasingly favored the stepparent in cases of contested adoption (Maddox, 1975; *In re Carson,* 1978).

The redivorce of the custodial parent is particularly troublesome for the courts. In the aftermath of a second divorce, the courts may be faced with a three-party dispute involving both biological parents and the stepparent. Upon the death of the custodial parent, the courts may be called on to settle a dispute between the surviving biological parent and the widowed stepparent. Different courts have resolved such disputes in favor of each party: the "parental priority" approach favors the biological parent as custodian, except in those cases where the parent has forfeited the rights of parentage (*Cox v. Young,* 1966) or is found to be unfit (*Leroy v. Odgers,* 1972). Adherents of this approach argue that the divorce or death of the custodial parent effectively terminates the stepparent–child relationships. Proponents of the "best interests of the child" approach, on the other hand, argue that a stepparent may obtain custody in cases where the stepparent has established a parental bond with the child prior to the demise of the marriage (*In re Allen,* 1981) and stepparent custody is the child's best interest (*Gorman v. Gorman,* 1981). One compromise solution is to grant custody to the biological parent and visitation rights to the stepparent (*Carter v. Broderick,* 1981). Another is to grant legal custody to the biological parent and stepparent (*Stanley D. v. Deborah D.,* 1983).

A MULTILEVEL/MULTIVARIABLE PERSPECTIVE ON CUSTODY ARRANGEMENTS AND CHILDREN

The effects of custody arrangements on children depend on a number of variables, which can be conceptualized at multiple levels of analysis. Bronfenbrenner (1977) proposed four levels of the ecological environment that might influence child development: (1) the microsystem, or the child's immediate physical setting; (2) the mesosystem, or the variety of micro-systems (e.g., family, school, neighborhood) in which the child is regularly immersed; (3) the exosystem, or informal social networks (e.g., kin, friends) and formal institutions (e.g., work settings, legal system); and (4) the macrosystem, or the overarching institutional patterns of the culture or subculture (e.g., cultural beliefs and attitudes regarding work, the family, etc.). He viewed these levels as interdependent (variables at one level could affect variables at another) and concentric (the exosystem contains the various mesosystems).

Since Bronfenbrenner's influential article, variations of his conceptual framework have been applied to several developmental issues, including research on children's adjustment to divorce (Kurdek, 1981) and the effects of joint custody on children (Clingempeel & Reppucci, 1982). We borrow from both the Kurdek (1981) and Clingempeel and Repucci (1982) adaptations of Bronfenbrenner's scheme, and propose that the effects of custody arrangements on children are mediated by multiple variables at three levels of analysis: ontogenic, divorced family, and social system. The ontogenic level includes the individual characteristics of parents and children (age, sex, personality traits, social and cognitive competencies); the divorced family level includes the nature of interrelationships among divorced parents and their children, and the social and physical dimensions of each parent's home; the social system level consists of informal social networks and formal or quasi-formal institutions (policies of work settings, the schools, the mass media) that may have an impact on variables at the divorced family and ontogenic levels of analysis.

The Ontogenic System: Child Characteristics

Individual characteristics of children, including age, sex, and personality variables, may interact with custody arrangements to mediate the child's adjustment to divorce.

Sex of Child

Custody arrangements may have different effects depending on the sex of the child. Several studies of mother-custody families found that boys experience more intense and enduring divorce-related adjustment problems (e.g., Hetherington et al., 1978; Wallerstein & Kelly, 1980). Hetherington and colleagues (1978) found that two years after divorce, boys—but not girls—continued to exhibit more behavioral and interpersonal problems than children from nuclear families.

Custody decision-making biases that result in mothers gaining custody of both sexes may account for the greater postdivorce adjustment problems of boys. Santrock and Warshak (1979) investigated the social development of six- to 11-year-old boys and girls living in mother custody, father custody, and nuclear-family homes. They found that children living with the opposite-sex parent were more demanding and less warm, and exhibited more antisocial behavior than children living with the same-sex parent. Thus the general finding that boys have greater difficulty adjusting to divorce may stem from the extant custody policy.

Wallerstein and Kelly (1980) obtained evidence that the same-sex parent–child relationships may be more important to children's postdivorce adjustment than opposite-sex parent–child relationships. This finding, however, depended on the age of the child. For school-age children, the boy's psychological adjustment correlated more highly with the quality of the father–child relationship, whereas the girl's adjustment correlated more highly with the quality of the mother–child relationship. For younger children, however, the psychological adjustment of children of both sexes was more highly correlated with the quality of the mother–child relationship.

The quality of parenting by custodial mothers may contribute to the poorer adjustment of boys. Both major longitudinal studies of divorce (Wallerstein & Kelly, 1980; Hetherington et al., 1978) found that mothers more often exhibit poor parenting practices with sons than with daughters. Moreover, Wallerstein and Kelly speculated that, in some cases, sons may symbolize the absent father and thus become a surrogate target for marital hostilities.

Greater adjustment difficulties for boys may also be due to sex differences in the pre- to postdivorce continuity of nonresidential father–child relationships. Father–son relationships have been shown to change more dramatically after divorce than father–daughter relationships (Wallerstein & Kelly, 1980). Consequently, boys may face greater adjustment demands.

Age of Child

Children of different ages differ in social and cognitive competencies, important settings in which they are immersed, and developmental tasks they face. As a result, responses to custody arrangements may vary as a function of age. While studies have not yet compared age-related responses across different custody types, Wallerstein and Kelly (1980) examined reactions of children of different ages in mother-custody families. In the absence of research, we can only speculate on how variations from mother custody would alter the Wallerstein and Kelly results.

The divorce-specific responses of the preschool (aged three to five) child often include fears of abandonment, sadness, and self-blame. Custody arrangements that permit regular and frequent contact with both parents may reduce fears of abandonment and self-blame cognitions, but they may also fuel fantasies of reconciliation. Further, frequent shifts of primary caregivers may result in stress, confusion, and disruption of attachment bonds.

The most frequently observed response of young school-aged children (six to eight years) was pervasive sadness. In addition, many children felt abandoned and rejected by their fathers, and feared the loss of their families. Loyalty conflicts and wishes for reconciliation were also common. At the 18-month follow-up, depression was related to infrequent visitation in boys, and poor mother–child relationships in girls. For young school-aged children, joint-custody arrangements might attenuate feelings of abandonment, loss, and rejection. While increased contact with the father could be especially helpful to boys, it might also be beneficial to girls, particularly those who have problematic relationships with their mothers. As with preschool children, however, joint custody might also heighten wishes for reconciliation.

Older school-age children responded to their parents' divorce with an intense anger toward one or both parents, and feelings of loss, rejection, and loneliness. Nine- to 12-year-olds were also more likely than children of other ages to join in alignments with one parent against the other, and thus become embroiled in interparental conflicts. Moreover, interparental hostilities were strongly associated with adjustment problems for these children. Boys of this age experienced the greatest postdivorce deterioration in father–child relationships. Feelings of loss, anger, and rejection might have been reduced by custody arrangements that distributed the time with each parent more evenly. This, however, is speculative and awaits future research.

Adolescents responded to divorce with initial feelings of loss and anger, loyalty conflicts, and anxieties regarding heterosexual relationships. Custody arrangements, however, may have less effect on adolescents than on younger children because of their expanded social networks, their extrafamilial activities, and their greater mobility (Clingempeel & Reppucci, 1982).

Personality Variables

Personality characteristics of children may also alter the effects of custody arrangements. Kurdek and his colleagues have shown that interpersonal reasoning and locus of control influence children's adjustment to divorce (see Kurdek's chapter in this volume for a detailed discussion). Children who exhibit low levels of ego resiliency and low tolerance of ambiguity may have greater difficulty adjusting to certain types of custody arrangement—those, for example, that require frequent changes in visitation patterns. Divorce and the custody decision-making process may also engender personality changes in children. Several researchers, for example, have speculated that divorce may produce a more external locus of control to the extent that children have no input into custody arrangements and other divorce-related life changes (Cantor, 1977; Duke & Lancaster, 1976; Kulka & Weingarten, 1979; Rotter, 1966; Wallerstein & Kelly, 1980).

The temperament of children may affect their adjustment to postdivorce custody arrangements (Clingempeel & Reppucci, 1982; Hetherington et al., 1978). Rutter (1979) has noted that temperamentally difficult children are more vulnerable to the effects of life changes and stressors. Hetherington and colleagues (1978) found that children who had been rated (by mothers) as having been more difficult infants had the most difficulty in adjusting to divorce. While the alternations in residence associated with joint custody may exacerbate the difficulties of the temperamental child (Abarbanel, 1979), the increased role of the father in child rearing may be helpful. Furthermore, custody arrangements that provide regular access to both parents may reduce feelings of loss and loneliness, and benefit the temperamentally difficult child (Clingempeel & Reppucci, 1982).

Divorced Family Level

Four major classes of variables that operate at the divorced family level and may mediate the effects of custody arrangements on children include: the parent–child relationship, the interparental relationship, the postdivorce change in resources, and the pattern of alternations in caregivers and caregiving environments.

Parent–Child Relationships

Two major longitudinal studies have examined parent–child relationships and child outcomes in divorced, mother-custody families. Hetherington and co-workers (1978, 1979a, 1979b) conducted a two-year study of 48 divorced families with a preschool child, and a matched sample of 48 nondivorced families. Details of this study are provided in the chapter by Hetherington, Arnett, and Hollier in this volume. Wallerstein and Kelly (1974, 1975, 1976, 1980) conducted a five-year study of 60 divorced families with 131 children aged three to 18 years. Clinical interviews were conducted shortly after the final separation and 1.5 and five years later. Information was also gathered from the children's teachers. Several methodological limitations should be noted: (1) lack of an intact control group; (2) unclear methods of data analysis; and (3) heavy reliance on clinical impressions.

Both Hetherington and colleagues and Wallerstein and Kelly have found that the frequency of child contacts with the nonresidential father decreases over time. These findings have been substantiated by a recently completed National Survey (Furstenburg et al., 1983), which revealed that one-third of children from divorced families had had no contact with their nonresidential parent in five years.

The frequency of visits from nonresidential fathers may be related to the postdivorce adjustment of children. Hetherington and colleagues (1978) found that, overall, frequent visitation was related to positive divorce adjustment. Wallerstein and Kelly (1976, 1980) reported that frequent visitation was related to positive adjustment of children of all ages, but especially younger and preadolescent children. Furthermore, five years after the divorce, they found that many unvisited or infrequently visited children felt rejected and unloved, and exhibited lower self-esteem. In at least two studies, however, frequency of visitation was unrelated to postdivorce outcomes in children (Hess & Camara, 1979; Kurdek et al., 1981).

The quality of the child's relationship with the nonresidential parent may be a better predictor of postdivorce outcomes than the frequency of visits. Hess and Camara (1979) compared 16 divorced, mother-custody families (whose biological parents had been separated for two to three years) with 16 intact, white, middle-class families. All 32 families had a child between the ages of nine and 11. They investigated the relative effects of three family process variables (affective relationships between the child and each parent, and the level of interparental harmony) on child outcomes (social relations with peers, aggression, work style at school, and stress). Higher quality relationships with one or both parents were related to lower levels of stress and aggression, better work effectiveness at school, and healthier social interactions. Higher quality relationships may also be related to higher self-esteem and less depression (Wallerstein and Kelly, 1980).

Divorce and mother custody may have a detrimental effect on long-term father–child relationships. Fine and colleagues (1983) compared perceptions of current relationships with fathers among 100 college students who experienced parental divorce before they were 11 years old and 141 students from nondivorced nuclear families. Findings revealed that students from divorced families perceived their fathers as more distant and less affectionate than students from intact families.

Several studies have found that the frequency of visits and the quality of the nonresidential father–child relationship are related (e.g., Clarke-Stewart, 1977; Furstenberg et al., 1983). The strength of this relationship, though, may be mediated by the age of the child and the amount of time since the divorce. Wallerstein and Kelly (1980) found that, for children of all ages, the frequency of visits and the quality of the relationship were highly correlated shortly after the divorce. Five years later, however, frequency and quality were strongly correlated only for children who were preschoolers at the time of divorce. It is possible that younger children may depend longer on frequent contacts for assurance that the non-custodial father still cares.

Custody arrangements may mediate the postdivorce quality of the non-residential father–child relationship. When custody is awarded solely to the mother, the limited frequency and duration of nonresidential parent–child interactions, permitted under most traditional "every other week-end" arrangements, may contribute to the diminution in the quality of the father–child relationship. Time constraints on father–child interactions may be painful for fathers who care most for their children. Wallerstein and Kelly (1980) observed that the depression experienced by many fathers often resulted in less frequent visits, with children feeling hurt, disappointed, and angry. Even when fathers visited frequently, their removal from the day-to-day activities of the child often led to communication problems and a lower quality relationship.

Arrangements that result in a more even distribution of interactions between the child and each parent may foster greater continuity in the father–child relationship. Fathers could continue to interact regularly with the child without the frustrating status of the marginal parent. More frequent and longer-lasting interactions would allow fathers to keep more in touch with the day-to-day changes in the child's life, thus, enhancing communication.

The quality of the custodial mother–child relationship is also important for the child's divorce adjustment (Hetherington et al., 1978; Hess & Camara, 1979; Wallerstein & Kelly, 1980). High-quality mother–child relationships have been associated with childrens' competent ego functioning, successful school performance, and social maturity (Wallerstein & Kelly, 1980), while low-quality relationships have been related to more dependency demands, less compliance and more antisocial behavior (Hetherington et al., 1978).

The quality of many custodial mother–child relationships deteriorates subsequent to divorce. Hetherington and colleagues (1978) found that mothers with sole custody made fewer maturity demands, showed less affection, were less likely to communicate well, and were more inconsistent in disciplining their children than mothers from nondivorced families. Although many of these problems in parenting improved during the second year after the divorce, the quality of the mother–child relationships in the divorced families was still poorer (particularly with boys) than that found in the nuclear family group. Also, Wallerstein and Kelly (1980) reported that two-thirds of the mother–child relationships in their study deteriorated shortly after separation. Moreover, five years after the divorce mother–child relationships were still problematic in 40 percent of the families.

The quality of the mother–child relationship may also be mediated by custody arrangements. Role strain and task overload problems, often reported by sole-custody mothers (Brandwein et al., 1974; Glasser & Navarre, 1965; Hetherington et al., 1978; 1979a), as well as emotional stresses associated with the marital disruption, may account in part for the deterioration in parenting practices and mother–child relationships. Arrangements that engender a more even distribution of child-rearing responsibilities may reduce task overload problems and stress, and, consequently, relationships may not be as adversely affected by the divorce.

The effects of custody arrangements on parent–child relationships and child outcomes may be mediated by parental psychopathology. Hetherington (1981) has suggested that children in single-parent families may be more susceptible to the negative effects of a custodial parent's psychopathology, because the nonresidental parent may not be sufficiently involved in the child's life to serve as a "protective buffer" between the child and the emotionally unstable parent. Furthermore, when a noncustodial parent is disturbed, frequent visitation may be inimical to the child's psychological adjustment (Hetherington et al., 1978; Wallerstein & Kelly, 1980)

In cases where one parent suffers from severe, chronic psychopathology, arrangements that involve alternations between parental homes may be contraindicated. Yet if the disturbance of one or both parents is acute but not severe, such arrangements may benefit children. Recently Clingempeel and Reppucci (1982) speculated that while joint-custody parents may not "serve as 'protective buffers' on a day-to-day basis, regular shifts to the home of the parent with whom the child *currently* has a positive relationship may serve as emotional support at times when staying with the other parent is particularly stressful and nonrewarding" (p. 109).

Future research that compares different structural types of joint- and sole-custody arrangements (e.g., joint legal custody with mother physical custody; joint legal custody with father physical custody; mother custody, father visitation; father custody, mother visitation; joint physical custody) on parent–child relationships is needed. This research should assess the frequency, quantity, and quality of parent–child interactions and the psychological health of parents as potential mediators of parenting practices and child outcomes. The extent to which parents serve as "protective buffers" under specific custody arrangements should also be investigated.

The Interparental Relationship

Interparental conflict often precedes marital dissolution and may not cease with the divorce decree (Hetherington et al., 1978; Westman et al., 1970). Parental disharmony has been related to adjustment problems of children in both divorced families (e.g., Hetherington et al., 1978; Wallerstein & Kelly, 1980) and nuclear families (e.g., Porter & O'Leary, 1980; Rutter, 1979). Moreover, empirical evidence has accumulated suggesting that children who live in high-conflict intact homes may experience more adjustment difficulties than children who live in low-conflict divorced homes (Hetherington et al., 1978, 1979a; McCord et al., 1962; Nye, 1957; Power et al., 1974; Rutter, 1979). Conflict may be especially detrimental to children in divorced families, as it has been found to vitiate the positive effects of frequent visitation (Hetherington et al., 1978; Wallerstein & Kelly, 1980) and/or result in the child's withdrawal from one or both parents (Wallerstein & Kelly, 1980). In a recent review of the empirical literature, Emery (1982) concluded that hostilities between parents may be the most powerful variable mediating the postdivorce adjustment of children.

Few studies have investigated the relation between custody arrangements (as they vary in frequency of child contacts with each parent and distribution of child-rearing responsibilities) and postdivorce interparental conflict. In the absence of empirical research, we offer three speculations on how custody arrangements that involve a more even distribution of child-care responsibilities may affect the postdivorce relationship between parents.

First, conflict may be exacerbated. A more even distribution of child-care duties may increase demands for interparental communication, and parents thus may have more opportunities to rekindle predivorce hostilities. New disagreements may also arise over differences in parenting practices, philosophies, and values. Second, conflict may be attenuated. The task overload problems of one parent and the feelings of loss and emptiness of the other may be reduced. As a consequence there may be less resentment between parents. Moreover, a greater need for interparental cooperation may pressure parents to separate ex-marital issues (and concomitant hostilities) from their current parental relationship. Third, conflict may be unaffected. Divorced parents may either successfully separate marital hostilities from shared parenting tasks, or carry out parental tasks independently of one another, with a minimal amount of contact.

Recently, investigators have attempted to determine the effects of custody arrangements on postdivorce interparental conflict by comparing relitigation rates in joint and sole custody families. The extant studies, however, (Ilfeld et al., 1982; Phear et al., 1984) have yielded contradictory results. Ilfeld and colleagues (1982) investigated the court records of 414 consecutive custody cases handled by a Los Angeles court over a two years, including 276 sole-custody cases and 138 joint-custody cases. They found significantly lower relitigation rates for joint-custody families (16 percent) than for sole-custody families (32 percent). However, in a study of 119 mother-custody and 65 joint-custody families in Massachusetts, Phear and colleagues (1984) found that significantly more joint-custody families returned to court, either to modify the original agreement or to resolve child-related conflicts.

These relitigation studies are difficult to interpret for at least two reasons. First, relitigation is not a direct measure of the frequency and intensity of interparental conflict. A decision to relitigate is probably related to other factors, including the parent's financial status, the parent's perception of the probability of winning, and the content of disagreements. Moreover, the number of parents in conflictual relationships who did not seek relitigation is unknown. Second, these studies did not examine relations between de facto arrangements and relitigation rates. Both sole- and joint-custody families vary as to the frequency of contacts with each parent, the degree of cooperative parenting, and the mechanics of alternations between parental homes. The actual patterns of contact between the child and both parents are related to, but not determined by, legally designated custody arrangments.

Leupnitz (1982) compared 18 joint-custody, 16 mother-custody, and 16 father-custody families (with a total of 91 children) across a number of general dimensions, including interparental conflict, demographics, and child outcomes. All families had been separated for at least two years prior to the interview and had one or more children under the age of 16. Among the joint-custody subsample, physical custody arrangements ranged from daily to yearly alternations between parents, with a split-week arrangement the most common.

The three custody arrangements did not differ on the level of parent-rated interparental conflict. They did differ, however, in the frequency of relitigation over child-support payments, with one-half of sole-custody families, but none of the joint-custody families, returning to court. Moreover, all noncustodial fathers—but only one joint-custody father—perceived financial arrangements as unfair.

Custody arrangements that give fathers more contact with their children and a greater role in child rearing may encourage compliance with child-support payments. As financial issues are often a major area of postdivorce conflict (Wallerstein & Kelly, 1980; Kurdek & Blisk, 1983; Ahrons, 1981), at least one source of hostility may be attenuated. It is also possible though that the most child-oriented fathers are both more likely to gain "shared responsibility" arrangements, and to make regular support payments.

The relationship between ex-spouses in a joint-custody situation may improve or become less conflictual over time. Preliminary results from one study of 201 joint-custody parents (Irving et al., 1984) suggest that relationships with former mates shifted from high conflict at the time of separation (as reported retrospectively) to "moderately" or "very friendly" several years later.

The success of custody arrangements that distribute child-rearing duties evenly between parents may depend in part on the parents' ability to separate the parental and ex-marital dimensions of their relationship (Clingempeel & Reppucci, 1982). Irving and coworkers (1984) have found that many joint-custody parents avoid conflict by to their communications with one another to what is essential for child rearing. Some parents, however, may be unable or unwilling to separate ex-marital hostilities from their parental relationship (Ahrons, 1981; Irving et al., 1984), and joint custody may be contraindicated.

Taken together, exploratory studies of joint custody (or comparisons of joint and sole custody) have not consistently revealed greater probabilities of postdivorce interparental conflict for either custody type. Preliminary analyses of a National Survey of Children (Furstenberg et al, 1983) revealed that the frequency of contacts between nonresidential parents and children was unrelated to the frequency of contacts between parents or the degree of interparental conflict. Furstenberg and colleagues (1983) found that few divorced parents discussed matters involving children, even when the nonresidental parent visited frequently. They speculated that "parallel" parenting, in which each parent operates as a self-contained unit, may be the most appropriate term for describing the vast majority of postdivorce parenting relationships.

Future studies should examine longitudinally the relations among various custody arrangements (e.g., joint physical custody, joint legal custody, father physical custody, mother physical custody), interparental conflict, and child outcomes. They should obtain measures of interparental conflict from both spouses and children, and should describe and compare de facto variations of legally designated types. Factors that may predict a parent's willingness to separate marital hostilities from the tasks associated with shared parenting after divorce need to be identified. Finally, future studies should investigate the relations between the reliability of child-support payments and various custody arrangements.

Change in Resources.

Marital separation and divorce are often accompanied by changes in economic, physical, and social resources, which may contribute to the adjustment problems of parents and children. Sole-custody mothers usually experience a precipitous drop in income after divorce (Espenshade, 1979). In addition, sole-custody mothers usually move after a divorce, often to less adequate housing (Colletta, 1983; Hetherington, 1979; Kriesberg, 1970; Wallerstein & Kelly, 1980). Both the geographical mobility, which may remove parents and children from support systems (Marsden, 1969; Pearlin & Johnson, 1977), and the reduced physical resources, may be related to adjustment difficulties. Postdivorce reductions in physical resources have been associated with discontinuity in parenting practices (Colletta, 1983; Hetherington et al., 1978; Goode, 1956; Kriesberg, 1970; Wallerstein & Kelly, 1980) and child-adjustment problems (Bane, 1976; Colletta, 1979; Desimone-Luis et al., 1979; Espenshade, 1979; Hetherington et al., 1978; Wallerstein & Kelly, 1980). The mother-custody divorced family may also experience a reduction in the number of people in the household, which may result in a narrower range of intrafamilial cognitive and social stimuli.

The total amount of pre- to postdivorce environmental change may be an important variable mediating child outcomes. Two studies (Stolberg, 1980; Kurdek & Blisk, 1983) have investigated the relations between environmental change and child outcome in mother-custody families. Stolberg (1980) measured the environmental change in 30 families by asking mothers to provide information regarding pre- and postdivorce financial and social conditions (e.g., monthly income, monthly rent or mortgage, number of people in the home, number of hours per week each parent spends with children). He found that high degrees of environmental change were related to psychological adjustment problems—such as depression, social withdrawal, and aggression—and a more external locus of control. Furthermore, children who experienced greater overall change in their environments also tended to view their custodial parents as "lacking control over their lives," a factor that may be related to postdivorce behavioral problems (Tooley, 1976). A higher degree of overall environmental change after divorce has also been associated with lower self-esteem and maladaptive, divorce-related thoughts (Kurdek & Blisk, 1983).

The magnitude of environmental change may vary as a function of custody arrangements. The reduction in economic resources after divorce may be less dramatic in custody arrangements that distribute child-care duties between parents more evenly. A major problem in sole custody, is the failure of nonresidential fathers to pay child support; studies show that less than one-third continue to support their families (Kriesberg, 1970; Winston & Forsher, 1971). To the extent that custody arrangements permit fathers, as well as mothers, an active role in child care, delinquent child-support payments may be less likely. At least two studies of joint custody (Leupnitz, 1982; Irving et al., 1984) have found that fathers are likely to continue support payments. Furthermore, visitation frequency and regularity of child-support payments are strongly correlated (Furstenberg et al., 1983).

Custody arrangements that distribute child-care duties more evenly between parents may also reduce the task overload problem of custodial mothers. This would give mothers, as well as fathers, some opportunity to pursue their own educational and career goals, and thus increase their chances for upward economic mobility.

Postdivorce Alternations in Care Givers and Care-Giving Environments

Custody arrangements vary in the frequency of the child's alternations between care givers and care-giving environments. Traditional single-parent legal agreements usually call for the child to spend 14 days with the custodial parent, followed by two with the noncustodial parent. Joint physical custody arrangements, however, may prescribe much more frequent alternations between parental homes, (every 3½ days, for example).

Frequent alternation between parental homes distributes the time the child spends with each parent more evenly, and may preserve the psychological and social roles of both the mother and father. But critics of regular or frequent separations and reunions from primary care givers argue that the continuity of parent–child relationships and the attachment bond may be disrupted. Allegedly, children would have inadequate opportunities to develop psychological ties to parents (Goldstein, et al., 1973) or to "get to know" either parent very well (Alexander, 1977; Clarke-Stewart, 1977; Jenkins, 1977).

Empirical evidence that children form multiple attachments (Lamb, 1976a, 1976b, 1976c), attenuates some of these concerns. But whether alternations between primary care givers after divorce result in two insecure attachments, as opposed to one secure attachment, is still unclear.

Children in daycare experience frequent separations and reunions with primary care givers; thus, research on the effects of day care may be relevant to debates on the mechanics of alternations. Several studies (Belsky & Steinberg, 1978; Kagan, 1979; Cochran, 1977; Kagan et al., 1978; Kagan, 1979) found that daily separations and reunions with primary care givers did not have deleterious effects on children. There are qualitative differences, though, between the patterns of alternation associated with day care and with joint physical custody: day care, unlike joint custody, involves daily separations and reunions with both parents, and any extrapolations should be viewed cautiously (Rutter, 1979).

Methodologically adequate studies of parent–child attachments in families with frequent alternations in primary care givers have not yet been conducted. But descriptive, hypothesis-generating studies suggested that children remain attached and "strongly loyal" to both parents (Steinman, 1981), and that parent–child relationships improve after divorce (Leupnitz, 1982).

Alternations between homes may affect children independently of the continuity of parent–child attachments. Two studies found that 25 percent of children in joint-custody situations either express anxiety about switching homes (Steinman, 1981) or are upset for a time following a shift in residence (Irving et al., 1984). Whether children experience problems with frequent changes in residence may depend on the differences between home environments. Clingempeel and Reppucci (1982) speculated that alternations may be problematic if home environments differ in the following areas: child-rearing and disciplinary practices; daily household routines; peers and potential peers; and physical/economic characteristics.

Empirical studies have not yet examined the relation between the magnitude of such differences and the psychological adjustment of children. One descriptive study of joint custody (Leupnitz, 1982) found that differing sets of rules (i.e., differences in acceptable behavior) across parental homes did not pose problems for children. Apparently, children were able to recognize and adapt to the different expectations.

Interparental inconsistencies in disciplinary practices have been related to behavioral problems for children in two-parent households (Clarke-Stewart, 1977). In joint physical custody, however, where the child alternates between two single-parent households, *intra*parental consistency may be most salient. Unlike the situation in a two-parent household, interparental differences would be circumscribed both temporally and contextually.

Intraparental consistency from pre- to postdivorce may also mediate children's divorce adjustment. At least one study (Leupnitz, 1981) found that joint-custody parents were less likely than sole-custody parents to alter discipline styles following divorce. To the extent that alternations between homes preserves the disciplinary role of both parents, there is less need for one parent to compensate for the other. Future research should examine the relations between custody arrangements, inter- and intraparental consistency in disciplinary practices, and child outcomes.

Social System Level

Divorced families are not isolated from, but linked to and affected by, the larger social context. Both informal social networks (e.g., kin, friends) and formal social institutions (e.g., schools, mass media) may affect how custody arrangments influence children's adjustments.

Informal Social Networks.

The social networks of parents can influence, directly or indirectly, the adjustment of children to divorce. Indirectly, the availability of kin and friends as sources of support may prevent the development of psychopathology in parents (Chiriboga et al., 1979; Raschke, 1977; Spanier & Casto, 1979)—an adult outcome that has been related to social adjustment problems in children (Hetherington et al., 1979a; Wallerstein & Kelly, 1980). But the frequency of interactions with friends and kin that is best for parent adjustment is not necessarily best for child adjustment. Hetherington (1984) reported data suggesting that mothers who interacted frequently with network members and who exhibited "self-oriented" coping styles—meaning that they maintained an active social life and continued "full force" toward career goals—were themselves very well adjusted, but their children were often poorly adjusted. But mothers who sacrificed their own psychological well-being and who used "child-oriented" coping styles—meaning that they focused almost exclusively on being a good parent and interacted rarely with network members—also had children with serious adjustment problems. The coping styles of mothers that brought about the most positive child outcomes involved a balance between child-oriented and self-oriented activities. The relations between the level of parent involvement with network members and children's divorce adjustment seem, therefore, to be curvilinear, and not linear.

Custody arrangements (such as joint physical custody) that distribute parental child-care duties more evenly would give both parents time off from child rearing. Mothers as well as fathers would thus have more time for developing social relationships. Joint-custody parents could also schedule the majority of social activities at times when the child is in the physical custody of the other parent. The improved social life of the parent would not then have to come at the expense of the child.

Parental social networks may also benefit children directly. Cochran and

Brassard (1979) postulated that larger and more diverse social networks may enhance specific cognitive and social competencies of children. Custody arrangements that approximate joint physical custody may expose children more regularly to the social networks (kin and friends) of both parents. Consequently, children's skills in making friends and adjusting to novel situations may be fostered.

Peers are potential sources of support for children following divorce. Several studies, however, have found that divorce-related adjustment problems in children may lead to negative social behaviors and, consequently, a deterioration in peer relationships (e.g., Wallerstein & Kelly, 1980; Hetherington et al., 1979a). Although antisocial behaviors may decrease by one or two years after divorce, school peers may continue to perceive these children (particularly boys) negatively, and peer relationships thus may remain poor (Hetherington et al., 1979b). Custody arrangements may mediate the quality of the child's postdivorce peer relationships. Wallerstein and Kelly (1980) found that when postdivorce parent–child relationships were healthy and supportive, peer relationships were not as adversly affected by divorce. Custody arrangements, then, that result in more positive parent–child relationships may be beneficial to the child's peer relationships.

The attitude toward the divorce by members of the parents' social network may also influence the outcome of custody arrangements. At least one study (Kitson et al., 1982) found that kin were less likely to provide financial, moral, or service support to members of the divorced family if they disapproved of the divorce decision. In considering joint custody, Clingempeel and Reppucci (1982) speculated, "If significant relatives or friends of the father view his postdivorce obligations to his children entirely in terms of support payments and occasional visits, and/ or if the mother's kin or friends view her negatively for not wanting sole custody, then the likelihood of a successful joint custody arrangement is probably reduced" (p. 118).

Formal Social Institutions

Formal social institutions may mediate the effects of custody arrangments. The policies of schools and characteristics of teachers may be particularly important. A school environment with structured activities and regular schedules may provide a sense of stability and continuity for children experiencing unpredictable custody arrangements and family lives (Hetherington et al., 1978; Wallerstein & Kelly, 1980). Further, if custody arrangements involve alternations between parental homes, policies of schools regarding flexibility in transportation—for example, allowing different buses to be used when living with each parent—and the mailing of correspondences (Ahrons, 1981) may be important factors.

Warm and sensitive teachers who promote supportive classroom environments may help to alleviate divorce-related adjustment problems. The attitudes of teachers regarding family life may also be important. For example, teachers who advocate traditional sex-role distinctions vis-à-vis divorce—which have women getting custody, men giving child support—may exacerbate adjustment problems for children in joint custody families (Clingempeel & Reppucci, 1982).

The employment conditions and policies of work settings of biological parents also may alter the effects of postdivorce custody arrangements. Work schedules that are more flexible and allow time off for child care may increase the likelihood that variations of joint custody will be successful. Employment that permits parents to live for an extended time in the same community may increase potentially successful custody options, whereas work that requires frequent moves or extensive travel may create problems with custody arrangements that require regular alternations between parental homes. Futher, the availability of work-sponsored day care and split work shifts may increase the probability of both parents playing an active role in child rearing.

The mass-media portrayal of postdivorce custody arrangements may affect children. Radio and television shows, newspaper articles, children's books, and popular parents' books on "coping with divorce" often present images of the divorced family that may help or hinder the postdivorce adjustment of children. Certain stereotypes (e.g., the mother is always the superior parent) can create more problems for the joint- or father-custody family, while others (e.g., father-absent homes are deviant) may be more detrimental to divorced, mother-custody families. Media portrayals may affect the way that human service professionals (teachers, clergy, psychologists) and the lay public relate to divorced family members, and thus affect, both directly and indirectly, how divorced family members perceive themselves. In a survey of divorce-related attitudes of lawyers, clergy, and psychotherapists, Kressel and colleagues (1978) found that these professionals were often distrustful of a continuing relationship between divorced parents. Ahrons (1981) speculated that this distrust reflects "the prevailing stereotype that former spouses must, of necessity, be antagonists; otherwise why would they divorce?" (p. 426). A perpetuation of this stereotype by "experts" may discourage parental cooperation and reduce the likelihood of successful joint-custody arrangements.

REMARRIAGE, CUSTODY ARRANGEMENTS, AND CHILD OUTCOMES

The effects of custody arrangements on children and families may change over time and in concert with predictable changes in the family life cycle. One such change for the majority of divorced parents is remarriage. Yet studies of postdivorce custody arrangements have treated divorce as a terminal rather than transitional event (Furstenberg, 1979). Consequently, possible alterations in custody arrangements and their effects, when one or both biological parents remarry—the next stage in the life cyle for 80 percent of divorced persons—have been ignored.

In this section we discuss conceptual and empirical issues relevant to two research questions. First, what are the effects of remarriage of one or both biological parents on pre-remarriage custody arrangements (including quantity and quality of child contacts with the nonresidential biological parent, relationship between ex-spouses, and shifts in parent with custody)? Second, what are the effects of custody arrangements (or the child's relationship with the nonresidential parent) on the quality of relationships within the household of the remarried residential parent (e.g., the stepparent—stepchild relationship)? Custody arrangements function as the dependent variable in the first question and the independent variable in the second question.

Effects of Remarriage on Pre-remarriage Custody Arrangements

Remarriage of one or both parents may engender changes in child-care arrangements. Two longitudinal studies—a study of central Pennsylvania families (Furstenberg & Spanier, 1984a) and a National Survey of Children (Furstenberg et al., 1983)—have examined the effects of remarriage on the nonresidential parent–child relationship.

Furstenberg and Spanier (1984a) conducted structured interviews with 104 central Pennsylvania parents shortly after marital separation and 2½ years later, when 35 percent had remarried and 13 percent were cohabiting. Their findings suggested that remarriage decreased the frequency of visitation. Sixty-seven percent of nonresidential parents continued to see their children at least several times a month when neither parent remarried, but this dropped to 40 percent when one parent remarried and to 34 percent when both remarried. Remarriage of either parent was also associated with a diminution in the quality of the nonresidential parent–child relationship; but a greater decline occurred when the nonresidential parent entered a second conjugal union. Furstenberg and Spanier speculated that concomitant geographical moves and the diversion of energies from parenting to new relationships could account for the effects of remarriage.

Findings from the recently completed National Survey of Children (Furstenberg et al., 1983) suggest that remarriage has relatively little effect on the nonresidential parent–child relationship. Furstenberg and colleagues (1983) conducted a five-year longitudinal study with a nationally representative sample of 2279 children between seven and 11 years of age. In 1976 structured interviews were conducted with the child and one primary care giver (usually the mother). School information was obtained via questionnaires mailed to one of the child's teachers. Reinterviews were conducted five years later, when the children were between 12 and 16 years old, with three subsamples: (1) all children who had experienced a marital disruption since the earlier interview; (2) all children whose parents had previously reported a high-conflict marriage; and (3) a randomly selected subsample of children from stable marriages with low to medium conflict. The total reinterview sample consisted of 1377 children from 1047 families. Most reinterviews of parents and children were conducted by telephone. Teacher data were obtained for 83 percent of children reinterviewed.

Furstenberg and colleagues (1983) found that remarriage of either parent had virtually no effect on the degree to which the nonresidential parent participated in child rearing, or on the overall quality of the nonresidential parent–child relationship. Remarriage of the residential parent also had no effect on the frequency of visits by the nonresidential parent. Nonresidential parents who remarried, on the other hand, saw their children less frequently than nonresidential parents who remained single. Withdrawal from the child was most evident when the nonresidential parent remarried and the residential parent did not.

Remarriage of the residential parent was associated with less frequent visits from nonresidential parents in the Furstenberg and Spanier (1984a) but not in the Furstenberg and colleagues (1983) study. Collapse across subgroups in the more heterogeneous National Survey, sample may have obscured differential "effects" of the remarriage. In fact more fine-grained analyses of the Furstenberg and colleagues (1983) data suggested that remarriage sometimes resulted in more contact, sometimes in less contact, and sometimes had no effect on the frequency of nonresidential parent–child interactions. Future research should attempt to determine factors that best distinguish among these three types of "effects."

Remarriage changes a one-parent into a two-parent family, and this alteration may cause shifts in the custodial parent. In the central Pennsylvania study, Furstenberg and Spanier (1984a) found changes in custody disposition in approximately 20 percent of cases where one or both parents remarried. Most changes were from mother custody of all children to father custody of one or more children.

Virtually no studies have reported findings on the effects of remarriage after divorce on the relationship between ex-spouses. Remarriage of one parent might possibly trigger resentment in the nonremarried parent and exacerbate interparental conflict. The stepparent could also play a role in fueling hostilities between the formerly married couple. It is also possible, however, that remarriage would attenuate conflict. The new stepparent could serve as an intermediary and mediator on child-related issues and thereby have a positive effect on the relationship between ex-spouses.

Remarriage after divorce may also affect children's kinship systems, including relationships with grandparents. Theoretically remarriage increases the number of persons who could serve as social-emotional supports and sources of cognitive stimulation for children (Fast & Cain, 1966; Furstenberg, 1979). When divorced parents remarry, children may inherit an expanded social network consisting of four biological grandparents, four stepgrandparents, two stepparents, stepsiblings, and other consanguinal kin of stepparents. The expanded kin system following remarriage may have beneficial consequences for children. As noted earlier, a larger social network with a greater diversity of members (terms of personal characteristics and social roles) may operate both directly and indirectly to enhance specific cognitive and social competencies in children (Cochran & Brassard, 1979).

A greater number of potential kin does not mean that more kin are functional in the lives of children. Two questions are critical: (1) Do kin of the nonresidential parent, including nonresidential grandparents, maintain contact and play a role in the child's life after divorce and remarriage? (2) Do kin of the residential stepparent, including stepgrandparents, play an active role in the child's life? An overarching question is whether stepkin replace or augment the blood kin of the nonresidential biological parent.

Furstenberg and Spanier's (1984a) study addressed both questions. They obtained reports from residential parents on the frequency of contact between children and their residential grandparent (parents of the residential parent), and stepgrandparents (parents of the residential stepparent). They also obtained qualitative data from 25 intensive case studies of remarried couples. The children in this sample saw their residential grandparents much more frequently than their nonresidential grandparents; but nonresidential grandparents still maintained periodic contact with their grandchildren. At 2½ years after the marital separation, approximately 75 percent of the children saw their nonresidential grandparents at least a few times a year.

Children may actually have more frequent contact with nonresidental grandparents than these data suggest. Furstenberg and Spanier (1984) speculated that residential parents underestimate the amount of contact children have with blood kin of the nonresidential parent. Nonresidential parents may take children to see grandparents during the regular visits, and residential parents may not be aware of contacts between first and third generations. The frequency of contacts between adults and former parents-in-law thus may not always predict the frequency of contact between nonresidential grandparents and grandchildren.

Stepgrandparents can also become salient support systems and role models for children. Furstenberg and Spanier (1984a) found that children had almost as much contact with stepgrandparents as they did with biological grandparents on the side of the residential parent. But the frequency of children's interactions with stepgrandparents may not be a valid index of the quality of these relationships (Furstenberg & Spanier, 1984a). Encounters with stepgrandparents may be difficult or strained. Remarriage will thus give children a greater variety of grandparent figures at the expense of close emotional bonds. The conditions under which children develop close relationships with stepgrandparents (and other blood kin of the stepparent) and view them as relatives or nonrelatives is unclear and should be the target of future research.

Children may also have a fixed amount of time to spend with grandparents, so that more time with one set translates into less time with another (Furstenberg & Spanier, 1984a). Yet, Furstenberg and Spanier reported data that do not support this zero-sum principle of contacts with relatives. They found that the frequency of contact between biological kin and stepkin was positively rather than negatively correlated, suggesting that a rule of equity applies in which all grandparents are ensured access to grandchildren.

In summary, very few studies have examined the effects of remarriage on premarriage custody arrangements. Moreover, research has obtained few consistent findings. One exception is that negative effects of remarriage on the nonresidential parent–child relationship most often occur when the nonresidential parent remarries. Future studies should obtain and compare perceptions of several family members rather than relying on single informants (usually the residential parent). Particularly lacking are studies of nonresidential parent–child relationships that compare perceptions of both residential and nonresidential parents, and studies of grandparent–grandchild relationships that obtain the views of these generations (grandparents, parents, children). Future studies should also examine separately the effects of remarriage of each parent, residential and nonresidential, and examine the impact on other family relationships, including those between ex-spouses, residential parents and children, and siblings.

Effects of Custody Arrangements on Stepfamilies

The frequency of visits and the quality of the nonresidential parent–child relationship (the de facto custody arrangements) may mediate relationships within the stepfamily formed after the residential biological parent remarries. Empirical evidence and theoretical speculations suggest that both husband–wife and stepparent–stepchild relationships may be affected by the continuing involvement of the nonresidential biological parent in child care.

More frequent visits from nonresidential parents may necessitate more contact between ex-spouses, which may have deleterious effects on the quality of second marriages. Cherlin (1978) proposed that stepfamilies have a higher divorce rate than first-married families, because they are confronted with relationships with "quasi-kin" (a term coined by Bohannon, 1970, to refer to former spouses, husbands and wives of former spouses, and blood kin of former spouses) that are ambiguous and for which society offers no institutional guidelines. Further, more frequent visitation increases the likelihood that ex-spouses will interact and thereby encounter role strain in second marriages. Cherlin predicted that, if all else were equal, the greater the frequency of interaction between former spouses, the higher would be the probability of separation and divorce in the remarriage.

Three studies have reported findings relevant to Cherlin's prediction (Clingempeel, 1981; Clingempeel & Brand, 1985; Furstenberg et al., 1983). Clingempeel (1981) conducted a multimethod study of frequency of face-to-face contact with quasi-kin and marital quality in 40 stepfather families in Virginia. Instead of the linear and negatively correlated relationship predicted by Cherlin, Clingempeel found a curvilinear pattern. Persons in stepfather families who maintained moderate frequencies of contact with quasi-kin exhibited better marital quality than those who maintained either high or low frequencies of contact. Cingempeel and Brand (1985), however, replicated the study with a Pennsylvania sample of stepfather families, and found no connection between frequency of contact with quasi-kin and marital quality. Furthermore, data from the National Survey of Children (Furstenberg et al., 1983) revealed that relationships with the ex-spouse rarely caused problems in the second marriage. Findings from these studies suggest overall that frequent visitation need not have a negative effect on the quality of remarriages.

The child's relationship with the nonresidential biological parent may also mediate the quality of the stepparent–stepchild relationship. Frequent visits from the nonresidential parent can reduce children's fears that the stepparent is a parent replacement, and result in more positive stepparent–stepchild relationships and better outcomes for children. Frequent contacts with the nonresidential parent might also increase role ambiguities for the residential parent and stepparent (because of the increased probability of interactions between ex-spouses and between residential stepparent and nonresidential biological parent), prevent the development of a cohesive stepparent-stepchild relationship, and ultimately translate into negative consequences for children. A third possibility is that an active child-care role by the nonresidential parent can result in the stepparent developing more of an "adult friend" than "acquired parent" relationship with the stepchild.

Only two studies have examined the relations between frequency of child contact with the nonresidential parent and the quality of the stepparent–stepchild relationship (Clingempeel & Segal, 1986; Furstenberg et al., 1983). In a multimethod study of stepparent–stepchild relationships in stepmother and stepfather families, Clingempeel and Segal (1986) found that for girls in stepmother families more frequent visits with the nonresidential mother was associated with less positive stepmother–stepdaughter relationships. The connection between frequency of visits and quality of the stepparent–stepchild relationship was not apparent for boys in stepmother families or for children of both sexes in stepfather families.

Furstenberg and Seltzer (1983) reported findings from the National Survey of Children that corroborated the Clingempeel and Segal data. In stepfather families, he found that regular contact with nonresidential fathers did not adversely affect stepfather–stepchild relationships. In stepmother families, though, regular contact with nonresidential mothers was connected to lower quality relationships with stepmothers. Furstenberg did not report results separately for male and female stepchildren.

The greater interdependence (and negative correlations) between visitation patterns and quality of stepparent–stepchild relationships in stepmother families (particularly for girls) might may be due to the unique characteristics of this group. Sole custody of children is awarded to fathers in only 10 percent of divorces (Sanders & Spanier, 1979), and probably occurs most often in cases where the mother has especially difficult relationships with her children. Given cultural stereotypes, stepmothers may try even harder and earlier on than stepfathers to assume a parental role with stepchildren. They may try even harder with stepdaughters, whom they perceive as having more difficult relationships with biological mothers. The combination of premature attempts at parenting and frequent visits from biological mothers may maximize loyalty conflicts: stepchildren may fear that the stepmother is trying to replace the biological mother. The stepmother is viewed less positively to the extent there is competition between the two mother figures.

Visitation patterns may also mediate children's relationships with non-residential grandparents and other kin of the nonresidential parent. Non-residential parents may be instrumental in providing access to their kin. Anspach (1976) and Spicer and Hampe (1975) found that children's contact with kin of the noncustodial father was directly proportional to the frequency of his visits. Furstenberg and Spanier (1984a) found that the amount of contact children had with kin of noncustodial parents was related to both the amount of contact children had with the nonresidential parent and that between parents (former spouses). Grandparent–grandchild relationships continued after remarriage as long as parent–child relationships continued. Furstenberg and Spanier speculated that, for practical and emotional reasons, it can be difficult for extended kin of the nonresidential parent to continue contacts with children without the sponsorship of the nonresidental parent.

Nonresidential grandparents, however, may continue to see their grandchildren even when nonresidential parents no longer visit their children and play a mediating role. There is recent evidence that grandparents suffer from their children's divorce and from lessened contact with grandchildren (Kornhaber & Woodward, 1981). Concerns regarding the negative effects of divorce on grandparents are reflected in recent trends in family law that guarantee legal visitation rights for nonresidential grandparents (Furstenberg & Spanier, 1984b).

Anecdotal evidence from Furstenberg and Spanier's 25 case studies suggested that when nonresidential grandparents encourage their own children to maintain contacts with their grandchildren, they play an important role in preserving the bilaterality of the child's kinship network. Furstenberg and Spanier noted that the nonresidential grandparents' view regarding responsibility for conjugal dissolution might be a factor in determining the grandparents' role in the child's kinship system. Nonresidential grandparents are probably more likely to maintain contact with their grandchildren independently of their own child when they side with their son or daughter-in-law on marital dissolution issues.

CONCLUSIONS

We have argued that programmatic research on the effects of custody arrangements on children should focus on variables at three levels of analysis: ontogenic, divorced family, and social system. Studies have, for the most part, focused on "divorced family" and "ontogenic" variables, and ignored "social system" influences—especially the effects of formal institutions. Future studies should examine how the policies of schools, family courts, the mass media, and work settings mediate the effects of custody arrangements on children.

We have also argued that studies of postdivorce custody arrangements should examine what happens when one or both biological parents remarry. Two kinds of research questions should be addressed: First, what are the effects of remarriage on pre-remarriage custody arrangements? Second, what are the effects of custody arrangements on stepfamilies? The treatment of divorce as a transitional rather than terminal event is more than overdue.

REFERENCES

Abarbanel, A. (1979). Shared parenting after separation: A study of joint custody. *American Journal of Orthopsychiatry, 49,* 320–329.

Abel v. Hadder, 404 So. 2d 64 (Ala. App. 1981).

Ahrons, C. R. (1981). The continuing coparental relationship between divorced spouses. *American Journal of Orthopsychiatry, 51,* 415–428.

Albright v. Albright, 437 So. 2d 1003 (Miss. S. Ct. 1983).

Alexander, S. J. (1977). Protecting the child's rights in custody cases. *Family Coordinator, 26,* 377–385.

In re Allen, 24 Wash. App. 637, 626 P. 2d 16 (1981).

Anspach, D. F. (1976). Kinship and divorce. *Journal of Marriage and the Family, 38,* 323–330.

Bane, M. J. (1976). Marital disruption and the lives of children. *Journal of Social Issues, 32,* 103–117.

Beck v. Beck, 86 NJ 480, 432 A. 2d 63 (1981).

Belsky, J., & Steinberg, L. D. (1978). The effects of day care: A critical review. *Child Development, 49,* 929–949.

Bezio v. Patenaude, 410 N.E. 2d 1207 (Mass. 1980).

Bodenheimer, B. M. (1977). Progress under the Uniform Child Custody Jurisdiction Act and remaining problems: Punitive decrees, joint custody, and excessive modifications. *California Law Review, 65,* 978–1014.

Bohannon, P. (1970). The six stages of divorce. In P. Bohannon (Ed.), *Divorce and After* (pp. 33–62). Garden City, New York: Doubleday.

In re Boyer, 83 Ill. App. 3d 52, 403 N.E. 2d 796 (1980).

Brandwein, R. A., Brown, C. A., & Fox, E. M. (1974). Women and children last: The social situation of divorced mothers and their families. *Journal of Marriage and the Family, 36,* 498–514.

Bronfenbrenner, U. (1977). Toward an experimental ecology of human development. *American Psychologist, 32,* 513–531.

Bronfenbrenner, U. (1979). *The Ecology of Human Development: Experiments by Nature and Design.* Cambridge, Mass.: Harvard University Press.

Canacakos, E. (1981). Joint custody as a fundamental right. *Arizona Law Review, 23,* 785–800.

Cantor, D. W. (1977). School based groups for children of divorce. *Journal of Divorce, 1,* 183–187.

In re Carson, 382 N.E. 2d 1116, 1116 (Mass. App. Ct., 1978).

Carter v. Broderick, Ala. Sup. Ct. 5/14/82.

Cherlin, A. J. (1981). *Marriage, Divorce and Remarriage. Social Trends in the United States.* Cambridge, Mass.: Harvard University Press.

Chiriboga, D. A., Coho, A., Stein, J. A., & Roberts, J. (1979). Divorce, stress, and social supports: A study in help-seeking behavior. *Journal of Divorce, 3,* 121–136.

Clarke-Stewart, A. (1977). *Child Care in the Family.* New York: Academic Press.

Clingempeel, W. G. (1981). Quasi-kin relationships and marital quality in step-father families. *Journal of Personality and Social Psychology, 41,* 890–901.

Clingempeel, W. G., & Brand, E. (1985). Quasi-kin relationships, structural complexity and marital quality in stepfamilies: A replication, extension and clinical implications. *Family Relations, 34,* 401–409.

Clingempeel, W. G., & Reppucci, N. D. (1982). Joint custody after divorce: Major issues and goals for research. *Psychological Bulletin, 91,* 102–127.

Clingempeel, W. G., & Segal, S. (1986). Step-parent-stepchild relationships and the psychological adjustment of children in stepmother and stepfather families. *Child Development, 57,* 474–484.

Cochran, M. M. (1977). A comparison of group day care and family child-rearing patterns in Sweden. *Child Development, 48,* 702–707.

Cochran, M. M., & Brassard, J. A. (1979). Child development and personal social networks. *Child Development, 50,* 601–616.

Colletta, N. D. (1979). The impact of divorce: Father absence or poverty? *Journal of Divorce, 3,* 27–36.

Colletta, N. D. (1983). Stressful lives: The situation of divorced mothers and their children. *Journal of Divorce, 6,* 19–31.

Complainant v. Defendant, 10 Fam. L. Rep. (BNA) 1097 (Va. Cir. Ct. 1983).

Cox v. Young 405 S.W. 2d 430 (Tex. Civ. App. 11th District, 1966).

In re Custody of Yuhas, 87 Ill. App. 3d 521, 409 N.E. 2d 148 (1980).

Daniel v. Daniel, 239 Ga. 466, 238 So. 2d 108 (1977).

Desimone-Luis J., O'Mahoney, K., & Hunt, D. (1979). Children of separation and divorce: Factors influencing adjustment. *Journal of Divorce, 3,* 37–42.

DiStefano v. DiStefano, 60 A.D. 2d 976, 401 N.Y.S. 2d 636 (1978).

Duke, M. D., & Lancaster, W. A. (1976). A note on locus on control as a function of father absence. *Journal of Genetic psychology, 129,* 335–336.

Edel v. Edel, 97 Mich. App. 266, 293 N.W. 2d 792 (1980).

Emery, R. E. (1982). Interparental conflict and the children of discord and divorce. *Psychological Bulletin, 92,* 310–330.

Espenshade, T. J. (1979). The economic consequences of divorce. *Journal of Marriage and the Family, 41,* 615–625.

Fast, I. & Cain, A. (1966). The stepparent role: Potential for disturbances in family functioning. *American Journal of Orthopsychiatry, 36,* 485–496.

Farmer v. Famer, 439 N.Y.S. 2d 584 (Sup. Ct. 1981).

Fine, M. A., Moreland, J. R., & Schwebel, A. I. (1983). Long-term effects of

178   *Effects of Custody Arrangements on Children*

divorce on parent-child relationships. *Developmental Psychology, 19,* 705–713.

Finlay v. Finlay, 148 N.E. at 626 (1925).

Furstenberg, F. F. (1979). Recycling the family: Perspectives for researching a neglected family form. *Marriage and Family Review, 2,* 1–22.

Furstenberg, F. F. (1981). Remarriage and intergenerational relations. In R. W. Fogel, E. Hatfield, S. B. Kiesler, & T. Shanus (Eds.), *Aging: Stability and Change in the Family* (pp. 115–142). New York: Academic Press.

Furstenberg, F. F., Jr., Nord, C. W., Peterson, J. L., & Zill, N. (1983). The life course of children of divorce: Marital disruption and parental contact. *American Sociological Review, 48,* 656–668.

Furstenberg, F. F., & Seltzer, J. A. (1983). *Divorce and child development.* Paper presented at a Meeting of the Orthopsychiatric Association, Boston, Mass.

Furstenberg, F. F., & Spanier, G. B. (1984a). Remarriage and reconstituted families. In M. B. Sussman & S. K. Steinmetz (Eds.), *Handbook of Marriage and the Family* (pp. 149–162). New York: Plenum.

Furstenberg, F. F. & Spanier, G. B. (1984b). *Recycling the Family: Remarriage after Divorce.* Beverly Hills: Sage.

Glasser, P., & Navarre, E. (1965). Structural problems of the one-parent family. *Journal of Social Issues, 21,* 98–109.

Glick, P. C. (1980). Remarriage: Some recent changes and variations. *Journal of Family Issues, 1,* 455–478.

Goldstein, J., Freud, A., & Solnit, A. (1973). *Beyond the Best Interests of the Child.* New York: Free Press.

Goode, W. J. (1956). *After Divorce.* Glencove, IL: Free Press.

Gorman v. Gorman, 400 So. 2d 75 (Fla. Dist. Ct. App. 1981).

Gottsfield, R. L. (1984). Private lives, public issues. *Family Advocate, 6,* (4), 36–38.

Gouge, M. (1980). Joint custody: A revolution in child custody law? *Washburn Law Journal, 20,* 326–343.

Grubbs v. Grubbs, 5 Kans. App. 2d 694, 623 P. 2d 5464 (1981).

Hall v. Hall, 95 Mich. App. 614, 291 N.W. 2d 143 (1980).

Haralambie, A. M. (1983). *Handling Child Custody Cases.* Colorado Springs, Colo.: Shepard's/McGraw-Hill Book Company.

Hess, R. D., & Camara, K. A. (1979). Post-divorce relationships as mediating factors in the consequences of divorce for children. *Journal of Social Issues, 35,* 79–96.

Hetherington, E. M. (1979). Divorce: A child's perspective. *American Psychologist, 34,* 851–858.

Hetherington, E. M. (1981). Children and divorce. In R. Henderson (Ed.), *Parent-child Interaction: Theory, Research, and Prospects* (pp. 33–58). New York: Academic Press.

Hetherington, E. M. (1984). Presentation at May 25–28 meeting of the Remarriage and Stepparenting Work Study Group, Lexington, Ky.

Hetherington, E. M., Cox, M., & Cox, R. (1978). The aftermath of divorce. In J. H. Stevens, Jr., & Mathews (Eds.), *Mother-child, father-child relations* (pp. 149–176). Washington, D.C.: National Association for the Education of Young Children.

Hetherington, E. M., Cox, M., & Cox, R. (1979a). Family interaction and the social, emotional, and cognitive development of children following divorce. In V. C. Vaughn & T. B. Brazelton (Eds.), *The family: Setting priorities* (pp. 71–87). New York: Science & Medicine Publishers.

Hetherington, E. M., Cox, M., & Cox, R. (1979b). Play and social interaction in children following divorce. *Journal of Social Issues, 35,* 26–49.

Hutterli, C. G. (1982). *Grubs v. Ross:* Oregon's new approach to child custody forum determination. *Willamette Law Review, 18,* 519–533.

Ilfeld, F. W., Jr., Ilfeld, H. Z., & Alexander, J. D. (1982). Does joint custody work? A first look at outcome data of relitigation. *American Journal of Psychiatry, 139,* 62–66.

Irving, H. H., Benjamin, M., & Trocme, N. (1984). Shared parenting: An empirical analysis utilizing a large Canadian data base. In J. Folberg (Ed.), *Joint Custody and Shared Parenting: A Handbook for Judges, Lawyers, Counselors, and Parents* (pp. 128–135). Portland, Oreg.: Association of Family and Conciliation Courts.

Jacobson, D. S. (1978). The impact of marital separation/divorce: II. Interparent hostility and child adjustment. *Journal of Divorce, 2,* 3–19.

Jarrett v. Jarrett, 78 Ill. 2d 337, 36 Ill. Dec. 1, 400 N.E. 2d 421 (1979), rehearing denied, 100 S. Ct. 797 (1980), cert. denied, 499 U.S. 927 (1981).

Jenkins, R. L. (1977). Maxims in child custody cases. *Family Coordinator, 26,* 385–390.

Jenkins v. Jenkins, 376 So. 29, 1099 (Ala. Ct. App. 1979).

Kagan, I. (1979). Family experience and the child's development. *American Psychologist, 34,* 886–891.

Kagan, J., Kearsley, R. B., & Zelazo, P. R. (1978). *Infancy: Its Place in Human Development.* Cambridge, Mass.: Harvard University Press.

Kallas v. Kallas, 614 P. 2d 641 (Utah 1980).

K. B. v. S. B., 415 N.E. 2d 749 (Ind. App. 1981).

Kilgore v. Kilgore, 54 Ala. App. 336 (1976).

Kitson, G. C., Moir, R. N., & Mason, P. R. (1982). Family social support in crises: The special case of divorce. *American Journal of Orthopsychiatry, 52,* 161–165.

Kornhaber, A. & Woodward, K. L. (1981). *Grandparents-grandchildren: The Vital Connection.* Garden City, New York: Anchor Press, Doubleday.

Kressel, K., Lopez-Morillas M., Weinglass, J. & Deutsch, M. (1978). Professional intervention in divorce: A summary of the views of lawyers, psychotherapists, and clergy. *Journal of Divorce, 2,* 119–155.

Kriesberg, L. (1970). *Mothers in Poverty: A Study of Fatherless Families.* Chicago: Aldine.

Kulka, R. A., & Weingarten, H. (1979). The long term effects of parental divorce in childhood on adult adjustment. *Journal of Social Issues, 35,* 50–78.

Kurdek, L. A. (1981). An integrative perspective on children's divorce adjustment. *American Psychologist, 36,* 856–866.

Kurdek, L. A., & Blisk, D. (1983). Dimensions and correlates of mothers' divorce experiences. *Journal of Divorce, 6,* 1–19.

Kurdek, L. A., Blisk, D., & Siesky, A. E. (1981). Correlates of children's long-term adjustment to their parents divorce. *Developmental Psychology, 17,* 565–579.

Lamb, M. E. (1977). A reexamination of the infant social world. *Human Development, 20,* 65–85.

Lamb, M. E. (1976a). Effects of stress and cohort on mother- and father-infant interaction. *Developmental Psychology, 12,* 435–443.

Lamb, M. E. (1976b). Interactions between eight-month-old children and their fathers and mothers. In M. E. Lamb (Ed.), *The Role of the Father in Child Development* (pp. 307–327). New York: Wiley.

Lamb, M. E. (1976c). Twelve-month-olds and their parents: Interaction in the laboratory playroom. *Developmental Psychology, 12,* 237–244.

Lapp v. Lapp, 336 N.W. 2d 350 (N.D. 1983).

Leroy v. Odgers, 18 Ariz. App. 499, 503 P. 2d 975 (1972).

Leupnitz, D. A. (1982). *Child Custody.* Lexington, Mass.: Lexington Books, D. C. Heath & Co.

Lumbra v. Lumbra, 136 Vt. 529, 394 A. 2d 1139 (1978).

Maddox B. (1975). *The Half Parent.* New York: M. Evans.

Marsden, D. (1969). *Mothers Alone: Poverty and the Fatherless Family.* London: Allen Lane, Penguin Press.

Mastropole v. Mastropole, 181 N.J. Super. 128, 436 A. 2d 955 (App. Div. 1981).

McCord, J., McCord, W., & Thurber, E. (1962). Some effects of paternal absense on male children. *Journal of Abnormal and Social Psychology, 64,* 361–369.

Meyer, B. S., & Schlissel, S. W. (1983). Child custody following divorce—How grasp the nettle? Part II–III. *New York State Bar Journal, 55,* (1, 2), 32–41 and 36–40.

Mills, B. G., & Belzer, S. P. (1982). Joint custody as a parenting alternative. *Pepperdine Law Review, 9,* 853–875.

M.J.P. v. J.G.P., 640 P. 2d 966 (Okla. 1982).

M.P. v. S.P., 169 N.J. Super. 425, 404 A. 2d 1256 (1979).

Nye, I. F. (1957). Child adjustment in broken and unhappy, unbroken homes. *Marriage and Family Living, 19,* 356–361.

Palmore v. Sidoti, 426 So. 2d 34, rev'd 104 S. Ct. 1879 (1984).

Pearlin, L. I., & Johnson, J. S. (1977). Marital status, life strains, and depression. *American Sociological Review, 42,* 704–715.

Phear, W. P. C., Beck, J. C., Hauser, B. B., Clarke, S. C., & Whitney, R. A. (1984). An empirical study of custody agreements: Joint versus sole legal custody. In J. Folberg (Ed.), *Joint Custody and Shared Parenting: A Handbook for Judges, Lawyers, Counselors, and Parents* (pp. 142–156). Association of Family and Conciliation Courts. Portland, Oreg.

Raschke, H. J. (1977). The role of social participation in postseparation and postdivorce adjustment. *Journal of Divorce, 2,* 129–140.

Remarriage of parent as ground for modification of divorce decree as to custody of child (1980). American Law Reports Annotated Second Series Later Case Service Supplementary (40-43 Alr 2d). Rochester, N.Y.: Lawyers Co-operative Publishing.

In re Robert J., 113 R. I. 710, 326 A. 2d 16 (1974).

Robinson, H. L. (1982–83). Joint custody: An idea whose time has come. *Journal of Family Law, 21,* 641–685.

Roman, M., & Haddad, W. (1978). *The Disposable Parent.* New York: Holt, Rinehart & Winston.

Rotter, J. (1966). Generalized expectencies for internal versus external control of reinforcement. *Psychological Monographs, 80,* (1, Whole No. 609).

Rupp v. Rupp, 268, Pa. Super. 467, 408 A. 2d 883 (1979).

Rusin v. Rusin, 103 Misc. 2d 534, 426 N.Y.S. 2d 701 (1980).

Rutter, M. (1979). Protective factors in children's responses to stress and disadvantage. In M. W. Kent & J. E. Rolf (Eds.), *Primary Prevention of Psycho-*

pathology: Vol. III Promoting Social Competence and Coping in Children (pp. 49–74). Hanover, N.H.: University Press of New England.

Sanders, R. & Spanier, G. B. (1979). Divorce, child custody and child support. Current Populations Report U.S. Bureau of the Census. Series P. 23. No. 84.

Santrock, J. W., & Warshak, R. A. (1979). Father custody and social development in boys and girls. *Journal of Social Issues, 35,* 112–125.

Schulmann, J., & Pitt, V. (1982). Second thoughts on joint child custody: Analysis of legislation and its implications for women and children. *Golden Gate Law Review, 12,* 538–559.

Spanier, G. B., & Casto, R. F. (1979). Adjustment to separation and divorce: An analysis of 50 case studies. *Journal of Divorce, 2,* 241–253.

Spicer, J. W., & Hampe, G. D. (1975). Kinship interaction after divorce. *Journal of Marriage and the Family, 37,* 113–119.

Staley D. v. Deborah D., 10 Fam. L. Rep. (BNA) 1070 (N.H. Sup. Ct. 1983).

Steinman, S. (1983). Joint custody: What we know, what we have yet to learn, and the judical and legislative implications. *University of California at Davis Law Review, 16,* 739–762.

Steinman, S. (1981). The experience of children in a joint-custody arrangement: A report of a study. *American Journal of Orthopsychiatry, 51,* 403–414.

Stolberg, A. L. (1980). Environmental change and psychopathology in children of divorce. Paper presented at the meeting of the Southeastern Conference on Human Development, Alexandria, Va.

In re Marriage of Thompson, 96 Ill. 2d 67, 449 N.E. 2d 88 (1983).

Tooley, K. (1976). Antisocial behavior and social alienation post divorce: The "man of the house" and his mother. *American Journal of Orthopsychiatry, 46,* 33–41.

Tuter v. Tuter, 120 S. W. 2d 203, 205 (Mo. Ct. App. 1938).

Utley v. Utley, 3 F.L.R. 2047 (DC Ct. App. 1976).

Wallerstein, J. S., & Kelly, J. B. (1974). The effects of parental divorce: The adolescent experience. In J. Anthony & C. Koupernik (Eds.), *The Child and His Family: Vol. III Children at Psychiatric Risk* (pp. 479–505). New York: Wiley.

Wallerstein, J. S., & Kelly, J. B. (1975). The effects of parental divorce: Experiences of the pre-school child. *Journal of the American Academy of Child Psychiatry, 14,* 600–616.

Wallerstein, J. S., & Kelly, J. B. (1976). The effects of parental divorce: Experience of the child in later latency. *American Journal of Orthopsychiatry, 46,* 256–269.

Wallerstein, J. S., & Kelly, J. B. (1980). *Surviving the Breakup: How Children and Parents Cope with Divorce.* New York: Basic Books.

Weed, J. A. (1980). *National Estimates of Marriage Dissolution and Survivorship: United States.* Vital & Health Statistics, Series 3, Analytical Studies, No. 19. DHHS Publication No. (PHS) 81-1403, Hyattsville, Md.: National Center for Health Statistics, USDHHJ.

Wiggins v. Wiggins, 411 So. 2d 263 (Fla. Dist. Ct. App. 1982).

Winston, M. P., & Forsher, T. (1971). *Nonsupport of Legitimate Children by Affluent Fathers as a Cause of Poverty and Welfare Dependence.* New York: Rand Corp.

PART III
PERSONAL/DEVELOPMENTAL
FACTORS

6

Differences in Children's Divorce Adjustment Across Grade Level and Gender: A Report from the NASP-Kent State Nationwide Project

JOHN GUIDUBALDI

Family disruption and consequent single-parent child rearing are now widely recognized as two of the nation's primary mental health problems. Census data, such as those described by Glick in this volume, have alerted both mental and health professionals and the public to the rapid deterioration of family stability and of traditional family socialization practices. Mental health practitioners have also been sensitized to these problems through first-hand experiences in both schools and clinics, where maladaptive child behaviors appear disproportionately among children from divorced-family households. As one illustration, school psychologists routinely observe a very high incidence of the single-parent condition in special class populations, grade retentions, and referrals from teachers.

Unfortunately, practitioners have been compelled to deal with these problems without the prerequisite empirical understanding of the sequelae of divorce or the personal and ecological factors that moderate its impact

Special gratitude is extended to 144 members of the National Association of School Psychologists who provided the extensive data base for this project, and to graduate assistants and secretary, Jeanine Lightel, Bonnie Nastasi, and Bonnie Heaton. Portions of this chapter have been excerpted with permission from a previously published chapter in: B. Lahey & A. E. Kazdin (1984), *Advances in Clinical Child Psychology* (Vol. 7). New York: Plenum Press.

on children. Only in the past decade have researchers begun to generate data-based understandings of divorce adjustment; most early studies, moreover, have serious methodological weaknesses. Thus many questions that have relevance for psychologists, counselors, teachers, and parents remain unanswered. Are there reliable differences between the academic and social competencies of divorced and intact-family children? If differences are evident, do they occur nationwide, or are they restricted to regional subgroups? Do such differences occur for only a brief time following divorce, or do they persist for several years? Does the frequently observed decline in postdivorce household income sufficiently explain intact- versus divorced-group differences? Within the divorced-family population, are there sex or age-sex group variations in adjustment?

This chapter addresses such questions using age-sex group analyses to extend previously reported results from a large nationwide sample (Guidubaldi, 1983; Guidubaldi & Cleminshaw, 1985; Guidubaldi, Cleminshaw, & Perry, 1985; Guidubaldi et al., 1983; Guidubaldi et al., 1984; Guidubaldi & Perry, 1985; Guidubaldi & Perry, 1984; Guidubaldi et al. 1984a,b).

PREVIOUS RESEARCH FINDINGS

In an *Advances in Clinical Child Psychology* review article a few years ago, Atkeson and colleagues (1982) noted that their chapter entitled "The Effects of Divorce on Children" might be considered premature, given the limited set of research studies available. They appropriately suggest, though, that critical examination of existing studies will correct the misguided assumption that prevailing conclusions are well-supported by research. That review, as well as others (Clingempeel & Reppucci, 1982; Emery, 1982; Hetherington, 1979b; Kurdek, 1981, 1983; Levitin, 1979; Shinn, 1978), conclude that existing studies are flawed by limited data-gathering procedures, biased sample selection, inadequate or nonexistent controls, and other serious methodological weaknesses. Considering the breakdown of family stability and the historical importance of the nuclear family structure in the socialization of children, it is surprising that so little has been done to provide a strong empirical understanding of the impact of divorce on children.

Two major longitudinal studies are typically cited as having contributed the most to our understanding of children's adjustment to divorce (Hetherington et al., 1978, 1979a, 1979b, 1982; Kelly & Wallerstein, 1976;

Wallerstein & Kelly, 1974, 1975, 1976, 1980a, 1980b). More recently, an additional series of multidimensional longitudinal research findings has been reported (Kurdek & Berg, 1983; Kurdek et al., 1981; Kurdek & Siesky, 1980a, 1980b). The impressive consensus of these studies is that divorce results in negative stresses for both children and parents. This chapter will focus specifically on children's adjustment to divorce rather than to father absence or single-parent status, as the latter two can be caused by such other factors as unmarried mothers, death of a parent, or separation (see Biller, 1976; and Lamb, 1981, 1982 for reviews of father-absence literature).

The often-cited longitudinal work of Wallerstein and Kelly (1974, 1975, 1976, 1980a, 1980b) suggests that children of divorce adjust and respond differentially by age level. Their basic initial findings (1974, 1975, 1976) were as follows: (1) young preschoolers (2½ to 3¼ years) showed regressive behaviors; (2) middle preschoolers (3¾ to 4¾ years) displayed irritability, aggressive behavior, self-blame and bewilderment; (3) oldest preschoolers (five to six years) showed increased anxiety and aggressive behavior; (4) younger latency-aged children (seven to eight years) responded with sadness, grieving, fear, fantasies of responsibility and reconciliation, anger toward and loyalty to both parents; (5) older latency-aged children (nine to ten years) betrayed feelings of loss, rejection, helplessness, loneliness, shame, anger, and loyalty conflicts; and (6) adolescents (11 years and over) exhibited sadness, shame, embarrassment, anxiety about future and marriage, worry, individuation from parents, and withdrawal.

A followup study on the preschoolers by Wallerstein and Kelly (1975) found that much of this negative behavior ended a year later for children who experienced stable care giver environments. Yet 44 percent of the children in his age group experienced a deteriorated psychological condition at follow-up. Girls, in particular, were vulnerable to depressive reactions and developmental delays. While intensive feelings had abated for younger latency-aged children by one year after divorce, 23 percent of this group were evaluated as experiencing a deteriorated psychological condition (Wallerstein & Kelly, 1976). By comparison, 50 percent of older latency-aged children at one-year follow-up appeared to have achieved equilibrium in their lives and accepted the divorce with some sense of finality; 50 percent, however, still displayed troublesome, depressive behavior patterns. In contrast Wallerstein and Kelly (1974) report that at one-year follow-up adolescents were able to avoid loyalty conflicts, often by distancing themselves from both parents.

Perhaps the most interesting results are presented in the five-year follow-up study (Wallerstein and Kelly, 1980b). The following seven variables were identified as having a positive effect on children's adjustment to divorce: (1) parental ability to resolve postdivorce conflict and anger; (2) ability of the custodial parent successfully to resume the parenting role; (3) ability of the noncustodial parent to keep a mutually satisfying relationship with the child; (4) personality characteristics of the child and the ability to develop coping skills; (5) ability of the child to find and use support systems; (6) diminished depressive or angry responses by the child; and (7) age and sex of the child. Wallerstein and Kelly further report that boys from divorced families appear, more than girls, to need a positive relationship with their fathers.

In an attempt to compensate for the methodological problems in the Wallerstein and Kelly research (1974, 1975, 1976), Hetherington and colleagues (1978) employed a more comprehensive, multivariate two-year study on the impact of divorce on children. The results illustrate the severe stress and disorganization experienced by families in the first year after divorce (Hetherington et al., 1978, 1979a, 1979b, 1982). Divorced parents made fewer maturity demands on their children and illustrated less consistency in disciplining, and in reasoning and communicating with, their children. Children from these divorced families displayed higher levels of dependent, disobedient, aggressive, demanding, unaffectionate, and whining behaviors, compared with children from intact families. Mother–son interactions were especially affected by a decline in the mother's parenting skills.

More recently Kurdek and associates conducted ongoing studies of 70 children from divorced homes, emphasizing the importance of children's social and cognitive skills tht moderate divorce adjustment (Kurdek & Berg, 1983; Kurdek et al., 1981; Kurdek & Siesky, 1980a, 1980b). As noted in Lawrence Kurdek's chapter, these studies have consistently indicated that younger children experience greater divorce-related problems than do older children.

Other recent studies with a more restricted scope have produced additional data about parent–child relationships and family conditions that influence the impact of divorce on children. Children's divorce adjustment has been found to be facilitated by the following: an authoritative management style of the custodial parent (Santrock & Warshak, 1979); residing with a custodial parent of the same sex (Warshak & Santrock, 1983); the availability of the noncustodial parent, and positive relations between parents (Hess & Camara, 1979; Rosen, 1977); parent–child discussions of divorce-related topics (Jacobson, 1978a, 1978b); low interparental hostility prior to separation (Berg & Kelly, 1979; Jacobson, 1978a, 1978b, 1978c); and more time with father after separation (Jacobson, 1978a, 1978c). These studies have also provided general corroborative findings that divorce presents significant stressors for children and their parents.

It should be noted that several studies have produced contradictory results that further complicate the issues. Whereas the above studies report a negative impact, others report no detrimental—or even positive—effects of divorce on children's adjustment (Bernard & Nesbitt, 1981; Colletta, 1979; Kurdek & Siesky, 1980b; Reinhard, 1977; Rosen, 1977). These conflicting findings may be due to the limited scope of criterion measures employed in those studies, which included only child questionnaire and interview data. Further, these studies did not include a control group of intact-family children in order to investigate the effects of divorce more directly. Kurdek and colleagues (1981) found discrepancies between the reports of children's divorce-related adjustment by custodial parents and by children. A caution concerning the use of children's self-report data was recorded by Warshak and Santrock (1983): "Can the failure to report negative perceptions be the result of defensive responding?" (p. 32).

LIMITATIONS OF PREVIOUS RESEARCH

The principal methodological limitation of these major studies, and other related studies, is *restricted sampling*. Sample selections have been small, based on ambiguous criteria, and limited to specific settings or geographic areas rather than the general population. Samples have been described, for instance, as: 96 families from a white, middle-class preschool center in Virginia (Hetherington et al., 1978, 1979a, 1979b, 1982); 30 families from a mental health center in Los Angeles (Jacobson, 1978a, 1978b, 1978c); 74 families from a Dayton, Ohio, chapter of Parents Without Partners (Kurdek et al., 1981); and 60 families from Marin County in California (Wallerstein & Kelly, 1975, 1976, 1980a). Samples almost exclusively represent white, middle- and upperclass families with the mother having child custody. These studies have also employed samples described as nonclinical, although selection often involved volunteers from clinics or agencies. Other studies include only clinical populations (e.g., Kalter, 1977; McDermott, 1970; Westman, 1972). Emery (1982) has suggested that unknown mediating variables may account for children's divorce-related problems in clinic samples. In general there is a lack of control groups; and the one employed by Hetherington and colleagues (1978, 1979a, 1979b, 1982) was matched to a possibly biased divorced group sample. Considering such sampling limitations, results of previous studies cannot be generalized to the total population of divorced families. More important, the many potential environmental variables that may be critical for an understanding of divorce are not adequately controlled: the middle-class samples of previous research tend to be relatively homogeneous with regard to community social support systems, school environments, ethnic background, socioeconomic status, and culture, and other factors that may modify the effects of divorce.

The few large-scale studies also have serious limitations. The study of 18,000 students from 14 states conducted jointly by the National Association of Elementary and Secondary Principals and the Kettering Foundation (Brown, 1980; Lazarus, 1980; Zakariya, 1982) indicated impaired school performance by children from one-parent, as compared with two-parent, families. This study used such global school criteria as grade point average, attendance, suspensions, truancy, and referral for discipline problems, rather than more specific measures of academic or social competencies. A further limitation was that one-parent families were defined as resulting from multiple factors, and two-parent families included remarried family units. Similarly, data based on 7119 children included in a Health Examination Survey 1963–1965 indicate that father-absent children have lower Wechsler Intelligence Scale for Children (WISC) scores and poorer Wide Range Achievement Test (WRAT) performance than father-present children, when socioeconomic status (SES) and divorce were not controlled (Svanum et al., 1982). Socioeconomic measures were found to be important intervening variables in both studies; but they either were based on data from the 1960s (Svanum et al., 1982), or defined as children's participation in supported lunch programs (Brown, 1980). These studies were therefore poorly controlled, and cannot be considered an assessment of children's specific adjustment to divorce.

A second major limitation of previous research is the lack of psychometrically adequate indices of school-aged children's cognitive and social competencies. In studying preschool children, Hetherington and colleagues (1982) used multiple evaluative procedures (observations, ratings, and psychometric assessments) and multigroup input (child, parent, and teacher). But the divorce adjustment of school-aged children has been evaluated through clinical impressions, interview and rating data which generally lack standardization, established reliability, and validity (Jacobson, 1978a, 1978b, 1978c; Kelly & Wallerstein, 1976; Kurdek & Berg, 1983; Kurdek et al., 1981; Kurdek & Siesky, 1980a, 1980b; Wallerstein & Kelly, 1980b). Achenbach (1978) criticized existing clinical assessments, indicating that there is currently no adequate classification system for children's mental disorders. Kurdek (1983) further emphasized that the clinical interview may not be sensitive to developmental levels of children, since it is typically employed to elicit criteria for disorders.

Closely related is the scarcity of data on how the school climate moderates the adverse effects of divorce. Hetherington (1979a) notes that "the role of extrafamilial supports, peers, schools, neighborhoods, the church, and social groups such as clubs or athletic groups has barely been touched on." School-based support for children of divorce is clearly a priority intervention, yet we currently lack a detailed understanding of school-related criteria and the school environments that promote positive adjustment.

A further methodological problem is the failure of many studies to control simultaneously for SES, age, and sex (McDermott, 1968; Morrison, 1974; Sugar, 1970; Tucker & Regan, 1966; Westman et al., 1970). Adding to the difficulties of interpretation, inconsistent findings have been reported concerning age and sex differences. Kurdek and colleagues (1981) and Reinhard (1977), for example, have not found sex differences, while other studies found that boys from divorced homes experience greater difficulty both socially and cognitively (Hetherington et al., 1982; Kurdek & Berg, 1983; Wallerstein & Kelly, 1980a, 1980b).

Two more sources of confusion are age at time of divorce and length of time expired since divorce. Wallerstein and Kelly (1980b) suggest that divorce is related to negative adjustment at all age levels studied, though the manifested behaviors differ depending on age at the time of the divorce, and reactions are most acute at the youngest ages. Reinhard (1977), on the other hand, indicates that 12- to 18-year-olds do not demonstrate divorce-related maladjustment, and Kurdek and colleagues (1981) conclude that older children are relatively better adjusted than younger children. But the interaction of time elapsed since divorce and age at time of divorce was not controlled in any of these studies. In reference to the former, Hetherington and colleagues (1982) conclude that adjustment is a function of both sex and duration of time since divorce. Girls make earlier adjustments, and the negative effects for boys are "more pervasive and long lasting" (p. 261). Yet Wallerstein and Kelly (1975) contend, on the basis of a small sample of preschoolers, that girls display more adverse effects than boys at a one-year follow-up evaluation.

Unfortunately the major studies have also failed to determine whether children's postdivorce adjustment is merely a reaction to decreased family income. Several studies have indicated that declining SES accounts for the deleterious impact of single-parent status resulting from a divorce (Colletta, 1979; Svanum et al., 1982).

To provide more definitive conclusions about the impact of divorce on children, and to unravel the complex effects of such potential mediating factors as social class, sex, age, and family support systems, methodological refinements are clearly needed. The current study employed improved sampling techniques, a nationwide sample, a carefully selected control group, and multifactored assessments conducted by highly trained evaluators, in an attempt to provide a more comprehensive understanding of this critical mental health issue. Additionally, a two-year follow-up study was conducted on a subset of this sample to examine long-term effects.

INVOLVEMENT OF THE NATIONAL ASSOCIATION OF SCHOOL PSYCHOLOGISTS

The author designed and initiated the following study during his term as president of the National Association of School Psychologists (NASP). Initial reports of the major findings of the study have appeared in NASP publications (Guidubaldi, 1983; Guidubaldi et al., 1983). Many of the 8000 NASP members had been previously sensitized to the importance of this research issue because their caseloads included increasingly large numbers of divorced-family children. Like clinical child psychologists, this group of professionals was acutely aware that little conclusive research evidence existed to facilitate effective interventions for these children. Yet school psychologists were in optimal situations to perform such research on a nationwide basis. Relative to other professionals in education, they had unique assessment skills, better understanding of child development principles, and access to home environments. And relative to other psychologists, they had an understanding of school environments, greater support from school administrators, established relationships with teachers, and increased access to samples of normal children. Their employment in schools further provided the opportunity to implement data-based interventions in both home and school environments.

METHODS

Sample Selection

In an attempt to develop a geographically stratified sample of evaluators, NASP members were randomly selected from the association's membership roster by state in proportion to state population. Of approximately 1500 selected, 144 psychologists from 38 states agreed to participate in the study. Each of these evaluators randomly selected an elementary school within the respective school district, and then randomly selected a total of six children from grade lists—two first-graders, two third-graders, and two fifth-graders. One child from each grade level represented an intact-family situation (both biological parents present since birth of the child), and the other a currently divorced single-parent family. Some psychologists were unable to provide data on all subjects by the deadline for the study. Consequently a total of 699 children were involved in the study. The geographic distribution of the Time-1 sample is described in Table 6.1. Although close correspondence to census figures was not achieved in every region, this sample is clearly nationwide in scope, and matched within eight percentage points in seven of the nine regions. Demographic characteristics of the Time-1 sample are described in Table 6.2. As indicated, the sample was quite evenly divided by marital status, grade, and school characteristics; and fairly evenly divided by sex and race. Males were somewhat overrepresented in the divorced group, and whites were somewhat overrrepresented in the intact sample.

For the divorced sample at Time-1, the mean length of time since the parents' divorce was 3.98 years ($sd = 2.54$). As might be expected, older children had spent more years in a single-parent home than had younger children. The mean scores for first-graders, for example, were 3.47 years for boys and 2.98 years for girls, while comparable figures for fifth-graders were 4.6 years for boys and 4.16 years for girls. Considering the length of time the children had spent in residence in single-parent homes, at the

Table 6.1
Time-1 Sample Description by Census Region

Census Region	Region Population (millions)	Percent of U.S. Population	N in Sample	Percent of Sample
New England	12.2	5.4	39	5.6
Mid-Atlantic	36.9	16.3	44	6.3
East North Central	41.7	18.4	247	35.3
West North Central	17.3	7.6	74	10.6
South Atlantic	36.8	16.2	142	20.3
East South Central	14.7	6.5	43	6.2
West South Central	23.7	10.5	21	3.0
Mountain	11.4	5.0	44	6.3
Pacific	31.8	14.0	45	6.4

1980 census total population = 226.5 million
Total $N = 699$

time of the study, they could not be considered as still experiencing immediate effects of the divorce process.

At Time-2, two years later, a request for follow-up data was sent to psychologists who participated at Time-1. Because of time constraints, job mobility, and other reasons, only 32 were able to provide such data by the end of the 1983–84 school year. A similar number agreed to provide a second follow-up cohort during the 1984–85 school year. Demographic data for the present follow-up sample of 137 children are presented in Table 6.3. Eleven of these subjects had experienced parental remarriage since Time-1, and three others who were in intact families now have separated parents. These 14 subjects were excluded from analyses for this article. Chi-square and Z-test comparisons between the follow-up sample of 123 children whose family status had not changed and the original population of 699 children, were performed using Time-1 demographic

Table 6.2
Time-1 Sample Description

	Total		Intact		Divorced	
Variable	N	Percent	N	Percent	N	Percent
Parent						
Marital status	699	100.0	358	51.2	341	48.8
Child						
Sex						
Male	365	52.2	180	50.3	185	54.3
Female	334	47.8	178	49.7	156	45.7
Grade 1	235	33.6	120	33.5	115	33.7
3	234	33.5	118	33.0	116	34.0
5	230	32.9	120	33.5	110	32.3
Race						
White	615	88.0	322	89.9	293	85.9
Black	52	7.4	21	5.9	31	9.1
Hispanic	16	2.3	9	2.5	7	2.1
Other	5	0.7	1	0.3	4	1.2
No response	11	1.6	5	1.4	6	1.7
School						
Location						
Urban	165	23.6	84	23.5	81	23.8
Suburban	303	43.3	157	43.9	146	42.8
Rural	217	31.0	111	31.0	106	31.1
No response	14	2.0	6	1.7	8	2.3
Type						
Public	676	96.7	346	96.6	330	96.8
Private	3	0.4	2	0.6	1	0.2
Parochial	11	1.6	6	1.7	5	1.5
No response	9	1.3	4	1.1	5	1.5

Table 6.3
Time-2 Sample Description (*N* = 137)

Variable	Total N	Total Percent	Remained Intact N	Remained Intact Percent	Remained Divorced N	Remained Divorced Percent
Current marital status of parents						
Remained intact	77	56.2	77	100.0		
Remained divorced	46	33.6			46	100.0
Remarried	11	8.0				
Separated	3	2.2				
Sex						
Male	67	48.9	38	49.4	25	54.3
Female	70	51.1	39	50.6	21	45.7
Grade at Time-1						
1	49	35.8	27	35.1	19	41.3
3	44	32.1	24	31.2	15	32.6
4	1	0.7	0	0.0	0	0.0
5	44	32.1	26	33.8	12	26.1
Current grade						
2	4	2.9	2	2.6	2	4.3
3	45	32.8	24	31.2	18	39.1
5	43	31.4	25	32.5	14	30.4
7	44	32.1	26	33.8	12	26.1
Race						
White	123	89.8	69	89.6	42	91.3
Black	10	7.3	5	6.5	3	6.5
Hispanic	3	2.2	2	2.6	1	2.2
Other	1	0.7	1	1.3	0	0.0
School location						
Urban	25	18.2	17	22.1	7	15.2
Suburban	60	43.8	36	46.8	18	39.1
Rural	41	29.9	20	26.0	14	30.4
No Response	11	8.0	4	5.2	7	15.2
School type						
Public	124	90.5	70	90.9	40	87.0
Private	1	0.7	0	0.0	1	2.2
Parochial	9	6.6	6	7.8	3	6.5
No Response	3	2.5	1	1.3	2	4.3
	M	SD	M	SD	M	SD
Full-scale IQ	108.56	13.80	109.92	13.54	107.96	14.12
Number of years in single-parent household	5.77	2.62			6.39	2.31

characteristics of each group. These analyses were performed separately for each marital status group (i.e., divorced or intact) to determine whether the follow-up samples adequately represented their respective Time-1 populations. For both divorced and intact groups no significant differences were noted between Time-1 population and Time-2 sample with regard to Time-1 characteristics of grade, sex, race, respondent's and spouse's or ex-spouse's occupation rating and education level, family income, or length of time in a single-parent household. The mean length of time residing in a divorced, single-parent home for the Time-2 sample was 6.39 years ($sd = 2.31$).

Assessments

This study employed a multimethod and multifactored approach to evaluating children's intellectual, academic, social-behavioral, and adaptive characteristics, as well as family and school environments (see Nay, 1979). In addition to psychometric measures, assessments included teacher-rating scales, child and parent interviews, and parent satisfaction assessment. Data collected from school records were grades, attendance, standardized group test scores, and special services provided to the child. School and community environment variable were also included. Providers of direct psychological services in the schools administered assessments, conducted interviews, and coordinated ratings.

To compensate for the acknowledged scarcity of well standardized social-emotional and adaptive behavior instruments, this multisource approach was deemed necessary to provide internal validity checks and to increase confidence in findings. It also provided the opportunity to examine the complex interactions among environmental conditions that have typically been neglected in previous research. The composite data base utilized here, moreover, parallels legally mandated multifactored assessment procedures employed by psychologists in schools (see Guidubaldi et al., 1979).

Psychometric Assessments

The Wechsler Intelligence Scale for Children—Revised (WISC-R; Wechsler, 1974) and Wide Range Achievement Test (WRAT; Jastak et al., 1978) were administered by participating school psychologists to gain well-established measures of intellectual and academic functioning.

Social-Behavioral Assessment

Assessment in this area was especially comprehensive, involving ratings by psychologists, teachers, and parents, as well as selected items from the child and parent interviews. In addition to direct child assessments, data from parent and teacher rating scales have been found reliable and valid in both clinical child and educational psychology research. For example, Achenbach and Edelbrock (1978, 1981) found two general maladaptive factors in childhood pathology that are included in present ratings. These are overcontrol characteristics, involving anxiety and withdrawal, and undercontrol factors, involving aggressive acting out and conduct disorders. It has also been well established that attentive, task-oriented behavior, as well as positive social relationships, predict academic success and adjustment in school (Bloom, 1976; Perry et al., 1979; Stevenson et al, 1976). Parent and teacher measures incorporating these adaptive and maladaptive domains were therefore included. Instruments employed were the Hahnemann Elementary School Behavior Rating Scale, or HESB (Spivack & Swift, 1975), the Sells and Roff Peer Acceptance-Rejection Rating, or PAR (Sells & Roff, 1967), a locus of control measure derived from the Harvard Project on Family Stress, or LC (Belle, 1982), and an optimism–pessimism scale, or OPTI, abridged from Stipek et al. (1981).

The HESB scale (Spivack & Swift, 1967) is a 60-item scale with a scoring system for 16 subscales. The teacher rates either the frequency of occurrence of a behavioral item or the degree to which a given behavior describes the child. The 16 subscales include both task-related and interpersonal behaviors. Selection of this instrument was based partly on the relevance of the subscales for clustering into school-related and diagnostic clinical factors. The subscales related to school tasks are orginality, independent learning, involvement, productivity with peers, inattention, and academic achievement. The domains considered here to be associated with undercontrol or conduct disorders include negative feelings, critical/competitive, social overinvolvement, and unreflectiveness. Overcontrol or anxiety-withdrawal characteristics are defined as the profile pattern comprised of failure anxiety, holding back/withdrawn, intellectual dependency, and low frequencies of productivity with peers. [Further description of this and the abovementioned assessment devices has been presented in previous publications (e.g., Guidubaldi, et al., 1984b).]

Adaptive Behavior

A standardization edition of the Vineland Teacher Questionnaire (VTQ) developed by Sparrow and colleagues (1981) was used as a measure of adaptive behavior. Form A, used for first grade, included 240 items. Form B included 199 items, and was used for third- and fifth-grade children. The items are rated by teachers on a three-point scale, ranging from "never or very seldom performs the activity" to "satisfactorily and habitually performs the activity." The items are divided into four factors of adaptive behavior, representing daily living, social, communication, and motor skills.

Child Interview

All children were interviewed by school psychologists. The interview instrument employed was adapted from the Harvard University Stress and Families Survey (Belle, 1982). Structured questions were developed to assess peer relations and parent–child relationships. Other relationships were also evaluated, including activites and interactions with siblings, friends, and adults other than parents. The peer relations section assessed both school and neighborhood peer relations.

Parent Interview

Parents from both intact and divorced families were interviewed by school psychologists. The interview instrument used was a structured questionnaire designed to ascertain relevant family data. Five major areas were evaluated: family environment, support systems, quality of life, child rearing, and divorce arrangements. The family environment domain dealt with information on residence, family composition, work and social arrangements, marriage and home routines. Data pertinent to relatives, friends, organizations, and activities, as well as school assistance, were included in support systems. The quality-of-life area pertained to family health, income level, transportation, and life changes. The section on child rearing was divided in terms of the developmental level of the child (e.g., perinatal period) and included assessments of parental approaches to discipline and parent–child relationships. The last section on divorce arrangements, was given only to parents with divorced status. Questions were related to custody arrangements, pre- and postdivorce interactions between spouses and between parents and children, and adaptations to the divorce of both parent and child.

Parent Satisfaction Scale.

The Parent Satisfaction Scale (PSS) (Cleminshaw & Guidubaldi, 1981) was given to all parents to complete and return to the school psychologist. It is a 50-item Likert-type instrument that assesses the parent's perception of satisfaction in the parent role. The scale is composed of five separate factors—spouse support, child—parent relationship, parent performance, child discipline and control, and general parenting satisfaction. A total score and separate scores for each factor are derived from the scale. The higher the total score, the greater is the perceived parent satisfaction.

School Environment

General school characteristics included size of school population, type of school population (ethnic and racial background), setting of school (urban, suburban, rural), type of school (private, public, parochial), school organization (neighborhood, consolidated, number of grades within school building), and transportation to school (walked or number of miles bused). The classroom characteristics included structure (open or traditional) and size of classroom. Additional school and classroom climate criteria were derived from the "effective schools" research movement (e.g., Brookover & Lezotte, 1977; Edmonds & Frederikesen, 1978). These were labeled as follows: safe and orderly environment, clear school mission, instructional leadership, high expectations, opportunity to learn and student time on task, frequent monitoring of student programs, home–school relations, and reinforcement practices. These dimensions were evaluated by the school psychologists on a five-point Likert Scale.

Time-2 Assessments

Data-gathering instruments at Time-2 included an expanded parent interview and psychologist's rating form; a modified child interview that deleted the Time-1 optimism versus pessimism scale, but added other items relating to such issues as life changes, stresses or worries, and the child's perception of the divorce and the single-parent home environment; the Achenbach Child Behavior Checklists and Parent and Teacher Report forms (Achenbach & Edelbrock, 1983); the HESB Scale; the WRAT; and an LC scale. For this time period, a total of 48 social-emotional and 27 academic criteria was used. Once again all assessments were performed and coordinated by school psychologists in the child's school district.

RESULTS

This project has yielded a very large volume of data that affords the opportunity to examine the complexities inherent in children's divorce adjustment. Because of the broad array of data, however, analyses are ongoing, and several important relationships have yet to be examined.

Moreover the second follow-up cohort study, currently in the data-gathering phase, is expected to yield extensive longitudinal information on approximately 100 additional children.

Analyses for this chapter focus on one of the most powerfully demonstrated findings of the project—that of age-sex variations in adjustment to divorce. Following a brief overview of Time-1 total group marital-status differences, sex differences in adjustment to divorce are summarized, and marital status differences by grade-sex category are presented in detail. Time-2 ANOVAs and ANCOVAs are then presented separately for each sex group, to illustrate the longitudinal continuity of sex differences in divorce adjustment.

Marital Status Differences for Total Group at Time-1

Detailed descriptions of total group marital status differences have been presented elsewhere (e.g., Guidubaldi et al., 1984b). An overview of these results, however, provides a useful context for grade-sex comparisons. Consistent differences were observed between total intact and total divorced groups on both social-emotional and academic-intellectual criteria. ANOVA results indicate that intact-family children performed better on 15 of the 16 Hahnemann classroom behavior ratings, as well as on Vineland communication, daily living, and social scales. They were absent less frequently, had higher peer popularity, according to both parent and teacher ratings, and demonstrated more internal locus of control, higher full-scale IQ, and higher WRAT reading, spelling, and math scores. Their grades in reading and math were higher, and they were less likely to repeat a school grade. All in all, intact-family children showed superior performance on 21 of 27 social competence, and eight of nine academic competence comparisons.

When covariance controls were employed for parents' educational, occupational, and family-income status, substantial differences between intact- and divorced-family children were also found on both social and academic competence criteria. For example, with family income controlled, intact-family children performed better on ten of the 16 Hahnemann ratings of classroom behaviors. Although one of these ratings pertained to academic achievement, no main effects of marital status were observed for academic criteria, as defined by teacher grades or WRAT test scores. Once again full-scale WISC-R IQ differences favored the intact group, as did teacher ratings of peer popularity.

When the parent questionnaire respondent's educational level was controlled, intact-family children showed superior performance on 15 of 16

Hahnemann teacher ratings, as well as on Vineland communication and social scores. They were less likely to repeat a school grade, had higher grades in reading and math, and better WRAT reading, spelling, and math scores. They were absent from school less often, had higher internal locus of control, and had better peer relations as judged by parent and teacher ratings.

When educational level of the child's other parent was controlled, intact-family children surpassed divorced-family children on 14 of 16 Hahnemann ratings as well as in Vineland communication and social scores. They also had less school absence and higher popularity ratings.

Covariance controls for respondent's occupational level revealed differences in favor of intact-family children on 14 of 16 Hahnemann ratings, all four Vineland scores, absence frequency, peer popularity, WRAT reading and spelling scores, grades in math and reading, and regular versus special class placement.

With occupational level of the other parent as the control variable, intact-family children showed better performance on 13 of 16 Hahnemann ratings, Vineland communication and social scores, grade in reading, absence frequency, and peer rejection index.

A number of other marital status differences were examined through correlations and chi-square analyses. Intact parents, for example, scored higher on all five parent satisfaction scales included in the parent interview. Divorced-family children were far more likely to have been previously referred to a school psychologist (chi square $= 17.58$, $p < 0.001$), to be in programs for reading difficulties (chi square $= 3.55$, $p < 0.05$), and to have repeated a school grade (chi square $= 6.27$, $p < 0.01$).

Sex Differences in Postdivorce Adjustment at Time-1

Although the number of marital status differences in total group analyses were convincing evidence of the negative effects of divorce, it quickly became apparent that children of divorce differed greatly in adjustment depending on such factors as age and sex. Early analyses, for example, illustrated powerful sex differences.

Within divorced-family households, girls consistently demonstrated better adjustment than boys. Divorced-group ANOVAs revealed that girls showed superior performance on 11 of 16 Hahnemann measures; Vineland daily living score; peer popularity; the optimism versus pessimism score; grades in reading, math, and classroom conduct; and WRAT reading, spelling, and math test scores. They were also less likely to have repeated a school grade or to be in special class placement.

Sex differences also persisted when IQ was controlled in analyses of covariance. Girls performed better on ten of 16 Hahnemann ratings, Vineland daily living skills, grade in conduct, peer popularity, and optimism, as well as on several academic criteria, including WRAT reading and spelling, grades in reading and math, and history of repeating a school grade. When family income was controlled in covariance analyses, girls performed better than boys on 11 Hahnemann ratings; Vineland daily living and social skills; grades in conduct, reading, and math; WRAT reading and spelling subtest scores; peer popularity; and optimism. They were also less likely to have repeated a school grade.

Marital Status Differences by Grade-Sex Category at Time-1

Because girls generally perform better than boys at these age levels, and because age and sex differences were frequently observed in large group analyses, separate T-test analyses were performed for each of the six grade-sex subgroups at Time-1. These comparisons of intact- and divorced-family children by grade-sex subgroups provide a more precise examination of postdivorce social-emotional and academic adjustment. Such precision has been impossible in previous research, because of the sampling limitations mentioned; its absence has caused many of the sweeping generalizations that surround this controversial topic.

Social-Emotional Criteria

Tables 6.4, 6.5, and 6.6 illustrate differences between intact-and divorced-family children by sex groups in first, third, and fifth grades respectively. When comparing results for the social performance variables, it is important to notice that, compared with intact-family children, both first-grade males and females from divorced families perform worse in the classroom as measured by teacher ratings. Males, for example, achieve significant lower scores on five of the 15 Hahnemann social profiles, and females on eight of 15, when compared with their peers from intact families. The results begin to vary by sex for third-graders: males from divorced families scored significantly lower than their counterparts from intact families on ten profiles, while the females scored significantly lower on only five profiles. This difference becomes even more dramatic by fifth grade, where males from divorced families scored significantly lower on 11 profiles, while females scored lower on only one. These results illustrate a dramatic sex difference, with divorced family females performing closer and closer to intact-family females as they progress through elementary grades. Males from divorced families, on the other hand, show an increasing number of differences from intact-family males at the higher grade levels.

In reviewing additional indices of social performance, it is evident that when compared with their peers from intact families, divorced-family first- and third-grade girls performed lower on Vineland social performance, and divorced-family third-grade girls performed lower on Vineland communication and had more peer rejection. There were, however, no family status differences in these measures for fifth-grade females.

In contrast, boys from divorced families received higher scores on a teacher measure of peer rejection at all three grade levels. In addition, peer popularity parent rating was lower for both first- and third-grade divorced-family boys, and a measure of peer contact was lower for divorced-group first-graders. Divorced-family boys in the first grade had significantly more school absenteeism than did intact-family boys. In addition, scores on the

Table 6.4
Time-1 T-Tests on Marital Status for First-Grade Males and Females

| | Males | | | Females | |
Variable	T-Value	Two-tailed Probability	Variable	T-Value	Two-tailed Probability
		Social-Emotional			
Hahnemann Profiles			Hahnemann Profiles		
Unreflectiveness	2.26	0.026	Independent learning	−2.71	0.008
Irrelevant talk	3.26	0.001	Involvement	−2.15	0.034
Social overinvolvement	2.69	0.008	Intellectual dependency	2.19	0.031
Critical/competitive	2.30	0.023	Failure anxiety	2.93	0.004
Inattention	2.88	0.005	Unreflectiveness	2.19	0.031
Absence	2.89	0.005	Social overinvolvement	2.42	0.018
Peer rejection (Teacher rating)	2.49	0.014	Holding back/ withdrawn	2.68	0.009
Peer popularity (Parent rating)	−2.93	0.004	Inattention	3.76	0.000
Peer contact (Child rating)	−2.56	0.012	Vineland domain Social (z score)	−2.38	0.020
		Academic-intellectual			
Academic achievement (HESB rating)	−2.30	0.023	WRAT reading	−3.33	0.001
			WRAT spelling	−2.68	0.009
			WRAT math	−3.24	0.002

Table 6.5
Time-1 T-Tests on Marital Status for Third-Grade Males and Females

Variable	Males		Variable	Females	
	T-Value	Two-tailed Probability		T-Value	Two-tailed Probability
Social-Emotional					
Hahnemann Profiles			Hahnemann profiles		
Originality	−2.54	0.012	Independent learning	−2.20	0.030
Independent learning	−2.49	0.014	Irrelevant talk	2.01	0.047
Intellectual dependency	3.48	0.001	Social overinvolvement	2.24	0.027
Unreflectiveness	2.97	0.004	Negative feelings	2.60	0.011
Social overinvolvement	2.70	0.008	Blaming	2.69	0.009
Negative feelings	2.31	0.023	Vineland domains		
Holding back/withdrawn	2.26	0.026	Communication (z score)	−3.02	0.003
Critical/competitive	2.69	0.008	Social (z score)	−2.44	0.016
Blaming	2.83	0.005	Peer rejection (teacher rating)	2.03	0.045
Inattention	2.84	0.005			
Vineland domains					
Communication (z score)	−2.44	0.016			
Daily living (z score)	−2.06	0.042			
Peer rejection (teacher rating)	2.55	0.012			
Peer popularity (parent rating)	−3.01	0.003			
Academic-intellectual					
WRAT reading	−2.53	0.013	Grade in reading	−2.14	0.036
Grade in reading	−2.57	0.012	Grade in math	−1.97	0.053
Academic achievement (HESB rating)	−2.72	0.007	Academic achievement (HESB rating)	−2.49	0.015

Table 6.6
Time-1 T-Tests on Marital Status for Fifth-Grade Males and Females

	Males			Females	
Variable	T-Value	Two-tailed Probability	Variable	T-Value	Two-tailed Probability
		Social-Emotional			
Hahnemann Profiles			Hahnemann profiles		
Independent learning	−2.73	0.007	Involvement	−1.98	0.051
Intellectual dependency	2.36	0.020			
Failure anxiety	3.30	0.001			
Unreflectiveness	2.23	0.028			
Irrelevant talk	2.22	0.028			
Social overinvolvement	2.61	0.010			
Negative feelings	3.06	0.003			
Holding back/ withdrawn	3.20	0.002			
Critical/competitive	2.52	0.013			
Blaming	3.16	0.002			
Inattention	3.17	0.002			
Vineland domains					
Social (z score)	−2.29	0.024			
Peer rejection (teacher rating)	2.14	0.034			
		Academic-intellectual			
Grade in math	−2.11	0.038	No significant differences		
Academic achievement (HESB rating)	−3.06	0.003			

Vineland were lower for third- and fifth-grade boys from divorced homes. Third-graders did worse on communication and daily living, and fifth-graders did worse on social performance.

Academic-Intellectual Criteria

Academic-intellectual results showed that females from divorced families had lower scores on all three WRAT scores at the first-grade level. For third-grade divorced-family girls, lower scores occurred in both reading and math, as well as in teacher's ratings of overall academic achievement. There were no academic differences for fifth-grade females.

By comparison, first-, third-, and fifth-grade males from divorced families all received significantly lower ratings from their teachers on overall academic achievement than did males from intact families. Both third- and fifth-grade divorced-male samples achieved lower teacher-assigned grades—third-graders in reading, and fifth-graders in math. Reading subtest scores on the WRAT were also lower for boys in third grade on the reading subtest.

ANCOVA Results for Grade-Sex Groups

The discovery of substantial variations in postdivorce adjustment by age-sex groups led to a number of additional questions about possible sex differences in responsiveness to environmental mediating factors such as SES conditions. Consequently ANCOVA analyses were conducted to examine marital status differences within age-sex groups, using controls for both parents' educational and occupational levels and family income. All observed differences favored the intact groups, with three exceptions noted below.

Tables 6.7, 6.8, and 6.9 illustrate marital status differences for each age-sex group when education level of the parent questionnaire respondent was controlled. This parent was the mother in intact families and the custodial parent (91 percent mothers) in divorced homes. At the first-grade level, both male and female divorced-family children demonstrated markedly lower performance than did intact-family children. For boys lower scores were evidenced on ten of 27 social-emotional variables, and one out of nine academic competence criteria. For girls, lower scores occurred on 12 of the social-emotional and four of the academic criteria. At third-grade level, divorced-family boys performed lower on 13 social-emotional and three academic criteria, whereas divorced-family girls surprisingly showed no differences from intact-family girls on any of the 36 criteria. The same pattern of sex difference was found at the fifth-grade

Table 6.7

Time-1 Analysis of Covariance by Marital Status—Controlling for Respondent's Education—for First-Grade Males and Females

Variable	Males F	p	Variable	Females F	p
			Social-emotional		
Hahnemann profiles			Hahnemann Profiles		
Independent learning	3.867	0.052	Independent learning	9.566	0.003
Irrelevant talk	7.814	0.006	Involvement	6.315	0.014
Social overinvolvement	6.725	0.011	Intellectual dependency	6.625	0.012
Holding back/withdrawn	4.949	0.028	Failure anxiety	10.670	0.001
Critical/competitive	4.599	0.034	Unreflectiveness	5.806	0.018
Inattention	9.042	0.003	Irrelevant talk	4.620	0.034
Absence	6.944	0.010	Social overinvolvement	7.709	0.007
Peer rejection (teacher rating)	6.283	0.014	Holding back/withdrawn	8.859	0.004
Peer popularity (parent rating)	6.658	0.011	Blaming	4.576	0.035
Peer contact (child rating)	5.510	0.021	Inattention	15.514	0.000
			Vineland domains		
			Communication (z-score)	4.055	0.047
			Social (z-score)	4.144	0.045
			Academic-intellectual		
Academic achievement (HESB rating)	4.760	0.031	WRAT reading	12.842	0.001
			WRAT spelling	8.639	0.004
			WRAT math	13.212	0.000
			Academic achievement (HESB rating)	4.880	0.029

Table 6.8

Time-1 Analysis of Covariance by Marital Status—Controlling for Respondent's Education—for Third-Grade Males and Females

Variable	Males		Variable	Females	
	F	p		F	p
Social-emotional					
Hahnemann profiles					
Originality	4.355	0.039			
Independent learning	4.262	0.041			
Intellectual dependency	9.244	0.003			
Unreflectiveness	9.063	0.003			
Social overinvolvement	6.965	0.009			
Negative feelings	4.557	0.035			
Holding back/withdrawn	3.856	0.052			
Critical/competitive	6.977	0.009			
Blaming	7.382	0.008			
Inattention	6.740	0.011			
Vineland domains					
Communication	4.401	0.038			
Peer rejection (teacher rating)	5.844	0.017			
Peer popularity (parent rating)	6.782	0.010			
			No significant differences		
Academic-intellectual					
WRAT reading	4.527	0.035	No significant differences		
Grade in reading	4.985	0.028			
Academic achievement (HESB rating)	5.389	0.022			

Table 6.9
Time-1 Analysis of Covariance by Marital Status—Controlling for Respondent's Education—for Fifth-Grade Males and Females

	Males			Females	
Variable	F	p	Variable	F	p
Social-emotional					
Hahnemann profiles			No significant differences		
Independent learning	6.158	0.015			
Productive with peers	3.982	0.049			
Intellectual dependency	5.065	0.027			
Failure anxiety	6.748	0.011			
Unreflectiveness	4.298	0.041			
Irrelevant talk	5.271	0.024			
Social Overinvolvement	6.290	0.014			
Negative feelings	10.219	0.002			
Holding back/withdrawn	11.172	0.001			
Critical/competitive	8.815	0.004			
Blaming	8.290	0.005			
Inattention	7.712	0.007			
Vineland domains					
Social (z-score)	6.104	0.015			
Peer rejection (teacher rating)	6.263	0.014			
Academic-intellectual					
Grade in math	5.003	0.028	No significant differences		
Academic achievement (HESB rating)	8.262	0.005			

level, where divorced-family boys were lower on 14 social-emotional and two academic criteria, while girls again showed no differences.

Considering the education level of the other parent as a control variable, a similar pattern of marital status differences exists at each grade level for both boys and girls. As shown in Tables 6.10, 6.11, and 6.12, at first-grade level divorced-family boys scored lower on eight social criteria and girls lower on six social and three academic indices. At third grade, divorced-group boys were lower on 11 social and two academic criteria, while the female groups showed no differences. Similarly no differences were evidenced for girls at fifth-grade level, while divorced-group boys performed worse than intact counterparts on one academic and 11 social-emotional criteria.

Differential gender responses were also observed when occupation levels of questionnaire respondents and spouses were controlled (see Table 6.13 through 6.18). With respondent's occupation level controlled at

Table 6.10
Time-1 Analysis of Covariance by Marital Status—Controlling for Spouse's Education—for First-Grade Males and Females

Variable	Males		Variable	Females	
	F	p		F	p
Social-emotional					
Hahnemann profiles			Hahnemann profiles		
Irrelevant talk	4.674	0.033	Independent learning	4.711	0.032
Social overinvolvement	4.326	0.040	Failure anxiety	10.080	0.002
Holding back/withdrawn	4.710	0.032	Social overinvolvement	4.529	0.036
Inattention	5.859	0.017	Holding back/withdrawn	6.243	0.014
Absence	6.622	0.012	Inattention	9.741	0.002
Peer rejection (teacher rating)	5.186	0.025	Locus of control	3.901	0.051
Peer popularity (parent rating)	4.206	0.043			
Peer contact (child rating)	7.012	0.009			
Academic-intellectual					
No significant differences			Repeated school grade	4.133	0.045
			WRAT reading	7.630	0.007
			WRAT math	10.779	0.001

first-grade level, divorced-family boys were lower on 13 social-emotional and two academic criteria, and divorced-group girls were lower on three social and two academic measures. At third grade divorced-group boys showed relative deficiencies on 15 social and four academic comparisons, while girls again showed no difference. By fifth-grade level, 14 social and two academic criteria were lower for divorced-group boys, in contrast to only one social difference for the girls' groups.

With spouse's occupation level controlled, first-grade divorced-group boys exhibited lower scores on seven social measures, and divorced-group girls on three social and three academic assessments. At third grade girls showed no differences, whereas divorced-family boys had lower scores on

Table 6.11

Time-1 Analysis of Covariance by Marital Status—Controlling for Spouse's Education—for Third-Grade Males and Females

	Males			Females	
Variable	F	p	Variable	F	p
Social-emotional					
Hahnemann profiles			No significant differences		
Independent learning	4.312	0.040			
Intellectual dependency	8.928	0.003			
Unreflectiveness	9.427	0.003			
Social overinvolvement	7.969	0.006			
Negative feelings	5.214	0.024			
Critical/competitive	8.753	0.004			
Blaming	8.746	0.004			
Inattention	5.951	0.016			
Vineland domains					
Communication (z-score)	5.021	0.027			
Peer rejection (teacher rating)	4.900	0.029			
Peer popularity (parent rating)	7.123	0.009			
Academic-intellectual					
Grade in reading	3.821	0.054	No significant differences		
Academic achievement (HESB rating)	5.368	0.022			

nine social and one academic index. In the fifth-grade samples, divorced-family boys were lower on ten social-emotional measures. Divorced-group girls were lower on two social-emotional criteria, but, unexpectedly, were higher than intact-group girls on the optimism measure.

The final set of SES covariance analyses controlled household family income (Custodial household for divorced-family children). This variable clearly accounted for more of the variance in boys' performance than did the other SES indicators (see Table 6.19). For the three grade levels, divorced-group boys showed no differences at first grade, lower performance on three social-emotional criteria at third grade, and lower performance on five social-emotional criteria at fifth grade. Divorced-group girls were lower on five social-emotional and two academic criteria at first grade, and one social-emotional criterion at fifth grade. At the third-grade

Table 6.12

Time-1 Analysis of Covariance by Marital Status—Controlling for Spouse's Education—for First-Grade Males and Females

Variable	Males		Variable	Females	
	F	p		F	p
Social-emotional					
Hahnemann profiles			No significant differences		
Intellectual dependency	4.454	0.037			
Failure anxiety	4.008	0.048			
Irrelevant talk	3.984	0.049			
Social overinvolvement	4.116	0.045			
Negative feelings	7.321	0.008			
Holding back/withdrawn	8.748	0.004			
Critical/competitive	5.400	0.022			
Blaming	5.845	0.018			
Inattention	6.241	0.014			
Vineland domains					
Social (z-score)	6.516	0.012			
Peer rejection (teacher rating)	5.191	0.025			
Academic-intellectual					
Academic achievement (HESB rating)	5.432	0.022	No significant differences		

Table 6.13

Time-1 Analysis of Covariance by Marital Status—Controlling for Respondent's Occupation—for First-Grade Males and Females

	Males			Females	
Variable	F	p	Variable	F	p
Social-emotional					
Hahnemann profiles			Hahnemann profiles		
Independent learning	5.834	0.018	Failure anxiety	4.939	0.029
Unreflectiveness	9.095	0.004	Unreflectiveness	3.878	0.053
Irrelevant talk	8.109	0.006	Inattention	4.357	0.040
Social overinvolvement	9.394	0.003			
Holding back/withdrawn	4.993	0.029			
Inattention	13.231	0.001			
Vineland domains					
Communication (z-score)	4.408	0.039			
Social (z-score)	6.399	0.014			
Motor (z-score)	4.090	0.047			
Absence	4.192	0.046			
Peer rejection (teacher rating)	9.985	0.002			
Peer popularity (parent rating)	5.861	0.018			
Peer contact (child rating)	8.252	0.005			
Academic-intellectual					
WISC-R full scale IQ	4.352	0.041	WRAT reading	4.110	0.046
Academic achievement (HESB rating)	9.064	0.004	WRAT math	4.963	0.029

Table 6.14

Time-1 Analysis of Covariance by Marital Status—Controlling for Respondent's Occupation—for Third-Grade Males and Females

Variable	Males		Variable	Females	
	F	p		F	p
Social-emotional					
Hahnemann profiles			No significant differences		
Independent learning	7.826	0.006			
Intellectual dependency	6.022	0.016			
Unreflectiveness	7.767	0.007			
Irrelevant talk	4.046	0.048			
Social overinvolvement	9.062	0.003			
Negative feelings	3.983	0.049			
Holding back/withdrawn	4.005	0.049			
Critical/competitive	11.517	0.001			
Blaming	5.254	0.024			
Inattention	7.121	0.009			
Vineland domains					
Communication (z-score)	4.469	0.038			
Daily living (z-score)	8.007	0.006			
Optimism	4.243	0.043			
Peer rejection (teacher rating)	9.441	0.003			
Peer popularity (parent rating)	6.856	0.011			
Academic-intellectual					
WRAT reading	8.206	0.005	No significant differences		
WRAT spelling	5.297	0.024			
Grade in reading	5.300	0.025			
Academic achievement (HESB rating)	10.328	0.002			

Table 6.15
Time-1 Analysis of Covariance by Marital Status—Controlling for Respondent's Occupation—for Fifth-Grade Males and Females

Variable	Males		Variable	Females	
	F	p		F	p
Social-emotional					
Hahnemann profiles			Absence	6.956	0.011
Independent learning	3.967	0.050			
Productive with peers	7.308	0.009			
Intellectual dependency	6.065	0.016			
Failure anxiety	5.085	0.027			
Unreflectiveness	4.095	0.047			
Irrelevant talk	5.131	0.027			
Social overinvolvement	4.363	0.040			
Negative feelings	8.532	0.005			
Holding back/withdrawn	12.693	0.001			
Critical/competitive	6.272	0.015			
Blaming	6.553	0.013			
Inattention	6.158	0.015			
Vineland domains Social (z-score)	5.221	0.025			
Peer rejection (teacher rating)	6.246	0.015			
Academic-intellectual					
Regular class placement	4.775	0.032	No significant differences		
Academic achievement (HESB rating)	4.843	0.031			

level they demonstrated a better approach to the teacher than did intact girls.

These ANCOVA results extend previous findings by controlling for SES, age, and sex, in assessing the impact of divorce on children. The interaction of these three factors illustrates the complexity of divorce adjustment, and adds substantially to our understanding of this process.

Marital Status Differences by Sex at Time-2

The first cohort of follow-up subjects did not include enough divorced-family children at the upper-grade levels to permit separate analyses for grade-sex groups. ANOVAs for each total sex group were conducted, however, to determine if Time-1 marital status differences and sex differentials in adjustment persisted after two more years of single-parent child rearing. Table 6.20 illustrates that, even after an average of 6.39 years in single-parent homes, divorced-group boys continue to show poorer

Table 6.16

Time-1 Analysis of Covariance by Marital Status—Controlling for Spouse's Occupation—for First-Grade Males and Females

	Males			Females	
Variable	F	p	Variable	F	p
	Social-emotional				
Hahnemann profiles			Hahnemann profiles		
Irrelevant talk	5.430	0.022	Independent learning	3.900	0.051
Social overinvolvement	6.715	0.011	Failure anxiety	8.055	0.006
Inattention	4.826	0.031	Inattention	5.649	0.020
Absence	5.536	0.022			
Peer rejection (teacher rating)	4.561	0.035			
Peer popularity (parent rating)	5.792	0.018			
Peer contact (child rating)	11.724	0.001			
	Academic-intellectual				
No significant differences			WRAT reading	9.795	0.002
			WRAT spelling	5.985	0.016
			WRAT math	9.320	0.003

adjustment than intact-family boys, on a wide assortment of criteria. On ten social-emotional criteria and ten academic criteria, intact-family boys showed superior performance. Once again, divorced-family girls did not demonstrate such widespread adverse effects. Intact-group girls surpassed them on only four social-emotional, and on no academic criteria.

Using covariance analyses to control for family income, no academic differences between marital status groups were noted for either sex group. As shown in Table 6.21, for males, seven social-emotional differences favoring intact-family children were observed. In contrast, only two social-emotional differences were observed for females, and one of them, locus of control, favored divorced-family children. Time-2 analyses thus replicate Time-1 findings, demonstrating again that the adverse effects of divorce are experienced primarily by boys, and that family income accounts for much of the variance in adjustment measures, particularly on academic achievement indices.

Table 6.17

Time-1 Analysis of Covariance by Marital Status—Controlling for Spouse's Occupation—for Third-Grade Males and Females

Variable	Males		Variable	Females	
	F	p		F	p
Social-emotional					
Hahnemann profiles			No significant differences		
Intellectual dependency	6.816	0.010			
Unreflectiveness	5.798	0.018			
Social overinvolvement	7.109	0.009			
Negative feelings	6.224	0.014			
Blaming	8.950	0.003			
Inattention	4.311	0.040			
Vineland domains					
Communication (z-score)	4.007	0.048			
Peer rejection (teacher rating)	3.923	0.050			
Peer popularity (parent rating)	4.443	0.038			
Academic-intellectual					
Grade in reading	4.156	0.045	No significant differences		

DISCUSSION

The deterioration of marital stability has drastically altered traditional approaches to childrearing. Educators, psychologists, and other professionals who work daily with children are painfully aware that children from divorced homes comprise a disproportionately large segment of their "problem" cases. Yet very little reliable evidence has been provided by researchers to improve practitioner services for this increasing population of troubled youngsters. Research activity has been limited and perhaps subdued by such obstacles as invasion of privacy or concerns about confidentiality—substantial issues in many postdivorce households, where custody and financial settlement matters may be unresolved sources of vulnerability. Those researchers who have dared to tread on this sensitive ground have provided a valuable service, by increasing our awareness of the magnitude of the problem and its potentially far-reaching

Table 6.18

Time-1 Analysis of Covariance by Marital Status—Controlling for Spouse's Occupation—for Fifth-Grade Males and Females

	Males			Females	
Variable	F	p	Variable	F	p
Social-emotional					
Hahnemann profiles			Hahnemann profiles		
Intellectual dependency	5.949	0.017	Social overinvolvement	4.710	0.033
Failure anxiety	5.193	0.025	Blaming	4.654	0.034
Irrelevant talk	4.049	0.047	Optimism	3.988	0.049
Social overinvolvement	3.895	0.052			
Negative feelings	6.674	0.011			
Holding back/withdrawn	5.584	0.020			
Critical/competitive	3.844	0.053			
Blaming	4.931	0.029			
Inattention	4.700	0.033			
Peer Rejection (teacher rating)	3.818	0.054			
Academic-intellectual					
No significant differences			No significant differences		

consequences. The nationwide research project described in this chapter was initiated to resolve some of the major disputes and ambiguities generated from the limited set of prior studies. Using a large, randomly selected sample of children from 38 states, and an unusually extensive set of assessments, the NASP–Kent State Project has been able to examine precisely some of the complexities of children's adjustment to divorce. This chapter has extended previous reports from the project, focusing on sex differences in postdivorce adjustment.

The data strongly indicate that, compared with boys, girls make far better adjustments to divorced, single-parent home conditions. But this

Table 6.19

Time-1 Analysis of Covariance by Marital Status—Controlling for Family Income—for First-, Third-, and Fifth-Grade Males and Females

Variable	Males		Variable	Females	
	F	*p*		*F*	*p*
			First Grade		
			Hahnemann profiles		
No significant differences			Failure anxiety	9.931	0.002
			Unreflectiveness	5.489	0.021
			Social overinvolve-ment	5.520	0.021
			Blaming	4.184	0.043
			Inattention	5.281	0.024
			WRAT reading	4.240	0.042
			WRAT math	8.396	0.005
			Third Grade		
Hahnemann profiles			Hahnemann profiles		
Intellectual dependency	4.107	0.045	Approach to teacher	4.767	0.032
Unreflectiveness	5.332	0.023			
Blaming	5.519	0.021			
			Fifth Grade		
Hahnemann profiles			Worry scale	4.141	0.045
Failure anxiety	6.294	0.014			
Negative feelings	8.826	0.004			
Critical/competitive	7.013	0.009			
Blaming	7.676	0.007			
Vineland domains					
Social (z-score)	3.812	0.054			

Table 6.20
Time-2 Analysis of Variance by Marital Status for Males and Females

Variable	Males F	p	Variable	Females F	p
		Social-emotional			
Achenbach (teacher rating)			Hahnemann profiles		
			Irrelevant talk	4.55	0.037
Work effort	13.67	0.000	Inattention	5.30	0.025
Appropriateness of behavior	10.37	0.002	Child discipline and control (parent satis-		
Child's happiness	12.44	0.001	faction scale)	5.07	0.029
Behavior prob- lems—total score	7.14	0.010	Father–child relations	4.67	0.035
Behavior problems— total score (Achen- bach–parent)	5.84	0.019			
Locus of control	4.70	0.034			
Father–child relations	22.06	0.000			
Parent satisfaction scale					
Child–parent rela- tionship	3.91	0.053			
Parent perform- ance	7.47	0.008			
Child discipline and control	9.45	0.004			
		Academic-intellectual			
Number of years in regular class	4.28	0.043	No significant differences		
Final grade in spell- ing (1981–82 school year)	7.54	0.009			
Final grade in math (1982–83 school year)	4.38	0.042			
Final grade in math (Fall 1983)	4.88	0.033			
Achenbach (teacher rating)					
Math (current aca- demic performance)	7.59	0.008			

Table 6.20 (continued)

Language (current academic performance)	5.30	0.025
Amount of learning	5.74	0.020
Achenbach (parent rating)		
Spelling (current academic performance)	3.88	0.054
Math (current academic performance)	7.37	0.009
Hahnemann Academic achievement	4.76	0.033

phenomenon is age related, in that male and female adjustment profiles in first grade are more similar than those occurring in later grades. By third- and fifth-grade levels, intact- and divorced-family boys show increasing numbers of adjustment differences, while girls from the two family situations become increasingly alike in adjustment profiles. As t-tests illustrate, profiles of fifth-grade divorced-family girls are almost indistinguishable from those of intact-family girls, whereas divorced-group boys were deficient on 13 of 27 social-emotional competence and two of nine academic competence criteria.

At Time-2, when subjects were at least two years older, this age-sex effect was strongly evidenced again through longitudinal comparisons. Whereas boys were different on ten areas of social-emotional adjustment and ten areas of academic competence, girls showed only four social-emotional and no academic competence differences. Since the youngest children from Time-1 (first graders) were at third-grade age level at Time-2, it was expected that the total groups of divorced and intact girls would show minimal differences—similar to older girls at Time-1—and that the total groups of divorced and intact boys would show substantial differences—similar to older boys at Time-1. These assumptions were supported by Time-2 analyses, further confirming the age–sex interactions initially observed. In contrast to some previous studies that describe divorced-family children as making better adjustments to single-parent family life on the basis of increasing time since divorce, these findings indicate strongly that such a conclusion holds only for girls, and that clearly the opposite conclusion holds for boys.

A sex difference was also found in the particular type of social behavioral adjustment to divorce. The present results indicate, for example, that boys from divorced families compared with both girls from divorced homes and boys from intact homes, have a behavioral pattern that indicates high frequencies of negative acting out or undercontrolled behavior. The specific Hahnemann domains of inattention, social overinvolvement, unreflectiveness, blaming, and critical-competitive behavior were often found for boys. Possibly as a result of the high frequency of acting-out behavior, peer relationships were more adversely affected for divorced-group boys than for girls at all grade levels.

The reasons for sex differences in adjustment to divorce are critical, but have not been adequately investigated. Kelly and Wallerstein (1976) suggested that boys are developmentally more vulnerable to such stressors as divorce. A sex-role modeling explanation is provided by Warshak and

Table 6.21
Time-2 Analysis of Covariance by Marital Status—Controlling for Income— for Males and Females

Variable	Males		Variable	Females	
	F	p		F	p
First Grade					
Achenbach (teacher rating)			Relationship with peers (Achenbach–parent)	4.02	.050
Work effort	5.33	.025	Locus of control	6.46	.014
Appropriateness of behavior	6.18	.016			
Child's happiness	6.13	.017			
Behavior with parents (Achenbach–parent)	4.84	.032			
Parent satisfaction scale					
Parent performance	3.90	.054			
Child discipline and control	4.86	.033			
Father–child relations	11.69	.001			
Academic-intellectual					
No significant differences			No significant differences		

Santrock (1983), who attributed differences to the opposite-sex child-custody relationship typical for boys. Hetherington (1979b) suggested that there may be sex differences in parenting styles, with custodial parents providing less emotional support for boys.

The age–sex interactions so prevalent in this study indicate that sequelae of divorce are more similar for the sexes at younger age levels. A plausible explanation is that custodial mothers offer nurturance and support to their younger children regardless of sex, but differentiate their parenting styles for boys and girls as they grow older. It is also possible that increasing sex-role differentiation as children progress through elementary grades results in boys displaying more stereotypical defiant, aggressive behavior that in turn generates more parent–child or teacher–child conflict. Considering sex-role modeling processes, these data would also suggest that boys increasingly require the same-sex parent's involvement as they approach puberty.

The mediating effects of SES were also found in these analyses to vary according to sex, age, and performance area. Both mothers' and fathers' education levels account for a substantial amount of the variance in marital status differences for older girls, but these effects are not apparent for boys or first-grade girls. A similar pattern was observed for occupation of mothers, although first-grade females showed fewer differences when this variable was controlled. Fathers' occupational classification did account for more of the variance in boys' marital status differences, but some male differences were also independent of this control factor. Females at the three grade levels again showed very few if any marital status differences when this covariate was used.

Family income was by far the most effective SES covariate in accounting for boys' marital status differences at each of the grade levels. As illustrated in ANCOVA tables, the list of differences diminished markedly. The same phenomenon was apparent in the Time-2 ANOVA and ANCOVA analyses, where a very extensive set of male group differences was reduced substantially through use of the income covariate (from 20 differences to seven). This finding may reflect for boys a greater dissatisfaction or anxiety about diminished postdivorce income, or possibly even a disrespect for the "provider" capability of the single-parent mother who is struggling financially. It may also relate to other factors pertinent to lower-SES groups, such as lower levels of support services and more defiant peer group norms. Since marital status comparisons without SES controls yielded far more significant differences for boys than girls, contrasts between the sexes in the amount of SES variance observed in ANCOVAs must be interpreted cautiously.

In most cases the amount of variance accounted for by SES factors was greater for academic than social-emotional criteria. It appears that the nonacademic behavioral problems are more resistant to these key environmental conditions. SES factors may exert their most powerful influence through academic encouragement and enrichment. An equally plausible explanation is that the effects of divorce are more noticeable in interpersonal interactions than in academic pursuits.

CONCLUSION

Results of the analyses presented here indicate that the adverse effects of divorce are far greater for boys than for girls by third-and fifth-grade levels. A major sex difference is also apparent in children's reactions to SES characteristics of mothers and fathers. Marital status differences between groups of girls at third and fifth grade are almost entirely eliminated when mothers' educational and occupational levels are controlled. These SES covariates, however, account for very little variance in male group differences.

Compared with mothers' characteristics, fathers' educational and occupational classifications appear to account for more of the variance in male performance. The family income variable is without question a major explanatory factor in divorce adjustment of boys.

These substantial age-sex differences appear to have considerable relevance for postdivorce decisions, such as child custody, support payments, and visitation schedules. In this study for example 68.5 percent of the initial divorced sample reported annual incomes of less than $15,000, with a median income of $10,000 to $14,999. Considering the pervasiveness of depressed incomes in single-parent divorced households, measures such as tax deductions for both custodial and noncustodial parents may be justified. Even stronger measures, such as recently enacted legislation to withhold child support payments from wages, seem to warrant support from mental health professionals.

Another means for maintaining predivorce income levels is more controversial, yet supported by the findings of this study. Despite the doubling of the divorce rate from 1970 to 1980, the percentage of father custody has not changed, remaining at 10 percent for the society as a whole in 1980. It is reasonable to expect that more equitable father-custody decisions would improve the financial status of the homes in which divorced-family children are reared. Joint custody might also enhance the financial support of children, since increased father involvement in child-rearing decisions may result in increased acceptance of financial responsibilities. Many states have facilitated this arrangement through legislation.

In addition to the possibility of alleviating financial distress, the father clearly plays an important role in facilitating the child's positive development. As stated previously, income level accounts more strongly for differences in academic than in social-emotional criteria. Beyond the enhancement of income level and related improvement of academic performance, the father may also play a crucial role in promoting appropriate social behavior. Other previously published findings from the NASP-KSU Project suggest that as boys mature, they have an increasing need for high-quality male parental contact. This is supported by evidence from such diverse measures as custodial parent's satisfaction with spouse's parenting, educational level of the father, quality of child's relationship with the father, visitation with the father, and decreased conflict between the parents (which can lead to more father–child contact).

Biller (1981) also supports greater father custody, particularly for boys. He cites research indicating that mother surrogates are more accessible than father surrogates, and presents data indicating that fathers are equally effective at parenting. Where father custody is not possible or is ill-advised, Biller (1981) recommends that father surrogates be provided through such organizations as Big Brothers, YMCA, and Boy Scouts. Recruitment of men in roles such as family therapists, preschool teachers, and public school educators is also suggested.

The startling pervasiveness of these sex differences across such a wide array of assessments and multiple data sources leads overwhelmingly to the conclusion that something must be done to assist boys in their adjustment to family disruption. Girls may also require assistance, even though empirical support for such a conclusion is lacking in this study. Researchers have suggested, for example, that adolescence is a particularly troublesome time for divorced-family girls, even though very few problems are observed in the preadolescent period. If this is the case, then the developmental transformations for girls may also shed some light on the reasons for boys' maladjustment.

It seems likely that prevailing sex-role stereotypes, particularly in lower-SES subcultures, encourage aggressive and possibly defiant behaviors for boys in both home and school settings, whereas such behaviors are rarely promoted by female sex-role stereotypes at any SES level. As girls develop more independence and self-sufficiency throughout the adolescent period, however, they may exercise their greater independence in defiant ways. During the preadolescent period, which is characterized by obedient behaviors, their adherence to the female cultural stereotype requires less exercise of power and authority on the part of parents and teachers, and they may fare well in mother-headed single-parent households. In adolescence, on the other hand, their diminished need for adult support, their greater independence from adult prescriptions, and their increased susceptibility to potentially defiant peer group norms may result in significantly reduced effectiveness of single-parent child-rearing procedures. Obviously, parental ability to monitor and control adolescent behavior is difficult even in two-parent families. Clinical practitioners testify that control problems are substantially compounded when only one parent is charged with the parenting responsibility, particularly when the chlld chooses to test the limits of parental authority.

While these conditions may prevail for girls in adolescence, they are likely to exist for boys at earlier levels, because of more defiant sex-role stereotypes. Testing limits of authority, particularly if that authority is a female parent or teacher, is far more likely to occur with young boys than girls, and the propensity may be exacerbated if boys begin to blame their mothers for the divorce. In such circumstances the single-parent mother faces serious behavior-control problems. The importance of structure and control in the postdivorce family has been documented in other analyses from this study (Guidubaldi et al., 1985), which demonstrate that such household routines as authoritative parenting style, earlier and regular bedtimes, and less television viewing, are related to better child adjustment. At this point in the mother's life, unfortunately, she is probably least likely to have the time, energy, or support necessary to exercise such control. The continuation of the father's parenting responsibility through sole or joint custody, or at least frequent visitation, may alleviate this problem. For these potential remedies to work effectively, however, we must first overcome a number of biases surrounding the divorce process. Our underdog mentality, which sometimes produces unjustified sympathies for mothers, and neglect of fathers' rights, must be addressed. We must also accept the reality that mothers, more often than fathers, require a period of job training and enhancement of occupational marketability after divorce. We must acknowledge that mothers have no monopoly on good parenting, that children's needs vary according to sex and developmental level, and that equitable custody decisions must be a national priority on legislative and judicial agendas.

Overall it appears that parental divorce *is* hurting America's children, particularly its sons. Rationalizations for adult egocentric behavior will continue to be generated, and answers to the legitimate question as to when divorce is less damaging than children's exposure to parental discord will still be sought. It should be clear, however, that divorced-family children in our society are currently vulnerable to behavioral and academic difficulties. Considering the many apparently irreversible changes in our society, a return to more stable child-rearing environments seems unlikely. The more tenable approach is to examine more assiduously the postdivorce environments that facilitate child adjustment and emotional security. This task requires no less than the full commitment of educators, social service personnel, and the psychology-related disciplines.

REFERENCES

Achenbach, T. M. (1978). Psychopathology of childhood: Research problems and issues. *Journal of Consulting and Clinical Psychology, 46,* 759–776.

Achenbach, T. M., & Edelbrock, C. S. (1978). The classification of child psychopathology: A review and analysis of empirical efforts. *Psychological Bulletin, 85,* 1275–1301.

Achenbach, T. M., & Edelbrock, C. S. (1981). Behavioral problems and competencies reported by parents of normal and disturbed children aged 4 through 16. *Monographs of the Society for Research in Child Development, 46,* Serial no. 188.

Achenbach, T. M., & Edelbrock, C. S. (1983). *Manual for the Child Behavior Checklist and Revised Child Behavior Profile.* Burlington, Vt.: University of Vermont, Child Psychiatry.

Atkeson, B. M., Forehand, R. L., & Rickard, K. M. (1982). The effects of divorce on children. In B. B. Lahey & A. E. Kazdin (Eds.), *Advances in Clinical Child Psychology* (Vol. 5) (pp. 255–281). New York: Plenum Press.

Belle, D. (Ed.) (1982). *Lives in Stress: Women and Depression.* Beverly Hills, Calif.: Sage Publications.

Berg, B., & Kelly, R. (1979). The measured self-esteem of children from broken, rejected, and accepted families. *Journal of Divorce, 2,* 363–369.

Bernard, J. M., & Nesbitt, S. (1981). An unreliable predictor of children's emotional predispositions. *Jounral of Divorce, 4,* 31–42.

Biller, H. B. (1981). The father and personality development: Paternal deprivation and sex-role development. In M. E. Lamb (Ed.), *The Role of the Father in Child Development.* (pp. 489–552). New York: Wiley.

Bloom, B. S. (1976). *Human Characteristics and School Learning.* New York: McGraw-Hill.

Brookover, W., & Lezotte, L. (1977). *Changes in School Characteristics Coincident with Changes in Student Achievement.* East Lansing, Mich.: Michigan State University, College of Urban Development.

Brown, B. F. (1980). A study of the school needs of children from one-parent families. *Phi Delta Kappan, 62,* 537–540.

Cleminshaw, H. K., & Guidubaldi, J. (1981). Assessing parent satisfaction. *Resources in Education.* ERIC: ED 200 858, *16*(9).

Clingempeel, W. G., & Reppucci, N. D. (1982). Joint custody after divorce: Major issues and goals for research. *Psychological Bulletin, 91,* 102–127.

Colletta, N. (1979). The impact of divorce: Father absence or poverty? *Journal of Divorce, 3,* 27–35.

Edmonds, R., & Frederikesen, J. (1978). *Search for Effective Schools: The Identification and Analysis of City Schools That Are Instructionally Effective for Poor Children.* Cambridge, Mass.: Harvard University, Center for Urban Studies.

Emery, R. E. (1982). Interparental conflict and the children of discord and divorce. *Psychological Bulletin, 92,* 310–330.

Guidubaldi, J. (1983, July). Divorce research clarifies issues: A report on NASP's nationwide study. *Communique.*

Guidubaldi, J., & Cleminshaw, H. (1985). Divorce, family health and child adjustment. In H. I. McCubbin & W. J. Doherty (Eds.), Family Health Care [Special Issue], *Family Relations, 34,* 35–41.

Guidubaldi, J., Cleminshaw, H. K., & Perry, J. (1985). The effects of parental divorce on children's and their parents' health. In J. E. Zins & D. I. Wagner (Eds.), Promoting physical and emotional well-being in educational settings; Innovative approaches and practices [Thematic Issue], *Special Services in the Schools, 1*(3), 73–86.

Guidubaldi, J., Cleminshaw, H. K., Perry, J. D., & Mcloughlin, C. S. (1983). The impact of parental divorce on children: Report of the nationwide NASP study. *School Psychology Review, 12*(3), 300–323.

Guidubaldi, J., Cleminshaw, H. K., Perry, J., & Nastasi, B. (1984). Impact of family support systems on children's academic and social functioning after divorce. In G. Rowe, J. DeFrain, H. Lingrin, R. MacDonald, N. Stinnet, S. Van Zandt, & R. Williams (Eds.), *Family Strengths 5: Continuity and Diversity.* (pp. 191–207). Newton, Mass.: Education Development Center.

Guidubaldi, J., Kehle, T. J., & Murray, J. W. (1979). Assessment strategies for the handicapped. *Personnel and Guidance Journal, 30,* 245–251.

Guidubaldi, J., Nastasi, B. K., Perry, J. D., Cleminshaw, H. K., Lightel, J., & Chiarella, D. (April 1985,). *Effects of Divorce on Children: The NASP-KSU Two-Year Longitudinal Study.* Symposium conducted at the annual meeting of the National Association of School Psychologists, Las Vegas, Nev.

Guidubaldi, J. & Perry, J. D. (1984). Divorce, socioeconomic status, and children's cognitive-social competence at school entry. *American Journal of Orthopsychiatry, 54,* 459–468.

Guidubaldi, J., & Perry, J. D. (1985). Divorce and mental health sequelae for children: A two-year follow-up of a nationwide sample. *Journal of the American Academy of Child Psychiatry, 24,* 531–537.

Guidubaldi, J., Perry, J. D., & Cleminshaw, H. K. (1984a). Divorce, socioeconomic status, and children's cognitive-social competence at school entry. *American Journal of Orthopsychiatry, 54,* 459–468.

Guidubaldi, J., Perry, J. D., & Cleminshaw, H. K. (1984b). The legacy of parental divorce: A nationwide study of family status and selected mediating variables on children's academic and social competencies. In B. B. Lahey & A. E. Kazdin (Eds.), *Advances in Clinical Child Psychology* (Vol. 7). (pp. 109–151). New York: Plenum Press.

Hess, R. D., & Camara, K. A. (1979). Post-divorce family relationships as mediating factors in the consequences of divorce for children. *Journal of Social Issues, 35,* 79–96.

Hetherington, E. M. (August, 1979a). *Children and Divorce.* Presidential Address, Division 7, American Psychological Association Convention, New York.

Hetherington, E. M. (1979b). A child's perspective. *American Psychologist, 34,* 851–858.

Hetherington, E. M., Cox, M., & Cox, R. (1978). The aftermath of divorce. In J. H. Stevens & M. Mathews (Eds.), *Mother/Child, Father/Child Relationships.* (pp. 149–176). Washington, D.C.: National Association for the Education of Young Children.

Hetherington, E. M., Cox, M., & Cox, R. (1979a). Family interaction and the social-emotional and cognitive development of children following divorce. In V. Vaughn & T. Brazelton (Eds.), *The Family: Setting Priorities* (pp. 71–87). New York: Science and Medicine Publishing Company.

Hetherington, E. M., Cox, M., & Cox, R. (1979b). Play and social interaction in children following divorce. *Journal of Social Issues, 35,* 26–49.

Hetherington, E. M., Cox, M., & Cox, R. (1982). Effects of divorce on parents and children. In M. E. Lamb (Ed.), *Nontraditional Families: Parenting and Child Development.* (pp. 233–288). Hillsdale, N.J.: Lawrence Erlbaum.

Jacobson, D. S. (1978a). The impact of marital separation/divorce on children: I. Parent-child separation and child adjustment. *Journal of Divorce, 1*(4), 341–360.

Jacobson, D. S. (1978b). The impact of marital separation/divorce on children: II. Interparent hostility and child adjustment. *Journal of Divorce, 2,* 3–19.

Jacobson, D. S. (1978c). The impact of marital separation/divorce on children: III. Parent-child communication and child adjustment, and regression analysis of findings from overall study. *Journal of Divorce, 2,* 175–194.

Jastak, J. F., Jastak, S. R., & Bijou, S. W. (1978). *Wide Range Achievement Test.* Wilmington, Del.: Jastak Associates.

Kalter, N. (1977). Children of divorce in an outpatient psychiatric population. *American Journal of Orthopsychiatry, 47,* 40–51.

Kelly, J. B., & Wallerstein, J. S. (1976). The effects of parental divorce: Experiences of the child in early latency. *American Journal of Orthopsychiatry, 46,* 20–23.

Kurdek, L. A. (1981). An integrative perspective on children's divorce adjustment. *American Psychologist, 36,* 856–866.

Kurdek, L. A. (Ed.) (1983). *Children and Divorce.* San Francisco: Jossey-Bass.

Kurdek, L. A., & Berg, B. (1983). Correlates of children's adjustments to their parents' divorces. In L. A. Kurdek (Ed.), *Children and Divorce* (pp. 47–60). San Francisco: Jossey-Bass.

Kurdek, L. A., Blisk, D., & Siesky, A. E. (1981). Correlates of children's long-term adjustment to their parents' divorce. *Developmental Psychology, 17,* 565–579.

Kurdek, L. A., & Siesky, A. E. (1980a). Sex role self-concepts of single divorced parents and their children. *Journal of Divorce, 3,* 249–261.

Kurdek, L. A., & Siesky, A. E. (1980b). Children's perceptions of their parents' divorce. *Journal of Divorce, 3*(4), 339–378.

Lamb, M. E. (Ed.) (1981). *The role of the father in child development* (2nd ed.). New York: Wiley.

Lamb, M. E. (Ed.) (1982). *Nontraditional Families: Parenting and Child Development.* Hillsdale, N.J.: Lawrence Erlbaum.

Lazarus, M. (1980). One-parent families and their children. *Principal, 60,* 31–37.

Levitin, T. E. (1979). Children of divorce. *Journal of Social Issues, 35,* 1–25.

McDermott, J. F. (1968). Parental divorce in early childhood. *American Journal of Psychiatry, 124,* 118–126.

McDermott, J. J. (1970). Divorce and its psychiatric sequelae in children. *Archives of General Psychiatry, 23,* 421–427.

Morrison, J. R. (1974). Parental divorce as a factor in childhood psychiatric illness. *Comparative Psychiatry, 15,* 95–102.

Nay, W. R. (1979). *Multimethod Clinical Assessment.* New York: Gardner Press.

Perry, J. D., Guidubaldi, J., & Kehle, T. J. (1979). Kindergarten competencies as predictors of third grade classroom behavior and achievement. *Journal of Educational Psychology, 71,* 443–450.

Reinhard, D. W. (1977). *Journal of Clinical and Child Psychology, 6,* 21–23.

Rosen, R. (1977). Children of divorce: What they feel about access and other aspects of the divorce experience. *Journal of Clinical Child Psychology, 6,* 24–27.

Santrock, J. W., & Warshak, R. A. (1979). Father custody and social development in boys and girls. *Journal of Social Issues, 35,* 112–125.

Sells, S. B., & Roff, M. (1967). *Peer Acceptance-Rejection and Personality Development.* Washington, D.C.: U.S. Department of Health, Education and Welfare.

Shinn, M. (1978). Father absence and children's cognitive development. *Psychological Bulletin, 85,* 295–324.

Sparrow, S., Balla, D. A., & Chicchetti, D. F. (1981). *Vineland Adaptive Behavior Scales: Classroom Edition* (research ed.). Circle Pines, Minn.: American Guidance Association.

Spivack, G., & Swift, M. (1967). *Devereux Elementary School Behavior Rating Scale.* Devon, Pa.: Devereux Foundation.

Spivack, G., & Swift, M. (1975). *Hahnemann Elementary School Behavior Rating Scale, Manual.* Philadelphia: Department of Mental Health Services, Hahnemann Medical College and Hospital.

Stevenson, H. W., Parker, T., Wilkinson, A., Hegion, A., & Fish, E. (1976). Predictive value of teacher ratings of young children. *Journal of Educational Psychology, 68,* 507–517.

Stipek, D., Lamb, M., & Zigler, E. (1981). OPTI: A measure of children's optimism. *Educational and Psychological Measurement, 41*(1), 131–150.

Sugar, M. (1970). Children of divorce. *Pediatrics, 46,* 558–595.

Svanum, S., Bringle, R. G., & McLaughlin, J. E. (1982). Father absence and cognitive performance in a large sample of six- to 11-year-old children. *Child Development, 53,* 136–143.

Tucker, J., & Regan, R. A. (1966). Intactness of the home and behavioral problems in children. *Journal of Child Psychology and Psychiatry, 7,* 225–233.

U.S. Bureau of the Census, Current Population Reports

Wallerstein, J. S. & Kelly, J. B. (1974). The effects of parental divorce: The adolescent experience. In E. Anthony & C. Koupernik (Eds.), *The Child and his Family (Vol. 3).* (pp. 479–505.). New York: Wiley.

Wallerstein, J. S. & Kelly, J. B. (1975). The effects of parental divorce: Experiences of the preschool child. *Journal of the American Academy of Child Psychiatry, 14,* 600–616.

Wallerstein, J. S. & Kelly, J. B. (1976). The effects of parental divorce experiences of the child in later latency. *American Journal of Orthopsychiatry, 46,* 256–269.

Wallerstein, J. S. & Kelly, J. B. (1980a). California's children of divorce. *Psychology Today, 13,* 66–76.

Wallerstein, J. S. & Kelly, J. B. (1980b). *Surviving the Breakup: How Children and Parents Cope with Divorce.* New York: Basic Books.

Warshak, R. A. & Santrock, J. W. (1983). The impact of divorce in father-custody and mother-custody homes: The child's perspective. In L. A. Kurdek (Ed.), *New Directions for Child Development: Children and Divorce* (pp. 29–46). San Francisco: Jossey-Bass.

Westman, J., Cline, D., Swift, W. & Krammer, D. (1970). Role of child psychiatry in divorce. *Archives of General Psychiatry, 23,* 416–420.

Zakariya, S. B. (1982). Another look at children of divorce: Summary report of the study of school needs of one-parent children. *Principal, 62,* 34–37.

7

Cognitive Mediators of Children's Adjustment to Divorce

LAWRENCE A. KURDEK

Because marital disruption and, particularly, marital discord have been connected to children's emotional and behavioral pathology (Bond & McMahon, 1984; Emery et al., 1984; Emery & O'Leary, 1984; Guidubaldi et al., 1984; Guidubaldi & Perry, 1984; Guidubaldi et al., 1983; Hetherington, et al., 1982; Kalter & Rembar, 1981; Links, 1983; O'Leary & Emery, 1984; Rutter, 1979), efforts have been made to integrate the available empirical literature in this area and develop conceptual models for understanding children's divorce-related experiences (Atkeson et al., 1982; Biller, 1981; Blechman, 1982; Clingempeel & Reppucci, 1982; Derdeyn & Scott, 1984; Emery, 1982; Emery et al., 1984; Furstenberg et al., 1983; Hetherington, 1979, 1984; Hetherington et al., 1979, 1982; Kanoy & Cunningham, 1984; King & Kleemeier, 1983; Leahey, 1984; Peterson et al., 1984; Voelker & McMillan, 1983; White & Mika, 1983). Kurdek (1981), for example, has been described children's divorce adjustment as being affected by four nested levels of factors: (1) ideologies about family life, (2) the stability of the postseparation environment and the availability of social supports to the single-parent family, (3) reciprocal changes in the parent–child roles in the postseparation family system, and (4) the child's own ability to deal with stress. The last level, which includes cognitive factors influencing divorce adjustment, is the focus of this chapter. It

The author would like to thank J. Patrick Schmitt, Sharlene Wolchik, and Paul Karoly for critical readings of the manuscript and Cyndi Dawson for typing the manuscript.

should be remembered, though, that these factors need to be considered within an interactive, ecological perspective.

The basis for a cognitive component of a model of children's divorce adjustments comes from two separate literatures. The first describes cognitive-developmental approaches to the study of development; the second emphasizes linkages between cognition and stress. Each will be discussed in turn; then attention will be directed to empirical support for a cognitive-developmental model of children's divorce adjustment, and to the practical application of such a model.

COGNITIVE-DEVELOPMENTAL APPROACHES

The basic premise underlying cognitive developmental models is that development proceeds parallel with, or as a consequence of, sequential changes in the structure and quality of underlying thought patterns (Kohlberg, 1969)—and thus, cognitive development is necessary but not sufficient for development in other areas. This approach has been most widely used to devise stagelike descriptions of growth, in the areas of perspective taking (Selman, 1980), distributive justice (Damon, 1977), interpersonal understanding (Selman, 1980), moral judgment (Colby et al., 1983), sex typing (Kohlberg, 1969), and understanding of family roles (Watson & Amgott-Kwan, 1984). More recently researchers have examined how cognitive development can aid in understanding and changing problematic behavior in children (Bobbitt & Keating, 1983; Harter, 1983; Selman, 1980; Urbain & Kendall, 1980). Empirical studies validating cognitive-developmental models have addressed two critical issues: (1) Does development occur in a stagelike fashion, such that longitudinal assessments reveal an invariant, forward progression, and no evidence of regression? (2) Is cognitive development necessary but not sufficient for development in other areas? Data regarding invariant progressive development have been confirmatory, especially in the areas of moral judgment (Colby et al., 1983), interpersonal understanding (Gurucharri & Selman, 1982), and distributive justice (Damon, 1980; Enright et al., 1984). Data regarding the necessary but not sufficient relation between cognitive development and other areas are neither extensive nor consistent (e.g., Enright et al., 1980; Enright et al., 1984; Krebs & Gillmore, 1982), and several authors have commented on the methodological problems involved in assessing this relation (e.g., Jamison & Dansky, 1979; Smolak & Levine, 1984). Perhaps because of such problems, researchers have more often sought to address the issue of requisite cognitive development by correlating cognitive development with growth in other areas (e.g., Colby et al., 1983; Selman, 1980) than by undertaking more stringent structural analyses (e.g., Edelstein et al., 1984; Jamison & Dansky, 1979; Krebs & Gillmore, 1982). Such correlational approaches, of course, provide evidence only for parallel development in two domains, and do not address issues regarding causal relations across diverse regions of psychological growth.

Cognitive developmental models of children's divorce-related experiences have been described by Longfellow (1979) and Neal (1983). Combining the work of Selman (1980) on social cognitive development with the work of Wallerstein and Kelly (1980) on children's reactions to divorce, these authors suggest that there are parallel developments between children's social cognition and their reactions to divorce. How children react to divorce, in other words, is influenced by the way they coordinate social perspectives and reason about social relationships. A developmental description of the role that social cognition plays in children's divorce reactions follows (see Shantz, 1983, for a more extensive description of social cognitive development).

Preschool children (three to six years old) have difficulty in distinguishing others' viewpoints from their own, and often confuse their own and others' subjectivity. They tend to consider one subjective state at a time, to view relationships in terms of concrete physical aspects, and to find it difficult to differentiate between inner motives and outward appearances. Given these cognitive limitations, preschoolers frequently react to divorce with fright, confusion, and self-blame. They are likely to focus on divorce as one parent's moving away, and may not be able to infer the complex motivations underlying the behavior of both parents. They may also find it difficult to identify and express their own feelings.

Although children of early-elementary-school age (seven to eight years) recognize that more than one subjective feeling can exist, such feelings are not directed toward the same person: one cannot, for example, feel happy and angry simultaneously toward the same parent. Persons are viewed in terms of context-specific feelings and actions, and relationships in terms of subjective appraisals of others' actions. Children at this age may thus experience divorce with sadness, loss, and rejection. While they may not blame themselves, they often develop pervasive negative evaluations of one or both parents, and have difficulty merging these negative feelings with the positive feelings that still exist. They may believe, further, that the parents could reconcile if they really wanted to and if they tried hard enough.

Older elementary-school-aged children (nine to ten years) recognize that conflicting feelings can exist simultaneously toward the same person. Inner motives are distinguished from overt action, and relationships are seen in terms of reciprocal attitudes and actions. Given the greater psychological sophistication of these children, they often construct an interpretation of divorce that focuses on parental conflict, incompatibility, and ambivalent feelings. They can be sensitive to each parent's need for distance from the other parent, but may also experience loyalty conflicts and intense anger toward one or both parents.

Young adolescents (11 to 13 years) and older adolescents (13 to 18 years) are capable of observing their own self-reflective process. This metacognitive skill enables them to adopt a "third person" viewpoint in considering their own and others' perspectives as they relate to each other. Persons are described in terms of enduring psychological traits, relationships are perceived as mutual. As one might expect, adolescents can construct a fairly realistic appraisal of divorce-related events, and can view the parents' decision to divorce as a consequence of a bad fit between two personalities, or in terms of lost mutuality and compatibility. Because their own social sphere is expanding, adolescents may react to divorce with anger, shame, and embarrassment, and may begin to question the durability of any marital relationship.

In sum, one argument for including a cognitive component within any model of children's divorce adjustment is that children's level of cognitive and social-cognitive development filters their perceptions of divorce-related events. Because these perceptions involve inferred psychological constructs (Barenboim, 1981) and the understanding of family roles (Watson & Amgott-Kwan, 1984), children's reasoning about divorce-related events should follow a stagelike progression similar to that found in other domains of interpersonal understanding (Selman, 1980).

COGNITION AND STRESS

The second literature source that provides a basis for examining the relation between cognition and children's divorce adjustment deals with the relation between cognition and stress. As a reflection of a larger concern with the role cognition plays in clinical practice and research (Arnkoff & Glass, 1982; Hollon & Kriss, 1984), focus has been directed toward cognition as a mediator of stress for both adults (e.g., Fleming et al., 1984) and children (e.g., Bernard & Joyce, 1984; Garmezy & Rutter,

1983). In view of the recent focus on children, studies concerning both adults and children will be discussed.

Cognition and Stress in Adults

Cognitive theories of stress in adults are relational and process oriented (Folkman, 1984), and emphasize the primacy of appraisal (Ellis, 1979; Lazarus, 1984; Lazarus & Folkman, 1984; Thompson, 1981). Stress is defined as a particular relationship between a person and the environment, where the person appraises an event as exceeding current resources, and then evaluates the range of coping strategies. Stress is thus embedded in a particular context, and appraisals of stress control are likely to change as a result of shifts both in the person–environment relationship (Folkman, 1984) and in the relative adequacy of available support and resources (Rofe, 1984).

Most of the data supporting the linkage between cognition and stress in adults have come from studies of attribution and depression. Generally these studies indicate that depressed people ascribe negative outcomes to internal, stable, and global causes (Anderson et al., 1983; Beck et al., 1979; Golin et al., 1981; Peterson & Seligman, 1984; Seligman et al., 1979). It should also be noted, however, that several studies have failed to predict subsequent depression from current cognitions (Coyne & Gotlib, 1983). Empirical support, then, for the causal priority of cognition over affect is not consistent (Zajonc, 1984). More recent studies have focused on daily experiences of stress—such as college examinations—and have found that appraisals of stressful events may involve the simultaneous experience of threat and challenge (Folkman & Lazarus, 1985), and that different kinds of coping may be appropriate for different types of stressors (McCrae, 1984).

Indirect support for the relation between cognition and stress in adults comes from interpretations of the consistent finding that the availability and use of social resources and support are positively related to general psychological adjustment (Cutrona, 1984; D'Augelli, 1983; Holahan & Moos, 1981; Lazarus & Folkman, 1984; Russell et al., 1984) and to divorce adjustment in particular (Caldwell & Bloom, 1982; Colletta, 1979; Daniels-Mohring & Berger, 1984; Kitson & Raschke, 1981; Richardson & Pfeiffenberger, 1983). One possible interpretation of this finding is that the utilization of social support activates cognitive processes and defensive styles that enable the stressed person to find meaning in the stressful experience, to gain mastery over the event, to diffuse responsibility, and to restore self-esteem through self-enhancing evaluations (Gottlieb, 1983; Pilisuk, 1982; Taylor, 1983). Such utilization may be most effective for individuals with an internal locus of control and for individuals who are not highly affiliative and dependent (Lefcourt et al., 1984).

Cognition and Stress in Children

As with adults, cognitive components have been implicated in children's general behavioral adjustment and divorce adjustment. Although appraisal has been an important component of how families adapt to crisis (McCubbin & Patterson, 1983), cognitive approaches to the study and treatment of stress in children are relatively recent (Bernard & Joyce, 1984; Ellis & Bernard, 1983; Garmezy & Rutter, 1983; Peterson et al., 1984; Selman, 1980).

Two major approaches to the study of cognition and stress in children can be identified. The first approach assumes a linkage between children's cognition and behavior (see Kohlberg & Candee, 1984; Turiel & Smetana, 1984), and argues that pathological behavior, such as delinquency, aggression, and social isolation, is due to the absence of certain skills. Ladd and Mize (1983) have identified three types of skills deficits: children may lack knowledge or concepts of appropriate social behavior; children may lack actual behavioral abilities due to lack of practice or opportunity; and children may have difficulty interpreting feedback about their social interactions. From this perspective the focus of intervention is on facilitating the acquisition of appropriate skills and knowledge (Conger & Keane, 1981; Ladd & Mize, 1983; Urbain & Kendall, 1980).

The second approach to the study of cognition and stress in children assumes that emotional and behavioral problems are the result of children's having constructed and internalized an incorrect interpretation of events. These interpretations are referred to as biases, errors, and distortions. Seligman and colleagues (1984) for example found that eight- to 13-year-old children who attributed bad events to internal, stable, and global causes were more likely to report depressive symptoms than children who attributed these events to external, unstable, and specific causes. Kaslow and colleagues (1984) also reported that among six- to 14-year-old children, depressed children make attributions as noted by Seligman and colleagues (1984), evaluate themselves negatively, have low expectations for performance, maintain stringent criteria for failure, and prefer punishment over reward.

The most clearly articulated presentation of this approach has come from proponents of rational-emotive therapy (Bernard & Joyce, 1984; Ellis

& Bernard, 1983), who argue that children's perception, representation, interpretation, and appraisal of events influence their psychological adjustment. Because cognitive factors such as expectations, attributions, beliefs, selective attention, and logical reasoning change with age, they are critical components of any developmental model of stress (see Kagan, 1984). A major assumption of this approach is that cognitive biases, errors, and distortions are central to both the understanding and the treatment of children's psychological disorders. This assumption has important consequences for understanding and treating children experiencing their parents' divorce.

Given the complexity of events leading up to parental separation and divorce, children's misinterpretation of these events can readily occur. Wallerstein (1983) in fact has listed cognitive mastery as a major task for children of divorced parents. This task involves acknowledging the reality of the marital rupture, resolving anger and blame, accepting the permanence of the divorce, and achieving realistic hopes regarding one's own future relationships. Peterson and colleagues note that such cognitive mastery can be affected by children's perception of the quality of their parents' marriage, the quality of the relationship between the children and their noncustodial parent, the tolerance with which parental divorce is greeted within the relevant subculture, and children's age and gender.

The acquisition of cognitive mastery can be difficult because of the irrational beliefs that children may hold about the divorce and about their role in the divorce decision. While there are many ways to classify the irrational beliefs of childhood (Bernard & Joyce, 1984), the scheme offered by Beck and colleagues (1979) captures many of the problematic attitudes of children experiencing divorce (Gardner, 1976; Tessman, 1978; Wallerstein & Kelly, 1980). These irrational beliefs, their definition, and divorce-related examples are presented in Table 7.1.

In addition to this list, Ellis and Bernard (1983) have identified three clusters of irrational beliefs that seem particularly relevant to children's behavior in the postdivorce period when a decrease in financial resources is apt to be experienced (Weiss, 1984). These beliefs are : "I must get what I want," "I must be comfortable and life should be fun," and "I must do well and be approved of."

Data supportive of a link between cognition and stress in children are not as extensive as those available for adults. Much of the data, in fact, are supportive of the skills deficit hypothesis, and indicate that poorly developed social cognitive skills—such as perspective taking, interpersonal understanding, social problem solving, intention cue detection, conversational skills, and moral reasoning—are related to low peer status (Bierman & Furman, 1984; Kurdek & Krile, 1982), aggression (Dodge et

Table 7.1

Irrational Beliefs and Illustrative Divorce-Related Comments

Belief	Description of Belief (from Beck et al., 1979)	Divorce-Related Comment
Arbitrary inference	Drawing a specific conclusion when the evidence is absent, or is contrary to the conclusion	"Mom and Dad can't care for each other anymore. If they did, they wouldn't be getting divorced."
Selective abstraction	Focusing on a detail taken out of context, ignoring other more salient features of the situation, and conceptualizing the whole experience on the basis of this fragment	"Dad called Mom today. Maybe they'll get back together soon!"
Overgeneralization	Drawing a general rule or conclusion on the basis of one or more isolated incidents and applying the concept across the board to related and unrelated situations	"Dad said he loves me, but he left. I'll bet Mom is gonna leave someday, too."
Magnification	Exaggerating the meaning or significance of an event	"I just can't face any of my friends now. They won't want to have anything to do with me."
Personalization	Relating external events to the self when there is no basis for making such a connection	"I know Mom and Dad divorced because of something I did."
Absolutistic, dichotomous thinking	Viewing experiences from only one of two opposing perspectives	"This divorce is either good or bad. It can't be both. It's bad!"

al., 1984), wide-ranging emotional disorders (Gurucharri et al., 1984), delinquency (Gibbs et al., 1984), and poor general adjustment (Kurdek & Krile, 1983). Although studies of the effect of social support provided directly to children are not extensive (Gottlieb, 1983; Stolberg & Cullen, 1983), positive effects could be interpreted in terms of meaning, mastery, and rebuilt self-esteem, as noted for adults.

In sum, recent theories of stress have suggested that cognition mediates stress for both adults and children, and that the positive effects of social support may be cognitively mediated. Supportive data for these views, however, are not extensive. A particular unresolved issue is the causal priority of cognition over affect. For children stress and pathological behavior have been thought to be the result of either a social skills deficit or an interpretation of events based on cognitive biases, errors, and distortions.

EMPIRICAL SUPPORT FOR A COGNITIVE-DEVELOPMENTAL MODEL OF CHILDREN'S DIVORCE ADJUSTMENT

As indicated, the study of cognitive mediators of children's adjustment to divorce has been based on both cognitive-developmental approaches to social cognition and research linking cognition and stress. Given the few empirical studies of children of divorce that have adopted a cognitive perspective, my colleagues and I have tested three predictions that would lend support to the validity of a cognitive-developmental model of children's adjustment to divorce. First, there should be age-related trends in how children reason about aspects of divorce. Second, given that marriage and divorce involve interpersonal relations, there should be a correspondence between children's general interpersonal understanding and their more specific reasoning about divorce. Third, if stress is alleviated by beliefs of mastery and control over problematic life events, then attributions of personal control should be related to positive divorce adjustment. Data relevant to each of these predictions will be summarized after a discussion of measurement issues.

Issues of Assessment

Currently there is no consensus on how best to define and assess children's views of divorce or their adjustment to divorce. Four strategies have been used to assess children's perceptions of divorce-related events—open-ended clinical interviews, structured interview schedules, objective self-report measures, and projective techniques. Two strategies have been used to assess children's adjustment to divorce: general behavioral adjustment has been assessed by parent ratings, teacher ratings, self-report self-esteem scales, and observation of parent-child interactions; and specific divorce adjustment has been assessed by parent ratings.

Assessing Children's Views of Divorce

In open-ended clinical interviews, the quality and richness of children's responses are given priority over a standardized procedure. Wallerstein and Kelly's (1980) Divorce Specific Assessment illustrates this strategy well. This assessment covered three broad areas. First was the child's response to and experience with parental separation and divorce. Of interest here were children's thoughts, fantasies, and emotional and behavioral reactions to the divorce; the situational specificity of reactions to the divorce; and the psychological defenses employed to deal with divorce-related stresses. The second area covered was the child's appraisal of relationships with both the custodial parent and the noncustodial parent, and the extent to which each relationship provided support and promoted development. The last area of concern was the availability of support systems outside of the home. Specific sources of support included siblings, peers, grandparents, extended family, school, teachers, and extracurricular activities.

Although this assessment is noted for its comprehensiveness, it does not readily lend itself to quantitative determinations of reliability. Thus while several studies have used subjective clinical interviews (e.g., Gardner, 1976; Tessman, 1978; Wallerstein, 1984; Wallerstein & Kelly, 1980), their empirical yield can be questioned (Levitin, 1979).

Structured interview schedules attempt to maintain the richness of data obtained through open-ended clinical interviews, while ensuring some degree of reliability and standardization. Fry and Leahey (1983), Warshak and Santrock (1983), Kalter and Plunkett (1984), and Kurdek and Siesky (1980) have employed this approach. Fry and Leahey (1983) asked adolescents to identify three upsetting and three pleasant events associated with the custodial parent. They were also asked to explain how and why the event was upsetting or pleasant for them. Warshak and Santrock's (1983) interview included questions regarding children's perceptions of parental roles, attitudes toward each parent, desire for more contact with each parent, feelings about separation from parents, understanding of the concept of divorce and reasons for the divorce, and predictions about their own eventual marital status. Kalter and Plunkett's (1984) interview was made up of ten questions that included general inquiry about behavior, feelings, peer relations, and the future. Kurdek and Siesky's (1980) questions focused on understanding the concept of divorce, reasons the child's parents no longer live together, parent reconcililation, blame for the divorce, negative and positive consequences of the divorce, descriptions of both parents, telling peers about the divorce, friends' reactions to the divorce, feeling different from peers, activities during the visits by the noncustodial parent, and the child's eventual marital status. In each study responses were content-analyzed and coded, and reports of interrater reliability were obtained.

Objective measures of children's perceptions of parental divorce have only recently been developed. Some measures have a general focus. Fry and Trifiletti (1983) had adolescents first identify stressful events associated with living in a single-parent family, and then rate each event on a five point bipolar rating scale. Hingst (1981) constructed a scale of 49 questions and provided five possible answers to each, from which children were to choose the one that most clearly approximated their feelings and/ or facts of the situation as they saw it. Ambert and Saucier (1983) had adolescents rate both parents on seven-point polar adjective scales. Other measures are more comprehensive and multidimensional. Reinhard (1977) devised a measure that required children to indicate how much they agree (e.g., 1 = strongly disagree, 5 = strongly agree) with 99 items. The items are grouped into subscales that include news of the divorce, acceptance of parents, loss of parent, changes in family relationships, post divorce conflict, emotional responses, peer reactions, need for counseling, and maturity. Plunkett and Kalter (1984) describe a 25-item scale in which children rated the extent of their agreement using a four-point scale. Items were combined into three composite scores: sad/insecure, active coping, and abandonment. Berg and Kurdek's 48-item Child Separation Inventory (Kurdek & Berg, 1983) requires yes or no answers and provides separate scores for peer ridicule and avoidance, paternal blame, maternal blame, self-blame, fear of abandonment, and hope of reunification. Such objective measures assess multiple dimensions of the divorce experience and allow the collection of traditional psychometric data, such as test–retest reliability and internal consistency.

A final type of measure used to assess children's perceptions of divorce is projective in nature. Warshak and Santrock's (1983) Projective Story task involves questioning children about events in pictures of divorce-related scenarios. Responses are scored for attribution of blame, reconciliation beliefs and wishes, attitudes toward custody arrangements, and attitudes toward parental remarriage. Although its reliability has not been assessed, the measure may be especially useful with the very young children or with children who are reticent to discuss the divorce. It may also be useful as a "warm-up" for the more objective measures described above.

Assessing Children's Adjustment to Divorce.

Measures of general behavioral adjustment have often been used as measures of divorce adjustment. These include standarized parent rating-scales such as the Child Behavior Checklist (Stolberg & Cullen, 1983), the Personality Inventory for Children (Kurdek et al., 1981), and the Louisville Behavior Checklist (Jacobson, 1978); standardized teacher rating-scales such as the Hahnemann Elementary School Behavior Rating Scale (Guidubaldi et al., 1983), the Health Resources Inventory (Kurdek & Berg, 1983), and the Kohn Social Competence Scale (Hetherington et al., 1982); and standardized self-report scales such as the Piers-Harris and Coppersmith self-esteem scales (Cooper et al., 1983; Kelly & Berg, 1978; Kurdek & Blisk, 1983; Lowenstein & Koopman, 1978). In addition, trained observers have rated parent–child interactions in a laboratory setting, and both free play and social interaction in a school setting (Hetherington et al., 1982).

Measures that specifically assess children's adjustment to divorce are not extensive. Kurdek and Siesky (1979) developed an open-ended structured interview for parents that covered conflict in the preseparation period, explaining divorce to the child, the child's immediate reactions to the divorce, children's present attitudes toward the divorce, and positive effects of divorce on children. More recently objective parent scales of children's divorce adjustment have been developed. These include the Parent Separation Inventory (Kurdek & Berg, 1983), the Single Parenting Questionnaire (Stolberg & Ullman, 1984), and the Divorced Parent's Questionnaire (Hodges & Bloom, 1984; Hodges et al., 1984). Each measure has adequate internal consistency for composite scores, but only Stolberg and Ullman report information regarding test–retest reliability, interrater reliability, and concurrent validity.

In sum, considerable progress has been made in developing measures appropriate for assessing children's perceptions of and reactions to divorce. Reliability and validity data, though, are limited. Consequently studies using these measures must be interpreted cautiously.

Age-Related Trends in Children's Understanding of Divorce

In our own studies, we have used two methods to assess age-related patterns in children's reasoning about various aspects of divorce.

First, we administered structured interviews to children, coded responses into categories derived through content analysis (with percent perfect agreement between two independent raters exceeding 96 percent), and cross-tabulated these response categories by age levels (Kurdek & Siesky, 1980). Second, we administered two objective measures to children, a modification of Reinhard's (1977) questionnaire (Kurdek et al.,1981) and the Children's Separation Inventory (Kurdek & Berg, 1983), and correlated these scores with children's age.

The questions and response categories for the structured interview are presented in the left-hand side of Table 7.2. To date, this interview has been administered to two independent cross-sectional samples (Kurdek & Berg, 1983; Kurdek & Siesky, 1980); to provide a more reliable assessment of age-related trends in children's responses, the two samples have been combined. This aggregated sample was divided into three age groups: six to eight years ($n = 55$), nine to 12 years ($n = 60$), and 13 to 18 years ($n = 78$). These age groups conform to those used by Wallerstein and Kelly (1980). The 98 boys and 95 girls of this sample were white, middle-class, and experienced parental separation an average of 31.78 months prior to the data collection.

Developmental trends in responses were assessed by contingency table analyses, in which the dimensions were developmental level (six to eight years, nine to 12 years, and 13 to 18 years) and response categories for the particular question of the interview (see Table 7.2). As shown in the right-hand side of Table 7.2, X^2 values were significant ($P < 0.05$) for 14 out of 18 analyses.

Generally the findings are consonant with developmental trends noted in the social cognition literature (Selman, 1980; Shantz, 1983), which indicate that older children's views of others are more likely than those of younger children to be abstract, psychological, and inferential. Specifically the significant effects can be summarized as follows: Older children were more likely than younger children (1) to define divorce in terms of psychological distance between parents; (2) to cite incompatibility as a reason for the parents not living together anymore and/or for the unlikelihood of parental reconciliations; (3) to attribute the blame for the divorce to one or both parents and not to themselves; (4) to cite loss of contact with the father as one of the bad things about the divorce; (5) to cite decreased parental conflict as one of the good things about the divorce; (6) to describe each parent as having positive and negative characteristics rather than neutral characteristics; (7) to tell friends about the divorce; (8) to view the divorce as not mattering to friends; (9) to see oneself as different from friends because of the divorce; and (10) to see parental divorce as irrelevant to their own marriage prospects. Table 7.2

Table 7.2
Questions and Responses from the Structured Interview and the Percentage of Children from Each Age Group Giving a Particular Response

Question and Response Categories	% From Each Age Group Giving Response*			χ^2	df	P
	6–8 years	9–12 years	13–18 years			
1. What does it mean when two people get divorced?				50.08	8	0.0001
Marriage dissolution: "They end their marriage."	6	13	21			
Physical separation: "They move far away from each other."	35	30	16			
Psychological distance: "They grow apart from each other and lose their bond."	27	49	61			
Child oriented: "I get real mad."	6	6	1			
"I don't know."	27	2	0			
2. Why don't your Mom and Dad live together anymore?				14.98	8	0.05
Incompatibility: "They didn't get along."	34	49	61			
Marriage dissolution: "They aren't married anymore."	35	13	20			
Loss of Love: "They don't love each other."	19	23	10			
Affair: "Dad fell for another lady."	4	4	4			
"I don't know."	8	11	5			
3a. Do you think your mom and dad will ever live together again?				5.68	4	0.22
"Yes."	15	13	4			
"No."	80	81	90			
"I don't know."	5	5	5			

				χ^2	df	p
3b. Why or why not?				32.15	8	0.001
Incompatibility: "No, they just don't get along."	26	45	55			
Remarriage: "No, Mom's married again."	13	17	29			
Parent report: "No, cause Mom said so."	10	6	3			
Child-oriented: "Yes, 'cause I want them to."	2	6	1			
"I don't know."	48	26	10			
4a. Do you think anyone is to blame for your mom and dad not being together like they used to be?				12.32	4	0.01
"Yes."	13	32	38			
"No."	83	60	61			
"I don't know."	4	7	1			
4b. Who?				9.74	10	0.46
Mom.	2	6	3			
Dad.	6	13	17			
"Both Mom and Dad."	4	6	12			
"Other" man/woman.	2	4	4			
Child.	2	2	1			
"I don't know."	85	69	64			
5. What are some of the bad things about your mom and dad not living together?				32.37	8	0.0001
Loss of contact with noncustodial father: "I don't get to see Dad that much."	31	57	74			
None: "There are no bad things about it."	8	8	7			
Adverse child feelings: "I get sad."	12	15	7			
Friends' reactions: "My friends feel sorry for me and pity me."	10	8	5			

Question and Response Categories	% From Each Age Group Giving Response*			χ^2	df	P
	6–8 years	9–12 years	13–18 years			
"I don't know."	40	13	8			
6. What are some of the good things about your mom and dad not living together?				32.01	10	0.0004
No parent conflict: "Mom and Dad don't fight with each other anymore."	27	43	48			
None: "There are no good things."	14	19	8			
Improved relations with custodial mother: "I'm much closer to Mom now."	2	6	13			
Child related: "I get away with a lot now."	25	17	5			
Happiness: "We all like things this way."	13	11	21			
"I don't know."	19	4	5			
7. What is your mom like? How would you describe her?				38.16	8	0.0001
Positive: "She's fun and nice and loves me."	62	74	57			
Negative: "She's mean and crabby."	0	2	12			
Positive and negative: "Sometimes she's nice, sometimes she's not so nice."	15	22	30			
Neutral: "She's tall and thin."	21	2	0			
"I don't know."	2	0	1			
8. What is your dad like? How would you describe him?				34.29	8	0.0001
Positive: "He's nice and takes me to neat places."	71	53	39			
Negative: "He never has time for me."	4	19	22			
Positive and negative: "Most of the time he's nice, but he can be mean."	4	19	31			

				χ²	df	p
Neutral: "He's kinda old and has a mustache."	15	2	4			
"I don't know."	6	7	4			
9. Have you told many friends that your mom and dad don't live together?				45.67	4	0.0001
Yes.	37	70	87			
No.	46	9	9			
Some.	17	20	4			
10. Does it matter to friends that your mom and dad no longer live together?				11.43	4	0.02
Yes.	19	23	17			
No.	67	67	83			
Some	14	9	0			
11a. Are there ways in which you think you're different from your friends?				3.96	4	0.41
Yes.	67	57	61			
No.	31	39	39			
"I don't know."	2	4	0			
11b. What are they?				13.93	4	0.007
Divorce related: "Yes, they live with their mom and dad, and I live with just Mom."	15	23	31			
Not divorce related: "Yes, we have different interests and ideas."	58	36	26			
"I don't know."	27	41	43			
12. What do you do when your dad visits?				15.39	8	0.05
Affection: "I hug him a lot."	21	13	4			
Talk: "We sit around and talk."	2	13	18			

Question and Response Categories	% From Each Age Group Giving Response*			χ^2	df	P
	6–8 years	9–12 years	13–18 years			
Avoidance: "I make myself scarce."	8	8	8			
Fun: "We have a real good time"	65	62	68			
"I don't know."	4	4	3			
13. What are some of the big differences between the way things are now between you and your dad and the way they were when your mom and dad lived together?				30.12	10	0.0008
Infrequent contact with father: "Now I hardly get to see Dad."	31	26	13			
More contact with father: "I get to see Dad more by myself."	4	15	16			
Personality changes: "Dad's much nicer now and more grown up."	10	17	16			
Emotional distance: "I feel less close to Dad now."	1	9	16			
Living arrangements: "Dad lives in a different house now."	25	5	5			
"I don't know."	29	26	35			
14a. Do you think you'll ever get married?				7.83	4	0.09
Yes	62	64	75			
No	27	15	10			
"I don't know."	12	20	14			
14b. Why or why not?				31.37	10	0.0005
Attachment: "Yes, because I'll fall in love and want to be with someone."	19	15	34			

Raise family: "Yes, I want to have lots of children."	8	21	20
Irrelevance of parents' divorce: "Yes, just because it didn't work for them doesn't mean it won't work for me."	0	2	12
Fear of divorce: "No, it wouldn't work out and we'd get a divorce."	8	11	7
Don't want to	8	4	0
I don't know	57	47	27

*The numbers of children in the 6–8-year, 9–12-year, and 13–18-year groups were 55, 60, and 78 respectively.

presents the percentage of children at each age level who gave a particular response. Gender differences were not significant.

With regard to our second strategy for assessing age-related trends in children's reasoning about divorce, we correlated age with responses to objective measures tapping understanding of, and feelings about, the divorce. Two studies are of interest. The first (Kurdek et al., 1981) included 58 white, middle-class, eight- to 17-year-old children whose parents had been separated about four years. These children were given a modified version of Reinhard's (1977) measure, which focused on their feelings about the separation and divorce. In this 34-item measure, children rated the extent to which they agreed or disagreed (1 = strongly agree to 5 = strongly disagree) with statements regarding the news of the divorce (e.g., "When I heard about the decision to divorce, I felt angry"); loss of the noncustodial parent (e.g., "When my father left, I felt I was being deserted"); peer relations (e.g., "I sometimes feel different from my friends because they have two parents"); family relations (e.g., "I feel I no longer need a father"); and emotional responses (e.g., "I sometimes feel that the divorce was because of me"). Cronbach's alpha for the summed composite score was 0.75. Neither the total score nor any of the component scores were reliably related to age. All relations to gender were also nonsignificant.

In the second study (Kurdek & Berg, 1983), we focused on children's understanding of the divorce rather than, as in the study just described, on their feelings about the divorce. This study involved 70 six- to 15-year-olds who were white, middle-class, and had parents who were separated by a mean of 13.17 months. These children were given the 60-item Children's Separation Inventory, which assessed their understanding of the divorce in six areas. These areas included: peer ridicule and avoidance (e.g., "It would upset me if other kids asked a lot of questions about my parents"); paternal blame (e.g., "My father caused the breakup of my family"); fear of abandonment (e.g., "Sometimes I worry that soon I may be left all alone with no one to take care of me"); hope of reunification (e.g., "Someday the whole family will probably live together again"); maternal blame (e.g., "It was usually my mother's fault when my parents had a fight"); and self-blame (e.g., "It's probably my fault that my parents are unhappy"). Children answered yes or no to each item. Cronbach's alpha for the summed composite score was 0.78.

Significant ($p<0.05$) correlations were obtained for age and the composite score ($r = 0.24$), as well as the following component scores: peer ridicule and avoidance ($r = 0.20$), fear of abandonment ($r = 0.24$), and hope of reunification ($r = 0.38$). In all cases older children had higher understanding scores than younger children. The correlation between the composite score and gender was also significant ($r=0.23$), with girls having higher understanding scores than boys.

In sum, we have generally found support for the prediction that there would be age-related trends in children's reasoning about divorce. The most consistent evidence has come from the structured interview and from questions that focus on children's cognitions—rather than feelings—about the divorce. It is of particular note that we found little evidence of self-blame at all age levels. But because we did not assess these children during the *actual* separation process, we cannot say that they never made self-accusatory attributions.

The Relation Between Interpersonal Understanding and Reasoning About Divorce

As noted both Longfellow (1979) and Neal (1983) have indicated that social cognition should be strongly related to children's notions about divorce. Social cognition covers reasoning about broad areas of interpersonal functioning; and parents' marriage and divorce are but one domain of that functioning. We have assessed the relation between reasoning about divorce and interpersonal understanding, in two separate studies (Kurdek & Berg, 1983; Kurdek et al., 1981). A similar procedure was followed in each study. Using responses to the structured interview described above, we generated a continuous Understanding Divorce score by assigning one point to each of the following "adjusted" responses: (1) defining divorce in terms of psychological separation; (2) stating that the parents no longer live together because of their incompatibility; (3) stating that the parents will not reconcile; (4) giving incompatibility as the reason for the unlikelihood of reconciliation; (5) not blaming oneself for the divorce; (6) providing positive or neutral (i.e., nonnegative) descriptions of each parent; (7) telling friends about the divorce; and (8) indicating that the divorce does not matter to friends.

For a measure of interpersonal understanding, we adapted a procedure developed by Selman (1980). Each child viewed a six-minute sound film-strip about Tom, who is faced with the problem of buying a birthday gift for his friend Mike, who has just lost his dog. Mike swears he does not want to see another dog again, but Tom happens to see an ad for a puppy sale. After viewing the filmstrip, the child was asked open-ended questions dealing with subjectivity, self-awareness, personality, and personality change, and the beginning, maintenance, and termination of friendship. Responses were coded as representative of a level of interpersonal understanding (see Selman, 1980), with 91 percent perfect agreement between two independent raters. Cronbach's alpha for the total composite score was 0.53.

In the Kurdek et al., (1981) study of 58 eight- to 17-year-olds, the Pearson correlation between the understanding divorce score and the interpersonal understanding score was 0.41 ($P<0.01$), with age partialled out. In the more recent study of 70 six- to 15-year-olds (Kurdek & Berg, 1983), in which a revised and expanded interpersonal understanding measure was used (interrater agreement at 96 percent and Cronbach's alpha for the total composite score = 0.70), the correlation between these two variables was 0.48 ($P<0.01$), with age partialled out. Because it could be argued that children use their own experiences with friendship termination as a basis for understanding parental divorce, it is significant that the highest correlation between the understanding divorce score and the component scores of the interpersonal understanding measure involved friendship termination ($r=0.36$, with age partialled, $P<0.01$).

In sum, we have found support for Longfellow's (1979) and Neal's (1983) position that level of interpersonal reasoning is related to level of understanding divorce. While these two authors might argue that interpersonal understanding sets the stage for the understanding of parental divorce, our data cannot address this prerequisite relation.

The Relation Between Attribution of Personal Control and Understanding Divorce

A final validating piece of information for a cognitive model of children's divorce adjustment is derived from a test of the relation between internal locus of control and understanding the divorce. Crediting one's effort, skill, and ability as reasons for outcomes in ambiguous situations might lead to a self-appraisal of controllability (see Doherty, 1983; Folkman, 1984; Kalter et al., 1984). In our two studies referred to above, we correlated the understanding divorce score with an internal locus-of-control score derived from the Nowicki–Strickland locus of control scale for children (Nowicki & Strickland, 1973). The Pearson correlations were significant ($P<0.05$) in both studies, 0.45 for the Kurdek et al. (1981) sample, and 0.30 for the Kurdek and Berg (1983) sample (age partialled out). We have therefore obtained support for the prediction that generalized feelings of mastery and control are related to positive divorce adjustment.

APPLICATIONS OF A COGNITIVE-DEVELOPMENTAL MODEL OF DIVORCE ADJUSTMENT

A cognitive-developmental model of children's adjustment to parental divorce has implications for the areas of assessment and intervention. Much work needs to be done in developing psychometrically sound measures of divorce adjustment. Although existing evidence does not provide a definitive rationale for the design of interventions, some guidelines can be provided.

Assessment

As noted above, cognitive-developmental models assume that children's growth occurs in an orderly, stage-related sequence. Research on children's reasoning about divorce is neither extensive nor systematic enough to warrant postulating fixed stages of reasoning in this area. The validation of such stages must await longitudinal data that document patterns of intraindividual change in children's reasoning. Although stage models of development have undergone critical review (Brainerd, 1978; Fischer, 1980; Flavell, 1982), the data reported here and by others (see Kurdek, 1986 for a review) indicate reliable age-related trends in the way that children reason about divorce.

Consistent findings of a positive relation between children's developmental level and their reasoning about divorce might lead one to conclude that older children are better adjusted to divorce than younger children. Such a conclusion is unwarranted for several reasons. First, as was indicated at the beginning of this chapter, children's cognitions about divorce comprise only one component of a multivariate model of their divorce adjustment. Potentiating, buffering, or compensating for the effects of children's cognitions are other intraindividual characteristics (e.g., temperament, stress threshold, emotional reactions), the child's postdivorce relationships with the custodial and the noncustodial parent, environmental stability and the availability of social support networks, and cultural ideologies regarding divorce and single-parent families (Bilge & Kaufman, 1983; Kurdek, 1981; Stolberg et al., in press). Second, children's reasoning about divorce becomes more abstract, complex, differentiated, and integrated with age, so that judgments of the normality of a child's reaction to parental divorce must be made within that child's developmental context (Achenbach, 1982; Sroufe & Rutter, 1984). While progress has been made in charting normative reactions to divorce for infants through adolescents

(Egeland & Farber, 1984; Hetherington et al., 1982; Vaughn et al., 1980; Wallerstein & Kelly, 1980), the samples have been rather small, and largely white and middle class. Applying the findings to lower SES groups, for whom divorce rates are particularly high, then, is questionable.

One practical consequence of representative normative data is their use in constructing developmentally anchored measures of children's divorce adjustment. Because children's reactions to divorce seem to follow a "crisis model" trend—from disequilibrium to restabilization (Hetherington et al., 1982),—such measures need to incorporate the amount of time passed since the parents' separation. Given that partners of distressed marriages are not likely to agree on the events occurring within their relationship (Elwood & Jacobson, 1982; Spanier & Thompson, 1984), assessment should also include reports from both parents, children themselves, and even teachers.

Intervention

Most traditional interventions for children of divorce have been developed from a family systems perspective (e.g., Bray & Anderson, 1984; Hajal & Rosenberg, 1978; Nichols, 1984; Rosenthal, 1979; Williams et al., 1983), in which the therapist, parent(s), and child work together to help the child deal with problems occasioned by the divorce. More recent programs have been designed for the children alone, and address the need for the child to develop peer support networks at school (Cantor, 1977; Kalter et al., 1984; Pedro-Carroll & Cowen, 1985; Pedro-Carroll et al., 1986; Stolberg & Garrison, 1985) or in the community (Guerney & Jordan, 1979; Hoorwitz, 1984).

As mentioned above, emphasis is currently being placed on developing cognitive interventions with children; rational-emotive approaches, in particular, are being designed for childhood problems (Bernard & Joyce, 1984). While these approaches may be helpful in treating children whose appraisal of events surrounding the divorce have occasioned problems of adjustment, their efficacy has yet to be assessed. Despite the fact that clinicians treating children's divorce-related problems have often noted that these children construct irrational beliefs (Gardner, 1976; Tessman, 1978; Wallerstein & Kelly, 1980), research on cognitive treatment strategies for these problems is limited. If a major task of children experiencing divorce is the achievement of cognitive mastery over a stressful sequence of events (Wallerstein, 1983), then future efforts would be well-directed in designing, implementing, and evaluating intervention strategies with a strong cognitive focus.

REFERENCES

Achenbach, T. M. (1982). *Developmental Psychopathology*. New York: Wiley.

Ambert, A., & Saucier, J. (1983). Adolescents' perception of their parents and parents' marital status. *Journal of Social Psychology, 120,* 101–110.

Anderson, C. A., Horowitz, L. M., & French, R. (1983). Attributional style of lonely and depressed people. *Journal of Personality and Social Psychology, 45,* 127–136.

Arnkoff, D. B., & Glass, C. R. (1982). Clinical cognitive constructs. In P.C. Kendall (Ed.), *Cognitive Behavioral Research and Therapy* (Vol. 1, pp. 1–34). New York: Academic Press.

Atkeson, B. M., Forehand, R. L., & Rickard, K. M. (1982). The effects of divorce on children. In B. Lahey (Ed.), *Advances in Clinical Child Psychology* (pp. 255–281). New York: Academic Press.

Barenhoim, C. (1981). The development of person perception in childhood and adolescence. *Child Development, 52,* 129–144.

Beck, A. T., Rush, A. J., Shaw, B. F., & Emery, G. (1979). *Cognitive Therapy of Depression*. New York: Guilford Press.

Bernard, M. E. & Joyce, M. R. (1984). *Rational Emotive Therapy with Children and Adolescents*. New York: Wiley.

Bierman, K. L., & Furman, W. (1984). The effects of social skills training and peer involvement on the social adjustment of preadolescents. *Child Development, 55,* 151–162.

Bilge, B., & Kaufman, G. (1983). Children of divorce and one-parent families: Cross-cultural perspectives. *Family Relations, 32,* 59–71.

Biller, H. B. (1981). Father absence, divorce, and personality development. In M. E. Lamb (Ed.), *The Role of the Father in Child Development* (pp. 489–552). New York: Wiley.

Blechman, E. A. (1982). Are children with one parent at psychological risk? *Journal of Marriage and the Family, 44,* 179–195.

Bloom, B. L., Hodges, W. F., & Caldwell, R. A. (1983). Marital separation: The first eight months. In E. J. Callahan & K. A. McCluskey (Eds.), *Lifespan Developmental Psychology: Nonnormative Life Events* (pp. 217–239). New York: Academic Press.

Bobbitt, B. L., & Keating, D. P. (1983). A cognitive-developmental perspective for clinical research and practice. In P.C. Kendall (Ed.), *Advances in Cognitive-Behavioral Research and Therapy* (Vol. 2, pp. 195–239). New York: Academic Press.

Bond, C. R., & McMahon, R. J. (1984). Relationships between marital distress and child behavior problems, maternal personal adjustment, maternal personality, and maternal parenting behavior. *Journal of Abnormal Psychology, 93,* 348–351.

Brainerd, C. J. (1978). The stage question in cognitive developmental theory. *The Behavioral and Brain Sciences 1,* 173–182.

Bray, J. H., & Anderson, H. (1984). Strategic interventions with single-parent families. *Psychotherapy, 21,* 101–109.

Caldwell, R. A., & Bloom, B. L. (1982). Social support: Its structure and impact on marital disruption. *American Journal of Community Psychology, 10,* 647–667.

Cantor, D. W. (1977). School based groups for children of divorce. *Journal of Divorce, 1,* 183–188.

Clingempeel, W. G., & Reppucci, N. D. (1982). Joint custody after divorce. *Psychological Bulletin, 91,* 102–127.

Colby, A., Kohlberg, L. Gibbs, J., & Lieberman, M. (1983). A longitudinal study of moral development. *Monographs of the Society for Research in Child Development, 48* (1, 2, Serial No. 200).

Colletta, N. D. (1979). Support systems after divorce. *Journal of Marriage and the Family, 41,* 837–846.

Conger, J. C., & Keane, S. P. (1981). Social skills intervention in the treatment of isolated or withdrawn children. *Psychological Bulletin, 90,* 478–495.

Cooper, J. E., Holman, J., & Braithwaite, V. A. (1983). Self esteem and family cohesion. *Journal of Marriage and the Family, 45,* 153–159.

Coyne, J. C., & Gotlib, I. H. (1983). The role of cognition in depression. *Psychological Bulletin, 94,* 472–505.

Cutrona, C. E. (1984). Social support and stress in the transition to parenthood, *Journal of Abnormal Psychology, 93,* 378–390.

Damon, W. (1977). *The Social World of the Child.* San Francisco: Jossey Bass.

Damon, W. (1980) Patterns of change in children's social reasoning. *Child Development, 51,* 1010–1017.

Daniels-Mohring, D., & Berger, M. (1984). Social network changes and the adjustment to divorce. *Journal of Divorce, 8,* 17–32.

D'Augelli, A. (1983). Social support networks in mental health. In J. K. Whittaker & J. Garbarino (Eds.), *Social Support Networks* (pp. 73–106). New York: Aldine.

Derdeyn, A. P., & Scott, E. (1984). Joint custody. *American Journal of Orthopsychiatry, 54,* 199–209.

Dodge, K. A., Murphy, R. R., & Buchsbaum, K. (1984). The assessment of intention cue detection skills in children. *Child Development, 55,* 163–173.

Doherty, W. J. (1983). Impact of divorce on locus of control orientation in adult women. *Journal of Personality and Social Psychology, 44,* 834–840.

Edelstein, W., Keller, M., & Wahlen, K. (1984). Structure and content in social cognition. *Child Development, 55,* 1514–1526.

Egeland, B., & Farber, E. A. (1984). Infant-mother attachment: Factors related to its development and changes over time. *Child Development, 55,* 753–771.

Ellis, A. (1979). The theory of rational emotive therapy. In A. Ellis & J. M. Whiteley (Eds.), *Theoretical and Empirical Foundations of Rational Emotive Therapy.* (pp. 33–60.). Monterey, Calif.: Brooks/Cole.

Ellis, A. & Bernard, M. E. (Eds). (1983). *Rational Emotive Approaches to Problems of Childhood.* New York: Plenum.

Elwood, R. W., & Jacobson, N. S. (1982). Spouses' agreement in reporting their behavioral interactions. *Journal of Consulting and Clinical Psychology, 50,* 783–784.

Emery, R. E. (1982). Interparent conflict and the children of discord and divorce. *Psychological Bulletin, 92,* 310–330.

Emery, R. E., Hetherington, E. M., & DiLalla, L. (1984). Divorce, children, and social policy. In H. W. Stevenson & A. E. Siegel (Eds.), *Child Development Research and Social Policy.* (pp. 189–266.). Chicago: University of Chicago Press.

Emery, R. E. & O'Leary, K. D. (1984). Marital discord and child behavior problems in a nonclinic sample. *Journal of Abnormal Child Psychology, 12,* 411–420.

Enright, R. D., Bjerstedt, A., Enright, W. F., Levy, V. M., Lapsley, D. K., Buss, R. R., Harwell, M., & Zindler, P. (1984). Distributive justice developmental: Cross cultural, contextual, and longitudinal evaluations. *Child Development, 55,* 1737–1751.

Enright, R. D., Franklin, C. C., & Manheim, L. A. (1980). Children's distributive justice reasoning. *Developmental Psychology, 16,* 193–202.

Fischer, K.W. (1980). A theory of cognitive development. *Psychological Review, 87,* 477–531.

Flavell, J. H. (1982). On cognitive development, *Child Development, 53,* 1–10.

Fleming, R., Baum, A., & Singer, J. E. (1984). Toward an integrative approach to the study of stress. *Journal of Personality and Social Psychology, 46,* 939–949.

Folkman, S. (1984). Personal control and stress and coping processes. *Journal of Personality and Social Psychology, 46,* 839–852.

Folkman, S., & Lazarus, R. S. (1985). If it changes it must be a process: A study of emotion and coping during three stages of a college examination. *Journal of Personality and Social Psychology, 48,* 150–170.

Fry, P. S., & Leahey, M. (1983). Children's perceptions of major positive and negative events and factors in single-parent families. *Journal of Applied Developmental Psychology, 4,* 371–388.

Fry, P. S., & Trifiletti, R. J. (1983). An exploration of the adolescent's perspective: Perceptions of major stress dimensions in the single-parent family. *Journal of Psychiatric Treatment and Evaluation, 5,* 101–111.

Furstenberg, F. F., Nord, C. W., Peterson, J. L., & Zill, N. (1983). The life course of children of divorce. *American Sociological Review, 48,* 656–668.

Gardner, R. A. (1976). *Psychotherapy with Children of Divorce.* New York: Jason Aronson.

Garmezy, N., & Rutter, M. (Eds.) (1983). *Stress, Coping, and Development in Children.* New York: McGraw-Hill.

Gibbs, J. C., Arnold, K. D., Ahlborn, H. H., & Cheesman, F. L. (1984). Facilitation of sociomoral reasoning in delinquents. *Journal of Consulting and Clinical Psychology, 52,* 37–45.

Golin, S., Sweeney, P. D., & Shaeffer, D. E. (1981). The causality of causal attributions in depression. *Journal of Abnormal Psychology, 90,* 14–22.

Gottlieb, B. H. (1983). Social support as a focus for integrative research in psychology. *American Psychologist, 38,* 278–287.

Guerney, L., & Jordan, L. (1979). Children of divorce—A community support group. *Journal of Divorce, 2,* 283–294.

Guidubaldi, J., Cleminshaw, H. K., Perry, J. D., Nastasi, B. K., & Adams, B. (October, 1984). *Longitudinal Effects of Divorce on Children:* Symposium conducted at the meeting of the American Psychological Association, Toronto.

Guidubaldi, J., & Perry, J. D. (1984). Divorce, socioeconomic status, and children's cognitive-social competence at school entry. *American Journal of Orthopsychiatry, 54,* 459–468.

Guidubaldi, J., Perry, J. D., Cleminshaw, H. K., & McLoughlin, C. S. (1983). The impact of parental divorce on children: Report of the nationwide NASP study. *School Psychology Review, 12,* 300–323.

Gurucharri, C., Phelps, E., & Selman, R. (1984). Development of interpersonal understanding. *Journal of Consulting and Clinical Psychology, 52,* 26–36.

Gurucharri, C., & Selman, R. L. (1982). The development of interpersonal understanding during childhood, preadolescence, and adolescence. *Child Development, 53,* 924–927.

Hajal, F., & Rosenberg, E. B. (1978). Working with the one parent family in therapy. *Journal of Divorce, 1,* 259–270.

Harter, S. (1983). Cognitive developmental considerations in the conduct of play therapy. In C. E. Schaefer & K. J. O'Connor (Eds.), *Handbook of Play Therapy* (pp. 95–127). New York: Wiley.

Hetherington, E. M. (1979). Divorce: A child's perspective. *American Psychologist, 34,* 851–858.

Hetherington, E. M. (1984). Stress and coping in children and families. In A. Doyle, D. Gold, & D. S. Moskowitz (Eds.), *New Directions for Child Development: Children in Families under Stress* (pp. 7–34). San Francisco: Jossey-Bass.

Hetherington, E. M., Cox, M., & Cox, R. (1979). The development of children in mother headed families. In D. Reiss & H. A. Hoffman (Eds.), *The American Family: Dying or developing?* (pp. 117–156). New York: Plenum.

Hetherington, E. M., Cox, M., & Cox, R. (1982). Effects of divorce on parents and children. In M. E. Lamb (Ed.). *Nontraditional Families: Parenting and Child Development* (pp. 233–287). Hillsdale, N.J.

Hingst, A. G. (1981). Children and divorce: The child's view. *Journal of Clinical Child Psychology, 6,* 161–164.

Hodges, W. F., & Bloom, B. L. (1984). Parents' report of children's adjustment to marital separation. *Journal of Divorce, 8,* 33–50.

Hodges, W. F., Tierney, C. W., & Buschbaum, H. K. (1984). The cummulative effect of stress on preschool children of divorced and intact families. *Journal of Marriage and the Family, 46,* 611–617.

Holahan, C. J., & Moos, R. H. (1981). Social support and psychological distress. *Journal of Abnormal Psychology, 90,* 365–370.

Hollon, S. D., & Kriss, M. R. (1984). Cognitive factors in clinical research and practice. *Clinical Psychology Review, 4,* 35–76.

Hoorwitz, A. N. (1984). Videotherapy in the context of group therapy for late-latency children of divorce. *Psychotherapy, 21,* 48–53.

Jacobson, D. S. (1978). The impact of marital separation/divorce on children. *Journal of Divorce, 1,* 341–360.

Jamison, W., & Dansky, J. L. (1979). Identifying developmental prerequisites of cognitive acquisitions. *Child Development, 50,* 449–454.

Kagan, J. (1984). *The Nature of the Child.* New York: Basic Books.

Kalter, N. Alpern, D., Spence, R., & Plunkett, J. W. (1984). Locus of control in children of divorce. *Journal of Personality Assessment, 48,* 410–414.

Kalter, N., Pickar, J., & Lesowitz, M. (1984). School-based developmental facilitation groups for children of divorce. *American Journal of Orthopsychiatry, 54,* 613–623.

Kalter, N., & Plunkett, J. W. (1984). Children's perception of causes and consequences of divorce. *Journal of the American Academy of Child Behavior, 23,* 326–334.

Kalter, N., & Rembar, J. (1981). The significance of a child's age at the time of parental divorce. *American Journal of Orthopsychiatry, 51,* 85–100.

Kanoy, K. W., & Cunningham, J. L. (1984). Consensus on confusion in research on children of divorce. *Journal of Divorce, 2,* 45–72.

Kaslow, N. J., Rehm, L. P., & Siegel, A. W. (1984). Social-cognitive and cognitive correlates of depression in children. *Journal of Abnormal Child Psychology, 12,* 605–620.

Kelly, R. R., & Berg, B. (1978). Measuring children's reactions to divorce. *Journal of Clinical Psychology, 34,* 215–221.

King, H. E., & Kleemeier, C. P. (1983). The effect of divorce on parents and children. In C. E. Walker & M. C. Roberts (Eds.), *Handbook of Clinical Child Psychology* (pp. 1249–1272). New York: Wiley.

Kitson, G., & Raschke, H. J. (1981). Divorce research. *Journal of Divorce, 4,* 1–37.

Kohberg, L. (1969). Stage and sequence: The cognitive developmental approach to socialization. In D. A. Goslin (Ed.) *Handbook of Socialization Theory and Research* (pp. 347–480). Chicago: Rand McNally.

Kohlberg, L., & Candee, D. (1984). The relationship of moral judgment to moral action. In W. M. Kurtines & J. L. Gewirtz (Eds.), *Morality, Moral Behavior, and Moral Development* (pp. 52–73). New York: Wiley.

Krebs, D., & Gillmore, J. (1982). The relationship among the first stages of cognitive development, role taking abilities, and moral development. *Child Development, 53,* 877–886.

Kurdek, L. A. (1981). An integrative perspective on children's divorce adjustment. *American Psychologist, 36,* 856–866.

Kurdek, L. A. (1986). Children's reasoning about parental divorce. In R. D. Ashmore & D. M. Brodzinsky (Eds.). *Perspectives on the Family.* (pp. 233–276.). Hillsdale, N.J.: Erlbaum.

Kurdek, L. A. & Berg, B. (1983). Correlates of children's adjustment to their parents' divorces. In L. A. Kurdek (Ed.), *New Directions in Child Development: Children and Divorce* (pp. 47–60). San Francisco: Jossey-Bass.

Kurdek, L. A., & Blisk, D. (1983). Dimensions and correlates of mothers' divorce experiences. *Journal of Divorce, 6,* 1–24.

Kurdek, L. A. Blisk, D., & Siesky, A. E. (1981). Correlates of children's long term adjustment to their parents' divorce. *Developmental Psychology, 17,* 565–579.

Kurdek, L. A., & Krile, D. (1982). A developmental analysis of the relation between peer acceptance and both interpersonal understanding and perceived social self competence. *Child Development, 53,* 1485–1491.

Kurdek, L. A., & Krile, D. (1983). The relation between third- through eight-grade children's social cognition and parents' ratings of social skills and general adjustment. *Journal of Genetic Psychology, 143,* 201–206.

Kurdek, L. A., & Siesky, A. E. (1979). An interview study of parents' perceptions of their children's reactions and adjustment to divorce. *Journal of Divorce, 3,* 5–18.

Kurdek, L. A., & Siesky, A. E. (1980). Children's perceptions of their parents' divorce. *Journal of Divorce, 3,* 339–377.

Ladd, G. W., & Mize, J. (1983). A cognitive social learning model of social skill training. *Psychological Review, 90,* 127–157.

Lazarus, R. S. (1984). On the primacy of cognition. *American Psychologist, 39,* 117–123.

Lazarus, R. S. & Folkman, S. (1984). *Stress, Appraisal, and Coping.* New York: Springer Publishing Company.

Leahey, M. (1984). Findings from research on divorce. *American Journal of Orthopsychiatry, 54,* 298–317.

Lefcourt, H. M., Martin, R. A., & Saleh, W. E. (1984). Locus of control and social support. *Journal of Personality and Social Psychology, 47,* 378–389.

Levitin, T. E. (1979). Children of divorce. *Journal of Social Issues, 35,* 1–25.

Links, P. (1983). Community surveys of the prevalence of childhood psychiatric disorders. *Child Development, 54,* 531–548.

Longfellow, C. (1979). Divorce in context. In G. Levinger & O. Moles (Eds.), *Divorce and Separation* (pp. 287–306). New York: Basic Books.

Lowenstein, J. S., & Koopman, E. J. (1978). A comparison of the self-esteem between boys living with single parent mothers and single parent fathers. *Journal of Divorce, 2,* 195–208.

McCrae, R. R. (1984). Situational determinants of coping responses. *Journal of Personality of Social Psychology, 46,* 919–928.

McCubbin, H. I, & Patterson, J. M. (1983). Family adaptation to crises. In H. I. McCubbin, A. E. Cauble, & J. M. Patterson (Eds.), *Family Stress, Coping, and Social Support* (pp. 26–47). Springfield, Ill.: Charles C. Thomas.

Neal, J. H. (1983). Children's understanding of their parents' divorces. In L. A. Kurdek (Ed.), *New Directions in Child Development: Children and Divorce* (pp. 3–14). San Francisco: Jossey-Bass.

Nichols, W. C. (1984). Therapeutic needs of children in family system reorganization. *Journal of Divorce, 2,* 23–44.

Nowicki, S., & Strickland, B. R. (1973). A locus of control scale for children. *Journal of Consulting and Clinical Psychology, 40,* 148–155.

O'Leary, K. D. (1984). Marital discord and children. In A. Doyle, D. Gold, & D. Moskowitz (Eds.), *New Directions in Child Development: Children in Families Under Stress* (pp. 35–46). San Francisco: Jossey-Bass.

O'Leary, K. D., & Emery, R. E. 1984. Marital discord and child behavior problems. In M. D. Levine & P. Satz (Eds.), Middle Childhood: Development and Dysfunction (pp. 345–364.). Baltimore: University Park Press.

Pedro-Carroll, J. L. & Cowen, E. L. (1985). The children of divorce intervention project: An investigation of the efficacy of a school-based prevention program. *Journal of Consulting and Clinical Psychology, 53,* 603–611.

Pedro-Carroll, J. L., Cowen, E. L., Hightower, A. D., Guare, J. C. (1986). Preventive intervention with latency age children of divorce. *American Journal of Community Psychology, 14,* 277–290.

Peterson, C., & Seligman, M. E. P. (1984). Causal explanations as a risk factor for depression: Theory and evidence. *Psychological Review, 91,* 347–374.

Peterson, G. W., Leigh, G. K., & Day, R. D. (1984). Family stress theory and the impact of divorce on children. *Journal of Divorce, 7,* 1–20.

Pilisuk, M. (1982). Delivery of social support. *American Journal of Orthopsychiatry, 53,* 20–31.

Plunkett, J. W., & Kalter, N. (1984). Children's beliefs about reactions to parental divorce. *American Academy of Child Psychiatry, 23,* 616–621.

Reinhard, D. W. (1977). The reaction of adolescent boys and girls to the divorce of their parents. *Journal of Clinical Child Psychology, 6,* 21–23.

Richardson, R., & Pfeiffenberger, C. (1983). Social support networks for divorced and stepfamilies. In J. K. Whittaker & J. Garbarino (Eds.), *Social Support Networks* (pp. 219–250). New York: Aldine.

Rofe, Y. (1984). Stress and affiliation: A utility theory. *Psychological Review, 91,* 235–250.

Rosenthal, P. A. (1979). Sudden disappearance of one parent with separation and divorce. *Journal of Divorce, 3,* 43–54.

Russell, D., Cutrona, C. E., Rose, J., & Yurko, K. (1984). Social and emotional loneliness. *Journal of Personality and Social Psychology, 46,* 1313–1321.

Rutter, M. (1979). Maternal deprivation, 1972–1978: New findings, new concepts, new approaches. *Child Development, 50,* 283–305.

Seligman, M. E. P., Abramson, L. Y., & Semmel, A. (1979). Depressive attributional style. *Journal of Abnormal Psychology, 88,* 242–247.

Seligman, M. E. P., Peterson, C., Kaslow, N. J., Tanenbaum, R. L., Alloy, L. B., & Ambramson, L. Y. (1984). Explanatory style and depressive symptoms among children. *Journal of Abnormal Psychology, 93,* 235–238.

Selman, R. L. (1980). *The Development of Interpersonal Understanding.* New York: Academic Press.

Shantz, C. U. (1983). Social cognition, In J. H. Flavell & E. M. Markman (Eds.), *Handbook of Child Psychology, Vol. 3. Cognitive Development* (pp. 495–555). New York: Wiley.

Smolak, L., & Levine, M. P. (1984). The effects of differential criteria on the assessment of cognitive-linguistic relationships. *Child Development, 55,* 973–980.

Spanier, G. B. & Thompson, L. (1984). *Parting; The Aftermath of Separation and Divorce.* Beverly Hills, Calif: Sage Publications.

Sroufe, L. A., & Rutter, M. (1984). The domain of developmental psychopathology. *Child Development, 55,* 17–29.

Stolberg, A. L., Camplair, C., Currier, K., & Wells, M. J. (in press). Individual, familial, and environmental determinants of children's post-divorce adjustment and maladjustment. *Journal of Divorce.*

Stolberg, A. L., & Cullen, P. M. (1983). Preventive interventions for families of divorce: The Divorce Adjustment Project. In L. A. Kurdek (Ed.). *New Directions for Child Development: Children and Divorce* (pp. 71–82) San Francisco: Jossey-Bass.

Stolberg, A. L., & Garrison, K. M. (1985). Evaluating a primary prevention program for children of divorce. *American Journal of Community Psychology, 13,* 111–124.

Stolberg, A. L., & Ullman, A. J. (1984). Assessing dimensions of single parenting. *Journal of Divorce, 8,* 31–45.

Taylor, S. E. (1983). Adjustment to threatening events: A theory of cognitive adaptation. *American Psychologist, 38,* 1161–1173.

Tessman, L. H. (1978). *Children of Parting Parents.* New York: Jason Aronson.

Thompson, S. Z. (1981). Will it hurt less if I can control it? A complex answer to a simple question. *Psychological Bulletin, 90,* 89–101.

Turiel, E., & Smetana, J. G. (1984). Social knowledge and action. In W. M. Kurtines & J. L. Gewirtz (Eds.), *Morality, Moral Behavior, and Moral Development* (pp. 261–282). New York: Wiley.

Urbain, E. S., & Kendall, P. C. (1980). Review of social cognitive problem solving intervention with children. *Psychological Bulletin, 88,* 109–143.

Vaughn, B. E., Gove, F. L., & Egeland, B. (1980). The relationship between out of home care and the quality of mother-infant attachment in an economically disadvantaged population. *Child Development, 51,* 1203–1214.

Voelker, R. M., & McMillan, S. L. (1983). Children and divorce: An approach for the pediatrician. *Developmental and Behavioral Pediatrics, 4,* 272–277.

Wallerstein, J. S. (1983). Children of divorce: The psychological tasks of the child. *American Journal of Orthopsychiatry, 53*, 230–243.

Wallerstein, J. S. (1984). Children of divorce. *American Journal of Orthopsychiatry, 54*, 444–458.

Wallerstein, J. S., & Kelly, J. B. (1980). *Surviving the breakup.* New York: Basic Books.

Warshak, R. A., & Santrock, J. W. (1983). The impact of divorce in father-custody and mother-custody homes: The child's perspective. In L. A. Kurdek (Ed.), *New Directions for Child Development: Children and Divorce* (pp. 29–46). San Francisco: Jossey-Bass.

Watson, M. W., & Amgott-Kwan, T. (1984). Development of family role concepts in school-age children. *Development Psychology, 20*, 953–959.

Weiss, R. S. (1984). The impact of marital dissolution of income and consumption in single parent households. *Journal of Marriage and the Family, 46*, 115–128.

White, S. W., & Mika, K. (1983). Family divorce and separation: Theory and research. *Marriage and Family Review, 6*, 175–192.

Williams, B. M., Wright, D., & Rosenthal, D. (1983). A model for intervention with latency-aged children of divorce. *Family Therapy, 10*, 111–1204.

Zajonc, R. B. (1984). On the primacy of affect. *American Psychologist, 39*, 117–123.

PART IV
INTERVENTIVE
APPROACHES

8

Mediating Parent–Child Postdivorce Arrangements

JESSICA PEARSON and NANCY THOENNES

Although a few writers note the positive aspects of divorce for children and families, most literature focuses on its pathological effects. Researchers frequently note that children from divorced families tend to be disobedient, aggressive, and lacking in self-control. Others report evidence of internalized problems, such as depression (Clingempeel & Reppucci, 1982; Emery, 1982; Kurdek, 1981; Hetherington et al., 1979). As increasing numbers of parents with minor children enter the ranks of the divorced population each year, the problem of helping children to adjust to this new life situation becomes more pressing. Mediation has been proposed as one means of assisting those children whose parents not only divorce, but formally contest the custody or visition arrangement.

According to its critics, the adversarial process fails to promote the cooperation, communication, and compliance behaviors that are necessary if individuals are to work together as parents after they cease to be spouses (Kaufman, 1976; Milne, 1978). Critics also contend that legal

The authors would like to thank the following individuals for their help: William Hodges, Margaret Little, Eleanor Lyon, Maria Ring, A. Elizabeth Cauble, Clarence Dong-Rosten, Mary Hayes, Judith Spendelow, Ann Abeloff, Virginia Harlan, Nancy Garnaas.

This chapter was prepared with the support of a grant from the Administration of Children, Youth and Families of the United States Department of Health and Human Services that was administered by the Research Unit of the Association of Family and Conciliation Courts. An earlier version of this article was presented at the 22nd annual conference of the Association of Family and Conciliation Courts, May 23–24, 1984, in Denver, Col. Details of data analysis and significant findings may be obtained by writing to the authors at the Association of Family and Conciliation Courts/Research Unit, 1720 Emerson Street, Denver, CO 80218.

proceedings pose potential stressors for children, since they often increase parent conflict, raise uncertainties about future contact with both parents, and affect the child's fantasies about reconciliation (Wallerstein & Kelly, 1980). Many divorcing parents agree that their experiences in the legal system exacerbate their problems (Spanier & Anderson, 1979).

Mediation advocates argue, on the other hand, that this process stresses compromise rather than winning and losing, encourages honest and open communication, and allows parties to create agreements that reflect the specific circumstances of their case. As a result they propose mediation as a logical method of resolving divorce disputes while simultaneously teaching the skills of negotiation, compromise, communication, and cooperation that the parties will need in the years of child rearing that lie ahead. Indeed one of the hypothesized benefits of divorce mediation is superior adjustment for the children involved (Emery, 1982; Coogler et al., 1979; Haynes, 1978).

Although custody mediation services are organized in a variety of ways, most include the same general steps (Kessler, 1978; Black & Joffee, 1978). Typically the session begins with the mediator reviewing the concept of mediation, gaining the trust of the couple, and encouraging commitment to the process. The next step usually involves defining the issues in contention. The mediator explores the degree of conflict surrounding the issues presented by the parties as "the dispute," and may look for conflict over any divorce issue not explicitly mentioned, or any underlying problems that may have provoked the custody/visitation dispute.

During the "processing" stage, mediators help parties to make concrete proposals, concessions, and counterproposals. The techniques used to encourage such behaviors include positive reinforcement of all conciliatory behaviors, paraphrasing what is said (to encourage angry spouses to listen), refocusing discussions that wander away from problem solving, and offering options or pointing out areas of agreement.

Mediation, when successful, generally concludes with the mediator helping the parties write an agreement. The mediator may then encourage the parties to have their attorneys review the agreement, and may also explain the necessary steps to legalize it and the options open to the couple should problems arise. In unsuccessful mediations the final step is to help couples recognize the impasse and leave the mediation without a sense of failure.

To summarize, mediation is an alternative and nonadversarial means of dispute resolution in which a mutually acceptable third party helps disputants identify the issues in contention, clarify individuals' needs and goals, make and accept concessions, establish the full range of possible solutions, and recognize the cost and benefits associated with each. The mediator's most basic role is to persuade each party to accept the largest concession the other is willing to make (Pruitt, 1971).

This chapter is an empirical evaluation of court-based mediation as a means of resolving contested child-custody and visitation matters. Specifically we compare adjustment outcomes for children whose parents successfully mediated custody with those who attempted to mediate but failed to reach an agreement, as well as those who adjudicated and those who pursued a noncontested divorce. In addition we assess parent evaluation of their mediation experience and its immediate and long-term impact on interspousal and parent–child relationships.

PROFILE OF DATA COLLECTION SITES

The Divorce Mediation Research Project involved interviews with parents in several divorce dispute categories. One group consisted of those parents who divorced without formally contesting the issues of custody or visitation—they are here termed "noncontesting." A second group of parents formally disputed custody and/or visitation but were diverted from traditional legal channels into mediation sessions offered through the court—these are referred to as the "mediation" group. Ultimately about half of these parents became the "successful mediation" group, and the rest the "unsuccessful mediation" group. The final group of parents disputed custody/visitation issues but were not offered an opportunity to try mediation within the court system. These parents resolved their disputes on their own or with the aid of attorneys, custody evaluators, or court hearings—they comprise the "adversarial" category.

The noncontesting and adversarial samples were drawn from divorce filings in Colorado, where no court-based mediation services were available. The mediation samples were drawn from the client population of three courts with in-house mediation services—the Los Angeles Superior Court, Hennepin County Court in Minneapolis, and the Connecticut Superior Court. Although these programs are unique in many respects, they also have many characteristics in common.

The Los Angeles Conciliation Court, the oldest and largest conciliation court in the country, began to offer mediation on an experimental basis in 1973. In 1980 a statewide bill mandating mediation in all cases of contested child custody and visitation was passed. A staff of court-employed mediators handles approximately 5100 cases per year (McIsaac, 1983). Most families enter mediation on the day they make their first court appearance, but in recent months a rising proportion of cases have scheduled mediation appointments prior to the initial court hearing. Couples who reach an agreement commit it to writing as an interparty stipulation. If neither the parties nor their attorneys object to the agreement within ten days, it will be entered with the court. Couples who fail to reach an agreement can return to court for a hearing or an investigation by a separate staff of court evaluators.

In Hennepin County, mediation, known also as "custody resolution counseling," began in 1975. Cases are referred for mediation and/or custody studies by the judge and four court referees who comprise the family court. Judges and referees employ subjective criteria in making domestic relations referrals—some prefer mediations and others favor studies. To the extent that referrals are systematic, it appears that clients are referred for custody studies if the parties are perceived to be committed to fighting, and in known cases of abuse or neglect. Mediators notify attorneys and the court of all agreements reached in mediation. Unsuccessful mediation clients may be required by court order to submit to a custody investigation. At the time of our data collection, unsuccessful mediation cases were reassigned to a new counselor for a custody study. Today investigations are usually performed by the mediating counselor.

Mediation services in Connecticut began on an experimental basis in 1977 in the New London court. Mediation is now available statewide to all divorcing couples in dispute over custody or visitation as well as to couples who file a motion to modify custody and visitation arrangements. Mediations are conducted by teams consisting of a male and a female mediator. In practice, however, whether a case reaches mediation varies somewhat by court location; some judges show a preference to hear most contested matters. Agreements produced in mediation are sent to attorneys for review and promulgation as a court order. If no agreement is reached, the case is typically assigned for study by a counselor who did not participate in the mediation. With the parties' consent, a counselor who mediated the case may also conduct the investigation.

At all three court sites, mediation is a brief intervention. Frequently it consists of a single session lasting two to three hours. Yet despite its brief nature mediation produces a high degree of user satisfaction—a reaction not voiced by respondents when asked about court hearings and other litigation experiences. The reasons for public dissatisfaction with court processes are numerous and complex; it appears, however, that many parents object to private issues being treated in a public forum. Still others feel frustrated that as clients they are out of touch with what is happening and are by no means in control of the decision-making process. As one respondent put it: "It was impersonal and slipshod; all the deals were made in the halls and there was no concern about anyone's best interest."

When exposed to the alternative of mediation, most respondents perceived it as a preferred method of resolving disputes. Among points cited in its favor are: (1) the opportunity mediation provides for individuals to be heard and to voice their opinions, (2) the less tense and defensive atmosphere, (3) the fact that the process is less rushed and superficial, and (4) the ability of mediation to help parties understand the needs and feelings of their former spouses (see Table 8.1).

MEASURING CHILD ADJUSTMENT

At all three mediation sites, a sample of clients completed a questionnaire prior to the initiation of mediation. Subsequent interviews took place an average of three months and 12 months after this initial interview. Questionnaires were self-administered or administered over the telephone by trained interviewers.

In addition to eliciting information about the demographic characteristics of disputants, the questionnaires included items dealing with the

Table 8.1

Evaluations of Mediation Sessions and Court Hearings as Reported by Mediation Clients Exposed to Both Processes

Percent agreeing with statements:	Mediation Sessions, %	Court Hearing, %
It focused on the children's needs and welfare.	71	51
I had a chance to express my own point of view.	77	39
It was tension-filled and unpleasant.	58	77
It was rushed.	21	44
It helped me understand my ex-spouse's point of view.	25	13
I always felt on the defensive.	50	65
It brought issues and problems out into the open.	63	49

*paired t-tests of differences between item means significant at 0.05 or better

degree of dispute over custody, visitation, and financial matters; the mutuality of the divorce decision; the balance of power in the dyad; communication skills; level of agreement in parenting styles; visitation patterns; reactions to mediation; experiences with and attitudes toward attorneys and courts; relitigation; and parent and child adjustment to divorce.

In assessing parental perceptions of child adjustment, we chose to focus on a single child in each family. In families with two or more children, parents were asked to provide information on one child between the ages of six and 11. If there were no children in this age range, the oldest or youngest child was selected on a random basis.

Each questionnaire included two instruments designed to assess parents' perceptions of their child's adjustment. The first instrument consisted of 19 statements, some positive and negative, about the divorce and the custody situation. On a five-point Likert Scale, parents were asked to indicate the degree to which they agreed or disagreed with each statement. Some of these items were original, and others were developed by Olsen and colleagues (1979). We used factor analysis to test empirically for underlying dimensions shared by these items. The procedure yielded six factors. Of these, two factors consisted of single items, and these were not retained for further analysis. The remaining factors were used to create four indices (see Table 8.2).

The first index sought to measure the quality of the custodial parent's relationship with the child. It included such items as "my relationship with this child is good" and "it is easy for me to show this child affection." The

Table 8.2
Variables and Factor Loadings on Composite Indices of Child Adjustment

---

Factor 1 Quality of custodian–child relationship:
    My relationship with this child is good. (0.87)
    It is easy for me to show this child affection. (0.81)
    It is easy for me to talk to this child about his or her problems. (0.79)
    This child does not confide in me. (-0.78)

Factor 2 Child's perceived acceptance of the divorce:
    This child accepts the divorce. (0.87)
    This child is angry at mother because of the divorce. (-0.70)

Factor 3 Child's perceived satisfaction with custody arrangement:
    This child needs more routine and stability in his/her life. (-0.72)
    This child is satisfied with the visitation arrangement. (0.59)
    This child is satisfied with the custody arrangement. (0.57)

Factor 4 Child's perceived maturity:
    This child understands the divorce. (0.72)
    This child has become more mature as a result of the divorce. (0.58)
    I find myself confiding in this child. (0.51)

---

second was an index of the child's acceptance of the divorce. It consisted of the items "this child accepts the divorce" and "this child is angry at mother because of the divorce." The third factor sought to measure the child's satisfaction with the custody and visitation arrangement. It included such items as "this child needs more stability in his/her life" and "this child is satisfied with the visitation arrangement." The final index sought to measure the parent's perception of the child's maturity following the divorce. The items loading on this factor included "this child understands the divorce" and "this child has become more mature as a result of the divorce." The items and factor loadings are listed in Table 8.2.

Our second instrument of child adjustment was a 119-item checklist of child behaviors developed by Achenbach and Edelbrock (1981). This checklist can be used to create a variety of subscales measuring specific behaviors, as well as to yield an overall measure of the child's well-being. The authors reported separate subscales for girls and boys, as well as for three age groups: four- to five-year olds, six- to 11-year olds, and 12- to 16-year olds. Given the size of our sample and the number of dispute resolution categories we wished to compare, we restricted our analysis to those subscales that were common to all age groups. Further we created these subscales using only those items that appeared across all age groups and both sexes. As a result our indices vary substantially from those originally designed by Achenbach and Edelbrock. The modified substales employed in our analysis were depression, aggression, delinquency, social withdrawal, and somatic complaints. Table 8.3 lists the items that comprise each of these subscales.

In addition to these quantitative measures, in-depth interviews were conducted with a small number of parents in each divorce dispute category. The interviews included questions about the marriage, the dispute, the dispute-resolution mechanism, and the child's reactions and adjustment to the divorce. These interviews took place approximately three and 12 months after the administration of the initial questionnaire.

Finally a small number of in-depth interviews with six- to 11-year olds were conducted by therapists experienced in working with children. These interviews also took place at the three- and 12-month follow-up intervals. The topics discussed included the child's affective and cognitive reactions to the divorce and, where applicable, the custody dispute; and the dispute resolution mechanism used by the parents. We interviewed 11 children whose parents pursued a noncontested divorce, and nine children whose parents were part of our adversarial sample. Forty-three children (about 15 per site) whose parents used mediation were interviewed.

Throughout our analyses we obtained reports from parents who were either sole custodians or joint residential custodians at both the initial and final interviews. There is little existing research on the similarities and differences in custodial and noncustodial parents' perceptions of children. Yet, because such differences are quite plausible, and given the greater amount of time the custodian spends with the child, we limited the analysis to sole and joint residential custodians. In cases of joint residential custody where both parents were interviewed, we randomly eliminated one parent from the analysis. Not surprisingly in each dispute category our sample is predominantly (70 to 85 percent) female.

In the present analysis, we excluded those mediation cases that resulted in temporary or partial agreements, such as agreements to seek counseling, or agreements that the children would remain with the father or mother until the results from a custody evaluation were available. Given the wide range of agreements that might be termed partial or temporary we chose to restrict the comparison to those cases resulting in either complete agreements or no agreements.

Table 8.3
Items Composing Achenbach-Edelbrock Child Behavior Checklist Subscales*

Depression	Social withdrawal
Fears he/she might do something bad.	Withdrawn, doesn't get involved with others.
Feels he/she has to be perfect.	
Fears going to school.	Underactive, slow moving, lacks energy.
Feels others are out to get him/her.	
Feels worthless or inferior.	Stares blankly.
Too fearful or anxious.	Secretive, keeps things to self.
Self-conscious or easily embarrassed.	Refuses to talk.
Sulks a lot.	
Unhappy, sad, or depressed.	*Delinquency*
Worrying.	Steals outside home.
	Steals at home.
Aggression	Runs away from home.
argues a lot.	Lying or cheating.
Cruelty, bullying, meanness to others.	Hangs around with children who get into trouble.
Demands a lot of attention.	
Disobedient at school.	
Gets in many fights.	*Somatic complaints*
Stubborn, sullen, irritable.	Aches or pains.
Teases a lot.	Headaches.
Temper tantrums or hot temper.	Nausea, feels sick.
Threatens people.	Stomach aches or cramps.
Unusually loud.	Vomiting, throwing up.

*All items are scored "very or often true," "sometimes true," or "not true."

Description of the Sample Prior to Mediation and Final Hearings

The cases retained for analysis were: 78 noncontesting parents, 50 adversarial parents, 53 parents who were not able to reach agreements in mediation, and 68 parents who produced full agreements in mediation. Although our focus is on the child-adjustment reports provided by parents, we offer a brief description of responding parents and their dispute resolution experiences, to provide a backdrop to these reports. Elsewhere we provide greater detail on the characteristics and experiences of the clients of the court-based mediation services (Pearson & Thoennes, 1984a).

In each of the groups (successful mediation, unsuccessful mediation, adversarial, and noncontesting) the respondents are primarily white and 35 years of age or younger. About half of the respondents in each group had only one child, and another 30–40 percent had two children. In each group, 30–40 percent of the respondents had no more than a high school education. In the unsuccessful mediation and noncontesting groups, about 30 percent had completed college, compared with about 15 percent in the successful mediation and adversarial group. These differences, however, are not statistically significant.

One source of variation in the groups was the stage in the divorce process at the initial interview. Noncontested respondents were, of course, awaiting final orders. A substantial proportion of the cases involving custody disputes—whether in the adversarial group or in the mediation group—entered our sample following the promulgation of a divorce decree. Ultimately, however, cases that were mediated before final orders were more likely to reach settlements. As a result, a greater proportion of the successful than the unsuccessful mediation group was at an early stage in the divorce process: postdivorce cases accounted for 27 percent of the successful mediation sample and 43 percent of the unsuccessful mediation sample. The average time between the parental separation and the first interview was 25.3 months for those in the adversarial group, 20.2 months for those who unsuccessfully mediated, 13.5 months for those who successfully mediated, and 12.5 months for those in the noncontested sample.

Another difference in the groups at the initial interview was the greater level of spousal cooperation reported by the noncontested sample versus all other groups. Nearly 80 percent of the noncontested respondents said their relationship with an ex-spouse was either "friendly" or "strained" rather than "difficult" or "impossible." Among the successful mediation, unsuccessful mediation, and adversarial samples, only about one-third reported this much cooperation. Analysis of variance reveals the dif-

Table 8.4
Selected Background Characteristics of Respondents in Various Mediation and Divorce Dispute Categories

	Full Agreement in Mediation, %	No Agreement in Mediation, %	Adversarial, %	Noncontesting, %
Race				
Anglo/White	81	79	78	87
Black	6	11	2	5
Hispanic	13	4	18	7
Asian	—	6	2	—
Indian	—	—	—	1
Occupation (partial list)				
Professional	24	36	26	30
Managerial	14	10	—	12
Clerical	28	21	23	37
Service	20	9	26	12
Education level				
High school or less	43	32	36	30
Trade school or some college	41	36	52	41
College graduate	16	32	12	29
Number of children				
One	54	48	51	41
Two	31	39	35	40
Three or more	15	13	14	19
Marital status				
Still living together	12	6	—	1
Separated	61	51	62	87
Divorced	27	43	38	12
Cooperation with ex-Spouse				
Easy	5	2	6	33
Strained	30	30	36	44
Can't cooperate much	33	23	15	9
Impossible or don't even try	32	45	43	14

ference to be significant at better than the 0.01 level. Table 8.4 summarizes selected characteristics of respondents in each divorce dispute category.

Initial Parenting Behaviors

Parents reported a variety of visitation problems at the time of the initial interview. One common problem was the lack of regular, predictable visitation. About 20–30 percent of the respondents in each dispute category reported that visitation was sporadic, with the children seeing their noncustodial parent infrequently or on an uncertain schedule. Moreover proximity was not a reliable indicator of the regularity of visitation. Even among ex-spouses who lived within 30 miles of one another, visitation was reported to be infrequent, irregular, or both, in approximately 20 percent of the cases in each category.

The more amicable relationship reported by noncontesting parents was related to fewer visitation problems. Analysis of variance confirms that there are significantly (probability of 0.01) fewer problems in this group versus all others. Thus about half of the respondents in each mediation and adversarial category—but only 10 percent of noncontesting respondents—were concerned about their child's well-being while in their ex-spouse's care. Nearly 40 percent of the mediation and adversarial groups, but only 10 percent of the noncontesting respondents, worried about the ex-spouse verbally deriding them to the children.

Similarly, less than 10 percent of the noncontesting parents, about a quarter of the respondents in the unsuccessful mediation and adversarial categories, and 40 percent of the successful mediation cases, reported concerns about their children being spoiled as a result of the divorce. A noncustodial mother in Connecticut, for example, worried about taking her children to dinner and the movies. As she expressed it: "The kids are getting used to being dated. It's not a natural relationship." In Los Angeles a father reported that after he corrects his sons, "I backtrack five minutes later, because I don't want the boys mad at me."

Many of these visitation concerns reflect basic problems in coparenting. In fact about half of the mediation and adversarial respondents reported hostility during discussions with the ex-spouse about the children. The figure for the noncontesting group was considerably lower, although a quarter did report hostility. Analysis of variance reveals the difference between the noncontesting and all other groups to be significant at the 0.01 level. Nearly 30 percent of the noncontesting, 40 percent of the successful mediation, and 60 percent of the unsuccessful and adversarial groups also reported basic differences between parents regarding child rearing. Again the differences between the noncontesting group and all others are significant at the 0.01 level. Further, no more than 20 percent of the respondents in any dispute categories regarded their ex-spouse as a help in child rearing. In fact when asked what they liked about their ex-spouse as a parent, many respondents were unable to think of anything.

On the positive side, most parents felt that they related well to their children, and many admitted, sometimes grudgingly, that their ex-spouse also got along well with the children. As one mother said, "He is crazy about the kid. He just has a strange way of showing it." In addition custodians often reported that their own parenting had improved following the divorce, despite the fact that sole parenting was commonly described

Table 8.5
Initial Parenting Behaviors Reported by Respondents in Various Dispute Categories

	Successful Mediation, %	Unsuccessful Mediation, %	Adversarial, %	Noncontesting, %
Visitation takes place rarely or irregularly	23	27	31	37
Percent reporting that visitation occurs irregularly where parents live no more than 30 miles apart	21	25	26	19
Respondents indicated "often" being concerned about:				
Children being spoiled	40	21	25	7
Ex-spouse deriding you to children	33	48	40	10
Children's well being with other parent	49	53	54	10
Percent who say the following descriptions of parenting are "often" true:				
In discussions of parenting, the atmosphere is hostile	52	55	52	25
You and ex-spouse have basic child-rearing differences	44	56	59	30
Your ex-spouse is a help in child rearing	14	12	4	20
Percent reporting ex-spouse gets along well with children	57	39	33	60

as stressful. Table 8.5 presents initial parenting behaviors for respondents in each dispute category.

Initial Child Adjustment

At the time of the first interview, most families faced the typical upheavals that accompany a divorce—physical relocation of one or both parents, financial stresses, and uncertainty about the future. Understandably, many parents found themselves overwhelmed, and this made it more difficult for them to assess what their children were experiencing. In the words of one mother, "I didn't notice any immediate changes [in the children] but I might have been too busy trying to be competent and not fall apart myself, so I might not have noticed."

An analysis of the Achenbach scale by dispute category reveals no statistically significant differences among the groups at the initial interview on the composite measures of child adjustment. Most parents felt that they enjoyed a good relationship with the child selected for evaluation in the questionnaire. Most parents also felt that this child was making a satisfactory adjustment to the divorce and the new custody arrangment.

Nevertheless a sizable proportion of parents expressed concerns about the child. In all the groups about 20 percent of the parents reported that the child seemed angry with the mother over the divorce, and about the same percentage reported that the child was angry with the father. Anger with parents is a theme that emerged in the in-depth interviews with the children, as well. In some cases the anger grew directly out of the divorce experience. One eight-year-old boy, for example, admitted to being angry with his custodial father, and expressed the wish that his father would "take some responsibility instead of just being angry and upset all the time."

In other instances the child's anger seemed the result of longstanding family problems, including abuse. Although the mediation programs do not accept known cases of abuse, the presence of family violence sometimes goes undetected. In such cases the child's anger about the divorce may be mixed with more general feelings of anger, fear, and even, in the words of one mother, relief: "The divorce was a relief [to my son]. He had a list of people to call if Dad beat Mom. . .It's not a normal responsibility for a little boy. . ."

Loyalty conflicts were a problem in the eyes of many parents. There were no statistically significant differences across the groups on this variable. Overall, 16 percent of all parents indicated that the child had taken sides with one parent, and 17 percent indicated that the child was worried or upset at the prospect of having to do so. Most parents indicated that they tried to reassure the child that he or she would always have both parents. Some children, however, had good reason to be concerned about losing one parent, since such a loss had been implicitly, and occasionally even explicitly, threatened by an adult. As one mother put it, "The attorney told the kids it was fine if they wanted to live with their father, but they should choose up sides."

Another problem mentioned by a sizable percentage of parents was the child's unwillingness to discuss the divorce. About 30 percent of the parents in all groups indicated that this was a problem. The in-depth interviews with children confirmed that for many children the primary coping mechanism was avoidance. In the words of two children:

> I feel nothing about the divorce. . . I know they fought once or twice because I'd hear them yelling at each other. The divorce is okay. I don't ever think about it.
>
> I just didn't think of it [the divorce]—that's how I handle problems. I don't think about them and they go away.

Along the same line, only about 60 percent of the parents in most groups thought their child accepted the divorce. The exception was the successful mediation group, where this figure was much higher (86 percent). Analysis of variance reveals the difference between the successful mediation group and the other groups to be significant at the 0.01 level. In their interviews children repeatedly expressed a wish for parental reconciliations. Although many noted that they were relieved not to be in the midst of fighting, others indicated that even the fighting was better than the divorce. Most children who wished for a reconciliation also recognized the unlikeliness of this happening. "The odds are one in a thousand—make that a million—that my mom and dad will get married again. It would be nice if they did, though."

Finally, between 30 and 50 percent of the parents indicated that they thought their child's life could benefit from more routine and stability, although the groups did not differ significantly among themselves with regard to this opinion. This is no doubt in large part a reaction to the general stress of the divorce and to the changes—in residence, babysitters, and daily routines—that often accompanied the separation. At the initial interview, for example, about 30 percent of the respondents reported that the child had changed schools within the last year. As many reported that the child, along with the custodian, had moved. During the course of the study, about a third of the custodians reported that they began working outside the home, or increased their work hours (See Table 8.6).

Children and the Mediation Experience

At none of the three court sites does mediation mandate the direct participation of children. Although it is the official policy of each court mediation service to involve children, the degree and manner in which this occurs is up to the discretion of individual mediators. The director of the Connecticut program acknowledges that "the introduction of children into the mediation process is the most flexible aspect of the process" (Salius et al., n.d.).

Many factors determine whether the child participates. One obvious factor is simply whether the child accompanies the parents on the sched-

Table 8.6
Parental Perceptions of Child Adjustment at the Initial Interview

	Successful Mediation, %	Unsuccessful Mediation, %	Adversarial, %	Noncontesting, %
Percent agreeing with the following statements:				
I have a good relationship with my child.	89	90	98	92
My ex-spouse has a good relationship with the child.	57	39	33	60
Child feels responsible for the divorce.	14	29	11	2
Child worries about taking sides.	14	31	19	6
Child takes sides with one parent.	18	26	13	10
Child won't talk about the divorce.	38	27	25	23
Child accepts the divorce.	86	62	64	60
Child needs more routine and stability in his/her life.	37	51	30	29
I find myself confiding in this child.	11	18	18	21
Child is angry with mother because of the divorce.	27	19	24	20
Child is angry with father because of the divorce.	18	25	21	13

uled mediation day. Although mediators can postpone the session or schedule additional sessions if the child is not present, most mediators are reluctant to do so, generally believing that the child will benefit more from a speedy resolution to the dispute. In addition to this obvious factor, mediators may be influenced by the nature of the dispute. Some mediators specify that they routinely speak to children in cases where parents present widely divergent views of the child's needs or preferences. The child's age may or may not influence the mediator's decision to involve the child. Some mediators prefer not to see preschool children because their limited verbal skills make interviews difficult. Others prefer to meet with the entire family, even infants, because they feel that observations of family interaction patterns are helpful in understanding relationship dynamics.

About a fourth of the parents who tried mediation reported that the mediator did meet with their children. Further, to the extent that mediators spoke with children in the sample, most (87 percent) met with all the children in the family, although not necessarily simultaneously. These discussions were usually private (49 percent) and attended by only the children and the mediator. A number of the mediators met with the children privately and then jointly with parents and children (31 percent). Least common (20 percent) were instances in which mediators had no private time with the children, and met with them only in the presence of both parents.

Most parents (61 percent) who reported that the mediators had met with their children said that the mediators shared with parents the insights gained by these meetings. Mediators agree with this assessment, and report that the procedure typically is to ask the child's permission to share these thoughts with his or her parents. Most parents (83 percent) reported that they liked the idea of mediators including children in the proceedings, although some parents were apprehensive about the procedure and worried about "putting the children through all that."

Because most children had not spoken with a mediator, it is not surprising that the in-depth interviews with children whose parents mediated revealed only a limited understanding of the process. In some cases children were completely unaware of the fact that mediation had occurred. Because public sector mediation often takes place in the courthouse, some children were confused about whether they had been to "court" versus "mediation."

Most children who spoke to the mediator described the experience favorably. Typically they liked the idea that someone cared enough to elicit their input. At its very best, involvement in the mediation helped the children to deal with their emotions, and improved the family's ability to communicate. As one child explained: "It helped. I got my feelings out.

My dad didn't know how I felt about him. I can talk to him now because of mediation. I couldn't before.''

Children who disliked their experiences with mediation complained about a variety of factors. For some, the session was simply "boring." A few children who saw the mediator along with their siblings or parents wanted more privacy, and were inhibited about expressing their concerns or preferences. Some children found the mediation sessions emotionally charged and unpleasant; even in these instances, however, most children reported that the sessions were still informative and helpful. Fortunately the children we interviewed rarely indicated that they felt the mediator had asked them to choose between their parents; indeed in a number of instances children said that speaking with a mediator had helped to convince them that they would not be asked to choose sides.

It is less easy to discern the measurable effects of mediators seeing the children. But, based on t-tests of responses at the final interview, parents whose child spoke with the mediator, as compared with those whose did not, were statistically more likely to say the child had a good relationship with the noncustodian. A comparison of responses to this item at the initial interview, prior to mediation, reveals no such difference between the two groups.

Children and the Adversarial Experience

About 37 percent of the parents who were contesting custody reported that a custody study had been conducted. This study is an investigative and evaluative process conducted by court personnel and/or private mental health professionals designed to gather information and offer input that will aid the court in identifying the preferred custodial parent. In almost 90 percent of these cases, the evaluator spoke with some or all of the children. Although parents expressed a great deal of dissatisfaction with the evaluation process, interviews indicated that children were generally neutral or positive about the contact. A number of children indicated that they appreciated the fact that everyone involved in the divorce was interviewed. Most evaluators appeared to have been good listeners and sensitive to the child's concerns.

Few children had been to a court hearing; those who had, though, were generally less favorable about the experience than about custody studies, and viewed the court as imposing and formidable. Yet in the few instances where children were seen by the judge in chambers, there was no indication that they felt forced to choose sides. Several children volunteered that they were given a chance to express their opinions, but added that they were relieved that the judge had the difficult job of choosing. Interviews with parents reveal mixed reactions to children being seen in chambers.

One parent insisted that: "It's so uncalled for, so unnecessary to put little kids through something like that."

Yet other parents were angry that their children did not speak to the judge: "My wife and I asked for the children to be interviewed by the judge. He declined. He said the kids should not be involved. But the children were already involved!"

Postdivorce Parenting

One year after the initial interview, questionnaires were readministered to parents. When asked about their ability to cooperate with the ex-spouse, we find, among the successful mediation cases, a shift toward greater cooperation. Analysis of variance shows this group to have become significantly more cooperative than the unsuccessful mediation and adversarial groups. In the adversarial group, cooperation has in fact declined. In the noncontesting and unsuccessful mediation groups, there has been virtually no change since the initial interview. The result of this fluctuation is that the groups now fall along a continuum, where the noncontested parents report levels of cooperation significantly better than all other groups, followed by successful mediation cases, unsuccessful mediation cases, and the adversarial group. Our follow-up interviews with children suggest that, for some, the increased cooperation brings both relief and confusion: "They can talk; why can't they live together?"

Another measure of the quality of parenting is the number of problems surrounding visitation. An analysis of responses to questions about the incidence of problems reveals similar patterns for all respondents who had a custody dispute, and shows no particular benefits for those who used mediation. The only statistically significant differences thus are between the noncontesting group and all others. Once again we asked respondents about the frequency of problems with the children's safety/well-being, discipline/overindulgence, late return following visitation, a lack of activities during the visit, or one parent criticizing the other in the presence of the children. At the initial interview, prior to any intervention of either an adversarial or nonadversarial nature, about 55 percent of all respondents who were contesting custody/visitation reported that three or more of these issues were sometimes or often a problem. Among respondents in the noncontesting category, where custody/visitation was not in dispute, significantly fewer (17 percent) reported problems with three or more of these issues. By the final interview, the number of respondents reporting three or more problems had declined to 12–18 percent for all mediation and adversarial group respondents, and to 4 percent in the noncontesting group.

Three final measures of cooperative parenting address the degree to which parents comply with their final divorce orders: regularity of "visitation" or contact with both parents, regularity of child support, and frequency with which the child's parents return to court.

We find that the regularity of visitation has remained fairly constant from the time of the initial interview. At the one-year follow-up, about 20 percent of all those who tried mediation, and about 35 percent of the adversarial and of the noncontesting groups, report that visitation rarely or never takes place on a regular, predictable basis. When we control for the distance separating the ex-spouses, the percentages change only slightly. For those living within 30 miles of their ex-spouse, about 20–25 percent of all groups report irregular visitation.

For child-support payment patterns, we find that, across all dispute categories, about 25 percent of the recipient parents in the mediation and noncontesting categories report receiving support very irregularly. The figure is 53 percent for the adversarial parents.

Finally, an analysis of variance reveals significantly lower levels of relitigation by those who produce final arrangements in mediation than by the adversarial group; and lower levels also, for those who did not initially contest custody, than for the unsuccessful mediation and adversarial groups. Between the first and final interview, then, about 10 percent of the noncontesting and successful mediation respondents went back to court to file contempt citations, to take out temporary restraining orders, or to change custody, visitation, or child support agreements. Among those who reached no agreement in mediation and in the adversarial group, approximately 26 percent returned to court. Table 8.7 summarizes these parental cooperation, compliance, and relitigation patterns.

Child Adjustment at the Final Interview

At the one-year follow-up, most parents expressed the belief that their child had made progress during the past months and was adjusting to the divorce. Thus only 10–15 percent of the parents in any dispute category still perceived their children as angry with either parent.

Yet not all reports from parents were as optimistic. For example, parental concerns about the child refusing to discuss the divorce did not decline between the initial and final interviews, and were still mentioned by a sizable proporation (16–30 percent) of the parents in each group. The differences across groups are not statistically significant. Nor does the passage of time produce large declines in the percentage of parents who feel that the child's life is lacking in routine and stability.

Finally there has been no decline, but, in most groups, an increase in the number of custodians who indicate that the child is their confidante and listens to their worries and plans. This may be indicative of a parent—child role reversal or a home environment in which children are encouraged to "grow up in a hurry." There is no consistent wisdom on whether the accelerated responsibilities and maturity ensuing from a divorce are desirable or undesirable. Table 8.8 summarizes parent reports of child-adjustment patterns.

Analysis of variance comparing the final interview scores on the Achenbach global scale and subscales with the indices of acceptance of the divorce, quality of the custodian–child relationship, satisfaction with the custody arrangement, and perceived maturity, reveals no statistically significant differences among any of the groups. Moving beyond this simple

Table 8.7

Parental Cooperation, Visitation, Child-Support Payment Behavior and Relitigation for Respondents in Various Divorce Dispute Categories One Year Following the Initial Interview

	Successful Mediation, %	Unsuccessful Mediation, %	Adversarial, %	Noncontesting, %
Percent reporting that cooperation with ex-spouse is:				
Easy	16	6	6	39
Strained	46	38	29	37
Difficult	9	14	2	8
Impossible	29	42	63	17
Problems with visitation:				
Children's safety	26	32	48	9
Spoiling children	25	15	19	10
Late return	23	24	26	10
Lack of activities	8	13	2	4
Criticizing each other	25	27	43	10
Percent reporting that three or more issues are problems	40	24	44	14
Percent reporting that visitation is highly irregular	17	23	32	35
Percent with irregular visitation patterns, living less than 30 miles apart	19	19	27	23
Percent reporting child support is very irregular	27	28	53	28
Percent reporting a return to court	11	26	26	9

comparison of groups, we next employed multiple regressions to identify the factors that best explain the variance in our measures of child adjustment at the final interview.

The dependent variables again included the global Achenbach score and the subscale scores of aggression, depression, social withdrawal, delinquency, and somatic complaints; and the indices created through factor analysis that appear to measure quality of the custodian-child relationship, the acceptance of the divorce, the satisfaction with the custody arrangement, and the maturity as a result of the divorce. Our list of possible predictors of child adjustment included a variety of items that have been mentioned in the literature. These independent variable fell into five major categories: (1) general background of the family (2) dispute/divorce spe-

Table 8.8
Parental Perceptions of Child Adjustment at the 12–Month Followup Interview

	Successful Mediation, %	Unsuccessful Mediation, %	Adversarial, %	Noncontesting, %
Percent agreeing with the following statements:				
I have a good relationship with my child.	100	93	98	99
My ex-spouse has a good relationship with the child.	66	69	43	70
Child feels responsible for the divorce.	7	9	8	—
Child worries about taking sides.	30	22	33	19
Child takes sides with one parent.	18	6	7	11
Child won't talk about the divorce.	30	20	19	16
Child accepts the divorce.	82	75	86	78
Child needs more routine and stability in his/her life.	29	28	34	39
I find myself confiding in this child.	26	13	28	33
Child is angry with mother because of the divorce.	12	16	12	14
Child is angry with father because of the divorce.	7	16	12	7

cific variables (3) characteristics of the child (4) variables related to custody and visitation and (5) characteristics of the parental relationship. The specific items included in each category are shown in Table 8.9.

Using the backward model of regression, variables were entered simultaneously and removed step-by-step until the optimum combination remained to explain the variance in the dependent variable. This technique allowed us to explain 10–16 percent of the variance in each of the Achenbach subscales as well as the global scale.

Table 8.9
Items Introduced as Independent Variables in Multiple Regressions to Predict Child Adjustment

Background characteristics

Level of financial strain experienced by custodian (first interview).

Custodian began working outside home.

Distance separating spouses (first and final interviews).

Custodian's interest in reconciling (first interview).

Custodian's educational level.

Age of custodial parent.

Number of children in the family.

Level of violence during the marriage.

Dispute/divorce variables

Number of times appeared in court (first interview).

Noncontested divorce.

Adversarial divorce.

Successful mediation.

Unsuccessful mediation.

Date of separation.

Mediator spoke with child.

Stage in the divorce proceedings (first interview).

Characteristics of the child

Child's sex.

Age of child.

Number of disruptions in child's life (moving, changing custody, new school, held back a grade) (initial, second, and final interviews).

Child's awareness of parental anger (final interview).

Custody/visitation variables

Children spend too much time with ex-spouse's new partner during visitation (final interview).

Child living with parent of the same or opposite sex.

Noncustodian disparages custodian to the children during visitation (first and final interviews)

Custodian remarried.

Noncustodian remarried.

Frequency of visitation (first and final interviews).

Characteristics of the parental relationship

Cooperation level between spouses (first and final interviews).

Custodian's attachment to ex-spouse (first and final interviews).

Custodian believes parents have basic differences in child rearing (first interview).

Custodian's perception of ex-spouse's anger level (final interview).

The explained variance was similar for the indices of quality of the parent–child relationship, acceptance of the divorce, the child's satisfaction with the custody arrangement, and maturity following the divorce. The adjusted R^2 were 0.08, 0.13, 0.20, and 0.12, respectively. Tables 8.10–8.19 display the variable contributing to each regression.

In looking across all ten regressions, we find five variables that appear in more than half. These variables are, in descending order of frequency: the parent's degree of interest in reconciling at the initial interview; the level of physical violence in the home during the marriage; custodian's financial stress as reported at first interview; the parent's level of cooperation at the first interview; and the parent's level of cooperation at the final interview. The pattern is for better adjustment in those families where parents are cooperative. Despite the mixed messages that may have been sent, we find better adjustment in homes were reconciliation was considered at the time of the initial interview. Adjustment is also greater in families with no history of violence, and where custodians did not experience high levels of financial stress at the initial interview.

Nine more variables appeared in half the regressions: the custodian's attachment to the ex-spouse at the initial interview; the noncustodian

Table 8.10
Summary of Regression of Independent Variables on Global Achenbach Scale

Variable	Beta	Significance
Parental cooperation level (final interview)	0.246	0.001
Divorce is noncontested	0.198	0.028
Custodian's attachment to ex-spouse (first interview)	0.161	0.044
Parents in adversarial group	0.136	0.046
Custodian's interest In reconciling (first interview)	0.125	0.109
Parental cooperation level (first interview)	0.118	0.116
Child living with same-sex parent	0.117	0.113
Level of violence in home during the marriage	0.117	0.091
Unsuccessful mediation group	0.111	0.158
Changes in child's routine (second interview)	0.110	0.085
Child's sex	0.110	0.146
Ex-spouse berates custodian when talking to children (final interview)	0.107	0.107
Frequency of visitation (final interview)	0.104	0.103
Successful mediation group	0.086	0.301
Parents have differences in childrearing (first interview)	0.086	0.227
Custodian's attachment to ex-spouse (final interview)	0.068	0.306
Age of parents	0.064	0.298

Adjusted $R^2 = 0.12$

berating the custodian to the children during visitation; the age of the parents; the age of the child; the child's sex; the number of changes in the child's life reported at the second interview; the regularity of visitation at the final interview; parents being in the noncontested group; and parents being in the adversarial group. Among these variables we find that child adjustment is associated with higher initial levels of custodian attachment to the ex-spouse; regular visitation at the final interview; no berating of the custodian parent to children during visitation; younger parents and children; fewer changes reported in the child's life (moving, changing schools) at the second interview; no dispute over custody; and nonadversarial group membership. We also find better adjustment for girls than for boys.

These analyses suggest that variables dealing with family dynamics, child characteristics, and the parent–child relationship, as well as those related to the dispute resolution category, are relevant in understanding children's adjustment.

DISCUSSION

The majority of the respondents with whom we spoke recognized and appreciated the fact that mediation allows for a more personal and private

Table 8.11
Summary of Regression of Independent Variables on Aggression Scale

Variable	Beta	Significance
Level of cooperation (final interview)	0.289	0.001
Parents in adversarial group	0.222	0.005
Custodian's attachment to ex-spouse (first interview)	0.215	0.008
Divorce is noncontested	0.212	0.003
Custodian's interest in reconciling (first interview)	0.191	0.014
Child's sex	0.154	0.015
Changes in child's routine (second interview)	0.143	0.024
Number of children in family	0.093	0.129
Custodian's financial strain (first interview)	0.089	0.153
Level of violence in home during the marriage	0.086	0.192
Parental cooperation level (first interview)	0.081	0.262
Frequency of visitation (first interview)	0.081	0.214
Frequency of visitation (final interview)	0.077	0.220
Custodian's attachment to ex-spouse (final interview)	0.074	0.262
Date of separation	0.073	0.239
Distance separating parents (final interview)	0.072	0.275

Adjusted $R^2 = 0.13$

resolution of disputes between nonstrangers than is afforded by normal court procedures. The formal and complex atmosphere of the legal system is perceived by many of our respondents as a cold, indifferent, and confusing setting in which to deal with a former spouse and the children. The court setting, too, is frequently perceived to undermine whatever degree of cooperation may exist between the spouses. Creating agreements in a semiprivate setting such as mediation is thought by users to be less unpleasant and less detrimental to the relationship between exspouses.

Despite these positive patterns, our study of child adjustment to divorce found only limited differences according to the formal dispute status of the parents or their exposure to mediation versus more traditional adjudicatory processes. There are several possible reasons for these results. One lies with the duration of our study. We measured child adjustment over a 12- to 15-month period, using a variety of parent-report items, including the Achenbach-Edelbrock child behavior checklist. Although previous research has documented an increased risk of emotional problems for children of divorce and an overrepresentation of such children in the outpatient psychiatric and psychological treatment populations (Zill, 1983), there is also evidence that psychological difficulties do not necessarily manifest themselves at the time of divorce or within 15 months.

Table 8.12
Summary of Regression of Independent Variables on Depression Subscale

Variable	Beta	Significance
Parental cooperation level (final interview)	0.216	0.004
Child's age	0.214	0.001
Parental cooperation level (final interview)	0.189	0.008
Custodian's attachment to ex-spouse (first interview)	0.161	0.029
Custodian's educational level	0.153	0.013
Level of violence in home during the marriage	0.122	0.069
Parents have differences in child rearing (first interview)	0.121	0.091
Amount of visitation (final interview)	0.120	0.060
Custodian's interest in reconciliation (first interview)	0.114	0.129
Ex-spouse berates custodian when talking to children (first interview)	0.109	0.139
Children's awareness of anger between parents (final interview)	0.099	0.146
Child's sex	0.088	0.220
Amount of visitation (first interview)	0.084	0.174
Changes in child's life (final interview)	0.075	0.213
Child placed with same-sex parent	0.075	0.298
Divorce is noncontested	0.069	0.316

Adjusted $R^2 = 0.162$

According to one study, treatment referrals for children of divorced families are made an average of five years after the divorce (Kalter & Rembar, 1977). On the other hand, another study reports only short-term social and emotional difficulties following divorce, which typically fade within two years (Hetherington et al., 1981). Thus while the duration of our study may simply have been too short, it is not clear what time period would have been optimal.

Another problem that may explain a lack of differences in adjustment outcomes by dispute category is that we altered the scales in the Achenbach-Edelbrock instrument and reduced the number of items that comprised each subscale. Our sample size simply did not permit us to analyze the data using the age- and sex- sepcific subscales. Instead we limited our analysis to those subscales and the items within each subscale common to boys and girls and children of all age groups. We should note, however, that when exploratory analyses were conducted using the original subscales reported for boys and girls in one age group (six- to 11-year-olds), no differences in adjustment outcomes by parental dispute category could be detected at either the initial or final interview.

Another possible explanation for the absence of differences in adjustment across dispute categories concerns parental conflict level. Data published from the New York Longitudinal Study revealed that parental divorce or separation was not related to the child's level of adjustment as a young adult when the effects of conflict were taken into account (Chess et al., 1983). Several investigators have found that children from relatively

Table 8.13
Summary of Regression of Independent Variables on Delinquency Subscale

Variable	Beta	Significance
Parents in adversarial group	0.187	0.018
Divorce noncontested	0.181	0.012
Distance separating parents (first interview)	0.173	0.026
Distance separating parents (final interview)	0.161	0.037
Child's sex	0.150	0.015
Education level of custodian	0.140	0.026
Parental cooperation level (first interview)	0.124	0.071
Age of custodial parent	0.123	0.047
Custodian reports children spend too much time with ex-spouse's new partner (final interview)	0.107	0.082
Number of court appearances (first interview)	0.104	0.098
Custodial parent's financial strain (first interview)	0.102	0.100
Parental cooperation level (final interview)	0.088	0.198
Custodian began work in the last year	0.083	0.178

Adjusted $R^2 = .10$

conflict-free single—parent homes are generally better adjusted than children from conflict-ridden two-parent families (Hetherington et al., 1979; Emery et al., 1983).

There may also be too much variation in the adversarial experience to make the term meaningful. Research shows, for example, that while some divorce attorneys are "litigators" who push their clients to a full court battle, many are conciliatory and seek to minimize hostility (Kressel, Lopez-Morillas, Weinglass & Deutsch, 1979; Mnookin, 1975).

Finally, the absence of differences in child adjustment for the mediation and adjudication groups may simply be due to the format and scope of the mediation intervention. At all three court sites, mediation is a brief process that typically does not require the child's direct participation. Based on our sample of mediation users in Connecticut, the average number of mediation sessions was 1.5, and the average number of hours was 2.3. At the Los Angeles Conciliation Court, cases averaged 1.7 sessions and 3.0 hours, and in Minneapolis, where the process takes the longest and most typically involves the child, the average number of mediation sessions is 3.3. Clearly there are limits to the effects that can be expected from a brief intervention. Moreover, given the minimal contact that most children have with the mediator, it is probably liklier that the effects of the process will

Table 8.14
Summary of Regression of Independent Variables on Social Withdrawal Subscale

Variable	Beta	Significance
Age of child	0.182	0.017
Age of parent	0.171	0.017
Child living with same-sex parent	0.167	0.007
Custodian's interest in reconciling (first interview)	0.113	0.076
Changes in child's routine (second interview)	0.099	0.126
Children's awareness of anger between parents (final interview)	0.093	0.149
Changes in child's routine (final interview)	0.092	0.142
Mediator spoke with children	0.090	0.145
Custodian's attachment to ex-spouse (final interview)	0.089	0.154
Frequency of visitation (first interview)	0.088	0.168
Custodian reports children spend too much time with ex-spouse's partner (final interview)	0.074	0.239
Frequency of visitation (final interview)	0.073	0.287
Custodian's educational level	0.069	0.281
Number of children in family	0.068	0.302
Parents in adversarial group	0.067	0.282

Adjusted $R^2 = 0.13$

be most felt by the parents, and that children will benefit only indirectly through the enhanced wellbeing of parents.

Our experiences and findings lead to several recommendations regarding the direction of future research on child-adjustment patterns following divorce. There is a clear need for objective measures that are developed and tested with children who experience a parental divorce; measures developed with clinical and normal populations may not be sensitive to divorce outcomes. There is a need for measurements that reflect growth and positive outcomes following divorce, rather than focusing purely on the behavioral disorders and psychological problems reflected in traditional adjustment scales. There is also a need to conduct research with large samples and longer longitudinal perspectives. Such samples are necessary to allow for the statistical control of the many social, familial and custodial factors that affect children's divorce adjustment, as well as to detect the differences that can be expected for children of different ages and sexes.

Our research also reveals the need for multimethod assessment procedures that involve both objective measures and direct observations and interviews with children. This is, of course, costly and difficult to accomplish. Our clinical staff and field researchers encountered significant resistance from parents in attempting to schedule interviews with children. As a result the sample of children ultimately interviewed probably did not reflect the heterogeneity of the population captured in the survey of parents.

Table 8.15
Summary of Regression of Independent Variables on Somatic Complaints Scale

Variable	Beta	Significance
Age of child	0.223	0.001
Custodian's attachment to ex-spouse (first interview)	0.183	0.016
Parental cooperation level (final interview)	0.153	0.032
Custodian's interest in reconciling (first interview)	0.127	0.088
Changes in child's routine (first interview)	0.127	0.050
Custodian perceives ex-spouse as angry	0.122	0.075
Successful mediation group	0.110	0.100
Changes in child's routine (second interview)	0.090	0.181
Level of violence in home during the marriage	0.086	0.182
Custodian's financial strain (first interview)	0.073	0.242
Mediator spoke with children	0.071	0.285
Changes in child's routine (final interview)	0.065	0.311

Adjusted $R^2 = 0.11$

With respect to policy issues, it is important that mediators, program administrators, and advocates alike be realistic about the potential benefits of mediation. Although numerous accounts document impressive levels of user satisfaction, and there is evidence of improved compliance and reduced relitigation, mediation has a more limited impact on relationships between disputants (Pearson & Thoennes, 1984, 1985) and appears to

Table 8.16
Summary of Regression of Independent Variables on Index of Child's Acceptance of Divorce

Variable	Beta	Significance
Ex-spouse has remarried	0.192	0.002
Custodian's attachment to ex-spouse (final interview)	0.191	0.004
Ex-spouse berates custodian when talking to children (final interview)	0.130	0.044
Frequency of visitation (final interview)	0.129	0.049
Custodian began work in the last year	0.124	0.041
Custodian's attachment to ex-spouse (first interview)	0.113	0.091
Frequency of visitation (first interview)	0.109	0.096
Parental cooperation level (final interview)	0.101	0.154
Successful mediation group	0.099	0.147
Age of custodian	0.088	0.144
Divorce was noncontested	0.084	0.263
Parents in the adversarial group	0.082	0.227
Parental cooperation level (first interview)	0.069	0.311

Adjusted $R^2 = 0.13$

Table 8.17
Summary of Regression of Independent Variables on Index of Quality of Custodian–Child Relationship

Variable	Beta	Significance
Unsuccessful mediation	0.224	0.001
Child placed with same-sex parent	0.159	0.011
Ex-spouse berates custodian when talking to children (first interview)	0.128	0.059
Custodian perceives ex-spouse as angry (final interview)	0.094	0.166
Custodian's financial strain (first interview)	0.086	0.162
Custodian's interest in reconciling (first interview)	0.073	0.238
Number of court appearances (first interview)	0.073	0.240
Age of child	0.073	0.233
Custodian has remarried	0.065	0.299

Adjusted $R^2 = 0.08$

have few measurable effects on children's adjustment. Like other researchers, we find that the more compelling predictors of child adjustment are parental conflict, parent–child contact, other stressors in the child's life, and general family dynamics, rather than formal legal status classifications. If more direct benefits to children are desired, mediation programs

Table 8.18
Summary of Regression of Independent Variables on Index of Child's Maturity Following the Divorce

Variable	Beta	Significance
Age of child	0.230	0.001
Unsuccessful mediation group	0.209	0.001
Number of children in family	0.199	0.003
Children's awareness of anger between parents (final interview)	0.151	0.022
Parent's stage in divorce process (first interview)	0.116	0.070
Custodian's financial strain (first interview)	0.115	0.065
Custodian's interest in reconciling (first interview)	0.095	0.127
Number of court appearances (first interview)	0.089	0.150
Violence in home during the marriage	0.064	0.298
Child's sex	0.063	0.301

Adjusted $R^2 = 0.12$

Table 8.19
Summary of Regression of Independent Variables on Child's Perceived Satisfaction with Custody Arrangement

Variable	Beta	Significance
Changes in child's routine (final interview)	0.246	0.000
Number of court appearances (first interview)	0.188	0.001
Custodian reports children spend too much time with ex-spouse's new partner (final interview)	0.188	0.002
Children's awareness of anger between parents (final interview)	0.165	0.014
Custodian's financial strain (first interview)	0.146	0.013
Parental cooperation level (first interview)	0.117	0.069
Successful mediation group	0.105	0.083
Level of violence in home during marriage	0.101	0.119
Number of children	0.091	0.131
Age of custodian	0.086	0.162
Distance separating parents (first interview)	0.079	0.177
Changes in child's routine (second interview)	0.080	0.193
Ex-spouse berates custodian when talking to children (final interview)	0.068	0.306

Adjusted $R^2 = .20$

should be modified to involve children routinely in ways that are understandable and meaningful to them.

Nevertheless, the potential benefits of mediation for child adjustment to divorce cannot be dismissed. Children remain central to the process of mediation. Parents who are exposed to the process are likely to say that it helped them focus on their children's needs but are far less likely to use this characterization to describe court hearings or other adversarial proceedings. The child-oriented focus and the information parents receive about parenting and the needs of their children are aspects of mediation that parents appreciate the most (Pearson & Thoennes, 1984, 1985).

REFERENCES

Achenbach, T. M., & Edelbrock, C. W. (1981). Behavioral problems and competencies reported by parents of normal and disturbed children aged 4 through 16. *Monographs of the Society Research in Child Development. 46* (188).

Black, M., & Joffee, W. (1978). A lawyer/therapist approach to divorce. *Conciliation Courts Review, 16,* 1–5.

Blechman, E. A. (1982). Are children with one parent at psychological risk? A methodological review. *Journal of Marriage and the Family, 20,* 179–195.

Chess, S., Thomas, A., Korn, S., Mittleman, M., & Cohn, J. (1983). Early parental attitudes, divorce and separation, and young adult income: Findings of a longitudinal study. *Journal of the American Academy of Child Psychiatry, 22,* 47–51.

Clingempeel, W. G., & Reppucci, N. D. (1982). Joint custody after divorce: Major issues and goals for research. *Psychological Bulletin, 91*(1), 102–137.

Coogler, O. J., Weber, R., & McKenry, P. (1979). Divorce mediation: a means of facilitating divorce and adjustment. *The Family Coordinator, 28,* 255–259.

Emery, R. E. (1982). Interparental conflict and the children of discord and divorce. *Psychological Bulletin, 92,* 310–330.

Emery, R., Hetherington, E. M., & Fisher, L. (1983). Divorce, children and social policy. In H. Stevenson & A. Seigel (Eds.), *Child Development and Social Policy.* Chicago: University of Chicago Press.

Haynes, J. M. (1978). Divorce Mediation: Theory and practice of a new social work role, Unpublished doctoral dissertation, Union Graduate School.

Hetherington, E. M., cox, M., & Cox, R. (1979). Play and social interaction in children following divorce. *Journal of Social Issues, 35* (4).

Hetherington, E. M., Cox, M., & Cox, R. (1981). Effects of divorce on parents and children. In M. Lamb (Ed.), *Nontraditional Families.* Hillsdale, N.J.: Lawrence Erlbaum.

Hodges, W. F., Wechsler, R. C., & Ballantine, C. (1979), Divorce and the preschool child: Cumulative stress, *Journal of Divorce, 3,* 55–68.

Kalter, N., & Rembar, J. (1977). The significance of a child's age at the time of parental divorce. *American Journal of Orthopsychiatry, 51,* 85–100.

Kaufman, I. R. (1976). Judicial reform in the next century. *Stanford Law Review, 29,* 1–26.

Kessler, S. (1978). *Creative Conflict Resolution: Mediation*. Atlanta: National Institute for Professional Training.

Kressel, K., Lopez-Morillas, M., Weinglass, J., & Deutsch, M. (1979). Professional intervention in divorce: The views of lawyers, psychotherapists, and clergy. In G. Levinger and O. C. Moles (Eds.), *Divorce and Separation*. (pp. 246–272). New York: Basic Books.

Kurdek, L. A. (1981). An integrative perspective in children's divorce adjustment. *American Psychologist, 36*, 856–866.

Kurdek, L. A., & Berg, B. (1983). Correlates of children's adjustment to their parents' divorce. In L.A. Kurdek (Ed.), *Children and Divorce;* (pp 47-60). San Francisco: Jossey-Bass.

McIsaac, H. (1983). Mandatory conciliation custody/visitation matters: California's bold strike. *Conciliation Court Review. 19*(2), 73–81.

Milne, A. (1978). Custody of children in a divorce process: A family self-determination model. *Conciliation Courts Review, 16*, 1–10.

Mnookin, R. H. (1975). Child-custody and adjudication: Judicial functions in the face of indeterminancy. *Law and Contemporary Problems, 39*, 226–293.

Olsen, D. H., Cleveland, M., Doyle, P., Reimer, R., Robinson, B., & Rockcastle, M. F. (1979). Unpublished instruments, Child Custody Research Project.

Pearson, J., & Thoennes, N. (1984). Mediating and litigating custody disputes: A longitudinal evaluation. *Family Law Quarterly, 17*(4), 497–524.

Pearson, J., & Thoennes, N. (1985). Mediation vs. the courts in child custody cases. *Negotiation Journal, 1*, 235-243.

Pruitt, D. (1971). Indirect communication and the search for agreement in negotiation. *Journal of Applied Social Psychology, 1*, 205–239.

Salius, A. J., Maruzo, S. D., & Hicks, R. R. (No date). The use of mediation in contested custody and visitation cases in the family relations court. Unpublished manuscript.

Shoemaker, R. M. (1984). Custody mediation: Including the children in the mediation process. Unpublished master's thesis, University of Colorado, Boulder.

Spanier, G. B., & Anderson, E. A. (1979). The impact of the legal system on adjustment to marital separation. *Journal of Marriage and the Family, 41*, 605–613.

Wallerstein, J. S., & Kelly, J. B. (1980). *Surviving the Breakup*. New York: Basic Books.

Zill, N. (1983). *Happy, Healthy and Insecure*. New York: Doubleday.

9

A Review of Treatment Methods for Children of Divorce

ARNOLD L. STOLBERG and PATRICIA WALSH

The effectiveness of intervention programs for children of divorce depends upon the extent to which the programs reflect important aspects of the divorce adjustment process. In this chapter, we present a temporal model of divorce adjustment. Current prevention and treatment programs for children of divorce are described and categorized by time of program introduction relative to the adjustment stage for which they are suited. Intervention programs are then evaluated on the extent to which they correspond to divorce adjustment demands, and on general treatment program development criteria.

NECESSARY COMPONENTS OF DIVORCE INTERVENTION PROGRAMS

Interventions intended to facilitate children's postdivorce adjustment must contain several elements if they are to meet outcome and dissemination requirements. First, interventions should be designed to reflect the unique set of problems that we know divorce poses for family members (Kurdek, 1981). Intervention programs should thus demonstrate a clear linkage between problems of divorce and program elements (Stolberg & Garrison, 1985). In addition divorce interventions share properties common to most structured prevention and treatment programs; reviews of programs for children of divorce must, therefore, consider these general elements in current and proposed interventions.

A TEMPORAL MODEL OF DIVORCE ADJUSTMENT

A temporal model of divorce adjustment has been proposed and evaluated that both clarifies processes that lead to adjustment problems in children, and helps in the design of comprehensive intervention strategies (Stolberg & Bush, 1985; Stolberg, Kiluk, & Garrison, 1986; Stolberg, Camplair, Currier, & Wells, in press). The five components of this model are: (1) the objective event of physical separation; (2) the temporal proximity to the separation; (3) the environmental, familial, and individual factors that mediate the impact of the separation; (4) the subjective evaluation of the separation; and (5) the individual's psychological responses to the event. The divorce adjustment process involves stages, each with its own set of demands. The stress experienced at each stage, and the consequent adjustment, are affected by environmental, familial and individual conditions.

Moderators of Children's Divorce Adjustment

Three classes of variables have been shown to predict children's postdivorce adjustment: (1) parental-familial factors, (2) environmental-extrafamilial factors, and (3) individual factors (Stolberg et al., in press). Parental-familial variables include predivorce martial hostility (Emery, 1982), parenting skills, the custodial parent's adjustment to the divorce, and the availability of the noncustodial parent to the child (Stolberg & Bush, 1985; Stolberg et al., 1986). Environmental-extrafamilial factors—such as divorce-related environmental changes, events, and time since the initial separation—also figure prominantly in the child's adjustment (Stolberg & Bush, 1985; Stolberg et al., in press). Individual variables that predict children's divorce adjustment include age, sex, and emotional predisposition of the child (Hetherington, 1979; Kurdek, 1981).

Divorce has been associated with high frequencies of objective and subjective changes in the children's lives, including moving to new neighborhoods, changing schools, and having the custodial parent take a new or first-time job (Stolberg & Anker, 1983; Stolberg et al., in press; Stolberg & Bush, 1985). Environmental change events often place demands on children for new skills, weaken their support systems, and result in feelings of anger and rejection (Stolberg et al., in press; Stolberg & Anker, 1983; Kurdek, 1981). Old friendships may be prematurely terminated and the development of new ones may be dependent on the acquisition of new social skills and attitudes; for example a child might move into a more socially and sexually precocious social system. Acceptance is dependent on developing new ways of interacting. New schools may have more advanced academic expections and thus also require new skill acquisition. The emotional support of parents and friends is frequently lost through divorce. At least one parent is no longer in the home while the other may be out of the home more often, meeting new job demands. Moving to new neighborhoods also means losing old friends. Finally the loss of satisfying the familiar elements of the previous environment, and the demand for the rapid acquisition of new skills and attitudes, may be particularly frustrating for the child and result in the inappropriate display of anger and aggression.

Parenting skills and parents' postdivorce adjustment are major determinants of children's adjustment (Hetherington et al., 1977; Stolberg & Bush, 1985). Parental adjustment determines the extent of emotional and physical availability of the custodial parent to the child (Stolberg et al., in press; Stolberg & Anker, 1983). Parenting skills include the parents' ability to effectively meet both the child's normal developmental needs, and the specific needs created by the divorce (Hetherington et al., 1977; Stolberg & Bush, 1985).

Interparental marital hostility has been found to correlate positively with maladaptation, the absence of prosocial skills, and poor self-concept (Emery, 1982; Stolberg & Bush, 1985; Stolberg et al., in press). High levels of parent hostility may, for example, provide a model for the child that encourages acting out (Steinmetz, 1977). Extremely hostile parents may further be expected to be less emotionally available to their children, as their energies are invested in their experience of overwhelming anger. In such situations parenting cannot be effectively achieved, and little support and buffering can be offered to the child.

The child's age at the time of the parents' separation identifies the developmental tasks most likely to have been interrupted by the marital dissolution (Kurdek, 1981; Wallerstein, 1983).

Stages of Divorce Adjustment and Intervention Programs

The temporal or stage notion of crisis reaction, around which a sequential model is built, proposes a mediating relationship between temporal proximity to the crisis, the psychological needs of the individual, and the individual's reaction to the event (Auerbach, 1986). Four stages are included in this model: (1) a "distal prestress period," or point at which the crisis event will occur in the anticipatable future; (2) a "proximal prestress period," or point at which the event will occur in the immediate future; (3) a "proximal poststress period," or time during which the crisis event has just concluded; and (4) a "distal poststress period," or period in which the identifiable crisis has been concluded in the somewhat distant past.

Operationalizing divorce as a series of time-linked stages explains the relationship between divorce-related events, the demands on the individual resulting from these circumstances, and the psychological adaptation of the individual (Hetherington et al., 1981; Wallerstein & Kelly, 1980). Such a definition easily fits Auerbach's (1986) and others' (Chiriboga & Cutler, 1977; Lazarus, 1966) temporal models. An anticipation or predecision period occurs before the separation. Although marital discord may be extreme, a decision to divorce has yet to be reached. An impact period or final separation period follows the physical separation, and may last for several months. The third adjustment stage, the period of adjustment to the separation, which may last several years, is not marked by objective events (such as separation from one's spouse), but by active attempts to master divorce-related demands (Hetherington et al., 1981). Divorce, unlike some other stressors, may be said to involve a fourth stage, the recovery-redefinition period, in which the individual redefines relationships with family members and others.

A strategy for crisis intervention is drawn from Auerbach's staged crisis-response theory (1986). In this theory, interventions are categorized according to the stages of the crisis event. Type 1 interventions are offered for individuals in the distal prestress period. Since emotional demands on the individual are low, educational and skill-building interventions are offered to assist individuals in anticipating the difficulties facing them. Emotional reactivity increases as temporal distance to the crisis event is reduced. Thus type 2 (proximal prestress period) and type 3 (proximal poststress period) interventions are designed to assist individuals with their more pressing emotional needs, and, somewhat less, with meeting the objective demands facing them. The rationale for the emphasis on emotional support is that emotional reactions of the individual in crisis interfere with meeting objective demands and acquiring skills; with increased temporal distance comes renewed objectivity and a greater potential to face objective demands. Thus type 4 (distal poststress period) interventions emphasize education and skill-building.

Divorce -adjustment interventions can be organized using Auerbach's four intervention types. Type 1 interventions are intended for families in the predecision period, and may be designed to help parents accurately assess and anticipate future divorce-related problems. Skills may be taught to help parents and children effectively meet future demands. Intervention in this stage may also be directed at the community at large. The goals of these second-order/community change programs (Watzlawick et al., 1974) are to shape the attitudes and behaviors of influencers of the divorcing family members' behavior (e.g., professionals, family members, and friends) to be consonant with psychological factors shown to facilitate children's divorce adjustment (Stolberg et al., 1986; Camplair & Stolberg 1987). Family members in late predecision periods might benefit most from type 2 interventions. Such interventions might be aimed at providing emotional support and tangible assistance in anticipating and planning for the soon-to-be-experienced life changes. Type 3 interventions are aimed at family members in the final separation period. Emotional support and relief from external demands, as well as efforts to gain mastery over new life demands, are the primary components of these programs. Increased temporal distance associated with the period of adjustment to the separation and divorce and the recovery redefinition period is accompanied by increased motivation and ability to master life demands. Educational and skill-building-oriented type 4 interventions are offered for these family members at these stages. In contrast to interventions in the first three periods, these divorce interventions may be either preventive or aimed at ameliorating existing adjustment problems. That is, treatment, and not prevention, is required for problems that may have been caused by an event in the somewhat distant past.

Essential Elements of Programmatic Interventions

The effectiveness of interventions for children of divorce may be maximized by directing program components at primary elements of the divorce-adjustment process. Program procedures must also face scrutiny through formal, empirical evaluation. It is not enough to say that a program "sounds good." To be considered effective, interventions must demonstrate their ability to achieve intended psychological outcomes. Such gains must also be demonstrated to be durable. Organizing program procedures in a format that facilitates dissemination and replication provides additional benefits. For example, the development of detailed program procedures manuals in the Divorce Adjustment Project has allowed the implementation of the program in other settings (Pedro-Carroll & Cowen, 1985; Stolberg & Garrison, 1985).

TYPE 1 INTERVENTIONS

Type 1 intervention programs are intended for families that may experience crisis events in the future (Auerbach, 1986). Distal prestress interventions for the crisis of divorce currently take two forms: those directed at the married couple, and those directed at society at large.

Behavioral Strategies for Preventing Marital Discord

Family-oriented interventions are aimed at preventing marital discord and divorce (Nyman, 1982, VanBuren, 1983). Interventions are intended for all married partners, generally before marital conflict is present; they attempt to teach skills and strategies that improve marital relationships. Conflict resolution, communication, and problem-solving skills are among the teaching activities in these programs. As discussed more fully in the chapter by Katzman and Karoly, this type of intervention strategy is in its infancy and available in few settings.

If prevention programs are successful, divorce and the related pathogenic processes are averted. Overt marital hostility is avoided, as conflict resolution and problem-solving skills are learned. Also parents learn successful ways of cooperating around family problems. Thus not only are pathogenic processes blocked, but interactional patterns are developed between parents that make them more effective in their role as parents.

The effectiveness of strategies to prevent divorce have only recently come under empirical review (VanBuren, 1983). Results of this evaluation are inconclusive, given its subjective nature and the small sample. The full potential of such programs is unrealized, because vehicles to assist in dissemination and replication of program procedures and benefits are absent (See also Katzman and Karoly's chapter in this volume).

Despite the potential strengths of such programs, there seems to be little public interest, as is also the case with many purely preventive programs—it is difficult to motivate people to participate in an intervention when no problem is present, and the contemplation of one's own potential divorce is obviously unpleasant. The future direction for this strategy should be to increase its popularity and seek out implementation sites where potential participants naturally gather (e.g., churches and synagogues). Interest in the program may be increased by helping potential participants understand the relevance of the intervention, by identifying very early markers that a problem may be developing. Most moderately well-functioning couples would argue their divorce is not imminent. They may agree, though, that communication patterns found to lead to divorce in others are present in their marriage. In addition, populations must be identified who are most receptive to, and may benefit from, participation.

Shaping Community Attitudes about Divorce

A couple's expectations about behaviors that may ensure their successful divorce adjustment are developed through interactions with professionals and nonprofessionals in their community (Coogler, 1978; Kappleman & Black, 1980; Deredyn, 1977). Attorneys, family members, and friends are the most frequently contacted and most influential decision shapers (Camplair & Stolberg, 1987.) Their recommendations, however, rarely reflect the real processes that facilitate children's divorce adjustment (Camplair & Stolberg, 1987). Anger at the former spouse, societal norms, and the adversarial requirements of the legal system are bigger influences on custodial, financial, and residential decisions than the factions that facilitate children's adjustment. As a consequence environmental change and interparent hostility tend to be maximized, and social supports, financial flexibility, parent availability, and coparenting arrangements tend to be minimized.

A prevention strategy has been proposed that is aimed at bringing the professional and personal activities of the "primary decision influencers" (attorneys, physicians, clergy, psychologists, family members, and close friends) in line with the psychological realities of divorce (Benn & Kalter, 1985; Stolberg, 1986; Camplair & Stolberg, 1987). Educational, skill-building programs are proposed that apprise the primary decision influencers of the psychological processes that mediate child adjustment and that consider the professional and practical constraints on the influencers' behavior.

For example, a preventive role for the pediatrician and family physician is based on the finding that physicians are perceived by custodial parents as very helpful when contacted (Camplair & Stolberg, 1987); yet they are contacted infrequently. Thus enhancing physicians' roles in promoting divorce adjustment must include increasing their awareness of divorce adjustment processes, increasing their sensitivity to signs of impending divorce in their patients, and teaching them how to offer appropriate types of assistance to patients before maladaptive processes are begun (Stolberg, in press). Such an intervention must also fit a prescriptive format in order to match the tight time constraints facing the physician.

Clergy, too, were found to be helpful when contacted. Their recommendations were generally in keeping with psychological determinants of adjustment. Again, they are used only occasionally. Religious leaders are more likely to be sought by families in conflict when they are *perceived* as being less bound by religious doctrine (Camplair et al., in press).

Enhancing the role of the primary decision influencer, as a strategy to prevent psychopathology in children of divorce, is very clearly aimed at the primary determinants of children's postdivorce adjustment. Interactional patterns of the divorcing couple are to be established that increase cooperation and consideration of all family members' needs. Minimizing environmental change, developing coparenting skills, and maximizing the noncustodial parent's contact with the child, to name a few, are the specific goals of this strategy.

This approach is, however, only hypothetical—much work is necessary to make it an effective and accepted intervention. The most frequently consulted primary decision influencers have been identified, and subjective, retrospective evaluations of their assistance have been conducted (Camplair & Stolberg, 1987). Little is known, however, about the practical and professional constraints that influence their recommendations. We know, for example, that physicians are perceived as helpful but are infrequently contacted. It may be that many physicians have little time to engage in mental health consultations with their clients, and so do not encourage or seek out such involvement.

Specific programs for the most powerful decision influencers remain to be developed; working relationships must be established with professional training programs, professional associations, and licensing boards, in order to develop, pilot, evaluate, and implement appropriate interventions.

TYPE 2 INTERVENTIONS

Type 2, (predecision period) interventions are aimed at families that will experience marital dissolution in the immediate future. Programs offered to families in this stage of the adjustment process are preventive in nature, when psychological problems are absent.

Adults' predecision period needs include emotional support, objective information, and assistance in making important divorce arrangements. Resolving self-perception conflicts, family castigations, and emotional distress is assisted by a stable support system (Wilcox, 1981). Evaluating the potential for the success of the marriage and separation requires an objective perspective on current circumstances and an informed awareness of future problems. Educational and supportive programs may assist in evaluating current and future circumstances, in building support systems, and in developing future career, economic, and family goals (Stolberg, et al., 1986).

The predecision period brings children a different set of problems. Parents' marital hostility is most extreme during this period, and may have deleterious long-term psychological consequences (Emery, 1982; Stolberg et al., in press): children need to be distanced or buffered from prolonged and direct exposure to interparental hostility. Further, only particularly strong parent–child relationships have been observed to mitigate the effects of marital turmoil and discord (Hetherington et al., 1979). Interventions must thus focus on maintaining or developing the quality of the parent–child relationship.

Existing predecision period prevention programs are of two types: those that assist adults in reaching the decision to divorce (Fine, 1980; Gardner, 1976), and those that assist the separating adults to make concrete postseparation living arrangements (Coogler, 1978).

Pre-divorce Counseling

Predivorce counseling involves an attempt to help adults involved in disintegrating marriages make a final decision about the future of their marriage. The Divorce Experience (1977) is a structured program —in contrast to most—for families considering divorce. Offered by the domestic relations staff of the family court of Minneapolis, the goals of this program are the development of support systems, and the facilitation of open, emotional expression in adult participants. The first two of three sessions are devoted to explaining the realities of the legal system and fostering expressions of loss. Adult members are helped to anticipate problems associated with divorce, through presentations made by previously divorced adults. Children's adjustment to divorce is the focus of the third session. Here participants are organized into small groups based on the age and developmental needs of their children.

There are no data on the effectiveness of the approach. While predivorce intervention would intuitively appear valuable, programs in other crisis intervention areas suggest treatment directions that are not reflected here. The brevity of the intervention, the relatively heavy weighting on adult decision making, and the minimal emphasis on parent–child interactions, leads one to question the usefulness of these programs. One wonders if two sessions aimed at decision making will produce results that apply to the conflicted home. Further, interventions for children in the medical setting (Kupst, 1986; Melamed & Bush, 1986), sexually abused children (Swift, 1986), and children of divorce (Stolberg & Garrison, 1985) are most effective at enhancing children's adjustment when primary emphasis is given to parent–child interactions and relatively little attention to adult adjustment and development. In summary, the intervention has potential, but systematic evaluation of its efficacy and greater attention to program development are needed.

Divorce Mediation

Divorce mediation is a process in which divorcing adults voluntarily seek the assistance of an impartial and highly trained third party in order to identify, discuss, and resolve disputes that result from divorce (Coogler, 1978; Emery & Wyer, 1987; Haynes, 1978; Kelly, 1983). This increasingly popular alternative to court-litigated divorces (Fine, 1980) is distinct from traditional court-mediated interventions in that a single professional is involved, its intent is cooperation rather than competition, and decisions are reached by the divorcing adults themselves, rather than being negotiated by attorneys or decided by a judge (Emery & Wyer, 1987). (See the chapter by Jessica Pearson and Nancy Thoennes in this volume for a more detailed discussion of mediation.)

A variety of mediation strategies exist, although all share the common thread of being goal focused, task oriented, and time limited (Kelly, 1983; Emery & Wyer, 1987). The diversity of approaches to mediation has been described as being as great as the number of approaches to psychotherapy (Kelly, 1983). While the methods may vary, goals generally include reaching divorce and custody settlements (when children are in the family) that are mutually beneficial and agreeable to both parties. Mediation is thus a *philosophy* for planning postdivorce arrangements, based on cooperation and concern for the future adjustment of all family members.

The mediation process often includes four activities: restructuring the interparental relationship so that cooperative and productive coparenting can occur, restructuring parent–child relationships to reflect the realities of the divorce, creating a model for problem solving that will be facilitative, and promoting the adjustment of all family members (Kelly, 1983). In contrast to many therapy modalities, the mediator takes a very active role, educating the clients, managing conflict, assisting in the development of bargaining proposals, and producing a written divorce agreement. Mediation differs from psychotherapy insofar as objective problem solving, rather than emotional expression and improving mental health, is the focus of the intervention (Kelly, 1983).

Mediation meets many of the criteria established here for effective divorce interventions. Most obviously the intervention is aimed at promoting the psychological adaptation of all family members. This is accomplished through cooperative efforts to develop living arrangements and parent–child and adult–adult interactional patterns that minimize environmental change and marital hostility, and maximize both cooperative problem solving and the children's contact with both parents.

Mediation has been exported to settings beyond the original development site. The dissemination of mediation procedures requires a significantly more complex plan than many of the interventions described in this chapter, primarily because of the level of sophistication required of the mediator. Extensive training programs are offered nationally to teach these complex procedures (Coogler, 1978).

Unfortunately, few systematic studies of the impact of mediation on children's divorce adjustment have been conducted. The results of the study presented in the chapter by Pearson and Thoennes suggest that mediation had few measurable effects on children's adjustment. Two other studies are currently under way. A court-based mediation program is being evaluated in the Charlottesville, Va., area by Emery and Wyer. Half of all families petitioning the court for custody or visitation hearings are randomly offered mediation. The remainder serve as the litigation contrast group. In a second study, a nonrandom sample of 150 self-selected mediation participants is being studied (Kelly, 1983). While no results are available on either project, it is clear that mediation, which is now being systematically evaluated, has already won general acceptance and shows great potential.

Future studies that address the question of for which divorcing adults mediation is most effective are needed. In contrast to the previously described community-oriented divorce intervention strategy, mediation puts a substantial demand on the divorcing couple. In the first author's clinical experience, many couples may not posses the prerequisite conflict resolution and problem-solving skills to enter into the process. Their feelings toward each other, and their expectations about appropriate behavior during the divorce process, may be so extreme that the cooperation required for successful mediation is unlikely. This question is currently being investigated in a study of a court sponsored mediation program in Richmond, Virginia (Camplair & Stolberg, 1986).

TYPE 3 INTERVENTIONS: PREVENTING PSYCHOPATHOLOGY IN CHILDREN OF DIVORCE

Children whose parents have recently separated, and who are passing through the final separation period and the period of adjustment to the separation, may benefit from type 3 preventive interventions (Stolberg et al, 1986; Stolberg & Garrison, 1985). The emotional state of the now separated adult dictates the content of final separation period interventions. Parents are less physically and emotionally available for children, yet their presence is required for children to master developmental tasks successfully (Wallerstein, 1983). Interventions that attempt to enhance the deteriorated parental role and help the child with the divorce-related stressors (Stolberg & Cullen, 1983) are required. The child also needs assistance in meeting normal developmental tasks (Stolberg & Cullen, 1983). Teaching single parenting skills, clarifying the child's role in the divorce, identifying and developing sources of stability and consistency in his or her life, and promoting the development of children's impulse control skills are important components.

Both the priority and perceived viability of prevention programs for families of divorce are demonstrated by the financial support provided recently by the National Institute of Mental Health. Preliminary results of these efforts are encouraging. Improved self-concept (Stolberg & Garrison, 1985), reductions in behavior problems and anxiety (Warren, Grew, Ilgen, Konanc, VanBourgondien & Amara, 1984), and improved social skills (Stolberg & Garrison, 1985) have been reported for child participants. Improved adjustment and greater control over environmental events have been observed in adult participants (Stolberg & Garrison, 1985).

Several strategies have been used to promote the adjustment of children of martial disruption. Interventions have been designed with children as the recipients of the intervention (Brogan & Maiden, 1984; Kalter, 1982; Pedro-Carrol & Cowen, 1985; Soehner, 1982; Stolberg & Garrison, 1985), parents/adults as participants (Lemmon & Farrell, 1983; Taylor et al., 1984; Stolberg & Garrison, 1985; Warren et al., 1984), and, in rare cases, parents and their children participating together (Warren et al., 1984). Several of these projects are conducted in schools and divorce courts, where the intended participants naturally gather (Brogan & Maiden, 1984; Pedro-Carroll & Cowen, 1985; Stolberg & Garrison, 1985; Warren et al., 1984). A representative sample of these programs will be reviewed in this section.

School-Based, Child-Directed Programs

The Divorce Adjustment Project: Children's Support Group (CSG) (Stolberg & Garrison, 1985), and the Children of Divorce Intervention Project (CODIP) (Pedro-Carroll & Cowen, 1985), are two similar school-based programs, the second being based on the first, and reflecting improvements in program procedures.

The constructive modification of children's responses to aspects of divorce that influence child adjustment was of primary consideration when designing these projects. While chronic marital hostility that has already taken place cannot be undone, the child's understanding of such interactions can be modified. Environmental changes, similarly, cannot be reversed. But the child's perception of these events can be modified; and the behavioral skills needed to meet the new circumstances can be taught.

Changes in immediate living conditions and family relationships are brought about by divorce. Intervention components were designed to assist children in adaptively responding to such events. Lost support systems must be replaced. Altered living circumstances, and reduced parental availability and financial resources, may result in increased anger and frustration in children. Communication skills, relaxation skills (Koeppen, 1974), and anger-control skills (Novaco, 1975) may help the child cope with such feelings. Helping children understand these confusing events should also serve to reduce their anger, frustration, and self-blame.

Normal developmental processes are interrupted by divorce (Wallerstein, 1983). Alternative systems must be developed to help children of divorce establish their identity and build internal control skills and teaching problem-solving skills may assist in this process (Finch & Kendall, 1979).

The CSG (Stolberg, et al., 1981) is a 12-session psychoeducational program designed to help seven- to 13-year-old children meet the behavioral and affective demands associated with divorce. Each one-hour session was divided into two sections. Part 1 involved discussion of a specific topic, e.g., Whose fault is it? What do I do on vacations? Do I worry about my dad? I wish my parents would get back together. Part 2 focused on the teaching, modeling, and rehearsing of specific cognitive-behavioral skills, e.g., problem-solving skills (Finch & Kendall, 1979), anger-control skills (Novaco, 1975), and communication and relaxation skills (Koeppen, 1974). The groups began by practicing basic, concrete applications (applying problem-solving skills to mathematics problems), and ended up with more complex skills, based on earlier ones, now applied to complex family problems (e.g., using communication, anger, and relaxation skills to solve the problem of what to say when your father doesn't make his Saturday visit).

Procedural revisions introduced in CODIP primarily reflect an increased emphasis on emotional support, and diminished attention to rehearsing concrete applications of cognitive-behavioral skills (Pedro-Carroll & Cowen, 1985). These changes are most apparent in the first three sessions. In addition, game playing was the primary vehicle used to teach skills.

The CSG and CODIP programs share an additional characteristic. Detailed manuals specifying all groups activities (Pedro-Carroll, 1984; Stolberg et al., 1981) have been developed to facilitate the implementation of the prevention programs in target schools, as well as serving as vehicles to disseminate program procedures to school systems outside of the districts where they were developed.

School-based interventions, as represented by the CSG and CODIP, meet many of the criteria for effective program design established in this chapter. Most important, evaluation data substantiate claims of the immediate and long-term effectiveness of these programs. Participants in the CSG, as compared with no-treatment control children, displayed significant improvements in self-concept at the end of intervention, which were maintained at the five-month follow-up. Significant increases in adaptive social skills were also identified at the follow-up (Stolberg, & Garrison, 1985). Significant reductions in problem behaviors such as acting out, and increases in competencies (e.g., effective learning and interpersonal functioning, adaptive assertiveness, appropriate school behavior, coping with failure and social pressures) occurred in children who participated in CODIP, as compared with those who did not (Pedro-Carroll & Cowen, 1985). Adjustment gains in program children were judged to have taken place by teachers, parents, group leaders, and the children themselves.

Both programs were founded on the research literature as a source of direction for program design. Their effectiveness may be attributed to the degree of correspondence between the needs of children during divorce and the procedures utilized.

Both manuals stand as useful program implementation tools for other service settings. The documents also allow for refinement of the intevention design, as in the case of the Pedro-Carroll and Cowen refinement of the CSG procedure, with a clear linkage between procedural changes and outcome improvements.

Community-Based Programs for Single Parents

Adults have been targeted as participants in programs intended to promote the adjustment of their children. These interventions have operated under two assumptions: that adults who have adjusted to their own divorce are good parents, and that children's divorce adjustment is enhanced when parent–child interactions are improved (Stolberg & Garrison, 1985; Taylor et al., 1984; Warren et al., 1984). The procedures used in parent-directed strategies reflect these assumptions. Enhancing adult adjustment is the goal of some programs (Lemmon & Farrell, 1983; Stolberg & Garrison, 1985; Warren et al., 1984), and enhancing single parenting and parent–child communication is the aim of others (Taylor et al., 1984; Warren et al., 1984). Components of the Parenting After Divorce Project (PAD, Warren et al., 1984) and the Divorce Adjustment Project: Single Parents Support Group (SPSG, Stolberg & Garrison, 1985) will be considered as representative of parent-directed strategies.

Two models of parent intervention have been developed by Warren and collegues (1984). The parent education component of the PAD project is a structured, five week, psychoeducational and support group for sets of five to seven single parents. A structured outline is used to direct participants in the discussion of topics relating to the effects of divorce on children, specific parenting skills (active listening, limit setting, and negotiation), and strategies to promote cooperative coparenting. The family education program includes parents and their children as participants. Single parents and their children met together with two leaders for six sessions; a seventh session was offered for the noncustodial parent, alone. The education and support focus was implemented by viewing a film on divorce, playing structured games to enhance communication, and then discussing family group activities. The PAD project components, therefore, emphasize single parenting: one involves the discussion of skills, and the other reflects the active rehearsal and shaping of optimal parent–child interaction patterns. Subjects were referred from the rolls of the local courthouse. Recently divorced parents and their children were invited to participate.

The PAD project meets some of the criteria established for optimal program design. First its intervention elements attend to a dimension of primary concern in children's postdivorce adjustment: altered parent–child interactions. Second it is sufficiently structured to allow for dissemination. Finally it has been subjected to rigorous, objective evaluation.

Comparisons of parent education group, family education group, and self-study control group participants demonstrated that participation in both interventions positively influenced children's overall adjustment, with participation in the family education program having the greatest positive effect (Warren et al., 1984). A composite, overall adjustment score was derived for each parent–child pair, based on changes in the child's functioning (anxiety, self-concept, social maturity, school affiliation, feelings about divorce, and behavioral adjustment), in parenting style, adult anxiety, and depression; and in family functioning. We conclude that direct efforts to shape parent–child interactions can positively influence children's postdivorce adjustment; further, the greater the opportunity for monitored application of the skills and interaction patterns, the more positive the effect will be.

The SPSG (Stolberg & Garrison, 1985) provides an important contrast to the procedures and results described by Warren and her associates. The Single Parents' Support Groups (Garrison et al., 1983) is a 12-week support and skill-building program for divorced, custodial mothers. Group procedures were intended to focus equally on the development of participants as individuals and as parents. Participants selected the topics for SPSGs based on a list of 20 options provided by group leaders (e.g., "The Social Me," "The Working Me," "The Sexual Me," "Controlling My Feelings," "Communicating with My Child," "Disciplining My Child," "Communicating with My Former Spouse About Childrearing Matters"). Procedures associated with each topic were described in a program procedures manual (Garrison et al., 1983).

Mothers in the SPSG were found to display better overall social and emotional divorce adjustment than subjects in child-only interventions and no-treatment controls (Stolberg & Garrison, 1985). They also reported fewer objective life changes and evaluated those changes that occurred more positively than did subjects in the comparison groups. In spite of these improvements, the adjustment of their children was not affected.

A more detailed review of topics discussed suggests that most sessions emphasized the development of the adult to the exclusion of parenting issues. Assessment indicated that parenting skills were not altered after intervention. Concurrent consideration of the Warren et al. (1984) and Stolberg and Garrison (1985) data leads to the conclusion that parenting skills and parent–child interactions must be modified if child adjustment is to be enhanced—facilitating adult adjustment does not automatically affect parenting effectiveness or child adjustment.

These data are consistent with others on divorce and other family crisis events. Path analysis of processes influencing children's postdivorce adjustment clearly indicates that the relationship between adult adjustment and parenting skills is not statistically significant (Stolberg & Bush, 1985). Hospital-based programs for families with a child with leukemia and for children receiving outpatient medical care are most effective when parenting behaviors and parent–child communication patterns are the direct focus of the intervention (Kupst, 1986; Melamed & Bush, 1986).

In summary, our review of type 3 preventive interventions suggests two successful directions for intervention: those aimed at the child and conducted in the schools, and those offered for parents. The latter programs have been demonstrated to be effective only when attention is directly focused on developing optimal parent–child interactions.

TYPE 4 INTERVENTIONS: PREVENTION AND TREATMENT

Type 4 interventions are intended for divorced families passing through the recovery-redefinition period. In contrast to interventions at earlier periods, type 4 interventions can be either preventive or aimed at ameliorating divorce-related adjustment problems. Prevention programs aim at redefining family relationships, and establishing permanent stability in the family. Enhancing family members' adjustment during this stage is substantially dependent on the successful resolution of earlier-stage demands. Treatment programs aim to ameliorate adjustment problems of children whose parents' divorce took place at some time in the past.

Structured programs of either sort are not described in the literature. Thus evaluating type 4 interventions cannot follow the format previously used in this chapter. Rather, clincial formulations of maladjusted children of divorce will be used in the development of a format for conceptualizing treatment. Consistent with the general evaluation strategy used here, processes leading to the common problems in children of divorce will be used to identify the important treatment components.

Adjustment problems in children of divorce tend to cluster around two dimensions—withdrawal and impulse-control deficiencies (Coddington & Troxell, 1980; Hetherington, 1979; Stolberg, et al., 1986). Hypermaturity, depression, guilt, anxiety, and somatic complaints are included in the withdrawal dimension (Gardner, 1976). Impulse-control problems and externalized behavior patterns include immaturity, loss of self-esteem, academic failure, peer problems, and anger-control problems (Emery, 1982; Gardner, 1976; Kurdek, 1981; Stolberg et al., in press).

The occurrence of adjustment problems this far into the divorce-adjustment process points to ongoing processes that interfere with the expected child development (Auerbach, 1986; Hetherington et al., 1981; Stolberg et al. 1986). The commonly identified stressors of father's initial exit from the home, fears of telling one's peers, and confusion about unforeseeable future events, are not the most significant determinants of enduring maladjustment. Relatively permanent changes in the child's experience are assumed the more detrimental processes. Such processes include the continued absence of a functional coparenting relationship, of effective single-parenting skills, and of a consistent relationship with the noncustodial parent (Stolberg & Bush, 1985; Wallerstein & Kelly, 1980); the continued hostility between the former partners (Emery, 1982); and the degree to which substantial and permanent changes in living conditions (e.g., moving to a new neighborhood, reduced discretionary funds in the family) have been experienced (Kurdek, 1981; Stolberg & Anker, 1983). The severity of the problems is further determined by the time elapsed since the pathogenic processes began. Prolonged lack of parents' control over children's behavior, for example, is likely to lead to more severe impulse-control problems, such as aggression, and academic failure.

Externalized pathology has been hypothesized to result from two processes—past and current displays of hostility between parents, and substantial environmental change (Emery, 1982; Stolberg & Anker, 1983). Anger and poor conflict-resolution skills displayed by the parents are incorporated into the child's repertoire. Substantial environmental alterations may result in increased exposure to frustrating situations (e.g., less money for activities that used to be routine, less physical and emotional availability of both parents, or moving to a new neighborhood and losing former peer groups). Children may not possess the skills (communication and impulse control) appropriately to express their feelings about these circumstances, so that anger is further heightened. Parents' decreased availability may result in the failure to complete homework or to work to get along with peers. Loss of parents and peers may be internalized as rejection. Poor self-concept may result from problems in school, inability to control anger, and perceived rejection by family and friends (Kurdek, 1981).

The less common pattern of internalized maladaptive responses may be due to a different set of processes (Gardner, 1976). Higher maturity demands (e.g., expectations to care for siblings and to perform household maintenance tasks) may be placed on the child that remove the child from desired play activities. The parent–child relationship may also become confused when the child and parent switch care-giving roles. Interparental conflict may be absent, with the parents' repression of feelings modeled by the child. The child's normal routine may be substantially altered, with the child having little control over the direction of the changes. Hypermaturity and the repression of perceived distress are thus the child's expected coping patterns.

Interventions for children in this stage of the divorce-adjustment process must focus on correcting the previously described dysfunctional processes that lead to the observed problems. Reductions in interparental hostility, and the development of a cooperative and responsible coparenting relationship are two important goals. A more normal pattern of interaction between the noncustodian and the child can be developed. The noncustodian can relieve the former spouse of parenting responsibilities when the latter is attempting to improve social and career opportunities. A key intervention goal would be to focus on the development of open and direct communications between parents and to reduce the reliance on adversarial systems such as attorneys and the courts.

Relationships with both parents must be improved. The custodial parent must develop a relationship with the child that includes control, consistency, and an acceptance of the parenting role. The child will be able to meet normal developmental demands when both parents accept their parental roles.

Finally impulse control, communication, and social and academic skills must be taught, to assist the child in meeting divorce-related demands. A format much like that of the Children's Support Groups (Stolberg & Garrison, 1985) may provide a structure for this intervention. Children whose parents had divorced as much as five years earlier participated in Pedro-Carroll and Cowen's CODIP project (1985), and realized substantial benefits.

SUMMARY

A stage model of divorce adjustment was used to categorize intervention programs for children of divorce. Three criteria were used to evaluate these programs. These were (1) the demonstration of a clear linkage between intervention strategies and more basic research on divorce adjustment, (2) the objective demonstration of program effectiveness, and (3) the availability of a vehicle for program dissemination.

Prevention programs implemented very early in the divorce-adjustment process showed the greatest promise. Particularly noteworthy were school-based prevention programs for children, and interventions specifically designed to promote competence in parenting skills. The success of programs may result from attention to processes that *directly* influence child adjustment: parenting skills and environmental change. Several of the less effective programs attended primarily to processes that only indirectly affect children's divorce adjustment (e.g., adult adjustment).

Future program development and evaluation efforts must answer several questions, as for example, "Do the benefits yielded from program participation last?" While followup data for some programs are available, such followup is generally of no more than five months in duration. Longer followup periods are mandatory truly to demonstrate program effectiveness. The question of who benefits from available intervention strategies also needs to be addressed. The characteristics of families that benefit from existing programs must be identified, and new programs for those who do not must be developed. Divorcing families with few job and social skills, for example, may find that the current array of programs does not meet their needs while dual professional-career, economically stable families may reap maximum benefits.

Several untested, primary prevention strategies merit further attention. Relationship-enhancement programs for recently married couples may both promote healthy marriages and prevent future divorces. Efforts to integrate psychological considerations into the activities of divorce and custody-decision influencers may minimize the intensity of such factors as marital hostility, environmental change, poor parenting skills, and poor coparenting relationships.

Finally dissemination programs must be designed and evaluated that will facilitate the implementation of effective interventions in applied settings. While the prevention programs cited in this chapter have training programs, none have been evaluated empirically, and few consider such factors as variations in skill level of service providers, and populations served.

REFERENCES

Auerbach, S. M. (1986). Stressful life events, psychological crises and crisis intervention: An empirical perspective. In S. M. Auerbach & Al L. Stolberg (Eds.), *Issues in Clincal and Community Psychology: Crisis Intervention with Children and Families.* (pp. 3-30). Washington, D.C.: Hemisphere.

Benn, R., & Kalter, N. (1985). Personal communication.

Brogan, J., & Maiden, U. (1984). Who gets me for Christmas: A course on separation, divorce and remarriage. Unpublished manual, Yorktown Heights, N.Y.

Camplair, C., & Stolberg, A. L. (1987). The role of the primary decision influencer in custody determination. *Journal of Divorce, 10,* 43–56.

Camplair, C. W. & Stolberg, A. L. (1986). Court sponsored divorce mediation: Evaluation from a family systems perspective. Unpublished manuscript, Virginia Commonwealth University, Richmond, Virginia.

Camplair, C., Stolberg, A. L., & Worthington, E. (in press). The role of family, friends, clergy and other professionals in decisions about child custody after divorce. *Journal of Pastoral Counseling.*

Chiriboga, D. A., & Cutler, L. (1977). Stress responses among divorcing men and women. *Journal of Divorce, 2,* 95–106.

Coddington, R. D., & Troxell, J. R. (1980). The effect of emotional factors on football injury rates—A pilot study. *Journal of Human Stress, 14,* 3–5.

Coogler, O. J. (1978). *Structured Mediation in Divorce Settlement: A Handbook for Marital Mediations.* Lexington, Mass.: Lexington Books.

Deredyn, A. P. (1977). Children in divorce: Interventions in the phase of separation. *Pediatrics, 60,* 20–27.

The Divorce Experience (1977). Unpublished manuscript, Domestic Relations Department, Family Court, Minneapolis, Minn.

Emery, R. E. (1982). Interpersonal conflict and the children of discord and divorce. *Psychological Bulletin, 92,* 310–330.

Emery, R. E., & Wyer, M. M. (1987). Divorce mediation. *American Psychologist, 42,* 472–480.

Finch, A. J., & Kendall, P. S. (1979). Impulsive behaviors: From research to treatment. In A. J. Finch & P. S. Kendall (Eds.), *Clinical Treatment and Research in Child Psychopathology* (pp. 137–156). New York: Spectrum Publications.

Fine, S. (1980). Children in divorce, custody and access situations: The contribution of the mental health professional. *Journal of Child Psychology and Psychiatry, 21,* 353–361.

Gardner, R. A. (1976). *Psychotherapy with Children of Divorce.* New York: Jason Aronson.

Garrison, K. M., Stolberg, A. L., Mallonnee, D., Carpenter, J., & Antrim, Z. (1983). The Single Parents' Support Group: A procedures manual. Unpublished manual, Divorce Adjustment Project, Virginia Commonwealth University, Richmond.

Haynes, J. M. (1978). Divorce mediator: A new role *Social Work, 23,* 5–9.

Hetherington, E. M. (1979). Divorce: A child's perspective. *American Psychologist, 34,* 851–858.

Hetherington, E. M., Cox, M., & Cox, R. (1977). The aftermath of divorce. In J. H. Stevens, Jr., & M. Matthews (Eds.), *Mother-Child, Father-Child Relations* (pp. 149–176). Washington, D.C.: NAEYC.

Hetherington, E. M., Cox, M., & Cox, R. (1979). Family interactions and the social, emotional and cognitive development of children following divorce. In V. Vaughn & T. Brazelton (Eds.), *The Family: Setting Priorities.* (pp. 71–87). New York: Science and medicine.

Hetherington, E. M., Cox, M., & Cox, R. (1981). Effects of divorce on parents and children. In M. Lamb (Ed.), *Nontraditional Families* (pp. 233–288). Hillsdale, N.J.: Erlbaum.

Kalter, N. (1982). Personal communication.

Kappelman, M. M., & Black, J. (1980). Children and divorce: The pediatrician's responsibility. *Pediatric Annals, 9,* 342–351.

Kelly, J. (1983). Mediation and psychotherapy: Distinguishing the differences. Unpublished manuscript, California.

Koeppen, A. S. (1974). Relaxation training for children. *Elementary School Guidance Counseling, 9,* 14–21.

Kupst, M. J., (1986). Coping in siblings of children with serious illness. In S. M. Auerbach & A. L. Stolberg (Eds.), *Issues in clinical and Community Psychology: Crisis Intervention with Children and Families.* (pp. 173-188). Washington, D.C.: Hemisphere.

Kurdek, L. A. (1981) An integrative perspective on children's divorce adjustment. *American Psychologist, 35,* 856–866.

Lazarus, R. S. (1966) *Psychological Stress and the Coping Process.* New York: McGraw-Hill.

Lemmon, G., & Farrell, A. D. (1983). Behavioral rehearsal of partner attention: Social skill remediation of loneliness among the separated and divorced. Unpublished manuscript, Virginia Commonwealth University, Richmond.

Melamed, B. G., & Bush, J. P. (1986). Maternal-child influences during medical procedures. In S. M. Auerbach & A. L. Stolberg (Eds.) *Issues in Clinical and Community Psychology: Crisis Intervention with Children and Families.* (pp. 123-143) Washington, D.C.: Hemisphere.

Novaco, R. W. (1975). *Anger Control: The development and Evaluation of an Experimental Treatment.* Lexington, Mass.: Lexington Books.

Nyman, J. A. (1982). Divorced: An area for planning of prevention work. *Nordisk Psykologi, 34,* 142–147.

Pedro-Carroll, J. L. (1985). The Children of Divorce Intervention Program: Procedures Manual. Unpublished manual, University of Rochester Center for Community Study, Rochester, New York.

Pedro-Carroll, J. A. L., & Cowen, E. L. (1985). The Divorce Intervention Project: An investigation of the efficacy of a school-based preventoin program. *Journal of Consulting and clinical Psychology, 53,* 603-616.

Soehner, G. (1982). The single Parent Family Project. Unpublished manuscript, Rochester, N.Y.

Steinmetz, S. K. (1977). *The Cycle of Violence: Assertive. Aggressive and Abusive Family Interactions.* New York: Prager.

Stolberg, A. L. (in press). The role of the pediatrician in children's divorce adjustment. *Journal of Pediatrics.*

Stolberg, A. L., & Anker, J. M. (1983). Cognitive and behavioral changes in children resulting from parental divorce and consequent environmental changes. *Journal of Divorce, 7,* 23–41.

Stolberg, A. L., & Bush, J. P. (1985). A path analysis of factors predicting children's divorce adjustment. *Journal of Clinical Child Psychology, 14,* 49–54.

Stolberg, A. L., Camplair, C., Currier, K., & Wells, M. (in press). Individual, familial and environmental determinants of children's post-divorce adjustment and maladjustment.. *Journal of Divorce.*

Stolberg, A. L., & Cullen, P. M. (1983). Preventive interventions for families of divorce: The Divorce Adjustment Project. In L. Kurdek (Ed.), *New Directions in Child Development: Children and Divorce* (pp. 71–81). San Francisco: Jossey-Bass.

Stolberg, A. L., Cullen, P. M., Garrison, K. M. & Brophy, C. J. (1981). The Children's Support Group: A procedures manual. Unpublished manual, Divorce Adjustment Project, Virginia Commonwealth University, Richmond.

Stolberg, A. L., & Garrison, K. M. (1985). Evaluating a primary prevention program for children of divorce: The Divorce Adjustment Project. *American Journal of Community Psychology, 13,* 111–124.

Stolberg, A. L., Kiluk, D., & Garrison, K. M. (1986). A temporal model of divorce adjustment with implications for primary prevention. In S. M. Auerbach & A. L. Stolberg (Eds.), *Issues in Clinical and Community Psychology: Crisis Intervention with Children and Families.* (pp. 105-119). Washington, D.C.: Hemisphere.

Swift, C. F. (1986). Community interventions in sexual child abuse. In S. M. Auerbach & A. L. Stolberg (Eds.), *Issues in Clinical and Community Psychology: Crisis Intervention with Children and Families.* (pp. 149-171). Washington, D.C.: Hemisphere.

Taylor, J. B., Green, A., & Frager, C. (1984). Divorce related pathology: A study in preventive intervention. Divorce Intervention Workshop, National Institute of Mental Health, Washington, D.C.

Van Buren, D. J. (1983, March). A behavioral approach for preventing marital discord. Southeast Psychological Association Annual Conference, Atlanta, Ga.

Wallerstein, J. S. (1983). Children of divorce: The psychological tasks of the child. *American Journal of Orthopsychiatry, 53,* 230–243.

Wallerstein, J. S. & Kelly, J. B. (1980). *Surviving the Breakup: How Children and Parents Cope with Divorce.* New York: Basic Books.

Warren, N. J., Grew, R. S., Ilgen, E. R., Konanc, J. T., Van Bourgondien, M. E., & Amara, I. (1984). Parenting after Divorce: Preventive programs for divorcing families. Divorce Intervention Workshop, National Institute of Mental Health, Washington, D.C.

Watzlawick, P., Weakland, J. H., & Fisch, R. (1974). *Change: Principles of Problem Formation and Problem Resolution*. New York: Norton.

Wilcox, B. L. (1981) Social support, life stress and psychological adjustment: A test of the buffering hypothesis. *American Journal of Community Psychology, 4,* 371–386.

Strengthening Marital Relationships via Communication Training:
A Critical Review of Competency-Based, Preventive Interventions

MELANIE A. KATZMAN and PAUL KAROLY

The psychologically damaging effects of divorce on children could be prevented unequivocally if "immature" individuals either did not marry, or, if they chose wedlock, did not procreate. A more rational (but equally unlikely) scenario would involve the prevention of marital discord and its aftermath by teams of mental health professionals, who would monitor all existing marriages (not just those of immature partners) to watch for "early warning signs" of distress and to be prepared to step in to mediate disputes before they escalated into permanent rifts. As implausible as these suggestions seem, they accurately mirror the classic biomedical (disease-centered) approach to prevention—that is, they presuppose the existence of a fundamental defect (e.g., immaturity) or a specific dysfunctional force or agency (such as stress) whose eventual disruptive effects upon "normal" processes (independent of context) can be assumed, unless a powerful technological intervention is introduced by trained experts. Quite a few mental health programs have been built upon such assumptions (Felner et al., 1983).

Currently a number of alternative models exist whose preventive goals are operationalized in terms of competence building (rather than defect elimination), collaboration (rather than focusing on the skills of the expert helper), and contextually relevant training (rather than relying on univer-

323

sally applicable, singular, high-potency, "magic-bullet"-type interventions). For the prevention of marital discord and family breakup, it is inappropriate to assume that the "body" (i.e., the marriage) is "healthy" unless and until it is underminded by structural weakness, or "attacked" by various sources of stress, whose nature and meaning are fully understood only by psychiatrists, psychologists, or other professional groups. On the contrary, we now know that the course of marital relationships is a declining one (that premarital bliss is rarely sustained), and that success at resisting the predictable decrease in relationship satisfaction requires continued efforts of both husband and wife to strengthen the interpersonal bond (see Markman et al., 1983; Stuart, 1980).

Our knowledge of the personal qualities and competencies that contribute to the maintenance of marriage is supported best by the results of longitudinal investigations. In one of the first predictive studies, Bentler and Newcomb (1978) examined the influence of varied personality and background variables in the forecasting of marital adjustment among 77 couples followed over a period of four years. These investigators found husband–wife similarity in background and personality traits to be a good predictor of marital stability, and found little evidence for the "need complementarity" (contrasting characteristics) hypothesis. In opposition to their expectation, the investigators found that couples' living together prior to marriage was not a useful predictor of subsequent marital adjustment—a finding viewed as "somewhat discouraging. . .in light of the currently growing movement toward trial or premarriages" (p. 1066).

Unfortunately for clinical interventionists, the Bentler and Newcomb (1978) study underscored the importance of relatively stable dimensions that are unlikely to yield to educative/preventive efforts. However, Markman and his colleagues, (e.g., Markman, 1979, 1981, 1984; Markman et al., 1984) employed a *cognitive-behavioral model* emphasizing the pivotal role of communication patterns among premarital couples. Other investigators have also sought to enhance transactional skills, but only among married, divorce-susceptible couples—those identified as "distressed"—and among "nondistressed" married couples. The purpose of this chapter is to evaluate critically the effectiveness of various programs in conjoint skills training for distressed and nondistressed married couples and for premarital couples.

Communication training, taught alone, or in conjunction with other behavioral skills, is the primary focus of many of the programs included in this review, because breakdowns in communication have been implicated as a cause of marital dysfunction in virtually every major theoretical model of marital distress. It is not surprising, therefore, that communication training comprises the core of a variety of marital treatment regimes, despite differences in theoretical underpinnings and in the timing of interventions relative to the marital cycle.

Despite a growing body of outcome research on marital interventions, only 26 studies qualified for review in this chapter. In order for change to be attributed to the effects of the marital intervention being studied, a control group design is required; as a result all studies that lacked a control group were excluded. Unfortunately a number of the early and seminal reports within the behavioral marital therapy literature had to be overlooked because they were uncontrolled studies (Azrin et al., 1973; Stuart, 1969; and Weiss et al., 1973). A detailed description of these papers can be found in comprehensive reviews by Jacobson and Martin (1976), Jacobson (1978a), and Jacobson and Margolin (1979). Studies in which only one spouse was treated are also omitted from this review, but are included in an article by Russell (1982) on individual and cojoint assertiveness training and its effects upon the marital relationship. Marital enhancement and premarital prevention programs that fail to teach or assess specific skills are also omitted (e.g., Marriage Encounter). Several reviews including such programs are available (Bagarozzi & Raven, 1981; Gurman & Kniskern, 1977, 1978; Hof & Miller. 1980; L'Abate, 1980; Olson et al., 1980). Finally most of the studies on the efficacy of the Minnesota Couple Communication Program (CCP) have appeared in relatively inaccessible sources such as doctoral dissertations and unpublished reports. Although these studies are not included in this review, readers may find them referenced in a review by Wampler (1982).

The first section of this chapter critically reviewed the outcome studies conducted with distressed, nondistressed and premarital couples, and draws conclusions about the efficacy of couples training for each of these samples. Brief attention is also given to methodological difficulties peculiar to each of the studies. The next section considers methological problems shared by most of the studies. The chapter concludes with a discussion of suggested directions for research in relationship-enhancement methods.

REVIEW OF
PROGRAMS FOR DISTRESSED COUPLES

The programs and outcomes to be discussed first are summarized in Table 10.1. The studies reviewed in this section fall roughly into two categories, those assessing communication training alone; and those

Table 10.1

Outcomes of Programs for Distressed Couples

Author	Type of Program,[a] Sample Size, Type of Sample	Outcome Criteria[b] (Source)	Results[c]	Follow-up
Baucom (1982)	1. Behavioral contracting (BC) 2. Problem-solving/ communication training plus contracting (PS/ C + BC) 3. Problem-solving/ communication training (PS/C) 10 weekly 1-hour conjoint sessions (18 in each of three E groups, 18 C) Distressed community sample	1. Marital adjustment (C) 2. Areas of change (C) 3. Communication patterns (positive) (J) 4. Communication patterns (negative) (J)	3 E groups superior to C on criteria 1, 2, 4. PS/C plus BC improved 1–4. PS/C improved on 1, 2, 4; BC improved on 1, 2.	3-month; all gains maintained, no difference between E groups on self-report measures
Hickman & Baldwin (1971)	1. Communication-based counseling 2. Programmed instruction in communication Both four twice-weekly one-hour conjoint	1. Relationship satisfaction (C) 2. Reconciliation agreements (C)	Significant improvement of counseled group over control on both measures. Counseled group significantly better than programmed group on criterion 1.	None

326

Study	Design	Measures	Results	Follow-up
	sessions (ten in each of two E groups, ten controls) Referred to reconciliation court		Programmed text group not significantly better than control group	
Jacobson (1977)	BMT Conjoint sessions for 8 weeks (5 BMT, 5 C) mildly distressed, university community	1. Marital adjustment (C) 2. Communication pattern (positive) (J) 3. Communication pattern (negative) (J)	BMT significantly better than C on all measures	1 year; gains in marital satisfaction maintained (behavioral measures not taken)
Jacobson (1978b)	1. BMT (2 variants: "good faith" and "quid pro quo" contracts) 8 weekly conjoint sessions (16 BMT, 8 NS, 8 C) Mildly distressed, university community	1. Marital adjustment (C) 2. Communication pattern (negative) (J) 3. Communication pattern (positive) (J)	BMT groups significantly better than wait list and nonspecific controls on all measures. BMT groups not different from each other	6 months; gains maintained for BMT on criterion 1 (behavioral measures not taken)
Jacobson (1979)	Problem-solving/ communication training Sessions once or twice a week for 1–2 hours over 15–30 weeks (6 E serving as separate single-subject	1. Spouse pleases and displeases (C) 2. Areas of change (C) 3. Communication pattern (positive) (J) 4. Communication pattern (negative) (J) 5. Communication	5/6 showed positive gains on all measures	6 months: 5/6 maintained changes on criteria 1, 2, 6 (behavioral measures not taken)

327

Table 10.1 (continued)

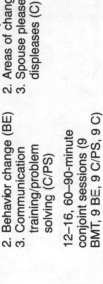

Study	Sample/Treatment	Criteria	Results
	experiment) Distressed in psychiatric hospital	pattern (neutral) (J) 6. Marital adjustment (C)	6 months: improvements maintained or increased on all measures for BMT and C/PS groups, BE groups deteriorated on all criteria
Jacobson (1984)	1. BMT 2. Behavior change (BE) 3. Communication training/problem solving (C/PS) 12–16, 60–90-minute conjoint sessions (9 BMT, 9 BE, 9 C/PS, 9 C) Mildly to severely distressed university community	1. Marital adjustment (C) 2. Areas of change (C) 3. Spouse pleases and displeases (C)	Significant gains for all treatments on criteria 1 and 2. Significant change on criterion 3 for BMT and BE. BE significantly better than C/PS and C on criterion 3
O'Leary & Turkowitz (1978a)	1. Communication training 2. Behavioral agreements plus Communication Training. Conjoint sessions (10 in each E group, 10 C) Distressed community sample	1. Marital adjustment 2. Communication pattern (C) 3. Feelings toward spouse (C) 4. Marital problems (C) 5. Spouse changes (C) 6. Problem solving (J)	Compared with controls, both treatments showed significant gains on criteria 2, 4, 5. Significant change for both E groups and C on 1 and 3. No difference between treatments	4 months: Significant increases on criteria 1 and 3 for both E groups (C not followed)

Study	Treatment/Sample	Measures	Results	Follow-up
Pierce (1973)	1. Communication training (Carkhuff model) 2. Insight counseling (both 12 weekly two-hour conjoint sessions) 5 CT, 16 IC, 4 C CT distressed community sample IC and C parents of emotionally disturbed children	1. Communication (J) 2. Self-exploration (J)	Significant change on criteria 1 and 2. Communication significantly better than insight and control on 1 and 2. Insight not significantly better than control.	None
Schindler et al. (1983)	1. Communication Training—conjoint couples 2. Communication Training—conjoint group (both 15 sessions) (16 CT conjoint, 19 CT group, 17 C) Moderately distressed German community sample	1. Quarreling (C) 2. Tenderness (C) 3. Communication (C) 4. Problem list (C) 5. General happiness (C) 6. Communication pattern (negative) (J) 7. Communication pattern (positive) (J)	CTC superior to CTCG and C on criteria 2, 3, 4. CTC and CTCG superior to C on criterion 5. CTC superior to CTCG and C on criterion 6	1 year: CTC maintained improvements on criterion 4 and 5, CTCG maintained gains on criterion 4. 17% of treated couples separated.
Tsoi-Hoshmand (1976)	2-stage Communication/ Negotiation training Approximately 8½-hour	1. Relationship satisfaction (C) 2. Caring (C)	Significant increase on criteria 1 and 2 (using individual, not couple, in	4 months: gains maintained in 70% of treated couples

Table 10.1 (continued)

weekly conjoint sessions (10 E, 10 C) Community and University samples	3. Learning in therapy (C)	analyses). (Increases in 3 correlated with increase in 1 and 2.) Criterion 2 increased significantly with stage-1 communication training

[a] All programs conducted in groups unless otherwise specified.
[b] C = client; T = trainer; J = trained judge
[c] "Significant change" refers to both pre- and postchange for experimental group, and greater change than control group.

based on behavioral marital therapy, which set out to examine either the effectiveness of an entire treatment package, or its components, including problem-solving/communications training and behavioral change.

Studies Evaluating Communication Training.

One of the earliest reports on the use of communication training with distressed couples was conducted by Pierce (1973). Couples were treated in groups, which focused primarily on imparting empathy skills. Through role-playing techniques, couples were taught to attend to one another's style of communication and to listen more accurately. Therapists provided feedback and communication skills, in addition to demonstrating appropriate skills (i.e., modeling effective communication). On two measures of outcome—skills in communication and degree of self-exploration—couples in the treatment group demonstrated significantly more positive change than did control group subjects.

Methodological difficulties in this study make interpretation difficult. First, a randomized control group was not used. Couples in the "control" groups were actually part of an earlier project and were not presenting with marital dysfunctions. In addition no validity data were presented with regard to Pierce's designated change measure. Finally, no followup data was collected.

Hickman and Baldwin (1971) investigated a slightly different approach to teaching marital skills: the potential of programmed instruction devoid of therapist contact. The investigators evaluated a programmed text that taught various communication skills, and compared it with a traditional marriage counseling procedure. In comparison with the untreated group, the traditional marriage counseling group demonstrated significant gains on a self-report semantic differential measure about the quality of the marital relationship. Reconciliation rates were 30 percent for the control, 50 percent for the programmed text, and 90 percent for traditional counseling.

Although the study paints a pessimistic picture of the ability of couples to improve without a therapist, the failure to control for variability in subject characteristics and to assess changes in communication skills makes the validity of these results questionable. It is interesting that the traditional counseling procedure had communication training as its primary focus. Given the impressive number of reconciliation agreements, it is unfortunate that the exact procedures used were not specified.

Schindler and colleagues (1983) evaluated yet another aspect of communication training. They compared the effectiveness of conjoint couples and conjoint group communication training, based on the Couples' Relationship/Enhancement Program (Guerney, 1977). These two procedures were compared with each other and with a waiting-list control group. Conjoint couples' treatment produced significant improvements relative to the conjoint group and the waiting-list control group, on measures of tenderness, communication, conflict resolution, and negative communication behaviors. Both experimental groups were superior to controls in producing change in general marital happiness. At the one-year follow-up, couples that were treated conjointly maintained gains on conflict resolution and general happiness, while group couples maintained their improvements in conflict resolution only. Unfortunately, no behavioral measures were taken at follow-up.

The apparent failure of the conjoint group treatment to produce change is probably the most striking outcome of this study, since this modality is commonly used in communication training. The authors suggest that the limited effectiveness of group treatment may reflect a "negative modeling effect," caused by severely distressed couples that did not change or changed slightly, thereby reducing the motivation for other group members. But the short-term superiority of conjoint procedures to group communication training did not hold during the follow-up period. Couples treated across both modalities failed to maintain changes. These unstable effects led the authors to suggest that additional treatment components are necessary to improve and maintain the durability of change in communication skills.

STUDIES EVALUATING BEHAVIORAL MARITAL THERAPY AND ITS COMPONENTS

The behavioral approach to marital therapy (BMT) is based on the assumption that distressed couples either lack or fail to emit the skills necessary to make desired changes in the marriage when conflicts arise. For example, rather than relying on positive control as the primary strategy for ensuring cooperation and compliance from the partner, spouses in distressed relationships make excessive use of aversive control tactics. As a result behavioral interventions are designed to teach couples how to bring about changes in their relationship in a more positive way.

Two types of skills are usually taught. First, problem-solving and communication skills are emphasized, in order that couples learn to converse more effectively, particularly around conflict areas. Second, contingency management or behavioral exchange skills—such as positive reinforcement, shaping, and pinpointing target behaviors—are included as part of the treatment package. "Pinpointing" involves translating abstract statements of intention (e.g., "You are always trying to hurt me") into operationalized statements (e.g., "Yesterday you criticized my driving in front of Fred and Lois"). It is believed that if expectations and dissatisfactions are clarified, the couples involved can be made more amenable to behavior change (Jacobson & Martin, 1976, p. 543).

Based on the model developed by the Oregon group (e.g., Weiss et al., 1973), Jacobson has completed four studies investigating the effectiveness of BMT. Two studies evaluated problem-solving/communication training and contingency contracting, and two studies evaluated these same components separately.

In his initial study, Jacobson (1977) compared couples receiving the standard, two-component BMT treatment package with a waiting list control group. On all three outcome measures, couples receiving BMT improved significantly, relative to the waiting list control group. Couples reported maintenance of these positive changes at one year follow-up. Ninety percent of the spouses reported scores within the normal range of marital adjustment after therapy, whereas, prior to therapy, only 20 percent reported scores within normal limits. Unfortunately this study involved only one therapist, had a small sample size, and did not control for nonspecific or placebo factors.

The difficulties noted were addressed in a subsequent study (Jacobson, 1978b) that compared two very similar behavioral treatments with a nonspecific control group, as well as with an untreated control group. The nonspecific treatment group involved procedures similar to those incorporated into the behavorial treatments, differing only in that couples in the nonspecific condition did not receive training in problem-solving and contracting skills. On two behavioral measures and one self-report measure, behaviorally trained couples improved significantly more than couples in either of the two control groups. Six-month follow-up data on the self-report measure indicated that differences between the behavioral groups and the control groups were maintained. Unfortunately the applicability of these findings from a mildly distressed, university sample, to a self-referred, severely distressed clinical sample is open to question. In addition the relative contribution of the various components was not assessed. A third study was therefore designed to examine problem-solving/communication training in isolation (Jacobson, 1979).

This experiment was conducted with a population of severely distressed couples, all treated by the author in a psychiatric hospital setting. Rather than employing the entire BMT package, a treatment intervention emphasizing training in problem-solving communication skills was tested against a nonspecific procedure in which the therapist instructed couples to change their behavior in positive ways. After receiving three sessions of the nonspecific procedure, problem-solving training was introduced in one conflict area at a time. The results, confirmed by self-report measures of marital relationships, indicated that all six of the treated couples improved significantly during the course of therapy. In five of the six cases, multiple baseline analyses confirmed that behavioral interventions were responsible for the improvement. Of the five couples helped by therapy, problem-solving/communication training was demonstrably necessary and facilitative for four. One couple did not respond favorably to problem-solving/communication, but did respond favorably to a more intensive focus on increasing positive behavior. On the basis of follow-ups, varying from six months to a year, five couples evidenced maintenance of treatment gains. Although couples maintained improvement in marital satisfaction up to a year after training, the degree to which this is associated with continued improvement in communication cannot be assessed, since behavioral measures of communication were not included at follow-up.

In a fourth study, Jacobson (1984) compared the relative effectiveness of BMT with its two major components, behavior exchange and communication/problem-solving training (C/PS), each presented in isolation. Couples were randomly assigned to one of these three treatments or to a waiting-list control group. The effects of treatment were evaluated using measures of global marital satisfaction, checklists of presenting problems, and spouse reports of behavior at home. Treated couples showed significant improvement, relative to untreated couples, on all three outcome measures. Complete BMT was no more effective than either behavior exchange or C/PS at posttest. Initially BE led to significantly greater increases in positive behavior than C/PS. At a six-month follow-up, however, there was a tendency for behavior exchange couples to reverse their progress. In contrast, couples receiving C/PS, either alone or in conjunction with behavior exchange, generally maintained their treatment gains or continued to improve. "The results suggest, at least in terms of immediate treatment effects, that the whole is not always more than the sum of its parts" (Jacobson, 1984, p. 304). They further suggest that although behavior exchange may be helpful in producing immediate behavior change, C/PS is a necessary condition for the maintenance and enhancement of treatment effects subsequent to termination.

Jacobson's research supports the general effectiveness of behavioral training with couples, with some suggestion that even severely distressed couples can derive considerable benefit from communication and problem-solving training alone. Jacobson's procedures, however, differ from nonbehavioral communication training procedures, like the ones employed by Schindler and colleagues (1983). In Jacobson's studies, couples were taught skills oriented toward making them more effective behavior modifiers. Training included how to use positive reinforcement in a problem-solving situation, through modification of both verbal and nonverbal behavior. Also couples learned more efficient strategies for solving problems and how to define solutions specifically and in behavioral terms. All of the elements of a behavioral exchange approach, except written contingency contracts, were employed. As a result, the role played by communication training distinct from problem-solving training cannot be established from these studies.

O'Leary and Turkowitz (1978a) compared a communication training procedure without instructions in contingency management with a condition that included, in addition to communication training, training in behavior exchange skills. The results of this study are somewhat confusing, because the two treatment groups did not differ, but improved significantly on half of the self-report measures of marital relations, and half of the self-report measures of marital communication. At a four-month follow-up, couples in both treatment groups reported a significant improvement in their communication patterns and in marital satisfaction relative to pretesting. Unfortunately a behavioral assessment was not conducted at follow-up.

O'Leary and Turkowitz, interestingly found an age by treatment interaction. Young couples benefited more from the combined program than they did from communication training alone, whereas older couples responded more favorably to communication training alone. Although any interpretation of these findings is pure speculation, Jacobson (1978a) suggested that younger distressed spouses still retain a significant amount of reinforcing power vis-à-vis their partners, whereas older couples have been more affected by satiation. Since behavior exchange procedures rely heavily on the ability of each spouse to provide positive behavior as a reinforcer for the other, the capacity of more recently acquainted couples to accomplish this could account for their positive response to such exchange training. The efficacy of communication training for spouses of different ages deserves future investigation.

While the studies by O'Leary and Turkowitz (1978a) and Jacobson (1979, 1984) suggest the efficacy of PS/C alone in achieving lasting increases in marital satisfaction, neither study employed behavioral measures at follow-up. The findings of the O'Leary and Turkowitz study are considerably more equivocal than Jacobson's, and are difficult to interpret due to the inconsistent results across measures.

Tsoi-Hoshmand (1976) compared a two-component behaviorally oriented marital intervention with a waiting-list control. Subjects were exposed first to instruction in problem solving and communication, followed by formal contractual negotiation training. Significant gains in caring and relationship satisfaction were found following communication training. At the end of treatment, statistically and clinically significant differences were found for treated couples on all three change measures. Subsequent testing indicated that changes in caring were associated with the first stage—communication training. Follow-up of between one and four months indicated improvement in 70 percent of the couples treated.

Unfortunately methodological difficulties preclude definite interpretation of the findings in this study. Couples were not randomly assigned to groups, only self-report measures were used, and statistical significance was achieved only when spouses were analyzed as individuals. Therefore, despite the positive findings, this study does not add significantly to our confidence in the effectiveness of BMT.

Baucom (1982) also conducted a comparison of behavior contracting and problem-solving/communications training. Distressed couples, screened for alcohol and sexual problems, were randomly assigned to one of four treatment conditions: (1) problem-solving/communication training plus behavior contracting (PS/C + BD); (2) problem-solving/communications training only (PS/C); (3) behavioral contracting only (BC); or (4) waiting-list control. In comparison with the control group, all treatment groups demonstrated significant improvement on self-report measures taken before, after, and three months following therapy. On observational measures significant gains relative to controls were demonstrated for negative communication only. Direct comparison of the three treatments showed no meaningful differences on any dependent measures. This finding is consistent with the findings of Jacobson (1979, 1984) and O'Leary and Turkowitz (1978a) that PS/C alone may be just as effective as PS/C with behavioral contracting. Similar to Jacobson (1984), Baucom failed to include a nonspecific treatment condition. As a result, factors common to almost any marital therapy (e.g., attention, concern for the couples) cannot be ruled out as factors that might have produced change. The evidence for change on negative communication in Baucom's study, along with increase in marital satisfaction, is especially notable, since negative behavior has been found to be a more potent predictor than positive behavior of daily marital satisfaction among distressed couples (Jacobson et al., 1980).

Through the use of different programs and assessment measures, the majority of studies suggest that distressed couples can be taught to increase their communication skills and to enhance preceptions of marital satisfaction. The results also suggest that couples can be trained to modify each other's behavior, at least temporarily.

Four well-designed studies evaluated the efficacy of behavioral prob-lem-solving/communication training (Baucom, 1982; Jacobson, 1979, 1984; O'Leary & Turkowitz, 1978a). Although three of these studies suggest that communication training alone is adequate for maintaining improvements in marital satisfaction, Jacobson's 1984 study suggests that behavior exchange may play an important role in producing immediate treatment effects. It should also be noted that more impressive outcome data were obtained from behavioral communication training (i.e, Jacob-son, 1984) than from nonbehavioral programs (i.e., Schindler et al., 1983). While the results of these studies support the efficacy of PS/C, the relative contribution of problem solving, as distinct from communication training, in BMT remains an area for further investigation. Unfortunately only one study included both a behavioral and self-support measure of communica-tion skill (O'Leary & Turkowitz, 1978a), and in this study significant change occurred on the self-report measure only. Future studies need to include behavioral as well as self-report measures of communication en-hancement.

All of the reported studies produced enchanced marital satisfaction; and, in those studies that included a follow-up, gains in this area were maintained (Baucom, 1982; Jacobson, 1977, 1978b, 1979, 1984; O'Leary & Turkowitz, 1978a; Schindler et al, 1983; Tsoi-Hoshmand, 1976). Five of the six studies (Baucom, 1982; Jacobson, 1979, 1984; O'Leary & Tur-kowitz, 1978a; Schindler et al., 1983; Tsoi-Hoshmand, 1976) empirically assessing both communication and satisfaction at the conclusion of therapy reported significant gains on both dimensions. Only seven studies included a follow-up, the longest of which was one year. It would appear necessary, however, to follow treated couples for periods of time longer than one year to assess, behaviorally and perceptually, the extended effects of treatment.

PROGRAMS FOR NONDISTRESSED COUPLES

A summary of the programs and results reviewed in this section can be found in Table 10.2. The two most widely researched programs for marital enhancement are the Minnesota Couples Communication Program, or CCP (Miller et al., 1976) and the Couples Relationship Enhancement Program or RE (Guerney, 1977). Five studies reviewed in this section have assessed the efficacy of RE with married couples, and three studies (to be reviewed in the next section) have tested its effectiveness with premarital

Table 10.2

The Outcomes of Marital Enrichment Programs

Author	Type of Program,[a] Sample Size, Type of Sample	Outcome Criteria[b] (Source)	Results[c]	Follow-up
Adam & Gingras (1982)	2-stage communication/ negotiation Training. 8 weekly 2½-hour sessions (19 E, 19 C) University community	1. Marital satisfaction (C) 2. Communication patterns (C) 3. Communication patterns (positive) (J) 4. Communication patterns (neutral) (J) 5. Communication patterns (negative) (J) 6. Communication skills (J) 7. Negotiation skills (J)	Significant gains on criteria 1–4 and 7 (criteria 1, 2 no change following stage-1 communication training)	2 months: gains maintained on criterion 1. 1 year: significant increase from pretest criterion 1, and gains maintained criterion 2 (behavioral assessment not conducted)
Brock and Joanning (1982)	1. Relationship enhancement (RE) 2. Minnesota Couples Communication Program (CCP) RE = 10 weekly 2-hour sessions CCP = 4 weekly 3-hour sessions (26 RE, 20 CCP, 8 C) Community	1. Marital satisfaction (C) 2. Communication patterns (C) 3. Communication skills (J)	RE superior to control and CCP on criteria 1–3, CCP on criteria 1–3, superior to control	3 months: RE gains maintained and superior to CCP on all criteria

Study	Treatment	Criteria	Results	Follow-up
Collins (1977)	Conjugal relationship modification (RE) 24 1½-hour weekly sessions (24 E, 21 C) University community	1. Communication skill (C) 2. Overall marital adjustment (C) 3. Communication pattern (C) 4. Acceptance and trust (C)	Significant change on criteria 1, 2	None
Ely et al. (1973)	Conjugal relationship modification (RE) 8 2-hour sessions (12 E, 21 C) Students	1. Acceptance and trust (C) 2. Communication pattern (C) 3. Feeling expression and responsiveness (C) 4. Feeling expression and clarification (role play task) (J)	Significant change on criteria 2–4	None
Epstein and Jackson (1978)	1. Assertiveness training (AT) 2. Insight training (IT) 5 1½-hour sessions over three weeks (6 in each E, 5 C) Community	1. Empathy (C) 2. Congruence (C) 3. Positive regard (C) 4. Assertive requests (J) 5. Attack (J) 6. Disagreement	AT significantly better than IT and C on criterion 4. IT and AT no different, but superior to control on criteria 5 and 6. AT superior to C on criterion 1	None
Garland (1981)	1. Communication training with active listening skills (CT-AL)	1. Marital satisfaction (C) 2. Communication patterns (C)	Significant gains for CT-AL on criterion 4	6 months: for both E groups self-reports of communication and

Table 10.2 (continued)

Study	Treatment	Criteria	Results	Follow-up
	2. Communication training without active listening skills (CT) 6 weekly 2½-hour sessions (7 CT-AL, 6 CT, 6 C) Seminary students	3. Active listening (J) 4. Perceptual accuracy (J)		satisfaction indicated improvement, whereas behavioral measures indicated deterioration. These effects were more pronounced for CT-AL
Jessee and Guerney (1981)	1. Relationship enhancement (RE) 2. Gestalt relationship facilitation (GRF) 12 weekly 2½-hour sessions (nine RE, 9 GRF) 22% students; community	1. Marital adjustment (C) 2. Communication patterns (C) 3. Trust and harmony (C) 4. Relationship change (C) 5. Relationship satisfaction (C) 6. Ability to handle problems (C)	Significant gains for both treatments on all variables. RE superior to GRF on criteria 2, 5, 6	None
Joanning (1982)	Minnesota Couples Communication Program (CCP) 4 weekly 3-hour sessions (17 E) University community	1. Marital adjustment (C) 2. Communication patterns (C) 3. Communication skills (J)	Significant gains on three criteria (no control)	5 months: perceived and rater-judged communication quality maintained, adjustment returned to pretest levels
Rappaport (1976)	Conjugal Relationship Modification (RE)	7 scales of relationship change, marital	Significant change on all criteria	None

Study	Treatment	Criterion measures	Results
	2 4-hour and two 8-hour sessions over eight weeks (20 E; two-week wait as own control) University community; 30% students	adjustment and satisfaction, communication skills, and problem-solving (all C); two scales of communication skills (J)	4 months: in both treatment groups perceived quality of relationship increased, but changes in communication were unstable
Russell et al. (1982)	1. Minnesota Couples Communication Program (CCP) 2. Behavioral exchange (BE) 6 2-hour weekly sessions (10 in each E, 10 C) 33% students; community	1. Marital satisfaction (C) 2. Marital tension (C) 3. Marital happiness(C) 4. Communication satisfaction (C) 5. Communication style (J) 6. Communication content (J)	Significant change on criterion: 6 (CCP husbands) 5 (CCP and BE wives) 2 (BE wives)
Wampler & Sprenkle (1980)	Minnesota Couples Communication Program (CCP) 6 weekly 2–5-hour sessions (22 E, 21 placebo, 9 C at posttest) (18 E, 11 placebo, 7 C at follow-up)	1. Open communication (J) 2. Empathy (C) 3. Positive regard (C) 4. Congruence (C) 5. Relationship inventory (C)	Significant gains for E on criteria 1 and 3–5 6 months: only positive changes in perceived quality of relationship persisted

Table 10.2 (continued)

75% students,
community; marital and
premarital mixed

[a] *All programs conducted in groups unless otherwise specified.*
[b] *C = client; T = trainer; J = trained judge.*
[c] *"Significant change" refers to both pre- and postchange for experimental group, and greater change than control group.*

342

couples. Three published studies evaluating the efficacy of CCP will also be reviewed in this section. A number of unpublished doctoral dissertations conducted over a decade ago have investigated the efficacy of these programs; the interested reader is referred to Gurman and Kniskern's (1977) review for a discussion of these works.

Relationship Enhancement draws upon Rogerian theory (Rogers, 1951). Couples are taught skills to enhance their use of empathic responses and unconditional positive regard—that is, to respect one another regardless of the situation. A group format is used wherein spouses alternate playing the roles of speaker and listener. While role playing, couples also practice the skills of expressing and clarifying feelings. The therapist first models the skills, then provides feedback during the practice sessions.

Theoretically CCP is based on Reubin Hill's family development theory and upon a systems theory approach that emphasizes the rule-governed nature of relationships (Miller et al., 1976). Like Guerney's program, the major objective is to teach self-awareness, reciprocity, and communication skills, though greater emphasis is given to awareness of the rules of a relationship, and education about metacommunication. This approach also uses a group format with behavior rehearsal and feedback.

Studies Evaluating RE

Rappaport (1976) evaluated RE in a study of couples participating in marathon group sessions. Subjects served as their own controls, in that they were tested twice prior to undergoing treatment, with a two-month intervening waiting period. On all variables studied, couples exhibited significant positive changes from pretest to posttest. No such changes were manifested during the waiting period. Although these findings suggest a treatment effect, a clear, causal relationship between treatment and outcome cannot be assumed. In order for studies that employ subjects as their own controls to be interpretable, it must be demonstrated that the changes that occurred in the treatment group were due to the treatment itself. This can best be accomplished through the use of a multiple baseline design.

Collins (1977) compared couples receiving RE with an untreated control group. They ranged from nondistressed to mildly distressed. The RE couples demonstrated significant improvement relative to controls on one measure of communication and on one measure of satisfaction. The absence of behavioral verification of change and of follow-up data in addition to the use of poorly validated measures, represent interpretive difficulties in the Collins study.

In a well-designed experiment using couples who were somewhat distressed, Ely and colleagues (1973) compared couples who were randomly assigned to a ten-week RE program with couples who remained on a waiting list. On both observational measures, and on two of the three self-report measures, significant differences were found that favored RE couples. Moreover, when control couples finally received the treatment, they too improved to a degree commensurate with the changes achieved by the first treatment group. Although self-report and behavioral measures both indicated significant improvement in communication, the measure of changes in the marital trust and acceptance (the Conjugal Life Questionnaire) did not show significant change. Follow-up data on treatment couples were not reported.

Three studies suggest, then, that RE is a promising procedure for training communication skills. However, its facility for effecting change in marital satisfaction is less clear, since not one of these studies was able to produce clinically significant changes in marital adjustment. Posttest scores on this variable in all three studies remained in the mildly distressed range.

In addition, although the use of multidimensional outcome criteria is admirable, the observational measures have not been sufficiently validated—a restriction that forces one to confine conclusions to self-report data. As such data are particularly vulnerable to alternative interpretations based on demand characteristics and placebo effects, it is unfortunate that nonspecific control groups, which might have ruled out such interpretations, were not included.

In an effort to assess the nonspecific effects of RE training, Jessee and Guerney (1981) randomly assigned 36 couples to group marital RE or to a group Gestalt relationship-facilitation treatment. Significant gains were made by the participants in both groups on all variables studied. In addition RE participants demonstrated greater gains than did the Gestalt relationship facilitation participants on measures of communication, relationship satisfaction, and ability to handle problems.

While these results suggest the superiority of the RE program, several factors render such a conclusion speculative: (1) the RE group scored uniformly lower on pretest measures than the Gestalt group; (2) RE group leaders were perceived as more enthusiastic than Gestalt leaders; and (3) a non-treatment control group was not included. The significant gains shown by participants in both treatment groups may thus have been due to the repetition of tests, experimenter demand effects, attention effects, or expectation effects. Only those variables on which the RE treatment was superior can truly be said to result from specific rather than nonspecific effects. Unfortunately these investigations also failed to include observational measures and to report follow-up data on either of the groups.

Brock and Joanning (1982) conducted a well-designed study, comparing RE and CCP treatment programs. The results of posttesting indicated that, compared with controls, RE was more effective in increasing marital satisfaction and communication, as measured by both self-report and observational measures. Compared with controls, CCP also produced significant increases in communication skills and satisfaction. However, RE was superior to CCP on self-reprt measures of communication and satisfaction. Results at a three-month follow-up evaluation, including 99 percent of the sample, showed that RE couples scored higher than CCP and control couples on all variables.

These results sugest that RE was a more effective intervention than CCP. However, CCP has been considered almost exclusively a marital enrichment program, whereas RE is a stragtegy considered applicable to couples reporting low marital satisfaction, as well as couples wishing to improve already satisfying relationships. Because the sample studied was composed primarily of mildly distressed couples, CCP may not have been assessed on the appropriate individuals. An alternative explanation of the results is that, for CCP to have maximal impact, the leaders should be more experienced with the program. After completing the study, leaders related greater difficulty in conducting CCP groups. If the leaders had been more experienced with CCP, results equivalent to those obtained by RE may have been obtained; RE, however, may be more "leaderproof," and thus more consistent in its impact on couples' relationships. Interestingly the RE leaders in the study by Jessee and Guerney (1981) were considered more enthusiastic than leaders in the alternate treatment.

Studies Evaluating CCP.

Wampler and Sprenkle (1980) conducted the first published follow-up study of the effects of CCP. Forty-three couples were assigned to a CCP or to an attention-placebo control group. Nine couples served in a no-treatment control condition. The immediate posttest results on a behavioral measure of communication indicated that CCP had a positive effect on the couples' use of open-style communication. The perceived quality of the relationship was also enhanced. The four-month follow-up indicated that changes in communication skills were not maintained, whereas the perceptual changes were. It appears that the continued use of a more open-style communication may not be related directly to relationship satisfaction, at least in terms of the measures used in this study. The improvements noted for CCP participants relative to the placebo and no-treatment control groups suggest that the continued positive change in the couples' perception of their relationship is due to participation in the CCP; but the particular aspect of the program that produced these changes is unclear. While these results attest to the immediate efficacy of the CCP program, the durability of these changes is an open question. The use of an attention-placebo control, as well as the reporting of follow-up results, are strengths in this study. Unfortunately Wampler and Sprenkle (1980) mixed engaged, married, and dating couples, and did not clarify whether the groups were matched on these and other important dimensions.

Joanning (1982) also assessed the immediate and long-term effects of CCP. Seventeen married couples, with self-report ratings of marital satisfaction ranging from well to maladjusted, were assigned to training groups. Couples improved significantly on all measures at posttest. Although marital adjustment returned to pretest levels by the five-month follow-up, couples' perceived communication quality and rater-judged communication quality maintained posttest levels. In response to an openended question concerning the impact of training on the couples' relationships, 16 couples reported feeling much closer during and immediately following training.

> This closeness or sense of intimacy seemed to be due to the large amounts of structured time during training that the couples had spent focusing on their relationships and observing other relationships. (Joanning, 1982, p. 466).

The failure of this study to include any control condition (attention-placebo or untreated control) precludes the attribution of change in communication or satisfaction to specific aspects of the training. An alternative explanation for the findings in this study is that focusing on communication skills and attitudes is a necessary but insuffcent method for improving and maintaining increased marital satisfaction. Although CCP provides some opportunity for couples to explore their relationships, the focus of the group is on communication. It may be necessary to expand the role of cognitive and emotional experiences in order to promote lasting marital satisfaction.

The question of whether CCP couples are at a disadvantage relative to couples who receive training aimed at resolving relationship issues is addressed by Russell and colleagues (1982), who compared CCP and a structured behavioral exchange (SBE) training program with a waiting-list

---

According to Wampler and Sprenkle (1980). Several published studies, however, (Dillon, 1975; Zimmerman & Bailey, 1977) reported preliminary positive long-term effects on self-report measures from ten weeks to five years.

control. Prior to training, couples' self-report of marital satisfaction ranged from maladjusted to well-adjusted.

While the general trend for both groups was one of improvement in marital satisfaction, couples in both treatments experienced a decline in perceived quality at least once during the posttest or 60-day follow-up. Perhaps "open and honest" communication sometimes brings with it information one would rather not hear, and, depending on the time of assessment, differential treatment effects may obtain. It is also interesting that these findings are similar to those reported by Jacobson (1984) and O'Leary and Turkowitz (1978a), in that the use of behavioral contracting did not produce more positive change than communication training alone.

The studies by Joanning (1982), Russell and collegues (1982), and Wampler and Sprenkle (1980) all indicate that CCP achieves its purpose of teaching couples skills and of increasing awareness about relationship issues. But, the failure of Joanning (1982) and Russell and colleagues (1982) to include controls at follow-up makes it difficult to attribute long-term changes to the program itself. Two studies reported maintenance of marital satisfaction in the absence of continued use of communication skills (Wampler & Sprenkle, 1980; Russell et al., 1982), and two studies reported anecdotally that participants had difficultly incorporating new skills into their daily routine (Joanning, 1982; Wampler & Sprenkle, 1980). If CCP is to effect long-term changes in communication skill, the program may need to be altered to increase the likelihood that the couples will continue to use the skills after program termination. Booster sessions at monthly or bimonthly intervals might be added, or additional time for skill practice could be build into sessions, along with the development of ways to encourage practice at home.

Studies Evaluating Other Training Regimes

Epstein and Jackson (1978) compared assertion-related communication training, insight training, and no-treatment, with couples being randomly assigned to treatment and control groups. The assertiveness/communication training group demonstrated a significant increase in assertive requests, compared with the insight training and no-treatment conditions. Both treatments reduced disagreements significantly. Communication training produced a greater decrease in attacks and a greater increase in spouse rate of empathy than the control condition; the insight training and no-treatment groups did not differ on these variables. On two of the three marital satisfaction subtests, no significant group differences were observed. It appears that the impact of communication training on spouses' perceptions of marital satisfaction was less dramatic than the behavioral changes noted by objective raters. Finally, while both treatment groups focused on increased understanding of interaction patterns between spouses, the assertiveness group specified and practiced alternate modes of communication. The greater gains accomplished by the assertiveness group suggest that delineation and practice of new communication skills may be helpful in achieving immediate behavior changes.

Garland (1981) compared two communication training programs with each other and with a waiting-list control condition. The training programs were almost identical, except that in one session the "experimental" group was taught active listening skills. At posttest, individuals trained in active listening skills did not actually use the skills any more than did the control group participants. Yet these trained individuals improved to a significantly greater extent than did control group participants in perceptual accuracy. These findings appear contradictory, since they suggest that couples increased their listening-based accuracy without actually using listening skills. In assessing changes in communication, however, only verbal behaviors were coded. Since one of the three active listening skills—attending—was not measured, it is possible that increases in attending were not reflected in the data. This difficulty highlights the need for investigators to include nonverbal as well as verbal measures of communication.

The short- and long-term effects of a marital enrichment program (MEP) were evaluated by Adam and Gingras (1982), using both self-report inventories and behavioral scales. Thirty-eight well-functioning couples were randomly assigned to either no-treatment control conditions or to the 20-hour-long MEP. At posttest, trained subjects were superior to control subjects on measures of marital satisfaction and communication. These gains were maintained for one year following posttest. Yet the expected superiority of the trained group over the control group following completion of the communication component was not supported by the data. Although trained couples did not show improvement in communication following completion of communication training, improvement was demonstrated in negotiation skills following the negotiation component. In comparison with the control group, MEP participants demonstrated a significant increase at posttesting in positive behaviors, and a significant decrease in neutral behaviors. No difference in negative behaviors was noted between groups. These results suggest that involvement in the program produced perceptual changes in marital satisfaction and communication. The behavioral ratings of improvement, however, are less impressive. Couples not only failed to increase communication skils—they did not decrease negative behaviors. This result is unfortunate, because the frequency of negative behavior rather than positive behavior appears to be correlated with marital distress (Birchler et al., 1975). While no immediate progress was observed in the couples' communication following exposure to the communication component, these observations do not necessarily attest to the ineffectiveness of communication training, since a reasonable period of time may be needed before the effects of learning become evident. These results, on the contrary, may suggest that increased communication in the absence of negotiation is insufficient in producing improvement in couples' interactions.

The present review of communication training programs with non-distressed couples may promote more confusion than clarity regarding the efficacy of treatment, given the diversity of methods used. Follow-up assessment was conducted in only six of the studies (Adam & Gingras, 1982; Brock & Joanning, 1982; Garland, 1981; Joanning, 1982; Wampler & Sprenkle, 1980; Russell et al., 1982), of which only four employed behavioral measures of communication (Brock & Joanning, 1982; Garland, 1981; Joanning, 1982; Wampler & Sprenkle, 1980). In only one instance was follow-up conducted one year after intervention (Adam & Gingras, 1982), and this study did not include behavioral measures. A large number of the studies employed dependent measures of questionable validity (Adam & Gingras, 1982; Ely et al., 1973; Garland, 1981; Rappaport, 1976; Russell et al., 1982); and, in four studies, results on objective measures of change in communication did not agree with self-report (Adam & Gingras, 1982; Epstein & Jackson, 1978; Garland, 1981; Russell et al., 1982). Changes in behavior generally tended to be more apparent to observers than to participants. Several studies suggest that improvements in marital satisfaction may persist despite the apparent instability of changes in communication patterns.

The above studies tentatively support the view that communication training can produce *statistically* significant and moderately durable changes in marital satisfaction, without necessarily producing subjective or lasting changes in communication. Clearly much more research needs to be done to test this conclusion. It is possible that the efficacy of training does not lie in the enhancement of skills, and that factors other than improvements in communication are necessary to induce clinically significant changes.

A REVIEW OF COMMUNICATION TRAINING WITH PREMARITAL COUPLES

Schlein (1971) developed one of the earliest premarital intervention program, called PRIMES (premarital relationship improvement by max-

imizing empathy and self-disclosure), which applies the Guerney relationship-enhancement (RE) approach to enhancing the self-awareness and
communication skills of premarital couples.

On behavioral measures of specific communication skills, PRIMES
couples, relative to controls, demonstrated significant gains in their ability
to show empathic acceptance and to express their feelings. On the two
self-report measures of general communication, no significant differences
were found. Relative to the control group, PRIMES couples also demonstrated significant changes in perceived warmth, ability to handle relationship problems, and improvements in the quality of their relationship.
No significant differences were found between groups on measures of trust
and intimacy, and relationship satisfaction.

The inconsistent findings across so many dependent measures create
some confusion in interpreting these results. The data suggest that training
can enhance specific communication skills, and that these skills help
couples handle problems. Yet, self-reports of communication and relationship satisfaction generally did not change.

Table 10.3 provides descriptive information on the empirical studies to
be outlined in the remainder of this section.

D'Augelli and colleagues (1974) reanalyzed the behavioral data from
Schlein's study, using the Carkhuff (1967) rating scales of empathetic
understanding, communication of respect, immediacy of the relationship,
and helpee self-exploration. Twenty-minute interactions—in which each
member of the couple was asked "What would you like to change in
yourself?" and "What would you like to change in your partner?"—were
coded by trained raters. Because of the high correlations between the
measures, only the results for empathy and self-exploration were reported.

The experimental group, in comparison with the control group, improved significantly on both measures. These results support Schlein's
findings that, with less than 20 hours of training, participants can increase
the efficacy of their general helping skills. Unfortunately, as indicated by
Schlein's study, the degree to which this improvement enhances relationship satisfaction is unclear.

Ridley and colleagues (1982) also assessed the efficacy of Guerney's
program with premarital couples. Their study adds to our knowledge by
including a credible alternate treatment group for control of nonspecific
treatment effects. Results indicated that the RE group demonstrated significantly better scores relative to the relationship discussion (RD) group
on all dependent measures. At posttest, participants in the RE group
increased on all measures of relationship quality, in contrast to the RD
group, which showed a decrease on these measures. In both groups couples discussed actual relationship problems, although only the RE group

Table 10.3

The Outcomes of Premarital Enrichment Programs

Author	Type of Program,[a] Sample Size, Type of Sample	Outcome Criteria[b] (Source)	Results[c]	Follow-up
D'Augelli et al. (1974)[d]	Conjugal relationship modification (RE) 8–10 weekly 1½–2-hour sessions (34 E, 34 C) Students: dating not engaged	1. Empathy (J) 2. Self-exploration (J) 3. Relationship improvement (C)	Significant change on criteria 1 and 2. Self-reported change on criterion 3	None
Ginsberg and Vogelsong (1977)	Conjugal relationship modification (RE) 8–10 weekly 1½–2-hour sessions (15 E, 27 C) Students: dating not engaged	1. Communication skill (2 measures) (J) 2. Communication pattern (2 measures) (C) 3. Problem solving (C) 4. Trust and intimacy (C) 5. Empathy and warmth (C) 6. Relationship satisfaction (C) 7. Relationship quality (C)	Significant change on criteria 1, 3, 7 (on criterion 5 significant change in self-perceived—not partner-perceived—empathy)	None
Markman, et al. (1983)	Premarital Relationship Enhancement Program	1. Relationship satisfaction (C)	Significant change on criteria 1, 2 (E males),	None

351

Table 10.3 (continued)

Study	Program / Sessions / Location	Criteria measures	Significant change[c]	Follow-up
	(PREP)	2. Perceived communication (C)	and 3–5	1-year; 100% of E and 60% of C still together; E significantly less decline in relationship satisfaction.
	5 sessions over 2½–5 weeks (14 E, 28 C)	3. Communication skill (2 measures) (J)		
	University community	4. Romanticism (C)		
		5. Love (C)		
		6. Problem intensity (C)		
Markman, Floyd et al. (1983)	Premarital Relationship Enhancement Program (PREP)	1. Relationship satisfaction (C)	No change	
	6 sessions (5 E, 5 C)	2. Problem intensity (C)		
	University community	3. Communication skill (C)		
		4. Problem solving (J)		
Ridley et al. (1982)	1. Conjugal relationship enhancement (RE)	1. Relationship adjustment (C)	RE had significantly greater increases on all criteria	6-month[e]: RE empathy and self-awareness lower than posttest, but greater than pretest and RD scores (criteria 1–4 not assessed)
	2. Relationship discussion (RD)	2. Trust and intimacy (C)		
	8 weekly 3-hour sessions for each (25 RE, 28 RD)	3. Empathy and warmth (C)		
	University community	4. Communication pattern (C)		
		5. Empathy (J)[e]		
		6. Self-awareness (J)[e]		

[a] All programs conducted in groups unless otherwise specified.
[b] C = client; T = trainer; J = trained judge.
[c] "Significant change" refers to both pre- and postchange for experimental group, and greater change than control group.
[d] Report based on Schlein (1971) data.
[e] Behavioral and follow-up data on this sample reported in Avery et al. (1980).

learned specific communication skills to be employed during problem solving. Satisfactory conflict resolution may have led to the observed increase in the quality of the relationship. While the RD group members increased their awareness of relationship realities, their lack of training in problem resolution may have been a factor in the decline in relationship quality.

Using data from these same couples, Avery and colleagues (1980) report that, relative to RD participants, RE members significantly increased on behavioral measures of self-disclosure and empathy skills. At six-month follow-up, RE participants maintained skills at a level higher than pretest, but lower than posttest. An interesting addition in the Avery et al. (1980) study was the use of a one-hour booster session five months after treatment. No significant differences between booster and nonbooster RE groups were found at follow-up, suggesting that skills can be maintained at a high level over time without the use of additional sessions. It is possible to conclude, however, that a one-hour booster session was too limited to produce desired results.

The positive results on the behavioral tests in the Avery et al. (1980) study and on the relationship quality indices in the Ridley et al. (1982) study indicate that premarital couples can learn self-disclosure and empathy skills, and that these skills do have a positive effect on the quality of these relationships. Unfortunately couples' satisfaction with their relationship was not reported at follow-up.

Based on his earlier laboratory findings, Markman developed a prevention program called PREP (Premarital Relationship Enhancement Programs), which includes both communication skills training and cognitive restructuring components. The specific communication skills included behavioral monitoring and contracting. Markman, Floyd, and co-workers (1983) compared the relationship satisfaction of five PREP and five waiting-list control couples both at posttest and one year later. The results indicated little difference between the PREP and control groups at posttest; yet self-report measures one year later indicated that PREP couples were more likely to maintain a stable relationship and less likely to experience a decline in relationship satisfaction from posttest to follow-up. At follow-up all of the PREP couples were still together, and four of the five married. Sixty percent of the control group couples had married, and two of the five had dissolved their relationships. This time-lagged effect highlights the importance of follow-up for program evaluation in prevention.

In an effort to replicate and improve upon this study, Markman and colleagues (1983) recruited couples planning to marry for the first time. A subset of these couples was later offered the PREP program. Couples were matched on several predictor variables (e.g., positivity of interaction) and randomly assigned to PREP or no-treatment control conditions. Following treatment PREP males demonstrated a significant increase in relationship satisfaction. A general question about relationship satisfaction further indicated that the PREP couples had increased their satisfaction, whereas controls tended to decline. There was a significant increase in skills for PREP couples, relative to controls, on two measures of communication. Although a posttest measure of problem intensity demonstrated improvement for the PREP group, the PREP couples also reported less intense problems than did controls at pretest. Control groups, in contrast, demonstrated a decrease on these dimensions.

These data generally suggest that the shortterm objectives of the program were met. They further indicate that prevention programs may be able to provide resources to help couples maintain their already high levels of functioning. There are several conceptual and methodological points worth considering, though. First, the absence of the follow-up data obscures our understanding of the programs' effectiveness in preventing later distress. Second, there is the possibility of a selection effect, since all PREP couples had the opportunity to decline the program, whereas control couples did not. To the extent that PREP couples were more motivated and were experiencing fewer relationship problems, the generalizability of Markman's findings is unclear.

Taken together the pattern of Markman's results raises the possibility that the positive effects of the intervention program were due to the prevention of a decline in couples' relationship satisfaction, which normally occurs over the life span (Rollins & Galligan, 1978). This hypothesis is consistent with a "bank account model," which posits that all couples start their relationship with a "sizable bank account," and those who become distressed slowly "withdraw" from the account through unrewarding interactions (Markman, 1979). Research with longer term follow-up is clearly needed, as well as replications of these preliminary findings. Markman and his associates are currently conducting a large N, longitudinal study to replicate and extend these intervention studies (Markman et al., 1983; Markman, et al., 1984).

Our review of communication training for premarital couples illustrates that the field of premarital training is yet in its infancy. Many of the available studies are nonexperimental (e.g., Hinkle & Moore, 1971; Meadows & Taplin, 1970; Van Zoost, 1973), and are therefore not reviewed in this chapter. Two of the studies employed the same population (D'Augelli et al., 1974; Ginsberg & Vogelsong, 1977). And one experimental study had a sample of five (Markman, Floyd, et al., 1983). Only two studies conducted follow-up assessments (Avery et al., 1980; Markman, Floyd, et al., 1983), and neither of these employed measures of both satisfaction and communication. The body of studies tentatively suggest that, in relatively short periods of time, couples can be taught to improve their communication skills. The available studies likewise suggest that the immediate effect of enhanced communication is improved perception of the quality of the relationship (Ginsberg & Vogelsong, 1977; Ridley et al., 1982). An important contribution of Markman and his associates is the evaluation of the same communication task by both the couples ("insiders") and objective raters ("outsiders"). This form of assessment should be continued.

These studies also point to the fact that couples involved in premarital training are already quite satisfied with their relationships, and that the most reasonable function of intervention may be maintenance rather than enhancement of marital happiness. Although premarital counseling programs are on the rise in the United States (Bargarozzi & Raven, 1981), no empirical data exist to support the notion that these programs reduce the incidence of divorce or separation for those couples who participate. This is primarily because the follow up evaluations that have been conducted have not allowed enough time to elapse after treatment to obtain a valid measure of treatment potency. In addition, we do not yet know whether premarital counseling practices serve a prophylactic function. Similarly we do not know if involvement in premarital counseling has a negative long-term effect on couples. Gurman (1980) has raised the concern that idealization is a necessity for young couples, and that intervention programs focused on potential problems "can be destructive to the very relationship one hopes to improve" (Gurman, 1980, p. 93).

METHODOLOGY

A familiar caveat emerges from this review of the literature on couples' communication: "Firm conclusions regarding the efficacy of training await replication of these results by studies with more adequate methodologies." Gurman and Kniskern (1978) have developed a design quality rating system to be used in evaluating the efficacy of marital therapy outcome studies. When these criteria were applied to the studies included in this review, only 35 percent received "very good" ratings. The majority of studies were rated as "good," or "fair," and one was rated as "poor" (see Table 10.4). Although a thorough discussion of all the methodological difficulties evidenced in these studies is beyond the scope of this chapter, the recurrence of similar problems across reports warrants a general

Table 10.4
Adequacy of Outcome Studies Using Gurman and Kniskern (1978) Rating System

---

Marital therapy
Very good:
   Baucom (1982)
   Jacobson (1984)
   Jacobson (1978b)
   Schindler et al. (1983)
Good:
   Jacobson (1977)
   Jacobson (1979)
   O'Leary & Turkowitz (1978a)
Fair:
   Hickman & Baldwin (1971)
   Tsoi-Hoshmand (1976)
Poor:
   Pierce (1973)

Marital enrichment
Very good:
   Adam & Gingras (1982)
   Brock & Joanning (1982)
   Epstein & Jackson (1978)
   Garland (1981)
   Wampler & Sprenkle (1980)
Good:
   Ely et al. (1973)
   Russell et al. (1982)
Fair:
   Collins (1977)
   Jessee & Guerney (1981)
   Joanning (1982)
   Rappaport (1976)   *Premarital enrichment*

Very good:
   None
Good:
   D'Augelli et al. (1974)
   Markman et al. (1983)
   Ridley et al. (1982)
Fair:
   Ginsberg & Vogelsong (1977)
   Markman, Floyd, et al. (1983)

review of methodology, and suggestions for future research. Drawing from the recommendations made by O'Leary and Turkowitz (1978b) in their review of methodological errors in marital treatment research, the following areas will be covered: selection of subjects, methods of assessment, and treatment specification.

Subjects

Few studies had 20 or more couples in the experimental condition (Brock & Joanning, 1982; Collins, 1977; D'Augelli et al., 1974; Rappaport, 1976). Small sample sizes may decrease the power of statistical tests in detecting clinically significant changes as a result of treatment. There are also limitations on the conclusions that may be drawn from the studies with small samples, because of the possibility of sampling bias.

O'Leary and Turkowitz report that "the problem of restricted patient populations is particularly salient in the controlled research on marital therapy" (O'Leary & Turkowitz, 1978b, p. 748). Almost all of the studies reviewed here involved young, well-educated, middle-class couples recruited from a university community, many of whom were students. Because age and number of years married can affect the outcome of different approaches to marital therapy (e.g., O'Leary & Turkowitz, 1978a), samples should include a wider range of participants. For studies in this area to have meaning for most clinicians, further research is necessary that evaluates couples' therapy in comparison with older clients and with clients from lower socioeconomic backgrounds.

A very common error was the omission of an adequate sample description. O'Leary and Turkowitz (1978b) recommend that, in addition to age, educational level, occupation, SES, and information regarding previous or concurrent therapy, authors should specify the fee paid, if any, for treatment, as well as the mean and range of years married, the number of children, and the number of previous marriages. Only seven studies included all of the suggested information, four of which were conducted by the same experimenter (Adam & Gingras, 1982; Epstein & Jackson, 1978; Joanning, 1982; Jacobson, 1977, 1978b, 1979, 1984). A related difficulty in the research on premarital counseling is the mixing of couples who are dating, engaged, or "planning to marry." To the extent that these terms represent varying levels of commitment to the relationship, differential outcomes may be expected. There has been little attempt, however, to define or separately analyze couples according to these differences.

Although only one study failed to report the method by which subjects were obtained (Russell et al., 1982), many of the studies employing multiple referral sources failed to report the percentage of subjects from each source. It is reasonable to expect that subjects obtained through different sources may not be comparable. For example a couple responding to an advertisement may be more motivated and have less problems than a couple seeking treatment or referred by the court.

Methods of Assessment

The lack of multiple outcome criteria is a frequently cited methodological error in marital treatment research. Only 25 percent of the studies reviewed relied solely on self-report data, however; and except for Jessee and Guerney (1981), these tended to be older studies.

Kniskern and Gurman (1984) have suggested that change in marital therapy be assessed from two perspectives: inside (the spouse) and outside (the objective observer) the treatment system. The rationale stems from recent studies that demonstrate that the objective impact of a partner's behavior may not be perceived in the same way by each spouse (see Markman, Jamieson & Floyd, 1983, for a more detailed discussion). While satisfaction with the relationship is generally considered a variable best measured by the insider, changes in communication skills are clearly amenable to multiple measures. Over one-third of the studies have employed both self-reports and behavioral assessments of communication. Only two of these, however, involved distressed couples (O'Leary & Turkowitz, 1978a; Schindler et al., 1983).

Positive change has generally been indicated when communication was measured by self-report. When multiple measures are employed, however, treatment outcome is less positive, and inconsistent findings are often reported (Adam & Gingras, 1982; Garland, 1981; Ginsberg & Vogelsong, 1977; O'Leary & Turkowitz, 1978a; Russell et al., 1982). Future investigations, including multiple evaluations from several perspectives, are needed to identify which aspects of communication arc modifiable by specific program components, and which changes lead specifically to increased satisfaction.

Gurman and Kniskern (1978), in their review of marital therapy, suggested that marital therapy may produce negative as well as positive or neutral effects. They reported deterioration in roughly 5–10 percent of the marital cases included in their review. The worsening of relationships as a result of therapy is a serious issue that must be addressed; yet only two studies included such an analysis (Brock & Joanning, 1982; Jacobson, 1984). Brock and Joanning (1982) were also the only researchers to conduct separate analyses for distressed and nondistressed couples. Given the range of disturbance reported in many of the investigations of marital enrichment, the use of such a breakdown would provide additional information as to which couples are best served by particular training methods.

In a recent article examining the effectiveness of BMT, Jacobson and colleagues (1984) highlight the importance of examining the clinical significance of treatment effects. In addition to reporting statistically significant indices of change, they suggest that authors report the proportion of couples who improved, as well as the number of "improved" couples who can truly be categorized as nondistressed. Anything less than a nondistressed level of marital satisfaction should not be acceptable to the client or the clinician.

Treatment Specification

Time and Group Format

Almost all of the studies reviewed used a structured time format for treatment—a methodological strength in that it makes the study more easily replicable. Within the structured formats, the studies differed in total number of treatment hours, as well as in the spacing and length of sessions (see Tables 10.1–10.3). The total number of treatment hours ranged from four hours (Hickman and Baldwin, 1971) to 30 hours (Jessee & Guerney, 1981). For all three kinds of studies, average meeting time was 18 hours. Ninety percent of the marital and premarital enchancement programs have been conducted in a group setting, with meetings held primarily on a weekly basis (75 percent) over an average duration of 14 weeks. In contrast, 30 percent of the communication training interventions for distressed couples were conducted in groups with an average duration (for group and conjoint treatment) of approximately 11 weeks. This variability in temporal format limits the comparisons that can be made between studies, and can function as a confounding variable when interpreting the results of a particular training method. Only one study (Markman et al., 1983) has addressed the question of optimal length of training by comparing weekly sessions with marathon programs.

Another important question involves the relative power of, and indications for, the use of extra-session tasks, as compared with the use of tasks or enactments within sessions (Aponte & Van Deusen, 1980, cited in Kniskern & Gurman, 1984). Although most programs employ "in-group" as well as "at-home" assignments, there are no data addressing whether assigning homework slows or speeds up therapy, or the conditions under which tasks of either sort are most productive. Several researchers report that couples had difficulty practicing new communication behaviors at home (Rappaport, 1976; Ridley et al., 1982; Wampler & Sprenkle, 1980), but little work has been done to develop ways of enhancing compliance to assigned tasks.

Component Analysis

The vast majority of studies used similar combinations of training techniques, but failed to isolate the relative effects of the different components in producing "therapeutic" change. Most of the programs can be classified as educacational, incorporating short lectures, behavioral rehearsal and feedback, and group discussion. The PREP program includes a cognitive restructuring component, and information on negotiation, whereas the RE program (e.g., Rappaport, 1976) includes some information on problem solving, in addition to communication training. The necessity of including these additional skills has not been assessed. The comparison between RE and an RD group (Ridley et al., 1982) suggests the importance of self-disclosure and empathy skills; yet no data were collected to indicate whether this was the only way in which groups differed. Garland's work (Garland, 1981) suggests the necessity for active listening skills; but no study has yet addressed the optimal way of teaching such skills.

Tsoi-Hoshmand (1976) attempted to evaluate the relative contributions of problem-solving and negotiation training, but only administered one of her measures following communication training, and this was not reflective of changes in communication skills. Similarly the experimental design employed by Adam and Gingras (1982) prevented clear attribution of changes to communication or negotiation training. The research projects of Baucom (1982), Jacobson (1984), and O'Leary and Turkowitz (1978a) represent viable steps in understanding the relative contributions of problem-solving/communication training and behavioral contracting. Unfortunately the relative contributions of problem solving versus communication training have not been assessed. The identification of active components in the various treatment packages represents a necessary task for future researchers.

Follow-up

A major weakness in half of the reviewed studies was the absence of a follow-up. When included, follow-up measures were generally administered 12 weeks after training, with only three studies including follow-up one year after training (Adam & Gingras, 1982; Jacobson, 1977; Markman 1983). Only one premarital study (Markman et al., 1983) tested couples 12 months after training.

Follow-up evaluations of one year or less are of limited value in determining the success of premarital counseling in preventing later marital distress or dissolution, simply because the majority of divorces in this country take place after the first year of marriage. (Norton & Glick, 1979).

FUTURE DIRECTIONS

Can marital therapy and enhancement programs prevent divorce? As this review indicates, we do not yet know. Our knowledge is limited by both the scant amount of data and various methodological inadequacies in the published research. The intent of the programs discussed was to inoculate couples against future relationship problems; yet conclusions about the actual impact of these interventions must be made quite tentatively.

The results generally indicate that involvement in training can produce enhanced and moderately sustained relationship satisfaction. But the limited behavioral data at the follow-up point to an inconsistent maintenance of improvements in communication skills. While the results of investigations that include alternative treatments and attention placebo control groups suggest that positive gains are attributable to some aspect of the training, the failure to obtain or maintain clinically signicant levels of relationship satisfaction raises several questions, and poses new directions for future studies. For one thing the available programs may be adequate, but in their present form not powerful enought to affect clinically significant change.

Second, as Markman and colleagues (1982) pointed out, "even if prevention programs are shown to be successful, we have to be careful and not make the logical error of affirming the consequent. That is, arguing that if skill training prevents problems, then a lack of skill causes problems'' (pp. 258–59).

While faulty communication, an inability to negotiate conflict, and the use of aversive behaviors to control one's mate have been implicated in the dissolution of many marriages, there has been very little work done on the *relative* importance of these behaviors in maintaining a successful relationship. As other aspects of a successful marriage are identified, their importance relative to communication and behavior exchange principles must be assessed, and ways of modifying these ingredients must be addressed.

Theory and research that address the etiology of marital distress as well as the dynamics of successful marriage are rare. In addition to information on the diffference between distressed and nondistressed groups, the field of marital relations must have data on how the implementation of certain communication practices affects marital interactions. There is a possibility, for instance, of overcommunication: some data suggest that misperceptions between intimately involved persons may at times be necessary for positive relationship adjustment (e.g., Levinger & Breedlove, 1966).

Another important direction for the field involves making more explicit the role of therapists as teachers. Attention is given to improving the efficacy of training and teaching skills, without incorporating information from the field of education. Clearly not all persons will learn the same way from identical packages. The use of primarily university-affiliated couples may have obscured the potential difficulties of trying to teach certain skills to less verbal or introspective individuals.

As Kniskern and Gurman (1984) have suggested, the structured nature of skills-training programs based on different theoretial orientations presents a slightly different, but exciting, avenue for future exploration. If effective programs, representing different approaches, could be organized, they could then be compared with one another. The most effective Rogerian-based program, for example, could be compared with the most effective behavioral program, to determine which approach is most useful with which problems.

Another issue of great practical import involves the timing of communication training/enrichment programs. Attempts must be made to define the point(s) in the developmental cycle at which these programs have the most profound and lasting effects. At present we do not know if programs are most beneficial before marriage, early in marriage and before parenthood, after childbirth, or at some point beyond. Furthermore, distinctly different types of enrichment experiences may be more suited to different stages in the marital life cycle.

In many of the reviewed studies, the investigators excluded couples experiencing sexual problems and couples within which one or both of the members exhibited severe psychological disturbances or alcohol abuse. Consequently our knowledge of program effectivenss is limited to *moderately* distressed clients.

The role of *self-selection* for the available training programs, too, needs to be explored further. The problem of selection effects impedes the generalizability and utility of many of the studies reviewed. Variables correlated with the selection of a training program (such as motivation and concern for the relationship) are unassessed, and may be correlated with performance on postassessment measures. Further, should the results reflect "true effects," the generalizability of these findings— as well as the very usefulness of couples' training programs for the prevention of marital distress—may be limited, to the extent that couples opting for training represent a select subsample. A greater effort should therefore be made to motivate a wider range of couples to participate in potentially helpful preventive programs.

The conclusions drawn in here parallel those of the preceding nine chapters. The processes involved in marital disruption, the effects of divorce on children, and the ingredients of effective remediation or prevention are all extremely difficult to identify, and even more difficult to reduce to a few serviceable generalizations. Certain reproducible trends, found across different populations and modes of data collection, do, however, provide a useful starting point for theory building and clinical application.

No matter how staunchly defended their opinions about divorce or marital dysfunction are, many clinical "experts" remain tied to limited data sets and narrow conceptual models. If the field is to advance beyond the preparadigmatic, "true believer" stage, every effort must be made to develop research procedures wherein rigor and precision are "happily wed" to representativeness of sampling and to the complexities inherent in marital interaction.

REFERENCES

Adam, D., & Gingras, M. (1982). Short and long term effects of a marital enrichment program upon couple functioning. *Journal of Sex and Marital Therapy, 8,* 97–118.

Avery, A. W., Carl, C. A., Leigh, L. A., & Milholland, T. (1980). Relationship enhancement with premarital dyads: A six-month follow-up. *American Journal of Family Therapy, 8,* 23–30.

Azrin, N. M., Naster, B. J., & Jones, R. (1973). Reciprocity counseling: A rapid learning-based procedure for marital counseling. *Behavior Research and Therapy, 11,* 365–382.

Bagarozzi, D. A., & Raven, P. (1981). Premarital counseling: Appraisal and status. *The American Journal of Family Therapy, 3,* 13–30.

Baucom, D. H. (1982). A comparison of behavioral contracting and problem solving/communication training in behavioral marital therapy. *Behavior Therapy, 13,* 162–174.

Bentler, P. & Newcomb,. M. (1978). Longitudinal study of marital success and failure. *Journal of Consulting and Clinical Psychology, 46,* 1053–1070.

Birchler, G. R., Weiss, R. L., & Vincent, J. P. (1975). A multimethod analysis of social reinforcement exchange between maritally distressed and nondistressed spouse and stranger dyads. *Journal of Personality and Social Psychology, 31,* 349–360.

Brock, G. W., & Joanning, H. (1982). A comparison of the Relationship Enhancement Program and the Minnesota Couple Communication Program. Unpublished manuscript, Texas Tech University, Lubbock.

Carkhuff, R. R. (1967). *Helping and human relations (Vol. 2). Practice and Research.* New York: Holt, Rinehart & Winston.

Collins, J. D. (1977). Experimental evaluation of a six-month conjugal therapy and relationship enhancement program. In B. G. Guerney, Jr. (Ed.), *Relationship Enhancement.* San Francisco: Jossey-Bass.

D'Augelli, A. R., Deyss, D. S., Guerney, B. G., Jr., Hershenberg, B., & Sborofsky, S. L. (1974). Interpersonal skill training for dating couples: An evaluation of an educational mental health service. *Journal of Counseling Psychology, 21,* 385–387.

Dillon, J. D. (1975). Marital communication and its relation to self-esteem. Unpublished doctoral dissertation, United States International University.

Ely, A. L., Guerney, B. G., & Stover, L. (1973). Efficacy of the training phase of conjugal therapy. *Psychotherapy: Theory, Research, and Practice, 10,* 201–207.

Epstein, N., & Jackson, E. (1978). An outcome study of short term communication training with married couples. *Journal of Consulting and Clinical Psychology, 46,* 207–212.

Felner, R. D., Jason, L. A., Moritsugu, J. N. & Farber, S. S. (1983). *Preventive psychology: Theory, research, and practice.* New York: Pergamon Press.

Garland, D. R. (1981). Training married couples in listening skills: Effects on behavior, perceptual accuracy and marital adjustment. *Family Relations, 30,* 247–306.

Ginsberg, B. G., & Vogelsong, E. (1977). Premarital relationship improvement by maximizing empathy and self disclosure. The PRIMES program. In B. G. Guerney, Jr. (Ed.), *Relationship Enhancement.* San Francisco: Jossey-Bass.

Guerney, B. G. (1977). *Relationship Enhancement.* San Francisco: Jossey-Bass.

Gurman, A. (1980). Behavioral marriage therapy in the 1980's: The challenge of integration. *American Journal of Family Therapy, 8,* 86–96.

Gurman, A. S., & Kniskern, D. P. (1977). Enriching research on marital enrichment programs. *Journal of Marriage and Family Counseling, 3,* 3–12.

Gurman, A. S., & Kniskern, D. P. (1978). Research on marital and family therapy: Progress, perspective and prospect. In S. Garfield & A. Bergin (Eds.), *Handbook of Psychotherapy and Behavior Change* (2nd ed.). New York: Wiley.

Hickman, M., & Baldwin, B. (1971). Use of programmed instruction to improve communication in marriage. *The Family Coordinator, 20,* 121–125.

Hinkle, E., & Moore, M. (1971). A student couples program. *The Family Coordinator, 20,* 153–158.

Hof, L., & Miller, N. R. (1980). Marriage enrichment. *Marriage and Family Review, 3,* 1–24.

Jacobson, N. S. (1977). Training couples to solve their marital problems: A behavioral approach to relationship discord. Part I. Problem solving skills. *International Journal of Family Counseling, 5,* 22–31.

Jacobson, N. S. (1978a). A review of the research on the effectiveness of marital therapy. In T. J. Paolina & B. S. McGrady (Eds.), *Marriage and Marital Therapy: Psychoanalytic, Behavioral and Systems Theory Perspectives.* New York: Brunner/Mazel.

Jacobson, N. S. (1978b). Specific and nonspecific factors in the effectiveness of a behavioral approach to the treatment of marital discord. *Journal of Consulting and Clinical Psychology, 46,* 442–452.

Jacobson, N. S. (1979). Increasing positive behavior in severely disturbed adult relationships. *Behavior Therapy, 10,* 311–326.

Jacobson, N. S. (1984). A component analysis of behavioral marital therapy: The relative effectiveness of behavior exchange and communication/problem solving. *Journal of Consulting and Clinical Psychology, 52,* 295–305.

Jacobson, N. S., Follette, W. C., Revonstorf, D., Baucom, H., Hahlweg, K., & Margolin, G. (1984). Variability in outcome and clinical significance of behavioral marital therapy: A reanalysis of outcome data. *Journal of Consulting and Clinical Psychology, 52,* 497–504.

Jacobson, N. S., & Margolin, G. (1979). *Marital Therapy: Strategies Based on Social Learning and Behavior Exchange Principles.* New York: Brunner/Mazel.

Jacobson, N. S., & Martin, B. (1976). Behavioral marriage therapy: Current status. *Psychological Bulletin, 83,* 540–556.

Jacobson, N. S., Waldron, H., & Moore, D. (1980). Toward a behavioral profile of marital distress. *Journal of Consulting and Clinical Psychology, 48,* 696–703.

Jessee, R. E., & Guerney, B. G. (1981). A comparison of Gestalt and relationship enhancement treatments with married couples. *American Journal of Family Therapy, 9,* 31–41.

Joanning, H. (1982). The long term effects of the couples communication program. *Journal of Marital and Family Therapy,* October, 463–468.

Kniskern, D. P., & Gurman, A. S. (1984). Future directions for family therapy research. In D. A. Bagarozzi (Ed.), *New Perspectives in Marital and Family Therapy: Issues in Theory, Research and Practice.* New York: Human Sciences Press.

L'Abate, L. (1980). Skill training programs for couples and families. In A. S. Gurman & D. P. Kniskern (Eds.), *Handbook of Family Therapy.* New York: Brunner/Mazel.

Levinger, G., & Breedlove, J. (1966). Interpersonal attraction and agreement: A study of marriage partners. *Journal of Personality and Social Psychology, 3,* 367–372.

Mace, D., & Mace, V. (1976). Marriage enrichment: A preventive group approach for couples. In D. H. L. Olson (Ed.), *Treating Relationships.* Lake Mills, Iowa: Graphic.

Markman, H. J. (1979). The application of a behavioral model of marriage in predicting relationship satisfaction of couples planning marriage. *Journal of Consulting and Clinical Psychology, 47,* 743–749.

Markman, H. J. (1981). Prediction of marital distress: A five-year follow-up. *Journal of Consulting and Clinical Psychology, 49,* 760–762.

Markman, H. J. (1984). The longitudinal study of couples' interactions. In K. Hahlweg & N. Jacobson (Eds.) *Marital Interaction.* New York: Guilford Press.

Markman, H. J., Floyd, F., Dickson-Markman, F. (1982). Towards a model for the prediction and primary prevention of marital and family distress and dissolution. In S. Duck (Ed.), *Personal Relationships—Dissolving Personal Relationships.* London: Academic Press.

Markman, H. J., Floyd, F. J., Stanley, S. M., & Jamieson, K. (1984). A cognitive behavioral program for the prevention of marital and family distress. Issues in program development and delivery. In K. Hahlveg & N. Jacobson (Eds.), *Marital Interaction*. New York: Guilford Press.

Markman, H. J., Floyd, F. J., Stanley, S., & Stephen, T. (1983). *Baby Steps Toward the Prevention of Marital and Family Distress*. Unpublished manuscript, University of Denver, Denver, Col.

Markman, H. J., Jamieson, K. J., & Floyd, F. J. (1983). The assessment and modification of premarital relationships: Preliminary findings on the etiology and prevention of marital and family distress. In J. Vincent (Ed.), *Advances in Family Intervention: Assessment and Theory* (Vol. 3). Greenwich, Conn.: JAI Press.

Meadows, M. E., & Taplin, J. F. (1970). Premarital counseling with college students: A promising triad. *Journal of Counseling Psychology, 17*, 516–518.

Miller, S., Nunnally, E. W., & Wackman, D. B. (1976). A communication training program for couples. *Social Casework*, 9–18.

Norton, A. J. & Glick, P. C. (1979). Marital instability in America: Past, present and future. In G. Levinger & O. C. Moles (Eds.), *Divorce and Separation: Context, Causes and Consequences*. (pp. 6–19). New York: Basic Books.

O'Leary, K. D., & Turkowitz, H. (1978a). Marital therapy from a behavioral perspective. In T. J. Paolino & B. S. McCrady (Eds.), *Marriage and Marital Therapy: Psychoanalytic, Behavior, and Systems Theory Perspectives*. New York: Brunner/Mazel.

O'Leary, K., & Turkowitz, H. (1978b). Methodological errors in marital and child treatment research. *Journal of Consulting and Clinical Psychology, 46*, 747–758.

Olson, D. H., Russell, C. S., & Sprenkle, D. H. (1980). Marital and family therapy: A decade review. *Journal of Marriage and the Family*, 973–993.

Pierce, R. M. (1973). Training in interpersonal communication skills with the partners of deteriorated marriages. *The Family Coordinator*, 223–227.

Rappaport, A. F. (1976). Conjugal relationship enhancement program. In D. H. L. Olson (Ed.), *Treating Relationships*. Lake Mills, Iowa: Graphic.

Ridley, C. A., Jorgensen, S. R., Morgan, A. G., & Avery, A. W. (1982). Relationship enhancement with premarital couples: An assessment of effects on relationship quality. *American Journal of Family Therapy, 10* 41–48.

Rogers, C. R. (1951). *Client Centered Therapy*. Boston: Houghton-Mifflin.

Rollins, B., & Galligan, R. (1978). The developing child and marital satisfaction in parents. In R. Lerner & G. Spanier (Eds.), *Child Influences on Marital and Family Interaction: A Life-Span Perspective*. New York: Academic Press.

Russell, R. A. (1982). Assertiveness training and its effects upon the marital relationship. *Family Therapy, 1*, 9–20.

Russell, C. S., Bagarozzi, D. A., Atilano, R., & Morris, J. E. (1982). A comparison of two approaches to marital enrichment and conjugal skills training: Minnesota couples communication program and structured behavioral exchange contracting. Unpublished manuscript, Kansas State University.

Schindler, L., Hahlweg, K., & Revonstorf, D. (1983). Short and long term effectiveness of two communication training modalities with distressed couples. *The American Journal of Family Therapy, 11*, 54–64.

Schlein, J. (1971). Training dating couples in empathetic and open communication:

An experimental evaluation of a potential preventive mental health program. Unpublished doctoral dissertation, Pennsylvania State University.

Stuart, R. B. (1969). Operant-interpersonal treatment for marital discord. *Journal of Consulting and Clinical Psychology, 33,* 675–682.

Stuart, R. B. (1980). *Helping Couples Change: A Social Learning Approach to Marital Therapy.* New York: Guilford Press.

Tsoi-Hoshmand, L. (1976). Marital therapy: An integrative behavioral learning model. *Journal of Marriage and Family Counseling,* April, 179–191.

Van Zoost, B. (1973). Premarital communication skills education with university couples. *The Family Coordinator, 22,* 187–191.

Wampler, K. S. (1982). The effectiveness of the Minnesota Couple Communication Program: A review of research. *Journal of Marital and Family Therapy,* 345–354.

Wampler, K. S., & Sprenkle, D. H. (1980). The Minnesota Couple Communication Program: A follow-up study. *Journal of Marriage and the Family,* 577–584.

Weiss, R. L., Hops, H., & Patterson, G. R. (1973). A framework for conceptualizing marital conflict, technology for altering it, some data for evaluating it. In L. A. Hamerlynk, L. C. Handy, & E. J. Mash (Eds.), *Behavior Change: Methodology, Concepts, and Practice.* Champaign, Ill.: Research Press.

Zimmerman, A., & Bailey, J. (1977). The Minnesota Couple Communication Program: An evaluation of the training and post-training communication behavior of its participants. Unpublished manuscript, University of Minnesota.

Subject Index

Achenbach Child Behavior Checklist,
94–96, 199
  correlation with Divorce Events
  Scale for Children, 130, *tables*
  4.6, 4.7, 131
  measuring child adjustment, 273
  items composing, *table* 8.3, 274
  scales altered, 292

Big Brothers,
  as father surrogate, 225
Birth rate
  decline of, 3
Boy Scouts
  as father surrogate; 225

Child Behavior Checklist
  assessing children's adjustment to
  divorce, 244
Children
  adaptation to divorce, 48–58
  adaptive impact of divorce, 35–37
  divorce adjustments, 185–227
    cognitive mediators, 244
  grandparents and divorce, 70
  impact of divorce on, 46–48
  living arrangements of, 26–29
  outcomes of divorce on, 91–99
    cognitive development, 98
    externalizing disorders, 93–95
    internalizing behavior, 95–97

racial differences in adjustment,
98, 99
self-concept, 91–93
social adjustment, 97, 98
post divorce environments, 111–
139
  adaptive tasks of, 134, 135
  environmental factors, 127
  individual child characteristics,
  126, 127
  ten least stressful events, *table*
  4.3, 121
  ten most stressful events, *table*
  4.2, 120
  relation between sex and living
  arrangements of, *table* 1.4, 29
and remarriage, 78
  treatment methods; *see* Treatment
Children of Divorce Intervention
  Project
  (CODIP), 310–312, 317
Child Separation Inventory, 243, 245
  children's understanding of
  divorce, 252
Cognitive developmental approaches
  application to divorce adjustment,
  255, 256
  assessing children's adjustment to
  divorce, 244
  assessing children's views of
  divorce, 242–244
  Child Separation Inventory, 243

369

effect of remarriage on nonresidential
and interparental conflict, 162
parent-child relationship, 170
relationships with ex-spouse and
problems in second marriage,
173
New York Longitudinal Study
parental conflict level and, 292

Optimism-pessimism scale (OPTI),
197

Parent and Teacher Report, 199
Parent-child relationship
nonresidential, 78–81
residential, 81–83
Parenting After Divorce Project
(PADP), 313
Parent Satisfaction Scale (PSS), 198
Parent Separation Inventory, 244
Partners of Opposite Sex Sharing
Living Quarters (POSSLQ), 7
Personal Attribute Inventory for
Children, 92
Personality Inventory for Children
assessing children's adjustment
to divorce, 244
Piers-Harris Self-Esteem Scale, 244
Post divorce
mediation of parent-child
arrangements, 267–297
children and mediation
experience, 281–283
children and the adversarial
experience, 283–284
initial child adjustment, 279–280
initial parenting behaviors, 277–
279
sample prior to mediation, 275–
277
parenting, 284, 285
Premarital Relationship
Enhancement Program (PREP),
353, 354
component analysis, 360
Premarital relationship improvement
by maximizing empathy and self-
disclosure (PRIMES), 349
Projective Story, 243

Psychological symptomatology
correlation of Divorce Events
Schedule for Children (DESC)
and adjustment problems, 133,
134
joint custody and, 128
Psychopathology
prevention of, in children of
divorce, 309–312

Remarriage
by age of divorce, 12, 13
demographics of, 71, 72
grandparent-grandchild
relationships and, 175
issues in family law, 147–152
as a life transition, 72–74
marital relationship in, 76–78
pre-remarriage custody
arrangements, effects of, 169–
173
rates of, *table* 1.2, 6
satisfaction with, 76, 77
stepfamilies, structural complexity
in, 69–71
trends of, 6, 7

Sells and Roff Peer Acceptance-
Rejection Rating (PAR), 197
Single Parenting Questionnaire, 244
Spearman
correlation with stress, 119, 120
Stepfamily
effects of custody arrangement on,
173–175
methodology in research of, 74, 75
sibling relationships in, 89–91
stepparent-stepchild relationship,
83–89
stepmothering, 88, 89
structural complexity of, 69–71
system, 75, 76

The Divorce Experience
pre-divorce counseling, 307
"Transitional-events,"
of divorce, 45, 46
model of, 41–45
Treatment
children's divorce adjustment

Author Index